Dying
To Hunt
In Montana

Nearly Two Hundred
Years of Hunting
Related Fatalities
in Montana

By Tom Donovan

First Printing: Fall of 2005
Printed by Data Reproductions Corporation

ISBN   0-9769718-0-1

Library of Congress Control Number: 2005905692

Portage Meadows Publishing
POB 6554
Great Falls, MT. 59406

Additional copies of this book are available through local bookstores
or they may be ordered directly from the publisher at the above
address.

Front Cover
Designed by: Portage Meadows Publishing
Created by: Astarna Inc. (www.astarna.com)
Cover photos: by Bonnie Donovan

The background is of the mountains in Teton County and the
tombstones are of Great Falls hunters, Fred Kent and Robert Smith.
Since their deaths occurred within days of each other in October of
1959, and because Fred Kent and Robert Smith were Army veterans
of World War II, they were buried side by side at the same cemetery
in Great Falls. Although these two young men were both born early
in 1927, they grew up in different parts of the state and didn't come
to Great Falls until after the war. While they probably didn't know
each other in life, they were brought together in death by their love of
hunting.

Dedicated
to

To my brother, Leroy Donovan,
one of the most dedicated hunters that I have ever known.
Leroy became lost in the Little Belt Mountains
in October of 1963 but fortunately
he found his way back to us.

And, to all those many hunters
who weren't as lucky.

MEL —
BOUGHT THIS BOOK FOR YOU; USING
MY FAMILY DISCOUNT! I REMAIN —
STAY HEALTHY — I REMAIN —
Your former Student
Always Good friend —
Leroy

Acknowledgments

Although a book of this type was obviously difficult to put together because of the delicate subject matter, I have many folks to thank for making it as easy as possible for me to get through it.

First of all, the publication of this book might not have come about without the encouragement of many of my family and friends, in particular my wife, Bonnie who also took all the photos except for the ones noted.

Of course, library personnel were indispensable at both the local and state level. A special thanks goes to the staff of the Great Falls Public Library, particularly John Finn, the head of Information Services; the reference librarian, Jeff Savage; library specialists, Sara Kegel and Carole Ann Clark, along with inter-library loan personnel, Shannon Smith and Jude Smith. This book wouldn't have been possible without their cooperation and assistance in the gathering of the reference and interlibrary materials. The State Historical Library at Helena also deserves a great deal of recognition for their marvelous collection of newspaper microfilm and other research materials.

A special thanks also goes to Thomas Baumeister, Education Bureau Chief with Montana Fish Wildlife and Parks for his cooperation and for opening up his files and other records to us.

Contents

List of Photographs   viii
Introduction   x
Preface   xiii
About the Author   xvi

Chapter 1: By Their Own Negligence   1

Chapter 2: Killed By Their Companion   59

Chapter 3: Lost or Missing   111

Chapter 4: Killed By Mistaken Identification   159

Chapter 5: From Health Reasons   197

Chapter 6: Water Deaths   227

Chapter 7: Killed by Animals   253

Chapter 8: Deaths By Other Causes   271

Mortality Tables
    1: How They Killed Themselves   333
    2: Companion Relationship   339
    3: Type of Companion Accidents   343
    4: Where They Became Lost or Missing 348
    5: Causes of Mistaken Identification 353
    6: Types of Fatal Animal Encounters   356
    7: Location of Water Deaths   357
    8: Water Deaths by Counties   359
    9: Health Related Deaths By Categories 363
    10: Categories of Deaths by Other Causes 367

Montana Hunting Fatalities by Year   375
Location of Montana Hunting Fatalities   405
Victim Index   433

LIST OF PHOTOGRAPHS

The "Dying to Hunt in Montana" list of fatalities would easily fill a large portion of a cemetery such as the New Highland Cemetery in Great Falls pictured above.

Chapter One: From Their Own Negligence   **page**

11/4/1928	Walter Griesbach	26
11/12/1928	Herschell A. Dockery	27
1931 (reported 1/2/1932)	William B. Burkhart	29
11/16/1936	Ray V. Doney	34
10/20/1939	William Smith	37
10/26/1969	David Lee Schonenbach*	49

Chapter Two: Killed by Their Companion

11/17/1928	Sgt. Paul B. Portis	81
10/19/1933	Walter L. Kulbeck	82
10/30/1941	Hezekiah VanDorn	85
10/9/1950	Caroline J. Ullery*	89
11/15/1950	Robert Wesley Brown	89

Dying to Hunt in Montana
Photographs

(Chapter 2 continued)
11/12/1957	Walter B. Sokoloski	95
10/19/1959	Robert Walker Smith	97
10/2/1977	Lewis P. Sprattler	103

Chapter Three: Lost or Missing
| 10/27/1959 | Fred Kent | 142 |
| 11/30/1981 | Wilbur and Vicki Stedman* | 151 |

Chapter Four: Killed By Mistaken Identification
| 11/4/1957 | Robert C. Jennings | 186 |

Chapter Five: From Health Reasons
10/29/1952	Alfred Sterner	211
10/16/1955	Silas H. Jerome	212
11/15/1955	Thomas Melton	213
9/19/1969	John A. McFarland	221
2/16/1983	William G. Nemeth	225

Chapter Six: Water Deaths
| 10/16/1947 | Clifford G. Hogan | 248 |
| 10/16/1947 | Albert L. Richardson | 248 |

Chapter Seven: Killed By Animals
10/22/1956	William K. Scott	264
10/31/1958	Sam Adams	266
11/1/2001	Timothy Hilston	268

Chapter Eight: Deaths by Other Causes
10/21/1908	Charles B. Peyton	290
10/31/1933	James V. Booth	306
10/29/1934	Emmitt C. Watters	307
10/21/1940	Donald P. Knapp	309
11/11/1967	Robert M. Barnes	317

*Photograph by Joyce Obland (www.graves-r-us.com)

Introduction

Over the years the mountains, prairies and wild animals of Montana have all taken their share of hunters. Many of the sportsmen have become lost in unfamiliar terrain, some have never been found while others have been located years later as just mere shreds of clothing and a few scattered bones. Some sportsmen have died from accidental discharges of their own rifles and shotguns while family members, friends, business partners and complete strangers have killed others. Many have been mistaken for deer, elk, bears, coyotes and other game animals and some have even been killed for just moving in the brush or for making sounds like an animal.

Vehicles of all kinds like wagons, sleds, trucks and automobiles seem to get involved in hunting accidents quite frequently especially when there are loaded weapons among the passengers. Hunters in Montana have utilized just about every means of dying while chasing wild game including stray and ricocheting bullets, avalanches, falling from cliffs, trees and from the air in airplanes. Some have drowned in rivers, lakes and reservoirs; they have died from affixation and from various health reasons. Most hunters have died violently in the old fashion ways like crawling through fences with their weapons or putting or removing their loaded firearms from their vehicle while a few have died in very unusual ways like from the bubonic plague, falling from a bicycle, being surprised in deer and bear traps and by being murdered by Indians.

With a subject matter as emotionally charged as hunting fatalities, why would anyone write a book like this? The quick answer to that question was purely by accident. I first became interested in this subject in 1995 while I was researching a story about a missing university student who became lost in the Mission Mountains in 1958 while doing a wildlife study. It was presumed that the 20-year-old wildlife student was killed and eaten by bears in the remote country northeast of Seeley Lake.

Introduction

I was just 10 years old at the time of the man's disappearance in 1958 and our parents persuaded my friends and myself from camping "by ourselves" because of the frightening story. Over the years I have shared that gruesome but quintessential Montana "campfire story" with many of my friends and acquaintances while in the Navy, at college, at work and in my travels.

Then in April of 1991 the missing man's final campsite was finally located but his remains have yet to be found. As a child, even though I had considered myself an expert on the story, I had never read a single newspaper account about the incident. To correct that omission I went about researching the story after selling my business in 1995. While I was following the story about the university student I found stories of four hunters who had also gotten lost that same year and four more hunters that became lost or missing in 1959.

As I was searching the 1958 newspapers for information on those 4 lost hunters I was amazed at the number of other sportsmen who had been killed or had died while they were hunting including 5 from gunshots, 7 from health reasons and another man who died after being mauled by a grizzly bear. From there on my research covered not only hunters who were gunshot victims, lost or missing, and sportsmen who died from health reasons but to fatalities from all other causes.

Thing were going along fine with my research project until my first interview with a widow of a hunter who had died 17 years earlier. While the woman was very nice and the many years had comforted her somewhat, I became disturbed to hear about what his death had done to her family. After that telephone conversation I suspended work on the project for over four years because I didn't want to open any more old wounds or heartaches.

Later when I realized that this book might actually save the lives of other hunters I decided to go ahead with the project by limiting my interviews and to use newspaper articles as my primary source of information. To make a greater impact on the hunters I increased the number of cases by expanding the time frame of the search and I broadened the categories to make it more interesting for the readers.

For the experienced hunter, these stories will probably stir memories of past situations and it may remind them of the unsafe hunting practices that they have participated in over the years. For the younger hunters who have only read about the dos and don'ts, they will have an opportunity to read about the hundreds of real life examples of people who have lost their lives because they didn't follow those rules.

For the parents and grandparents of young boys and girls considering the sport of hunting, these tragic stories might make them consider the youngster's maturity and judgment instead of just their age. Reviewing these real-life accounts with young hunters may reinforce the importance of their hunter's safety education, which could keep them safe. Lastly, these accounts may make all of us safer hunters, and by doing so, they might give some meaning to the tragic deaths of all the hunters who were the subjects of these sad stories.

There are well over 800 fatalities recorded in this book and every one of these tragic deaths had devastating effects on the family and friends of the victim. These incidents and the circumstances surrounding them are generally complicated and open to different interpretations, even among the participants involved. This record is of course incomplete. There will be many cases where someone had suffered an injury while hunting and then died later from complications of the wound. If you know of such a hunting fatality, or other hunting deaths not found in this book please write to me at Portage Meadows Publishing, POB 6554, Great Falls, MT. 59406.

Finally, the principle message of this book, besides the interesting history is to: **BE CAREFUL !**

Preface

Disclaimer

This work is about a piece of Montana history and it is by no means anti-hunting. Further more it is not anti-gun, and should not be construed as such as the facts here prove that more hunters have died from drowning and health reasons than from firearms.

It was not our intent to record every single hunting related fatality in the state of Montana, but enough of the tragedies to convey the feelings and emotions involved with unsafe hunting. To the best of our knowledge, the stories and the facts in this work are true.

In some cases it was next to impossible to verify the proper spellings of the names, the exact locations and specific dates of the accidents. For that reason and for reference purposes, we have listed the incidents by their reporting dates.

In some cases the hunter may have been fatally injured in one county and died in a hospital of another, in those incidents the location of the accident was indicated. We apologize if we have offended anyone regarding the subject and nature of this book, but we feel that these histories may save lives.

Using this book

The fatalities in this work have been categorized into eight different classifications and chapters; **Own Negligence, By Companion, Mistaken Identification, Lost or Missing, Health Reasons, Water Deaths, Animal Encounters** and **Other Causes.** To assist the reader navigate through this book there is a **Victim Index, Fatalities By the Year** and **By the Location** tables along with appendixes of the various types and causes for each of the categories.

If a person knows the name of a particular victim, but is not sure of how he met his death, he would first go to the Victim Index. There he will find the "when," "where" and the "how" and the category of the accident. By going to the appropriate category chapter, and then searching through the dates, which are in chronological order the person will find the story of the incident. The facts in the story are as they were reported in the newspaper or newspapers.

Other readers may be interested in knowing how many hunters have lost their lives in a particular county, year or in certain types of accidents. They only need to peruse through the appendixes and the By Year and Location tables.

Most readers will probably find the most interesting parts of this book are the different types of hunting fatalities in the appendixes for "Other Causes" and in "Animal Encounters."

Date of Incident

In some cases a hunter was wounded and later died from his injuries. There have been cases where the skeletal remains of a lost hunter were located years later but no specific account was found of when the individual was first reported missing. Because of these variables and since it is often difficult to determine specific dates we have listed the incidents by newspaper reporting dates as the reference date for the incident. If a specific newspaper is not listed it was found in the Great Falls Tribune.

Location of Incident

Since the state of Montana was established it has gone through many changes in the number counties and their borders. From the original 9 counties established in 1864 the number had doubled by 1889 and was at 26 in 1904, exploded to 43 counties in 1918 and settled with 53 at present.

While the incidents were in fact reported to the appropriate county authorities at the time, we have tried our best to list them in the present day counties for easier locating. For example, a hunting accident near Libby at the turn of the century would have been reported in Flathead County but it is in present day Lincoln County.

Preface

Graphic Descriptions

While many of the early-day newspaper articles dealing with hunting fatalities were very graphic and even bordered on gruesome, we have tried to be sensitive in describing these tragedies but we have maintained some of the original descriptions for their effect.

Errors, Omissions and other Variations in the Facts

As was stated in the earlier Disclaimer, it is impossible to verify names, exact locations and specific dates in these incidents. In many cases new facts come to light later, which may affect the cause of death etc.. These facts may come out days, weeks, months and even years later making it practically impossible to follow.

There have been cases like the one about the hunter who had been mortally wounded by his son. Not wanting his son to be blamed or traumatized further, the dying man claimed on his death bed that he had accidentally shot himself. Then some time later the boy admitted that he had accidentally fired the fatal shot.

Stories often change over the years. Forty years earlier a man may have shot himself while pulling his shotgun out of his pickup but 20, 30 or 40 years later the family recalls the story about great grampa being killed by his hunting partner.

We have made a concerted effort to get the stories correct, and again we apologize deeply for any errors or omissions that we might have made. We are also very sorry for your loss, and only hope that this work will bring some meaning to your departed loved ones by possibly saving other lives.

ABOUT THE AUTHOR
Tom Donovan

by Bonnie Donovan

While Tom mostly fishes these days, he has been a life-long sportsman having grown up in Montana, bagged a caribou in Alaska and while serving overseas he hunted and fished in various location in Asia.

Since he was a small boy, Tom has trapped some of the same waters that the early-day beaver trappers and mountain men had worked in western Montana. Over the years he has hunted and eaten just about everything that runs, fly or crawls including porcupine, owl and beaver tail.

Author with his Alaskan Caribou in 1967.

Before Tom was twelve years old he was trapping mice and other small rodents later turning his attention on big game, upland game birds and trapping muskrats, beaver and predators.

In his early teens, Tom's parents had so much confidence in his hunting and survival skills that they often dropped him off along some of the most remote sections of the Blackfoot and Bitterroot Rivers to hunt and trap.

Chapter One:

Killing Themselves While Hunting In Montana

Today, students taking hunter safety courses are taught to treat every firearm as if it were loaded; to always point the muzzle of their firearm in a safe direction; to always be certain of their target before shooting; the safe way to go through fences and to carry their weapons in a manner so not to injure themselves or others.

The young hunters also learn the proper way of handing off and accepting a firearm from another person; that they should never have a loaded gun in their vehicle and the importance of being familiar with the weapon that they will be using in the field.

After reading this chapter, **"By Their Own Negligence"** along with, **"Killed by Their Companion,"**
"Killed When Mistaken for Game" and the majority of the cases in **"By Other Causes"** chapter, the reader, especially the young hunters involved with hunting safety courses will quickly understand why they were taught these rules. This book is full of tragic stories of both young and old hunters who had violated these standard safety rules and unfortunately paid for it with their lives.

Although there were no age requirements to hunt until 1910 when children under 14 with firearms were required to be accompanied by a parent or guardian and the mandated hunting safety program wasn't initiated until 1958, there were still standard and recognized gun safety rules as early as 1891.

In November of 1891 Charles Hallock of "Forest and Stream," which later became "Field and Stream" was quoted in the Great Falls

Chapter One: BY THEIR OWN NEGLIGENCE

Tribune the following hunting safety advice:

"Having been asked by my friends frequently for advice for their boys on handling guns, I send you a digest of same:

"Empty or loaded, never point a gun towards yourself or anyone else.

"When a-field, carry your gun at half cocked. If in brush, let your hand shield the hammer from whipping twigs.

"When riding a horse from one shooting ground to another, or whenever you have your gun in any vehicle, remove the cartridges if it is a breech loader as it is so easy to replace them. If it is a muzzleloader, remove the caps, brush off the nipples and place a wad on each nipple, letting down the hammers on the wads. Simply removing the caps sometimes leaves a little powder on the nipple, and if the hammer is struck with something it may discharge.

"Never draw a gun towards you by the barrels.

"More care is necessary in the use of a gun in a boat than anywhere else, the limited and confined space and the uncertain motion making it dangerous at best. If possible no more than two persons should occupy a boat. Hammerless guns are a constant danger to persons boating.

Always clean your guns thoroughly as soon as you return from a day's sport, no matter how tired you feel. The consequence of its always being ready for service is ample return for the few minutes' irksome labor."

Chapter One: BY THEIR OWN NEGLIGENCE

Actual cases of hunting fatalities due to the hunter's own negligence:

April 30, 1881
John Brown of Rocky Gap accidentally shot and killed himself while he was hunting near a hot springs on the North Fork of the Sun River. The springs described in this account are probably the ones known as "Medicine Springs" on Arsenic Creek, which is located above Gibson Reservoir.

Initially Mr. Brown and his party were reportedly investigating the warm waters of the hot springs to determine their medicinal value on such ailments as rheumatism, which had troubled Mr. Brown, but while he was in the remote backcountry he decided to ride off and do some hunting.

The first reports into Fort Shaw were that Mr. Brown's horse had bucked him off and he was accidentally shot in a lung as he went down. Transportation was arranged and the hospital at the fort was being readied for the possible surgery on the injured man.

But later word came in that the hunter had only lived for about 30 minutes and that he was in fact shot in the chest when his weapon accidentally discharged while he was picking it up by the barrel.

Because of the remoteness of the area, the body brought out and so Mr. John Brown was buried in the mountains where he died. The last rights over his mountain burial were read by one of his good friends, the Reverend Mr. Hall.

October 15, 1884
(Helena Daily Herald)
David Austin lost his life when he accidentally shot himself just minutes after leaving his Missoula home to go hunting. The 50-year-old Missoula County commissioner was found with a bullet hole in his head from his needle gun[1].

3

Chapter One: BY THEIR OWN NEGLIGENCE

September 9, 1893
(Livingston Enterprise)
Eli Paulin, the 16-year-old son of Isaac Paulin of Grass Valley in Missoula County accidentally shot and killed himself Sunday afternoon while he was hunting.

Eli was reportedly pushing his shotgun through a fence ahead of him when it accidentally discharged into his abdomen, killing him instantly.

December 29, 1895
(Anaconda Standard)
John Whiting reportedly accidentally shot and killed himself near Philipsburg while he was hunting.

August 4, 1901
Sixty-year-old George E. Hailey accidentally shot and killed himself while he was hunting rattlesnakes on his mining claim, which was located on Upper Geyser Creek near White Sulphur Springs.

When Mr. Hailey failed to return to the cabin he was sharing with a Mr. Dean, a search was started the next morning and his body was found near his diggings. Mr. Hailey had told Dean that there weren't enough rocks to throw at all the snakes near his claim and so he was going to shoot some.

The evidence at the scene indicated that Mr. Hailey had sat down to rest, and he apparently grabbed his shotgun by the barrel as he got up. The weapon accidentally discharged into Hailey's thigh just above the knee. He tried to stop the flow of blood by tying a handkerchief around the wound but he eventually bled to death.

George Hailey was well known and well liked in Meagher County having resided there since 1888. He was a native of Louisiana and during the Civil war he had served in the Confederate Army.

Chapter One: BY THEIR OWN NEGLIGENCE

November 2, 1901
<u>James Gamble</u>, the only son of Mr. and Mrs. John T. Gamble of Chinook was accidentally shot and killed while he was hunting prairie chickens south of his hometown.

The Gamble boy was hunting with another young man when he scared up a covey of birds and he bagged two and crippled another. The wounded bird had flown into a clump of brush and while he entered the thick bushes his shotgun accidentally discharged into his right side just under his arm.

After hearing Gamble's shot his companion pushed his way through the brush and there he found the lifeless body of his friend. Dr. Hopkins was called to the scene but there wasn't anything he could do to save the boy's life. The next day the county coroner decided that it was clearly an accident and he didn't hold an inquest.

January 5, 1902
(Anaconda Standard)
Sixteen-year-old <u>William Stuart</u> died a few days after he had accidentally shot himself while he was hunting along the Bitterroot River near his home at Stevensville.

While he was walking with a friend they came across a section of ice, which he tried to break up with the butt of his .22-caliber rifle. The shock from one of the first blows caused the weapon to accidentally discharge and the bullet penetrated the left side of his chest near the nipple and then it lodged in his back.

September 10, 1902
<u>Reverend Leslie E. Armitage</u>, the former pastor of the Methodist Episcopal Church at White Sulphur Springs accidentally shot and killed himself while he was hunting near town.

Chapter One: BY THEIR OWN NEGLIGENCE

The 26-year-old Mr. Armitage had been hunting with the Harris brothers on Checkerboard Creek when he shot himself in the abdomen and quickly bled to death.

By the time Dr. Harris located his hunting partner he had already died. Mr. Armitage apparently tried to stop the blood flow as he was found holding a handkerchief over the wound.

Reverend Armitage was originally from Canada and he attended and then later taught at Montana Wesleyan University at Helens. He had recently resigned as pastor of his church in town to enter the clothing business in White Sulphur Springs.

October 5, 1902
Arthur Sharpe, the 16-year-old son of A.L. Sharpe, who lived on the family ranch on the Sun River Bench about 8 miles from Great Falls was accidentally killed while he was hunting near Cascade.

The boy left Cascade with the son of James Craig and a hired hand to hunt birds along Sheep Creek about 12 miles from town. After hunting the surrounding foothills for a while the boys decided to cross the creek and work the other side.

The three hunters entered the water together and when they were in the middle of the stream Sharpe apparently slipped on a stone and he lost his balance. The boy was carrying his loaded and cocked shotgun at eye level when it accidentally discharged as he was jerking it around while trying to regain his footing.

When the shotgun went off the muzzle was practically pointing directly at his face. Although the loud blast startled the other boys they were horrified at the sight of Sharpe's wounds to his throat and face. Sharpe fell into the stream and his frantic friends carried him to the safety of the bank but they weren't able to stop the blood gushing from his neck.

Chapter One: BY THEIR OWN NEGLIGENCE

The Sharpe boy tried to speak while his two friends were carrying him to a nearby small cabin but his lower face was totally gone. One of the lads stayed at the cabin with victim while the other boy ran to Cascade for help. It took about an hour and a half for the messenger to run to town and another thirty minutes for Dr. McLennan to arrive at the scene but Arthur Sharpe was dead by the time they arrived.

The father of the dying boy was in Great Falls at the time of the accident and after receiving word he secured a team of horses and he drove to the cabin to be with his fallen son.

November 5, 1902

John Malloy of Columbia Falls accidentally shot and killed himself while he was hunting ducks on Whitefish Lake. He had been hunting from the shore of the lake when he decided to take a small boat out onto the water. When he was placing his shotgun into the craft by the barrel it accidentally discharged into his side, which caused a huge wound.

Another hunter in the area went to Malloy's aid and he rushed him to the lake home of G.E. Baker. Dr. Robinson arrived from Columbia Falls but nothing could be done for the victim except to provide as much comfort as possible until he died.

September 19, 1903

Nick Simons Jr., 13, of Madison County accidentally killed himself when he was climbing over a fence with his gun while he was hunting near Rochester, not far from Virginia City. The shotgun blast literally separated his head from his shoulders.

August 15, 1904

Eighteen-year-old William Malard died from an accidental gunshot wound while he was hunting with his friends in Phillips County. Apparently the boy shot himself in the abdomen with his .22-caliber rifle while he was crawling through some rocks.

Chapter One: BY THEIR OWN NEGLIGENCE

November 22, 1904
Thirteen-year-old <u>Percy Glenn</u> of Fergus County accidentally shot and
killed himself while he was hunting near his home on McDonald
Creek about 13 miles southeast of Lewistown.

His little brother was with him at the time and he later said that Percy
had slipped on some loose rock while he was chasing after an animal
and his shotgun discharged as he went down.

The entire charge of the No. 5 shot entered his left leg just below
the knee, and the young boy described it as a horrible wound.
Unfortunately Percy Glenn bled to death before medical aid could
reach him.

September 2, 1905
<u>Frank Gonsior</u>, 17, of Monarch accidentally killed himself in
an unusual hunting incident near his hometown in the Little
Belt Mountains. The young man had been working on the John
Holsheimer Ranch when he left to go bird hunting before breakfast.

When Gonsior didn't return for his meal Mr. Holsheimer and his
son began searching for him. They found the dead body of Frank
Gonsior sitting next to a shock of grain at the edge of a field. The
victim had apparently bled to death from a shotgun wound to the leg
and after following the man's blood trail they located his weapon in a
patch of heavy brush.

At first it was believed that the boy had accidentally shot himself
with his double-barrel shotgun while he was pushing through the
thick brush, but after further investigation Mr. Holsheimer found
a wounded large hawk, which was described as being a "Rocky
Mountain" hawk[2].

The officials ruled that the young hunter had shot and wounded the
large bird, and when the injured hawk attacked Gonsior he began
clubbing at it with the butt of his loaded gun. Evidently the young

man had forgotten that the hammer of his gun was pulled back and the second barrel discharged while he was clubbing at the bird.

The full charge of birdshot went into Gonsior's right thigh inflicting a large wound. The injured boy drug himself out of the brush and into the open field where he leaned himself up against the shock of grain. The artery in his leg had been severed and he probably went into shock and quickly bled to death.

Frank Gonsior was born in Monarch and he had never left Cascade County. The body of the popular youth was taken to his bereaved parent's home in Monarch with a team and wagon.

September 27, 1907
Sheepherder, <u>William Powell</u> also met his death when he misused his firearm while he was hunting between Flat Creek and Cut Bank Creek about 30 miles southeast of Fort Benton.

Mr. Powell was herding sheep on the Engellant place when he apparently tried to kill a badger. The man was jamming the butt end of his loaded rifle down the badger hole when the weapon accidentally discharged into his neck.

October 8, 1908
(Missoulian)
<u>Louis Deckerville</u>, 50, of East Helena was accidentally killed when he was crawling under a barbwire fence with his loaded shotgun. Mr. Deckerville was taking a short cut to a lake to hunt ducks when he apparently drug his double-barreled shot gun by the barrel through the fence and he was struck with both barrels.

October 26, 1908
<u>Andrew J. Martin</u>, the 17-year-old son of Mr. and Mrs. Simon Martin died instantly after being accidentally shot with his own shotgun while he was duck hunting on the Missouri River near the Fifteenth Street Bridge in Great Falls.

Chapter One: BY THEIR OWN NEGLIGENCE

Young Martin left his home about 10 o'clock that morning with two of his friends and they secured a boat and were above the bridge when Martin reportedly got tired of rowing and he wanted to take a different position in the boat.

As he picked up his double-barreled 12-guage-shotgun by the barrel it accidentally struck the side of the boat and one of the barrels discharged into his abdomen. The powerful blast from the shotgun went through Martin's body and crashed into the bow of the boat.

Martin's two companions went into shock and all they could do was scream for help. They apparently became disoriented and they couldn't even bring themselves to row the boat. When they were found the boys were only gripping the craft and screaming their heads off.

Two other men were on the river near the scene at the time and after hearing the shot and the screams they helped the boys get to the shore and they delivered the dead boy's body to his home.

Andrew Martin was well known and he had just graduated from Great Falls High School that spring. The young man was just starting life and he was employed as a molder at the Great Falls Iron Works.

November 15, 1909
Fourteen-year-old George Clarence Beckman of Great Falls died at the Deaconess Hospital a few hours after being accidentally shot while he was on a duck hunt on the Missouri River.

Three other boys had accompanied Beckman that day and he and Hilmer Johnson were in one rowboat while Werth Dickenson and Albert Vinning were in a second craft. The boys had planned on collecting firewood and then they were going to build a bonfire on the island near Little Chicago and then hunt ducks from that location.

Chapter One: BY THEIR OWN NEGLIGENCE

Dickenson and Vinning were collecting wood on the north shore of the river and Beckman and Johnson had landed near the old pavilion adjacent to Gibson Lake (where the new skateboard park is now located). While Johnson began collecting scrap lumber and driftwood around the pavilion Beckman was putting his shotgun into the boat.

Beckman was holding the shotgun by the muzzle as he was placing it into the boat when it accidentally discharged. The blast tore into the left side of his chest, tearing through his lung and then coming out his back leaving a ghastly hole.

An agonizing scream from the victim brought the frantic Johnson to Beckman's side. While Beckman was bleeding badly from his wound Johnson began screaming for Dickenson and Vinning but at first they thought he was just clowning around.

After realizing that there was indeed trouble, the other two boys rushed across the river where Werth Dickenson was credited for taking charge of the situation. He immediately sent one of the boys to call the police and the other to bring back a doctor while he remained at the scene and tried to stop the bleeding of his friend's wounds.

The young wounded hunter was taken to the hospital in the new ambulance, which had been recently purchased with donations from the residents of Great Falls. It was equipped with the newest equipment including a swinging cot, a thermometer, a doctor's medical case and it was lighted by an oil lamp.

George Beckman died 2 hours after the accident but he lived long enough at the hospital to see his mother before he passed. The untimely death of the Beckman boy caused the community of Great Falls to reorganize its emergency procedures.

November 30, 1911
Walter B. Munroe was accidentally shot and killed in the kitchen of his home while he was cleaning his .32-caliber automatic Winchester

11

Chapter One: BY THEIR OWN NEGLIGENCE

rifle. The well-known Kalispell Dairyman had recently loaned the weapon to a neighbor who had gone hunting.

Mr. Munroe had just started his morning by lighting a fire at about 5 o'clock and then he began cleaning the weapon. Apparently he had thought his neighbor had emptied the gun before returning it, but there was still a shell left in the magazine, which automatically entered the chamber and it accidentally discharged as Munroe was starting to examine it.

The bullet entered the man's left rib cage; ranged upward through his lungs and heart; came out of his right shoulder and then lodged in the ceiling of his house. Mr. Munroe was about 38 years old and he left a wife and a 3-year-old daughter.

May 7, 1912
(Lewistown Daly News)
Floyd Ritch, the 22-year-old son of a well-known Fergus County rancher died at the St. Joseph Hospital in Lewistown from an accidental gunshot wound he received while he was hunting coyotes on the Lehman Ranch near Heath.

Mr. Ritch had located a den of coyotes on the spread and he went to the ranch house to borrow a pick, shovel and a .45-caliber revolver from Jason Apple who was the foreman of the place.

After returning to the den, Ritch started to dig down to the animals when he lost his footing and he fell to the ground. The old style Colt revolver, which had no safety, was in his hip pocket and when the hammer struck a rock it accidentally discharged into the boy's body.

The heavy slug entered the young man's back and then passed through his abdomen, tearing a big hole through his intestines before exiting through his belly. Mr. Ritch was able to make his way back to Apple's cabin and from there he was transported to the hospital in Lewistown.

Dying to Hunt in Montana
Chapter One: BY THEIR OWN NEGLIGENCE

Dr. Harry Wilson performed surgery on Floyd Ritch, but he didn't
believe the young man would survive the wound. Although the
victim's condition had initially improved, he died the next evening.

September 9, 1912
(Anaconda Standard)
Fifteen-year-old John Sagar of Butte was killed instantly when he was
accidentally shot in the head while he was hunting in the second
canyon north of the Columbia Gardens.

Earlier that Sunday morning the Sagar boy had attended services at
Holy Savior Church and then about noon he and his friends got a
.22-caliber rifle and they headed for the hills.

The other boys later told the authorities that Sagar had looked
down the barrel of the weapon as he was trying to dislodge a shell
in the rifle by tapping the butt of the rifle on a rock. The firearm
accidentally discharged from the pounding, and the bullet struck the
boy at the bridge of his nose; entered his brain and he tumbled over
dead.

At first his friends thought he was just stunned and they tried to
revive him by pouring water over his head while they begged him to
wake up and speak.

When John Sagar couldn't be aroused, the boys ran to the John
Korn place, which was just east of the Columbia Gardens. Mr. Korn
quickly hitched up a team of horses and he took the boy's body to the
saloon that his father owned and operated in Butte.

September 29, 1912
Augusta area farmer, Richard Jones accidentally shot and killed
himself in the Dearborn Canyon at about 6 o'clock on Friday,
September 27. There were no witnesses to the tragedy but from the
location of the gun and the man's body it appeared that he had died
shortly after he was shot.

Chapter One: BY THEIR OWN NEGLIGENCE

Mr. Jones had gone to a field to drive his cattle home and he had taken a gun along in case he ran across some game. It appears that when he drove his cattle to a gate he stood his gun up against the wire fence while he opened the latch. After closing the gate behind the animals he apparently pulled the gun through the fence by the barrel and the trigger caught on the wire and discharged.

The man and his wife lived alone on their farm, and when he didn't come home for supper Mrs. Jones started looking for him. She found the body of her husband about 40 feet from where he was shot, indicating that he had been crawling to his home when he died of his wounds.

October 2, 1912

Carelessness also caused the instant death of Martin McGraw of Great Falls while he was hunting prairie chickens with a friend near Monarch. Mr. McGraw and his companion, Louis Beckler had been sharing one gun while they were hunting on a ranch near Belt Park.

After leaving the ranch house, Mr. Beckler used the .22-caliber rifle to wound a prairie chicken and as they were chasing after that bird McGraw grabbed the weapon to killed another chicken that was perched in a tree. When they noticed the first crippled bird Beckler wanted his turn with the rifle to finish it off for good.

Mr. Beckler later explained to the authorities that McGraw didn't want to waste ammunition on a wounded bird and said he would club the chicken to death with the butt of the gun. According to Beckler, McGraw grabbed the barrel of the rifle and struck the bird, and at that very instant the weapon accidentally discharged and struck him in the chest. The fatal bullet entered McGraw's body about 2 inches above his right nipple and then it pierced his heart.

Martin McGraw had come to Great Falls in 1909 from Canada and ironically he owned and operated a shooting gallery business on Third Street South where he had always insisted that his patrons follow safe gun handling practices.

14

Chapter One: BY THEIR OWN NEGLIGENCE

November 26, 1912
(Anaconda Standard)
The body of 23-year-old <u>Harrison Allen</u> of Livingston was found
Sunday night, November 24 in the Boulder Country some 40 miles
from his home. Mr. Allen had been on an extended hunting trip with
Walter Clark and Clyde Bunnel at a hunting camp when he failed to
return to their cabin Saturday night.

The authorities believed that Mr. Allen had become lost and while
he was frantically trying to find his way out of the backcountry he
accidentally shot himself when he tripped and fell.

September 3, 1913
<u>Mrs. Dr. Hubert E. Houston</u>, of Kalispell was accidentally shot and
killed while she was on a hunting trip with her husband, his sister,
Miss Frances Houston and Charles H. Jennings near Spencer Lake.

The party was driving along a road when they backed into a log as
they were turning their vehicle around. The impact lodged Mrs.
Edna Houston's loaded gun under her seat, and when she was
pulling it out by the barrel the trigger caught on the lunch basket and
accidentally discharged. The bullet entered the woman's abdomen
and she reportedly died instantly.

Mrs. Houston left a husband and three lovable little daughters aged
6, 5 and one was about 11 months old. Ironically Dr. Houston had
been involved with another hunting tragedy when his friend B.F.
Egan died after becoming lost in November of 1902.

September 5, 1913
Fourteen-year-old <u>Leslie Dodds</u> of Dillon died in Murray Hospital at
Butte after holding on to life for 3 days after being accidentally shot
on the opening day of the 1913 Duck Hunting Season.

Mr. Dodds was shooting ducks with several of his friends at Red
Rock Lake a few miles south of Dillon when he was shot in the side

with his own weapon. Although Dodds was rushed to Butte the best medical attention at that time couldn't save him.

Leslie Dodds was the son of a Dillon minister and he was attending the preparatory school at the State Normal College[3] where he had earned distinction in athletics.

October 12, 1916
Ralph Belgrade of Craig was accidentally shot and killed in the home of his brother while he was borrowing a rifle to go hunting.

After a short visit at the home of Louis Belgrade, Ralph was carrying the weapon towards the door when it accidentally discharged sending the round into his right shoulder. The young man died a few hours later leaving a wife and 3 children.

December 10, 1916
Great Falls painter, Joseph A. Stuesse accidentally shot and killed himself while he was deer hunting along Canyon Creek about 7 miles northwest of Wilburn in Lewis and Clark County.

After working during the summer in Great Falls, Mr. Stuesse and fellow painter, Dave Whitcher had agreed to hunt, trap and prospect in the Trout Creek area during the fall of 1916. They packed most of their supplies into the area on their backs and Louis Houberg of Wilborn hauled in the rest of their gear for them on a packhorse.

The two men prospected for a couple of months in the early fall and then they ran their trap lines and began to hunt for their winter meat supply. The two men only had one rifle between them so they took turns hunting and checking their traps.

On December 8, Mr. Houberg visited their camp and he and Joe Stuesse went deer hunting together while Mr. Whitcher checked their traps. That afternoon Houberg heard a gunshot and he presumed that Stuesse had dropped a deer and he proceeded to join him to help out with the animal.

Chapter One: BY THEIR OWN NEGLIGENCE

After following Stuesse's tracks in the fresh snow he came across the man's dead body. Mr. Stuesse was partially propped up against a tree with his rifle at his side. Apparently he had tripped on one of the many fallen lodge poles in the area and he was shot in the groin with his 25-35-caliber Remington automatic rifle.

Joe Stuesse was originally from Canada and he had lived in Great Falls for about a year before his death. Mr. Stuesse took his last trip out of the woods that he loved over the back of a packhorse to Wilborn by his two friends.

October 24, 1918
Well-known Chouteau hunter and trapper, M.F. Stoughton was shot and killed in a peculiar accident while he was crossing the Missouri River on the Loma Ferry.

Stoughton had packed a loaded broken-down .22-caliber hammerless rifle in a sack and when he began shaking the weapon parts out of the bag the trigger apparently caught on something in the sack and it discharged into his abdomen. The 48-year-old outdoorsman reportedly died a short time later.

October 26, 1918
The body of Jack Smith was located about a week after he had accidentally shot and killed himself near the McManuamy's Lumber Mill, which was about 21 miles northwest of Kalispell. Mr. Smith's body was found along side of a log, which he had been crawling under when his rifle accidentally discharged. The charge had tore off a portion of his right hand and then entered his head.

Smith had been hunting with 15-year-old Tom Clark and when the young boy returned home alone a search began for the missing hunter the next day. Jack Smth was a single man who had lived alone on his homestead for about 15 years.

Chapter One: BY THEIR OWN NEGLIGENCE

October 10, 1919
The president of the Arrow Creek Livestock Company, <u>Alexander Stronach</u> died several days after being accidentally shot while he was coyote hunting on his ranch at Laird about 35 miles north of Chester.

Mr. Stronach and one of his hired hands left the ranch on October 6 in search of coyotes, which had been hanging around the place for sometime. After stopping their vehicle to take a shot at a coyote, Mr. Stronach was accidentally shot in the forehead while he was removing his rifle from the back seat.

After two physicians worked on Mr. Stronach at the ranch he was moved to the hospital at Chester. Alex Stronach had ranched in the Geyser area before he and other investors had purchased the Frank Laird ranch located in the northern portion of Liberty County near the Canadian border.

November 5, 1920
(Bozeman Daily Chronicle)
Fifty-six-year-old <u>Thomas A. Towery</u>, accidentally shot himself Tuesday evening November 2 while he was coyote hunting on his ranch near Sedan.

The rancher had told one of his neighbors that some coyotes had been bothering his cattle and he was going to ambush them. Taking his 22-special rifle he went into his field and he crawled to the top of a haystack in a small coral not far from his house.

Because Mr. Towery was alone the rest of the account was based on the evidence that the authorities found. Apparently Towery had stood his rifle against the logs of the coral as he watched for the coyotes to appear.

Either, Mr. Towery saw one or more coyotes and had reached for his rifle or else he had decided to give up and go home. As he picked

Chapter One: BY THEIR OWN NEGLIGENCE

up the weapon the hammer must have caught on something, and it accidentally discharged into his right cheek about an inch below his eye.

The condition of his body and clothing indicated that he had grabbed his face with his hand after being shot as his face, hands and parts of his shirt were covered with blood. The man's body was discovered the next morning about 8:30 o'clock and it was determined that he had been dead for several hours.

Mr. Thomas Towery was a single man and he had come to Montana from Texas to homestead his place in about 1900. The various books in his home indicated that Mr. Towery had been well educated and that he was fond of music. The man was considered a very good neighbor and he was quite prosperous. Before his death, Mr. Towery had planned to lease his property and to spend the winter hunting and trapping.

November 26, 1920
Charles L. Torrence of Simms was accidentally shot and killed with his own weapon while he was at a hunting camp with his foster-father, J.A. Phillips at Hot Springs on the north fork of the Sun River.

While working at the cook wagon at the camp the 27-year-old Mr. Torrence reportedly dropped a handgun, which he had been carrying in his shirt pocket. He reportedly picked the weapon up and later the same pistol fell to the ground again, this time it discharged into Torrence's chest. The young man was said to have died about 40 minutes later.

Ironically the pistol that ended Torrence's life was a souvenir that he had found while he was serving in the Argonne Forest with the 119th Field Artillery in France. Charles Torrence found the pistol in an abandoned German tank and he later brought it back to Montana.

Chapter One: BY THEIR OWN NEGLIGENCE

November 9, 1921
<u>Knute Knuteson</u>, 27, of St. Cloud, Minnesota was accidentally killed while he was hunting on the Clayton Ranch about 3 miles from Gregson Springs.

Mr. Knuteson was hunting alone on his stepbrother's ranch when his horse apparently stumbled and he fell to the ground and his .30-30-caliber rifle accidentally discharged. The bullet entered his right lung and it came out through the back killing him instantly.

When Mrs. George Clayton noticed Knute Knuteson's horse return without a rider she went to the scene where she found the man's body and she notified the authorities.

November 23, 1921
Devon area farmer, <u>Archie Blair</u> accidentally shot and killed himself while he was taking his shotgun from his buggy after returning from a hunting trip.

Mr. Blair apparently pulled the shotgun from the rig by the barrel when it accidentally discharged, striking him in the side and then through the heart. Archie Blair left a widow and one child.

August 7, 1922
(Northwest Tribune)
Thirty-one-year-old <u>Andrew Lubardo</u> accidently shot and killed himself while he was hunting rabbits when he apparently used his double-barreled shot gun to club a rattlesnake.

Andrew and his wife of only one month were visiting the John Lucas Ranch about 4 miles east of Bear Creek when he decided to go hunting. After failing to return to the ranch house a search party was organized.

Chapter One: BY THEIR OWN NEGLIGENCE

Apparently as Lubardo was making his way up a hillside he ran across a nest of rattlesnakes. He managed to shoot one snake and another eluded him by slithering between some large boulders.

As Lubardo was leaning over a large rock and striking at the snake with the stock of his weapon the hammer evidently struck the boulder and it discharged into his chest.

While Lubardo's body was being prepared for burial it was discovered that he had been bitten by a rattler after he had fallen to the ground. The authorities said that the man was probably already dead at the time he was bitten.

Being a veteran, Lubardo's funeral was conducted by the American Legion at the cemetery, which is near the edge of Bear Creek. In one of those freaky coincidences, after the firing squad had passed, a large rattlesnake crossed the road in front of the color guard. The men quickly killed the reptile.

September 2, 1923
(Anaconda Standard)
Ralph Ryan accidentally shot and killed himself while he was hawk hunting on his parent's ranch, which was about a mile and a quarter southeast of Piedmont.

For quite a while the Ryan's chickens had been under attack by hawks and it was a custom of Ralph and his two older brothers to hunt them during their spare time.

A hawk was seen swooping near the chicken house and the eleven-year-old boy took down the heavy .410-guage shotgun from the gun rack and he started for the barn where he took his position on the seat of the harrow.

Chapter One: BY THEIR OWN NEGLIGENCE

Ralph may have been holding the shotgun between his legs when it evidently slipped from his grasp and it fell and struck an iron cross rod on the farm implement. The boy apparently watched the weapon as it fell and when the gun accidentally discharged it took part of his forehead off.

When Ralph's mother heard the shot she went to the barn where she found her son still sitting on the harrow with his head slumped over. The young Ralph Ryan left behind his parents, his 2 brothers and a sister.

September 30, 1923
Winston area rancher, <u>John Szasv</u> died at a Helena hospital from an accidental gunshot wound he received at his ranch house after returning home from hunting.

Mr. Szasv reportedly shot himself in the abdomen while he was carrying his .30-30 rifle by the barrel as it struck the doorway to the kitchen of his home. The 33-year-old victim's wife was herself in the hospital at Townsend after giving birth to twins the day before his death.

<u>October 1, 1924</u>
<u>Larcey M. Lakar</u>, the 15-year-old son of Mr. and Mrs. Joe M. Lakar of Bear Creek accidentally shot and killed himself while he was hunting in the hills above Washoe.

Larcey and his brother, 17-year-old Tony Lakar were crawling through a fence when the full load from his newly acquired shotgun discharged into his heart.

October 8, 1924
The body of 15-year-old <u>Walter Wersall</u> was found in a bean field on his parent's farm near Drury Station on the Shepherd Railroad after accidentally killing himself while hunting.

Chapter One: BY THEIR OWN NEGLIGENCE

Walter had been hunting with several of his friends when they separated and he apparently accidentally shot himself in the head while he was either sitting down or getting up. The full charge of his shotgun struck him just above the bridge of his nose tearing away his forehead and much of his brains.

September 25, 1926
(Missoulian)
Seventeen-year-old <u>Samuel B. Clark Jr.</u> of Florence was accidentally killed when his own 12-guage doubled barrel shotgun discharged into his body while he was hunting near his home.

Clark, a senior at Florence-Carlton High School was duck hunting with brothers George and Claude Jones in the marshlands northeast of Carlton when the boys decided to spread out.

The Jones brothers later said that they had heard the shot that killed Clark but at the time they thought he had shot at a duck. When it was time to return home, the brothers called for Clark but their friend didn't answer.

They found Clark's body lying on one side of a log and his shotgun was on the other. Apparently the boy lost his footing on the log while he was holding the barrel of his weapon, which was resting on his shoulder. One of the two barrels discharged into Clark's groin when the gun struck the ground during the fall killing him in minutes.

The Jones boys immediately ran for help at the Sterrett Ranch and Clark's body was later taken to the ranch in a buggy. Coroner Forkenbrook reported that the full blast had struck the boy in the left groin, which badly mutilated the body and it probably caused instantaneous death.

Chapter One: BY THEIR OWN NEGLIGENCE

Sam Clark had 3 brothers at the time of his death and he had been living with the George Jones family near Florence.

November 16, 1926
The body of <u>William Lawrence</u> was discovered face down on the floor of his cabin after he was accidentally shot and killed with his own shotgun, as he was going hunting.

Mr. Lawrence was reportedly in the habit of keeping his loaded shotgun behind the door of his cabin and it apparently accidentally discharged as he grabbed it by the barrel.

His brother, John Lawrence took his body to their former home in Nebraska for burial.

September 30, 1927
Helena Forest supervisor, <u>Burr W. Clark</u>, 42, of Helena was killed when a loaded pistol accidentally discharged from inside his packsack. The vice president of the Montana Elks Association was loading the sack into his car at Radersburg when the weapon discharged into his body.

<u>**October 17, 1927**</u>
<u>Joseph J. Kosena</u>, the 16-year-old son of Mr. and Mrs. Kime Kosena of Anaconda was accidentally killed while he was hunting on Willow Creek about 12 miles east of the smelter city.

Joe Kosena was hunting deer with a party of five when he fell behind to rest. Apparently he was dragging his rifle or he was using it as a walking stick when it accidentally discharged and the round went through his heart. His brother, Mike Kosena was the first to reach the body after he heard the victim's shot.

November 15, 1927
Sixteen-year-old <u>Rex Roberts</u> of Hamilton died in a Hamilton hospital after severing an artery in his right arm with a shotgun blast while he was duck hunting with his brother, Fred and other

Chapter One: BY THEIR OWN NEGLIGENCE

companions at Lake Como. The Hamilton High School junior had just recovered from a fractured collarbone that he had sustained during football practice.

November 16, 1927
(Missoulian)
The body of <u>George Kennedy</u> was found November 15 near the Fehlberg Ranch, some 35 miles west of Kalispell, after he was reported lost on Sunday, November 13, while hunting near Lake McGregor.

When the body was found the searchers noted a single bullet hole in the man's head. Because Kennedy was lightly clothed and he wasn't carrying any food or matches the officials presumed that the man had shot himself rather than endure suffering from the hardships of being lost in the cold weather.

It was later determined by the county coroner that Mr. Kennedy had in fact accidentally shot himself while he was hunting. Men who had hunted with the victim before reported that he was in the habit of carrying his gun fully cocked while he was hunting.

Residents at the Fehlberg Ranch reported that they had heard a shot on the day of Kennedy's disappearance, and it was believed that it was the one that ended the man's life.

December 11, 1927
<u>Anton Schafer</u>, 15-year-old Judith Basin County rancher, was killed in a hunting accident on his father's place about 15 miles east of Stanford.

Anton and his younger brother had returned from a hunting expedition when he pulled his shotgun from their sled by the barrel and it accidentally discharged into his chest, killing him instantly.

Chapter One: BY THEIR OWN NEGLIGENCE

November 4, 1928
Thirty-year-old Great Northern section foreman, <u>Walter Griesbach</u> died at the St. Claire Hospital in Fort Benton after accidentally shooting himself near the Teton Station.

Mr. Griesbach and his 2-man crew were on a section car clearing an obstruction from the track when he observed something moving in the grass. Telling his men that he was going to "check it out" he grabbed the muzzle of his .16-guage shotgun and the weapon accidentally discharged into his abdomen near the hip.

The men rushed Mr. Griesbach to Fort Benton on the section car but he died about two hours later. He was conscious the entire time, and he said his goodbyes to his fellow workers and he sent messages of love to his wife at the Teton Station and to his parents.

Walter Griesbach had been a marine pilot during the First World War and he was the only surviving son of Henry W. Griesbach, a pioneer of Chouteau County for more than 50 years. Ironically all four of Henry's sons were gunshot victims. Besides Walter, one of Henry's boys was killed during World War One, another of his sons shot and killed a brother and then he committed suicide.

November 6, 1928
Helena Valley farmer and caretaker of the Stanchfield Hunting Preserve, <u>Bozo Masanovich</u> died at a Helena hospital from an accidental gunshot while he was hunting ducks.

Chapter One: BY THEIR OWN NEGLIGENCE

Mr. Masanovich was hunting alone on the shoreline of Stanchfield Lake when he slipped and fell and his shotgun discharged into his leg. By the time the wounded hunter was discovered he was suffering from exposure and had lost a great deal of blood.

Because of his condition the doctors weren't able to operate immediately and consequently gangrene set into his wounds. Even after a last minute operation to remove his injured leg Masanovich didn't survive. Ironically Mr. Masanovich had survived the entire war in Europe as an officer in the Czechoslovakia Army without a single injury.

November 12, 1928
Eighteen-year-old <u>Herschel A. Dockery</u> of Cascade was accidentally shot and killed while he was hunting in the Sheep Creek country about 25 miles southeast of Cascade.

The Dockery boy was hunting deer with Charles Hodson, Victor Swedblom and Swedblom's brother-in-law, all from Cascade. The men split up in the morning and they all met on a slope half way between the north and south forks of Sheep Creek.

While the men were talking, Herschel Dockery dropped his rifle and it started to slide down the hillside. He quickly grabbed the weapon and pulled it towards his body when it discharged into his right hip and then the bullet drove passed his heart. Dockery's friends carried his body the 3 miles out of the rough country on a stretcher.

November 25, 1929
Carbon County farmer, <u>Richard Allen</u> died at a Billing hospital after he accidentally shot himself in the right leg while he was hunting near Roberts, which is located on Rock Creek between Red Lodge and Laurel.

Chapter One: BY THEIR OWN NEGLIGENCE

The twenty-five-year-old Mr. Allen was taken to Roberts on a sleigh and then he was taken to Billings on the train where a number of blood transfusions, including one from his brother failed to save him. Richard Allen was the second fatality of the 5-day pheasant season of 1929.

September 28, 1930
Centennial Valley rancher, <u>Charles Montgomery</u>, 39, was the first hunting fatality in 1930 when he was accidentally killed while he was passing through a fence. Both barrels of Montgomery's shotgun reportedly went off into his stomach as he pulled it through the fence.

Mr. Montgomery's 12-year-old daughter, Roberta, ran 3 miles to the nearest ranch house for aid but her father had probably died in minutes. Charles Montgomery was married with the one child and he worked his ranch near Monida.

October 26, 1931
<u>Hollis B. Wiggin</u> of Frenchtown was accidentally shot and killed while he was duck hunting on the Clark Fork River with Charles Luedice and the latter man's son.

When they reached the shore Mr. Wiggin began passing out the weapons and when he was handing the boy his shotgun stock first, it accidentally discharged into his chest.

November 10, 1931
Twenty-three-year-old <u>Wallace Stone</u> was accidentally killed instantly while he was cleaning his hunting rifle in the parlor of his parents home about 3 miles east of Miles City on the Yellowstone Trail.

While his parents were in town Mr. Stone was cleaning his .32-caliber rifle when it accidentally discharged and struck him between the eyes.

Chapter One: BY THEIR OWN NEGLIGENCE

November 13, 1931
<u>Floyd Marble</u>, 31, of Bozeman was found dead from a hunting accident. He apparently shot himself in the abdomen with his shotgun when he slipped and fell on some loose shale on a trail near his hunting cabin. He was hunting alone and he bled to death as he tried to make his way back to his cabin.

November 22, 1931
(Missoulian)
<u>John C. Holland</u> of Bozeman was reportedly found dying in his automobile from an accidental shotgun blast. He apparently suffered the fatal wound while he was getting out of his car.

(1931) Reported on 1/2/1932
<u>William B. Burkhart</u>, 43, of Orchard Homes, Missoula was killed on November 21, 1931 when his rifle accidentally discharged when he slipped while he was stepping over a log.

October 4, 1932
The body of <u>Clarence E. Fahlgren</u> was found hanging in a fence about 100 yards from his home after he had accidentally shot himself while hunting ducks and rabbits.

The Greycliff rancher's shotgun apparently discharged as he was crawling through the fence and the blast tore away part of his face. Mr. A.C. Boyles found the body of the man the next day after a search was initiated when Fahlgren's widow called the neighbors explaining that her husband hadn't come home from a hunt.

November 2, 1932
(Missoulian)
<u>Oliver M. Johnson</u>, the 45-year-old caretaker at Georgetown Lake, was accidentally shot and killed as he was climbing through a fence.

Chapter One: BY THEIR OWN NEGLIGENCE

Mr. Johnson had been hunting alone when his shotgun apparently discharged while he was going through the fence that bordered the highway.

John Burlovich of Anaconda was walking along the road when he found the body of the man who had died from a massive gunshot wound to his abdomen.

November 29, 1932
Robert M. Bell, 45, of Butte died from a bullet wound through the heart when his .22-caliber rifle accidentally discharged as he was getting into his car after hunting rabbits with his son.

November 10, 1933
Donald Campbell was found dead, apparently the victim of his own rifle while he was hunting near Eureka. His body was discovered near his car and the authorities believed that he was killed while he was removing his weapon from the vehicle.

October 29, 1934
Charles Jacobs, 33, of Billings died in a local hospital after accidentally shooting himself while he was removing his shotgun from the rumble seat of his car while he was pheasant hunting.

November 4, 1935
Lawrence Dean, 34, of Bozeman was accidentally shot and killed while he was hunting pheasants near Manhattan with four of his friends.

The men were driving down a road when they spotted some Ringnecks and they stopped to get out. Apparently Mr. Dean's shotgun caught on something in the car and it accidentally discharged as he was removing it from the vehicle.

Chapter One: BY THEIR OWN NEGLIGENCE

November 6, 1935
Lawrence Carmack, 33, of Manhattan was accidentally shot
and killed while he was duck hunting near Dry Creek north of
Manhattan.

He had been hunting with two companions when he was struck in
the head and face from his shotgun while he was removing it from
his car.

November 8, 1935
Seventeen-year-old Sam Kahl of Ronan died in a Polson hospital
a day after he had been accidentally shot while hunting near his
hometown.

The young hunter reportedly was pulling his shotgun through a fence
when it accidentally discharged into his abdomen. He died without
ever regaining consciousness.

November 27, 1935
(Missoulian)
Philip Satterlee Terrio, 19, of Darby was accidentally killed while he
was rabbit hunting with three other men near Wisdom.

The men had just parked when Mr. Terrio was shot in the neck with
his .25-caliber rifle as he was removing it from the car. He was rushed
to a hospital at Hamilton where he died from his wound.

August 2, 1936
(Missoulian)
Harry Ernest Stradtzeck, 12, was fatality wounded while he was
hunting gophers near his ranch house about 7 miles from Niarada.

He had left his home about 3 o'clock in the afternoon with his rifle
and his mother thought he was just taking a nap when she saw him
lying in the shade next to a small stream.

Chapter One: BY THEIR OWN NEGLIGENCE

About an hour later she approached her son and she discovered that he had been shot in the head. The boy's father went for a doctor but Harry Stradtzeck was dead before help returned.

October 4, 1936
(Missoulian)

Eighteen-year-old John Fink of Warm Springs died at the state hospital after accidentally shooting himself while he was hunting jackrabbits.

While hunting about a mile from Warm Springs John Fink reportedly shot himself in the left arm just above the elbow as he was jumping off a fence. The young man died shortly after the medical staff had amputated his arm.

October 11, 1936
(Missoulian)

Edgar Hicks, 16, of Hamilton was killed when his shotgun accidentally discharged while he was hunting just six hours into the 1936 Duck-Hunting Season.

Hicks was killed instantly when the shotgun he was reaching for blasted into his neck and as he fell the barrel of the weapon penetrated the wound.

The accident occurred about 1 o'clock in the afternoon on the Riverside Bridge on Highway 3 about a mile north of Hamilton. Two young boys, Owen Rumley and Jack Centers were with Hicks at the time and they witnessed the tragedy.

When Coroner John Dowling and Under Sheriff A.C. Baker arrived at the scene Mr. Dowling removed the gun barrel, which was stuck about two inches or more into the lower jaw of the victim. The coroner said that death was due to the destruction of vertebra in the neck and at the base of the skull.

Chapter One: BY THEIR OWN NEGLIGENCE

The three boys had left their homes in Hamilton earlier that day and they had been shooting ducks from the bridge. Hicks had borrowed the Rumley boy's 410-guage single-barreled shotgun, and he had placed the weapon on the bridge railing. When the Hicks boy grabbed for the shotgun it accidentally discharged into his neck.

Four years earlier in October, Hicks' younger brother, Donald Hicks was killed by an automobile not far from the spot where Edgar met his own death. Edgar Hicks was born at Sula, Montana on January 28, 1920 and he was a junior at Hamilton High. His entire high school class attended his funeral.

October 17, 1936
Ruth Fraunhofer, 18, of Ulm was found dead with a bullet through her heart at her uncle's ranch, which was about 10 miles south of Ulm.

The young woman reportedly had left the ranch house telling her brother that she was going out to shoot some sparrows. Her brother was later searching for hen eggs and he found her near a haystack with the .22-caliber rifle under her body.

October 22, 1936
Edward Neumann, a 33-year-old Petroleum County rancher was killed when his shotgun accidentally discharged while he was duck hunting near Wild Horse Lake about 40 miles northeast of Lewistown.

The authorities reported that Mr. Neumann had been shot through the throat when he was removing a loaded shotgun from the back seat of his car. Apparently the trigger had caught on the door handle and it discharged.

November 10, 1936
Albert Booth, 27, of Fort Benton was killed instantly when his rifle accidentally discharged while he was on an elk-hunting trip in the Gallatin Canyon.

Evidently the man's firearm discharged as he was picking it up after he had stopped to build a fire to warm up. Other members of his hunting party later found his body.

November 10, 1936
Elmer E. Stockman Jr., 35, of Hamilton was shot and killed when the shotgun he was taking out of his car accidentally discharged. Mr. Stockman, who had organized the Boys Scouts in Hamilton some 15 years earlier, had just returned from pheasant hunting with Max Cook and Bill Newman.

November 15, 1936
Arthur T. Ridgeway, 45, of Denton was shot and killed while he was returning from a deer-hunting trip in the Little Belt Mountains with his friends. Mr. Ridgeway was sitting in the back seat of the vehicle when a rifle accidentally discharged into his abdomen, killing him within minutes.

November 16, 1936
(Missoulian)
Thirty-five-year-old Missoula-area-rancher, Ray V. Doney died at St. Patrict's Hospital in Missoula after he accidentally shot himself while he was hunting pheasants in the Jocko Valley.

While Mr. Doney was pulling his shotgun through a fence the weapon accidentally discharged into his legs. He was rushed to Missoula but he died that night.

July 13, 1937
(Missoulian)
The body of Andrew Danielson was found about 8 miles northwest of Kalispell on the A.R. Douglas Timberland property. Alex Danielson, the brother of the victim found the badly decomposed remains while he was in the area to collect firewood.

A .32-caliber rifle was found next to Mr. Danielson and the 69-year-old had been killed by a single gunshot to the chest just below the heart. Alex said that his brother had apparently shot himself accidentally while he was sitting under a tree waiting for a deer to come along.

November 23, 1937
(Missoulian)
Deep Creek rancher, <u>Berton Thompson</u> was accidentally killed while he was climbing through a wire fence along a highway. Mr. Thompson, who was about 50 probably died instantly after being struck in the head by a slug from his .306-caliber high-powered rifle.

September 23, 1938
(Missoulian)
<u>Earl Lyght</u>, 20, of Kalispell was killed instantly when his rifle accidentally discharged while he was hunting at the Sam Conners Logging Camp, which was about 25 miles west of Kalispell.

Mr. Lyght had returned to the camp with an elk he had killed and he then placed his rifle on a low roof of a barn. When the trigger of the weapon struck the edge of the roof the firearm discharged and the bullet struck Earl Lyght in the lower part of his neck.

October 23, 1938
<u>Mark Kaulbach</u>, 19, of Fort Benton was accidentally killed when a loaded shotgun discharged into his body as he was placing it into a car. He had been duck hunting with two of his friends at the Old Nichols Reservoir about 10 miles east of Fort Benton.

November 1, 1938
(Missoulian)
<u>Forrest Smurr</u>, 22, of Polson was killed on his birthday when he pulled a shotgun out of a car at the Fred Newgard Ranch about three miles south of Pablo. Mr. Smurr and his cousin, Leroy Hoepner were

driving Miss Josie Newgard home to the ranch after she had done some work at the Smurr place, and then they had planned to hunt pheasants when they got there.

While Miss Newgard was getting out on one side of the car, Forrest Smurr was removing his shotgun from the vehicle from the other side when it accidentally discharged. The full charge of the shot struck the young man in the head, killing him instantly.

December 3, 1938
(Missoulian)
Twenty-three-year-old <u>Fred Grinde</u> died at a Great Falls hospital after being accidentally shot a week earlier on a hunting trip in the Sun River Canyon.

Mr. Grinde was at his hunting cabin with his wife when he dropped a pistol, which discharged and struck him in the abdomen. Mrs. Grinde drove the 80 miles to Great Falls in an hour and a half on mostly icy Montana roads in an unsuccessful attempt to save her husband's life. Fred Grinde was the son of the late Martin C. Grinde, former mayor of Great Falls.

October 16, 1939
<u>Robert Phoenix</u>, 21, of Logan was killed instantly when his shotgun accidentally discharged while he was on a hunt about three miles north of Three Forks.

Mr. Phoenix was crawling through a fence and pulling his gun along, when the trigger apparently caught on the fence and the full charge struck him in the face.

October 20, 1939
Twenty-one-year-old <u>William Smith</u> died in a Missoula hospital from an accidental gunshot wound he had sustained while he was hunting west of Stevensville.

Smith's hunting companion, Robert Bruce said that Mr. Smith had stood up onto a stump to look around for deer and he was using his rifle as a support when it accidentally discharged into his abdomen.

William Smith was carried out of the woods on an improvised stretcher to a car and then down a rough 3-mile logging road to the main highway to Missoula.

November 3, 1939
Chauncey Bowdin of Moiese died four days later in a hospital after accidentally shooting himself while he was getting into his car to go pheasant hunting. His right jaw, part of his right cheekbone and three fingers of his right hand were torn away by the shotgun blast.

October 4, 1940
(Missoulian)
Hamilton rancher, Denise F. Kohner died in a local hospital from an accidental gunshot wound to his chest as he was cleaning a rifle at his home west of town.

Mr. Kohner was cleaning his .25-20-caliber Remington rifle in preparation to hunt some coyotes that had been preying on his band of sheep. After finding her wounded husband Mrs. Kohner called her neighbors by telephone and the man was taken to the hospital.

Mr. Kohner had served in the U.S. Navy during the First World War and he served nine months overseas. Denise Kohner and his wife were working on the Miles Romney Ranch since moving to the Bitterroot from Fort Peck three years earlier.

Chapter One: BY THEIR OWN NEGLIGENCE

October 20, 1940
(Missoulian)
Robert Reesman, 12, of Missoula was killed instantly when he was shot with his own rifle while he was horseback riding in the Lavalle Creek area about 15 miles north of town. The accidental shooting brought a tragic conclusion to a weekend camping and hunting trip for six young Missoula grade school boys.

While the other four lads went hunting in one direction, Reesman and Herman Montreuil were hiking in another when they found a horse in a field. The two boys caught the horse and they road it along a rode until they came across a gate.

The Montreuil boy reportedly dismounted the horse and opened the gate while Reesman started the horse through the entrance. While passing through the gate Reesman's .22-caliber rifle apparently slipped from his grip and it fell to the ground and discharged, hitting him between the eyes.

Young Montreuil ran to their camp and then he rode his bicycle about six miles to where a summerhouse was being built for Walter Pope of Missoula. At the house the boy told the two carpenters about the tragedy and they all drove back to the scene where they found the Whittier eighth grader dead. The three then drove to Missoula where they reported the incident to the sheriff's office.

The officers found the two boys' rifles at the scene and Reesman's weapon had been fired once and the empty cartridge still in the chamber. The victim was killed with a single-shot through the head.

November 18, 1940
Carl Shepka, 13, of Anaconda was killed while he was rabbit hunting with three other boys at Lost Creek about five miles north of the smelter city.

Chapter One: BY THEIR OWN NEGLIGENCE

Ten-year-old Larry Lescantz told the authorities that the Shepka boy was holding the gun while he was helping the other boys unload it when it discharged into his chest.

November 22, 1940
James Brice, 14, of Laurel died from a gunshot wound while he was on a Thanksgiving Day hunt with his older brother and a friend.

It was reported that Brice's shotgun had gotten jammed and while he was trying to clear the action the weapon exploded into his armpit, and he died about 5 hours later.

November 8, 1941
Riley Ray, 56, of Gage, Montana died in a local hospital as a result of a gunshot wound while he was bird hunting.

Mr. Ray and his hunting partner, Vern R. Patterson had spotted some pheasants and they had stopped to take some shots when the 12-guage shotgun that was in the front seat between them accidentally discharged into the victim's left hip.

November 7, 1942
The body of 54-year-old John Eichstadt of Anaconda was found at Georgetown Lake after he had been missing for two days. A search was called after Mr. Eichstadt didn't return from a hunting trip with his friends. John Eichstadt was found with a single-bullet wound to his forehead.

November 1, 1943
James Bowden, 11, of Corvallis was killed when the shotgun he was carrying accidentally discharged in his face while he was pheasant hunting.

Chapter One: BY THEIR OWN NEGLIGENCE

His hunting companion, Duncan Stewart later said that while the two boys were crossing a bridge Bowden's gun went off when it touched the bridge railing.

November 15, 1943
Gilbert John Pochervina, 14, of Butte died in a local hospital of a gunshot wound to the abdomen he received while he was hunting with his father.

The two had been duck hunting at Ruby Dam near Sheridan when Gilbert was accidentally shot while he was pulling his shotgun from a duck blind by the barrel.

October 14, 1944
Orit T. Forbes, 40, of Shelby died in a local hospital while he was under going surgery on a shotgun wound he had sustained while he was hunting near Valier.

Mr. Forbes' shotgun had discharged into his abdomen as he was removing it from his vehicle. He was able to crawl back into his car and drive himself a mile to his hunting partner, E.A. Lee who took him on to Shelby.

October 16, 1946
William Kercher Jr., 17, of Riceville accidentally shot and killed himself on the opening day of the 1946 Big Game season. He was reportedly killed when his rifle accidentally discharged when he slipped and fell on the highway 4 miles north of Neihart.

Mr. Kercher and his 20-year-old friend, Louis Osterman had been walking side by side to their car on the ice-covered road, when Kercher slipped and fell, his gun going off simultaneously. The bullet struck the victim in the forehead just above the right eye, killing him instantly.

Chapter One: BY THEIR OWN NEGLIGENCE

The two hunters' sisters, Helen Osterman and Leota Kercher, both 19, had been sitting in the car about 200 feet away and they witnessed the tragedy. Officials reported that the two hunters had left early that day and their sisters were to pick them up at the pre-arranged place and time.

November 8, 1947
Ralph Grosswiler, 40, of Kalispell accidentally shot and killed himself as he was removing snow from his rifle while he was big game hunting in the Coram area. At the time of the tragedy Mr. Grosswiler was hunting with a friend about 8 miles from the nearest road.

November 1, 1948
Jerry Brown, 24, of Broadus was accidentally killed while he was hunting with four companions near Broadus when his rifle discharged as he set it on the ground at their camp, striking him in the forehead.

October 17, 1949
William Patterson, 27, of Dillon was the first hunting fatality of the 1949 Big Game Hunting season when he was accidentally shot while removing his rifle from a vehicle.

His hunting partner, Robert Morey reported that the men were getting out of Patterson's car to go elk hunting when he heard a rifle shot. Mr. Morey said he ran to Patterson's side and asked, "What is the matter?" He then said that Bill Patterson said, "Everything is the matter!" and then he collapsed dead.

October 24, 1950
Frederick Portman Jr., 43, of Helena accidentally shot and killed himself while he was cleaning his rifle on the day before the 1950 Big Game hunting season.

Chapter One: BY THEIR OWN NEGLIGENCE

October 23, 1950
Flathead authorities reported that 31-year-old <u>Curtis Westrum</u> of Hungry Horse was accidentally killed by his own weapon while he was making his way through thick brush along Flossie Creek. The report stated that Curtis Westrum was probably accidentally shot in the head when a twig had tripped the trigger on his weapon.

October 27, 1951
<u>Raymond A. Kuaffman</u>, 16, of Kalispell was accidentally shot and killed while he was hunting with his father in the Mountain Brook area just east of Kalispell.

As Raymond and his father were preparing to drive to another hunting spot he was killed instantly when his .32-special rifle discharged while he was moving it around in the cab of his father's pick-up. The Flathead High School sophomore left his parents, two brothers and three sisters.

October 11, 1952
<u>Orville Clancy</u>, 17, of Wolf Point was accidentally shot and killed while he was pheasant hunting alone south of Wolf Point. The boy had been crawling through a fence when his 12-guage, double-barreled shotgun went off, blowing off the top of his head.

Young Clancy had one pheasant in one hand and another bird in his belt when he placed the butt end of his gun through the fence first. The officials reported that the weapon was quite old, held together with wire and tape and probably went off from the jarring it received as it was placed on the ground, or else the trigger may have caught a barb on the wire fence.

October 22, 1952
Sixty-year-old <u>Richard W. Gilber</u> of Troy, Montana was found dead in his cabin about 2 miles south of town. His underwear-clad body was found just inside the doorway of his cabin along with ten empty .303-caliber rifle cartridges.

Chapter One: BY THEIR OWN NEGLIGENCE

The authorities believed that Mr. Gilber must have heard a wild animal near his cabin, and he had gotten out of bed and began shooting from his open doorway. Some how one of the rounds entered his head at the base of his skull, taking the back of his head.

November 4, 1952
Kenneth Newton, 17, of Saco, Montana accidentally shot and killed himself while he was hunting near his hometown. The young hunter had gone hunting alone about 7 miles northwest of town when he parked along the road and he was shot in the head while he was reaching for his gun in the vehicle. When found, Ken Newton was lying on the front seat with his feet protruding from the car door.

October 13, 1953
Clarence Sivertson, 20, of Chinook was accidentally killed when the gun he was removing from his car accidentally discharged. Mr. Sivertson and George Willey had just returned from shooting when he grabbed the .22-caliber rifle by the barrel.

October 23, 1953
William Syblon, 37, of Roundup accidentally shot and killed himself while he was hunting near Gage, Montana. Mr. Syblon had parked along a road on his family's ranch when he was shot in the temple while he was getting out of his car.

November 1, 1954
Dean Williams, 18, of Lambert, Montana died from an accidental gunshot wound to the chest when he grabbed for a rifle in a truck. He had been deer hunting with Clinton and James Mullin also of Lambert.

When the men came to a fence, Williams had gotten out to open the gate to allow the truck to go through. While Williams was holding the gate open he saw a deer and he leaped back into the pickup to get his gun when it accidentally went off.

Dying to Hunt in Montana
Chapter One: BY THEIR OWN NEGLIGENCE

October 17, 1956
Miles Spaich, 41, of Orinda, California accidentally shot and killed himself while he was hunting northwest of Deborgia about 23 miles west of Superior. Mr. Spaich had been hunting with three of his friends about 7 miles up Flat Rock Creek at the time of the accident.

October 18, 1956
Raymond H. White, 42, of Billings died in a local hospital from an accidental gunshot wound to his left side while he was deer hunting in the Mystic Lake area.

Mr. White was alone when his .22-caliber pistol accidentally discharged either when he was loading it or returning it to its holster.

After being wounded he was able to drive himself to the Montana Power Company plant where he was transferred to another vehicle and taken to Billings.

October 7, 1957
Fifteen-year-old Arthur Shoberg of East Helena was killed when his shotgun accidentally discharged while he was hunting at Lake Helena about 15 miles north of the Capital City.

Arthur Shoberg was with three other boys from east Helena, John Neckowich, Richard Warren and Don Smith when they spotted a flock of ducks and they stopped their car. When the hunters were getting their guns out of the trunk Shoberg's weapon accidentally discharged into his chest.

October 20, 1958
Howard Gleason, 77, of Glendive was accidentally killed with his own rifle while he was hunting along the Yellowstone River about 7 miles south of Savage, Montana. Mr. Gleason's rifle apparently had gone off when it was either dropped or set on ground.

Dying to Hunt in Montana
Chapter One: BY THEIR OWN NEGLIGENCE

November 22, 1958

LeRoy Tucker, 41, of Lodgepole accidentally shot himself during a hunting trip in the Little Rocky Mountains about 35 miles south of Fort Belknap.

Mr. Tucker had been hunting with his younger brother, Bill when he shot himself in the right leg with his .30-40 rifle. Bill Tucker immediately went for help, but LeRoy had bled to death before assistance arrived.

November 24, 1958

Harold T. Farron, 57, of Missoula died en route to a hospital from a gunshot wound after he had stumbled and fell on his own rifle.

Mr. Farron had been hunting deer with his sons, Harry and Daniel about 18 miles west of Drummond. Daniel Farron later told the authorities that he and his brother had heard a gun shot and found their father shot in the left side.

November 1, 1959

Joseph Cadieux found the body of his hunting partner and brother-in-law, 44-year-old John Edward Grady in a deep snow-covered ravine just off the shoulder about three-quarters of a mile from the summit of Rogers Pass on Montana Highway 200.

After being shot in the head, Mr. Grady had fallen about 350 feet into the 600-foot ravine. The victim's .30-06 rifle was found broken from the fall from the sheer cliffs. A wrecker truck with a wench was called into recover the body.

November 18, 1959

Aloysius Racine, 14, of Heart Butte was killed while he was rabbit hunting about 20 miles south of Browning. He had been hunting with his brother when he accidentally shot himself in the head near his ear as he was pulling a rifle from his shoulder.

Chapter One: BY THEIR OWN NEGLIGENCE

November 1, 1960
John R. Dahl, 41, of Anaconda accidentally shot and killed himself with a .22-caliber pistol while he was leaving his parent's home in Garnet to go hunting.

October 2, 1961
James Gregory, 17, of Red Lodge was the first hunting victim of the 1961 hunting season when he was accidentally killed while he was bird hunting west of town. Members of his hunting party found his body with a gunshot wound to the chest, and his shotgun nearby with its barrel separated from the stock.

November 13, 1962
Edward Olson of Bozeman was accidentally shot in the head with his son's gun while he reached over the car seat to get it. His son, John Olson and another man rushed Edward to the hospital from where they had been hunting in the Bridger Mountains, but he was declared dead on arrival.

November 24, 1962
Thirteen-year-old Kenneth Eickoff of Grass Range died from shock and loss of blood after accidentally shooting himself in the thigh. The hunting party that found his body couldn't determine how long he had been dead.

September 27, 1963
Division chief accountant for the Montana Power Company, 53-year-old Charles William West of Butte accidentally shot and killed himself with his .22-caliber rifle while he was preparing to go hunting.

September 27, 1963
Fifteen-year-old Billy Johnson, the son of Mr. and Mrs. Walter Johnson of Malta was killed while he was cleaning his shotgun before going hunting.

Chapter One: BY THEIR OWN NEGLIGENCE

October 15, 1963
<u>Theodore Haynes</u>, 19, of Ballantine died of an accidental gunshot wound to the head from his .22-caliber rifle. He had been with a large party of hunters when one in the group killed a pheasant.

When Theodore was running down the bird he dropped his sawed-off rifle and it discharged as it hit the ground.

November 13, 1963
<u>Charles Nelson</u>, 63, of Missoula died at a Ronan hosiptal after suffering an accidental gunshot wound while he was hunting west of Ronan.

Mr. Nelson had originally planned on hunting with Victor Sager of Missoula but they missed connections and he went out alone. He was reportedly struck by an accidental discharge from his .20-guage shotgun while he was going through a gate in a fence.

Two women later found Mr. Nelson on the Round Butte Road about 8 miles from Ronan. When found the injured man was on his hands and knees, fully conscious but bleeding badly. Charles Nelson left a wife and two daughters.

November 20, 1964
The body of 48-year-old <u>William Popish</u> was found near his vehicle in Sawmill Gulch about 10 miles southwest of Missoula.

It appears that Mr. Popish was accidentally shot when he was placing his .30-06 rifle butt first into his car. Apparently when the weapon hit the floorboard it discharged point blank into the man's chest.

October 11, 1965
The body of <u>Egon Wagerer</u>, a 38-year-old tourist from Schweinfurt, Germany was found by a search party a day after he had been reported missing while on a bear hunt.

Chapter One: BY THEIR OWN NEGLIGENCE

The authorities believed that the victim had accidentally shot himself in the head after leaving the Uderian Guest Ranch, which was about 3 miles north of Lincoln.

October 24, 1966
William Allen Young, 32, of Lewistown died in a Harlowton hospital from an accidental gunshot wound. Mr. Young was accidentally shot while he was removing a gun from his pickup truck while he was hunting near Castle.

October 1, 1967
Twenty-two-year-old Michael P. Milelich of Butte was pronounced dead at a Butte hospital from an accidental gunshot wound while he was preparing to go bird hunting.

Mr. Mihelich was in his basement bedroom at his parent's home when his .22-caliber pistol accidentally discharged. Michael managed to make it up the stairs to tell his mother that he had shot himself and then he passed out.

October 16, 1967
Roy F. Warwood, 18, of Belgrade was accidentally killed after being shot in the lower abdomen while he was goose hunting about 2 miles east of the Madison River near Three Forks.

Warwood's 19-year-old friend and hunting partner, James H. McMilin later said that they were trying to free their boat from some brush along the river when Warwood's shotgun accidentally went off. He said he heard a muffled blast and then his friend yelling out, "I'm dying." McMilin ran to a near by ranch for help but the victim was dead when help arrived.

November 18, 1967
Clarence Stokes, 57, of Kalispell accidentally shot and killed himself while he was pulling his rifle out of his truck by the barrel. The man's body was found near his car.

Chapter One: BY THEIR OWN NEGLIGENCE

October 30, 1968
Raymond Rebich, 17, of Dillon was accidentally shot and killed while he was elk hunting in the Smallhom Creek area about 15 miles southeast of Dillon. Ray Rebich was found shot in the head by his .30-30-caliber rifle by his hunting companion.

October 26, 1969
David "Davi" Lee Schonenbach, 16, of Ashland accidentally shot and killed himself with his .25-35 rifle while he was preparing to go hunting.

October 26, 1969
Daniel Herron, 42, of Granger, Washington died in hospital as a result of an accidental gunshot wound to the foot while he was hunting in the Sheep Creek country. Mr. Herron shot himself in the ankle with his .357-magnum handgun about 3 miles from where Sheep Creek enters Wolf Creek.

Photo by Joyce Obland
(www.graves-r-us.com)

November 14, 1973
(Daily Inter Lake)
The body of 42-year-old Wesley Drollinger of Kalispell was found by members of a 40-man search party after being reported missing while hunting near Welcome Springs on the Flathead Mine Road.

The authorities reported that Mr. Drollinger had accidentally shot and killed himself as he was picking his weapon up by the barrel after he had either dropped or laid his rifle on the ground.
Sadly, Drollinger's 18-year-old son, Wade was accidentally shot and

killed in another hunting accident just 10 days later. The younger Drollinger was accidentally killed by another youth who shooting over their vehicle.

October 18, 1974
(Missoulian)
Richard L. Middleton, 17, of Santa Ana, California was accidentally shot and killed by a holstered pistol he had packed away in his packsack for hunting.

The county coroner reported that Richard Middleton had been struck by .41-caliber bullet when he placed his pack on the floor of a Gardiner convenience store. The bullet entered his abdomen and then ranged into his neck.

October 23, 1974
(Missoulian)
The body of 22-year-old Sam McDonald of White Sulphur Springs was found in the Wall Mountain area about 20 miles east of Townsend after he failed to return from a hunting trip.

Mr. McDonald accidentally shot himself with a handgun while he was hunting in the mountainous region where the Broadwater, Meagher and Gallatin County lines converge. His body was located near the railroad tracks about 50 yards west and just inside the Broadwater County line.

October 20, 1975
Twenty-three-year-old Robert Wright of Butte became the first hunting fatality of the 1975 Big Game Hunting Season when he was killed about 18 miles west of Silver Star.

Mr. Wright and his friend, Willard Sweet had shot a deer and they had brought it back to their camp when a .30-06 rifle accidentally discharged as they were drying it off with a towel. The shooting took place in their school-bus camper and the fatal round struck the victim in the lower torso tearing apart his liver.

Chapter One: BY THEIR OWN NEGLIGENCE

October 24, 1977
Thirteen-year-old <u>William J. Pierson</u> of Deer Lodge was killed when he fell on his weapon while he was hunting birds with his father, brother and a family friend in the Big Park area below Mount Powell west of their home.

November 5, 1979
After being missing since September 9, 1978, the remains of 17-year-old <u>David Wade Christianson</u> of Havre were found on a ranch near Chinook by Cut Bank hunter, Dale Luckner.

An investigation found that the young man had tripped on a dead fall and he was accidentally shot and killed by his .22-caliber pistol, which was still clutched in his hand when he was found.

October 29, 1980
<u>Walter Campbell</u>, a 58-year-old Bynum area rancher was killed in a hunting accident about 8 miles west of Pendroy. He had been hunting coyotes or rabbits in a field near the Old Rockport Huterite Colony when he was shot in the head while placing a rifle into his pickup.

Mr. Campbell was reportedly on his way to the Huterite colony to buy some fresh eggs when he apparently spotted some game in the field and he had stopped to take a shot.

September 30, 1986
<u>Jeff Thompson</u>, 24, of Lakeside died in a Kalispell hospital after accidentally shooting himself in the leg while he was bear hunting on Blacktail Mountain near Lakeside.

After stopping along the road, Mr. Thompson reached across the seat of his pickup to grab his .308-caliber rifle by the barrel and the trigger apparently came in contact with the emergency brake handle and the rifle accidentally discharged.

Chapter One: BY THEIR OWN NEGLIGENCE

The heavy bullet entered Thompson's left inner thigh and exited through the kneecap, nearly severing his leg. He was airlifted to Kalispell for surgery by the ALERT rescue helicopter.

October 2, 1986
Mark Lowell Burgett, 12, of Sheridan died from an accidental gunshot wound to the head when he was removing a handgun from a car.

November 6, 1986
(The Herald News of Wolf Point)
Twenty-nine-year-old Raymond C. Eagle died at Trinity Hospital at Wolf Point after accidentally shooting himself while he was hunting about 4 miles east of town with several of his friends.

The Roosevelt County authorities and the Bureau of Indian Affairs officers found the wounded man about 100 yards west of the main trail with a single gunshot wound to both of his legs. The bullet from his .30-30-caliber rifle had entered the man's upper thigh; then it traveled to the groin and then went through the other leg before leaving his body.

December 27, 1987
(Montana Standard)
Twenty-five-year-old Eastern Montana College student, Tayor Buck died from an accidental gunshot wound while he was fox hunting during Christmas break.

Mr. Buck was visiting his brother, Allen Buck when he decided to drive down to Alzada in the extreme southeastern corner of the state. He borrowed his brother's 4-wheel drive vehicle and took along a rifle in case he saw a fox on the way.

Apparently Taylor Buck fired one shot at a fox from inside the pickup as the authorities later found an empty .223-caliber shell inside the cab. About 15 miles north of Alzada the young man stopped on the gravel road to Camp Crook to probably take another shot at an animal.

A nearby rancher noticed the parked vehicle for sometime and he drove up to investigate. He found the body of Taylor Buck lying next to his truck, dead from a single shot to the face from a .223 rifle. Apparently the man had grabbed the barrel of the rifle as he was removing it from the vehicle.

April 23, 1988
(Billings Gazette)
The body of 48-year-old <u>Gerald B. "Two-Gun" Jensen</u> of Wolf Point was found on a rural road by a neighbor about a quarter mile from his home. Mr. Jensen had been killed by an accidental gunshot wound to his chest as he was getting out of his pickup truck.

Apparently Mr. Jensen grabbed the business end of his Winchester .243 rifle when it accidentally discharged into his chest. Before leaving home the life-long resident of Wolf Point had told his stepson that he was going to shoot a skunk near their place.

Gerald Jensen had served in the U.S. Army and he worked 24 years for Wolf Point Implement before his death. He left a wife, a son, three daughters and two stepchildren.

October 24, 1990
(Accident Report)
Thirty-six-year-old <u>Scott L. Jorgenson</u> died at a local hospital after being accidentally shot with a high-powered rifle that was in the front seat of his vehicle.

Mr. Jorgenson and his party were hunting antelope near Steve Funk's place, north of Hinsdale when he walked back to their vehicle. The victim reportedly placed his rifle on the front seat and it discharged as he was getting in to drive off.

Chapter One: BY THEIR OWN NEGLIGENCE

October 25, 1990
Thirty-four-year-old <u>Anita Louise Greenlee</u> of Billings was killed
northwest of Red Lodge when her hunting rifle accidentally
discharged into her chest. She had been hunting with her husband
and daughter, but she was alone when she was shot after accidentally
dropping her rifle.

October 31, 1990
<u>Anthony "Tony" Kar Tuss</u>, 44, of Bozeman was killed with his own
.12-guage shotgun while he was taking it out of his van after returning
from a hunt.

Mr. Tuss, a longtime hunter, had been bird hunting with some
friends in the Malta area. Officials later pointed out that the incident
was a classic scenario when a hunter, believing that the gun was
unloaded, and picking it up by the barrel.

November 26, 1990
(Missoulian)
Eighteen-year-old <u>Troy Steven Goldston</u> of Polson accidentally shot
and killed himself at his home after returning from a hunt.

The Lake County authorities reported that the accident was the result
of a combination of carelessness and alcohol. Goldston's younger
brother and cousin both witnessed the shooting.

Troy Goldston had just returned from a hunting trip and he had
been drinking that afternoon. Lake County Sheriff Joe Geldrich
said that the recent high-school graduate had taken the .357-Ruger
revolver from a pickup truck, and thinking it was unloaded he was
handling it carelessly when it discharged into his head.

October 18, 1991
<u>Donald B. Hambrick</u>, 43, of Stevensville was killed while he was
pheasant hunting with a friend northeast of Stevensville. The man

was shot in the chest when he pulled his shotgun threw a fence and a piece of wire apparently tripped the trigger.

November 1, 1991
Thirteen-year-old <u>Lucas Johnson</u> of Toston was accidentally shot and killed while he was preparing to go hunting with his older brother. The young boy was reportedly shot in the chest with a .22-caliber rifle.

November 5, 1991
The body of 29-year-old <u>James M. Jackson</u> of Missoula was found on a logging road north of Tarkio in the South Fork of Nemote Creek and about 2 miles from his parked vehicle.

The officials reported that Mr. Jackson had been shot twice from his bolt-action rifle when he fell down an embankment. Although the authorities wouldn't speculate on the incident, they reported that Jim Jackson was accidentally shot in the leg during the fall, and then he died instantly from the second shot.

December 20, 1991
<u>Harry D. "Tubby" Hilyard</u>, 52, of Plentywood died while he was hunting on his ranch about 4 miles from town. The well-known businessman reportedly was accidentally shot in the chest while he was climbing over a fence with his rifle.

"Tubby" Hilyard owned the Commercial Grain Company in Plentywood where he reportedly had 2 mountain lions that guarded his business at nights.

November 23, 1997
<u>Todd Slauson</u>, 29, of Missoula was found dead from an accidental gunshot wound after being reported missing for a week while he was on a day hunt in the Clinton area.

Mr. Slauson reportedly left his home to go hunting early on Sunday, November 16, and he was supposed to go to work that same afternoon. Because Slauson didn't tell anyone where he had gone, searchers weren't able locate his pickup truck until Tuesday evening about 10 miles up the Schwartz Creek Road south of Clinton.

A combined crew of the Missoula Search and Rescue and the Western Montana Mountain Rescue Team searched the area using the 'grid method," which is generally utilized for locating dead persons. Although this searching technique, which calls for the searchers to work a territory in close proximity of one another it is generally about 80 percent effective, but it is very time consuming.

May 7, 2000
(Missoulian)
Seventy-six-year-old William Cantrell of Flathead County was accidentally shot and killed while he was hunting coyotes in the rural farmland between Kalispell and Columbia Falls.

Mr. Cantrell received a single gunshot to the head when his weapon accidentally discharged when he lost his footing and fell down a 15-foot embankment. When the man didn't return home a family member drove to the area in a 4-wheel all-terrain vehicle and discovered his body at the foot of a muddy gully.

October 31, 2001
Dennis R. Nelson, 45, of Gallatin Gateway accidentally shot himself while he was hunting on Castle Rock Mountain in Gallatin County.

The Gallatin County authorities reported that Mr. Nelson must have tripped and fell discharging his Model 700 rifle into his body. Two other hunters found Nelson's body next to a fallen tree about 50 yards from the main trail. Dennis Nelson was born in the Gallatin Valley and he was reportedly an experienced hunter.

November 7, 2003
Fifty-five-year-old Gary Lee Truax of Missoula accidentally shot himself while he was hunting in the upper Miller Creek area south of town.

Dying to Hunt in Montana
Chapter One: BY THEIR OWN NEGLIGENCE

The Missoula County authorities located his body the following day in a steep area about 20 minutes from his car. The officials said that Gary Truax had apparently slipped and his weapon accidentally discharged into his head as he went down.

June 4, 2004
(Missoulian)
The body of 21-year-old Zachnary W. Mienk of Kalispell was found in a remote area of the Swan State Forest after being reported missing while bear hunting.

Apparently the Flathead Valley Community College student had stumbled and accidentally shot and killed himself.

November 29, 2004
(Daily Inter Lake)
Forty-four-year-old Joseph Holzapfel died at the Kalispell Regional Medical Center after accidentally shooting himself while he was removing firearms from his vehicle at his home in Evergreen.

Joe and his mother had gone hunting earlier that day and when he was removing their .30-30 Winchester and a .30-06-caliber rifle from the vehicle the latter weapon accidentally discharged into his abdomen. The slug entered Mr. Holzapfel's lower abdomen, exited his chest and entered his jaw and lodged in his lower left orbital.

According to the accident report Joseph Holzapfel's wife was in the house when she heard the shot and as she went to the door Joe stumbled to the porch and told her that he was sorry.

February 3, 2005
(Billings Gazette)
Fifty-three-year-old Bruce J. King of Plentywood accidentally shot and killed himself while he was removing a shotgun from the rear-window gun rack of his pickup.

Chapter One: BY THEIR OWN NEGLIGENCE

Mr. King had obtained permission to hunt coyotes on Joe Kavon's property north of Dooley and he was accidentally shot in the chest after spotting an animal. Later while doing his chores, Mr. Kavon drove out and found the body of Bruce King next to his pickup.

(Endnotes)

[1] Needle guns were a breach-loaded weapon with a cartridge primer, which was struck by a slender pin or needle. These long rifles were widely used in Europe since the 1860's.

[2] The "Rocky Mountain" hawk in this case was probably a Red-Tailed Hawk very common in the area.

[3] In the early years the state colleges in Montana also conducted high school programs along with college courses.

KILLED BY THEIR HUNTING COMPANION

Someone once said that hunting is really quite safe as long as you don't hunt by yourself or with someone else. All joking aside, while it is not safe to hunt alone it can really be dangerous if you are hunting with an unsafe partner. While two heads are generally better than one, two guns are by far more dangerous than a single weapon.

Probably the most emotional and devastating hunting accident is one in which a hunter is responsible for the death of his hunting partner. In most cases the partner was a husband, wife, father, son, brother, sister, uncle, nephew, cousin, life-long buddy or at least a fellow worker or just a good friend.

It is tragic enough to loose a loved one or a best friend who had been accidentally killed while hunting, but if you were the cause of his or her death the guilt, shame and grief would be unbelievable.

There is one case where a young man killed his older brother while they were hunting ducks near Great Falls. That was pretty much all that the newspaper reported about the accident but the caretakers at the cemetery later reported that the grieving father of the two boys visited the grave of his oldest son two or three times a week until his own death. One can only imagine the feelings and the relationship between the father and his surviving son, little alone what the mother went through.

September 23, 1893
(Livingston Enterprise)
Tom Tregoning of Radersburg was accidentally shot and killed by his hunting companion near Crow Creek in Broadwater County.

Mr. Tregoning was shot in the neck while the two men were jumping a ditch when Jim Williams' gun accidentally discharged. A brother of Tregoning had died just a few weeks earlier from injuries sustained in a mining accident at Marysville.

December 28, 1895
Paul Zias of Belt was accidentally shot by a companion while he was hunting with his friends about 7 miles from his home. While the party was passing through some brush the hammers of one of the men's shotgun caught on some boughs and both barrels accidentally discharged into the Finn's right thigh.

The blast tore away a great deal of the man's flesh and it shattered the thighbone. After being first treated at Belt, Mr. Zias was transported to Great Falls where he died ten days later at the Columbus Hospital.

August 11, 1897
Thirty-year-old William Keogh of Belt died at the Columbus Hospital in Great Falls as a result of an accidental gunshot wound he received on the Little Belt Creek about 8 miles from his home.

In preparation for the 1897 bird-hunting season Mr. Keogh and his friend, Alex Capewell drove out to the country to train one of his young dogs.

The men were preparing to return to town when Capewell shot a hawk, and as he was placing his Winchester repeating shotgun into the rear of the wagon it accidentally discharged. The full load of the No. 5 shot entered Keogh's side as he was seated on the wagon.

Chapter Two: KILLED BY THEIR COMPANION

Capewell left his friend at the wagon and he road to Belt and then returned to the scene with Doctors Vidal and Akmas. The men took the injured man to Belt where his wounds were dressed and Dr. Vidas later transported him to the Columbus Hospital.

In Great Falls Dr. Longeway assisted Dr. Vidal and the two surgeons did every thing possible, but they held out very little hope that Keogh would survive. The charge of shot had struck Keogh near the point of the hip and it ranged through the lower part of his abdomen.

Keogh was born in Canada and he had lived in Great Falls before moving to Belt where he was a representative of the Singer Manufacturing Company.

William Keogh was single and his only surviving relatives were his parents living at Kincardine, Ontario. Mr. Keogh's body was embalmed at a Great Falls mortuary and then it was sent to Ontario for burial.

September 2, 1901
Cascade County rancher, Henry C. Love died at the ranch of Jim Eastman about 25 miles south of Great Falls from an accidental gunshot wound while he was hunting prairie chickens with a party of his neighbors and friends from Great Falls.

On opening day, Henry Love had invited friends, Frank McGarry, day foreman of the Montana Central Smelter, William McMillan, a smelter yardman, Oliver Ross, boiler man at the mill and a man named Woodin from Great Falls along with his close friend and neighbor rancher, Leonard "Al" Herbolsheimer.

Mr. Love's ranch was located on Ming Coulee about 20 miles south of Great Falls and it consisted of 30 acres where he ran 40 head of cattle and 17 horses.

Chapter Two: KILLED BY THEIR COMPANION

At the ranch the party was laughing and talking as they were looking for birds with Mr. Love walking a few feet in front of Herbolsheimer when a flock of chickens sprang up. Both men wheeled to get a shot and when Mr. Herbolsheimer ejected a shell from his Winchester repeating shotgun it accidentally discharged into the hip of his friend and passed into his bowels.

Mr. Love cried out, "My God, Al, you have shot me," and then he fell and rolled into a ditch. Until that moment Herbolsheimer hadn't even realized that his weapon had discharged. He thought the shot he heard was Love shooting at the birds as they took off.

Everyone rushed to the aid of the wounded man who never lost consciousness until the time he died. The men picked him up and placed him in a wagon they had been using and then headed for the Eastman place, which was the nearest house.

On the way to the ranch house Mr. Love spoke optimistically and he only regretted spoiling the day's shooting for the others. "I am sorry boys," he reportedly said, "for all this will spoil your day. This will be a big doctor's bill for me and how am I going to pay it?" The men assured him that he wouldn't have to pay a thing for the incident. At one point Mr. Love asked the driver to slow down, stating that the jerking of the wagon hurt him.

Henry Love was carried into the Eastman house about 2:30 o'clock, about a half an hour after the accident and he only lived for another 30 minutes. His last words were again his regrets for spoiling his friend's day of hunting.

Mr. Herbolsheimer walked the 2 miles back to his ranch where he hitched up his horses and drove to Great Falls to inform Mrs. Love and her 2 children, 10-year-old Willie and Robbie, 4, of the tragedy. Herbolsheimer then notified the police and the coroner who held an inquest the following day.

Chapter Two: KILLED BY THEIR COMPANION

On the day of the hunt Mr. Love had told his wife that she could go to town to visit her friends and that was where Mr. Herbolsheimer retrieved her. On the way out of town he was interviewed about the incident and while he was describing the tragedy Mrs. Love fell off of the wagon seat and moaned and wept uncontrollably.

Henry Love and Mr. Herbolsheimer were close friends and they had helped each other constantly on their ranches. No one ever blamed Mr. Herbolsheimer for the accident. Mr. Love was about 40 years old, born in Missouri and he had lived in Montana for about 15 years.

The day after the shooting the undertaker from Great Falls prepared the body at the Eastman place and it was later moved to the Love Ranch where the funeral was held. Henry Love was buried at Red Cemetery, which is about 15 miles from Great Falls.

December 8, 1901
Frank Swingley, 15-year-old son of well-known Orr ranchers, Mr. and Mrs. G.H. Swingley was accidentally shot and killed when he and his brother were cleaning their shotguns in preparation to go hunting.

While Mr. Swingley had taken his wife to Great Falls for medical treatment their 4 sons were home alone to take care of the ranch and themselves. At the house were Eddie, 19; Frank, 15; Henry, 13 and 11-year-old Douglas, commonly called "Dudd."

About 5 inches of fresh snow had covered the area and Frank told his little brother, Douglas that they would go hunt jackrabbits, which were reportedly very plentiful on their place. Frank had a good shotgun but instead of borrowing one of his brother's guns the younger boy decided to utilize an old weapon that nobody else used.

Wanting to have his own weapon, Douglas decided to clean up and use an old muzzle-loading double-barrel shotgun that apparently had not been fired for many years, and had been lying around in storage.

Chapter Two: KILLED BY THEIR COMPANION

Since there was no chamber to open, the boys couldn't tell that the gun was in fact loaded.

Douglas noticed that the nipple was stopped up and after he couldn't clear it by blowing through it he apparently asked Frank for advice on how to clear it. The two boys decided that the firing of a new cap would probably clear the nipple. They placed a cap on the nipple and started outside to fire the shotgun.

As they were starting for the door, Frank led the way and he was about 8 feet ahead of Douglas who was anxiously pulling back the hammer, which was extremely stiff. The small boy's thumb wasn't strong enough to pull the old hammer back far enough to lock it and it slipped and fell down on the new firing cap.

The deafening blast of the shotgun sent all but 14 pellets of the large birdshot into Frank's right jaw, tearing away most of the lower bone and teeth. The blast severed the jugular vein and the large arteries in the neck, cutting the windpipe and it tore away the esophagus of the boy. Frank immediately collapsed to the floor unconscious and he died soon afterwards.

A neighbor was summoned to the house and he found young Frank lying in at least 4 quarts of his blood. After seeing that the other boys were all right the neighboring rancher went to Great Falls to inform the parents. Not wanting to upset his ill wife, Mr. Swingley only told her that Frank was sick and he was going to him.

The next day the county coroner investigated the scene and he found 14 pellets in the wall and a stovepipe and determined that the boy's death was due to their ignorance of the old style weapon and the little fellow's inability to hold back the hammer.

Chapter Two: KILLED BY THEIR COMPANION

Douglas became temporarily insane after the shooting and his family and friends were concerned if he would ever recover.

What made this incident even more unfortunate was that the family had always observed a strict rule of unloading every weapon before it was taken into the house. The antique gun had been around for so long that no one could remember when it was last used and it had never been considered loaded.

August 5, 1903
While hunting with his older brother on their parent's farm near Holt, 6-year-old Eddie Collins was accidentally shot in the head.

Just as his brother was shooting his .22-caliber rifle the young boy stepped into the line of fire and he took the bullet near his temple. The son of Mr. and Mrs. M.H. Collins died shortly after the physician arrived from Kalispell.

September 9, 1904
Twenty-five-year-old Sand Coulee stage driver, Iverson Vaughn died at the Rutter Ranch near Monarch from an accidental gunshot wound while he was hunting.

Mr. Vaughn had been hunting with a party from Sand Coulee but he was alone with H.A. Johnson at the time of the accident. Apparently Vaughn had run out of ammunition and he went over to Mr. Johnson to borrow some. His friend was also out of shells except for the ones in the magazine of his shotgun.

As Johnson was in the process of ejecting a couple of rounds from his weapon he inadvertently pointed the muzzle towards Vaughn. The Shotgun accidentally discharged into Vaughn and most of the charge went into his left leg but many of the shot entered his other leg. The bones in the left leg were completely shattered and the arteries in both legs were lacerated.

Johnson did everything he could for his friend at the scene but after realizing he couldn't stop the bleeding his friends helped him move the victim the 2 miles to the Rutter Ranch. By the time Dr. Foster arrived from Neihart Mr. Vaughn had bled to death. Before he died, Mr. Vaughn said that the shooting had been completely accidental.

Iverson Vaughn was married and he had a family living in Lewistown. He had recently moved to Cascade County and he had been driving the Sand Coulee stage to Great Falls for a few months before his death.

November 17, 1904
Ten-year-old Warren Hulbert of Thompson Falls was accidentally shot through the head by his companion, Earl Hardman near their home while they were hunting.

November 19, 1904
Harry Nagard, of Bozeman was accidentally shot and killed near his hunting camp in West Gallatin Canyon by his brother, George Nagard.

The two brothers had been hunting with several friends and on their way to their camp the men decided to do some target shooting. While George Nagard handed the gun to his brother muzzle first, the weapon accidentally discharged and the round went through Harry's body and he died minutes later.

December 19, 1904
Carroll Emmett Brooks of Missoula was killed instantly and his brother, Howard and another friend, Arthur Chandler were injured while they were hunting rabbits near the Garden City.

Chapter Two: KILLED BY THEIR COMPANION

The three boys were walking in a single file down a trail while two other boys were following behind them when one of their shotguns accidentally discharged towards the three leading the group.

Howard Brooks, who was the nearest to the weapon only received a slight injury while Carroll, who had been walking in the middle of the two received most of the charge in the side of the head behind his left ear. Chandler received only a slight injury from a few pellets in his back.

August 26, 1906
<u>Miss Ruth Bean</u> died from an accidental gunshot wound that she received while she was working in a kitchen of a ranch in the Centennial Valley near Dillon. Miss Bean was from the area and she was cooking for the Shambow ranch during the hay harvest.

The owner of the ranch, Levi Shambow reported later that thirteen-year-old Edward Lunger ran into the kitchen after a double-barrel shotgun because one of the ranch hands wanted it to shoot a hawk.

The gun was a hammerless type and the safety catch was not in place. As the boy took the gun from the gun rack he apparently touched one of the triggers and the weapon accidentally discharged into Miss Bean's right leg just below the knee.

A messenger was sent after a physician, but because of the distance to and from Dillon the young lady died before medical help arrived at the ranch.

Edward Lunger had been an orphan at the state orphanage home at Three Forks since he was nine years old. Mr. Shambow had adopted the Lunger boy from the orphan's home about 18 months earlier and he returned him to the home immediately after the incident.

Chapter Two: KILLED BY THEIR COMPANION

July 13, 1908
(Anaconda Standard)
<u>A.F. Moody</u>, 37, of Virginia City was accidentally shot and killed by his companion while they were squirrel hunting on Granite Creek.

Mr. Moody had been hunting with S.T. Crum, and they only had one shotgun between them. Moody was carrying the gun at full cock in readiness when they spotted a squirrel, which escaped into its hole.

Mr. Crum had pulled the gun up on the squirrel and while he was lowering it back down the hammer slipped from his thumb and it accidentally discharged as Moody was stepping in front of the muzzle. Moody was struck in the right leg with the full load of shot.

Mr. Crum immediately threw down the gun and began helping his friend. He made a tourniquet out of a handkerchief and then he ran the quarter of a mile to the Bottcher house where Moody was living at the time. At the ranch Crum secured a wagon to bring the injured man back to the house.

While Crum was getting the horses for the wagon Thomas E. Castle ran ahead to help Mr. Moody. He noticed that the handkerchief tourniquet wasn't very effective and he replaced it with a leather strap. Dr. Bradley of Virginia City and Dr. Clancy from Ruby were summoned but the man had bled to death before they arrived.

Mr. A. F. Moody had come to Madison County from Aberdeen, Washington where he had been a locomotive engineer. Before his death Mr. Moody had laid pipe for the Blaine Springs Power Plant and he later helped Fred Bottcher with his truck garden on Granite Creek for about 3 years. Mr. Moody married Mr. Bottcher's niece and he also left two brothers in Washington State.

January 1, 1909
(Republican Courier)
<u>Otto Roll</u>, the 12-year-old son of Mr. and Mrs. Edwin F. Roll of Springhill was accidentally shot and killed by 11-year-old Ottis Roll,

the half brother of Otto's father, while they were hunting with Otto's 17-year-old uncle near their home.

The three boys had been walking in single file with Otto in the lead and Ottis close behind him when a bird flew off in front of them. Otto fired at the bird but missed with his single-shot shotgun and then he dropped to a knee to reload.

In the meantime the bird continued its flight in front of the hunters. Not wanting the bird to get away before Otto could reload, Ottis pulled his shotgun to his shoulder and pulled the trigger just as Otto arose to take another shot and he received the full charge to the back of his head.

October 5, 1909
Mike Friel of Butte died in St. James Hospital after being accidentally shot by his cousin while they were hunting ducks on the flat outside of town.

The former deputy sheriff of Silver Bow County stepped into his cousin's line-of-fire as he was about to shoot at some birds and he took the full load in his right shoulder blade and lung.

As Mike Friel was on his deathbed he told his cousin that he shouldn't feel responsible, as it was his own fault for stepping into the way of the blast.

September 17, 1912
(Anaconda Standard)
Two weeks after being accidentally shot with a high-powered rifle while hunting, 24-year-old Edward Michaels died at St. John's Hospital in Helena.

Mr. Michaels was hunting with a friend in the mountains near Elkhorn when they were walking in a column. With Mr. Michaels in the lead the hunters began to go through some brush when the 30-

Chapter Two: KILLED BY THEIR COMPANION

30-caliber Savage rifle held by the other man accidentally discharged into the victim's back.

The bullet entered Michaels' back just to the right of the spine and it ranged upward grazing the kidney, liver, lower part of the lung and then went through the diaphragm. Edward Michaels was born and raised at Marysville but was he was living with his father at Elkhorn and he was employed as a stationary engineer.

December 2, 1914
Fred E. Woodworth, of Thompson Falls, and the under sheriff of Sanders County was accidentally shot and killed while he was hunting with a party of friends in the upper Thompson River country on November 25, 1914.

The party started out early Wednesday morning in different directions and later Albert Florin shot at a running buck deer in front of a brushy timbered area. Others in the party reported that they had heard 2 shots fired nearly simultaneously and they believed that Woodworth had also fired at the same deer. Mr. Florin shot twice more at the animal before it went down in the thick brush.

Florin went down the hill and into the thicket to find the deer but instead found the dead body of Fred Woodworth with a bullet hole through his head. Appalled by the sight of his dead friend, Mr. Florin reportedly became temporarily insane from grief and his cries and screams attracted the other members of the party who found the death scene and the dead deer nearby.

The body of Mr. Woodworth was brought out the 10 miles by pack animals to the country road where a team and wagon met them the next day.

Some strange facts involving Mr. Woodworth and his death revealed that a year earlier he had been accidentally shot through the shoulder by J.M. Chichton while they were hunting in the same territory that he was eventually killed in. Also while en route to the Thompson River on this fatal trip Mr. Woodworth narrowly escaped death when a rifle being unloaded accidentally discharged and barely missed his face.

It was also determined that Woodworth's rifle did in fact discharge and it was the second shot heard by members of the hunting party when Mr. Florin had fired at the deer. At first it was speculated that Woodworth had accidentally shot himself but it was determined that involuntary muscular contractions probably caused him to pull the trigger of his rifle at the time of his death.

County Coroner D.H. Billmeyer held a formal inquest and the jury found that the deceased met his death by an accidental gunshot wound and Albert Florin was exonerated from any and all blame connected with the tragedy.

October 7, 1916
Well-known barber, Joseph F. House, 42, of Great Falls died during surgery at Columbus Hospital after being accidentally shot by a companion while he was on a duck hunt.

Mr. House, John A. Delaat and Kenneth McGlenn drove to the Sun River southwest of the American Brewery where they met Mr. Stewart and they all went hunting. After getting only one duck the party returned to Mr. House's automobile.

The men began unloading their shotguns for the trip back to Great Falls when the weapon John Delaat was handling accidentally discharged into House's upper thigh, severing a major artery.

The men rushed the injured hunter to the Columbus Hospital where they found two surgeons on duty who immediately began working on Mr. House.

Mr. House remained conscious throughout the ordeal and he was very calm. As they were driving to the hospital he reportedly told his friends that he was hurt bad and probably wouldn't make it, but that he would be brave and try and pull through.

Joseph House had lived in Great Falls for about 3 years and he had come from San Jose, California. He had one of the best barbershops in the state and he was well liked.

What made the tragedy especially pathetic was the fact that Joe House had only been married for about a month before his death. He left his wife, a sister and three brothers.

October 13, 1916
Well-known Minneapolis grain buyer, <u>Oswald K. Sellar</u>, working out of Lewistown was accidentally shot and killed by a friend while they were returning from a hunt near Hilger.

The 35-year-old Mr. Sellar and his friend and granary builder, Clarence Napper were in a vehicle about to drive back to town when Mr. Napper pulled his large-caliber revolver out of its holster in order to shoot at rabbits along the road in their headlights.

The handgun accidentally discharged into the right side of Mr. Sellar who immediately lapsed into unconsciousness and he died in his friend's arms on the way to a Lewistown hospital. Mr. Oswald Sellar was a single man at the time of his death but he was to be married to a Duluth, Minnesota woman in a month or two.

December 16, 1916
Eighteen-year-old <u>Wilbert Shipman</u> of Bozeman was accidentally shot and killed on the last day of hunting season, Friday December 15, 1916.

Mr. Shipman had been hunting in the Upper West Gallatin Canyon about 64 miles from Bozeman with his seventeen-year-old cousin, William Philo Pace.

Chapter Two: KILLED BY THEIR COMPANION

Soon after leaving their camp the two men had wounded an elk and while they were chasing the animal Pace reportedly tripped over a couple of snow-covered lodge poles and his rifle discharged into the back of Shipman. Pace later told the authorities that as he fell into a ditch his weapon went off and he heard Shipman cry out.

The accident happened at about 5:30 in the evening just 200 yards from the Safley Hunting Lodge near Black Butte. The hunters at the lodge heard the shot and they reportedly commented that someone had shot an elk nearby the cabin. Philo Pace ran to the Safley Lodge for help and Shipman was moved to the cabin where he died at 6:20 p.m. that evening.

Dr. Gaertner of Three Forks and Dr. Carson of Wilsall, who had been staying at the nearby Wilson Hunting Camp, arrived a short time after Shipman's death and they determined that the bullet had entered the victim's body in the small of the back and it exited through the groin.

The next morning the party started out with the body of Wilbert Shipman by sled to Salesville, some 6 miles away where C.A. McIntyre, the undertaker was waiting with his automobile.

September 27, 1917
Gladys Bradley, 12, of Bannack was accidentally shot and killed by her hunting companion, Joe Collins. In the short news release it was reported that the little girl's head was almost taken off by the blast.

April 12, 1919
Ten-year-old Elijah Linn of Musselshell was accidentally shot and killed by his 17-year-old brother, Raymond while they were rabbit hunting just a few miles south of their home.

The older boy was carrying a shotgun as they were approaching a fence and when Elijah was opening the gate the weapon accidentally discharged into his groin. The boy survived the blast of the shotgun but he died before help could reach him.

October 2, 1919

Leroy S. Tupper of Kalispell was accidentally shot by his hunting companion and business partner, O.E. Bolon while they were hunting near Bowser Lake west of the city.

Mr. Bolon later told the authorities that he was shooting at a deer running through the timber and that he didn't notice Mr. Tupper between him and the animal. Mr. Tupper was shot through both legs and he was rushed to a hospital in Kalispell where one leg was amputated and he died a few hours later.

The following year Tupper's father brought a $25,000 lawsuit against Mr. Bolon for negligence and carelessness in the shooting death of his son. It was said that the three men had been in the real estate business together at Kalispell for many years.

November 4, 1921

(Bozeman Daily Chronicle)

James Pullman, 35, of Somers, Montana was shot and fatally wounded by his hunting partner, Bert Schlogel while they were stalking deer in the Loon Lake region on Tuesday, November first. Mr. Schlogel returned the dead body of his friend to Kalispell and reported the incident.

November 13, 1921

Sixteen-year-old Andrew Brae of Missoula was accidentally shot and killed while he was trapping muskrats west of town. Andrew was trapping with 14-year-old Fred Jamieson when his partner dropped his rifle killing him instantly.

December 9, 1922

Paul Russell, 18, of Libby died at St. Luke's Hospital at Spokane, Washington from an accidental gunshot wound while he was hunting on November 21.

Chapter Two: KILLED BY THEIR COMPANION

Russell was accidentally shot in the shoulder by his hunting companion, Paul Boothman and at first his condition improved but died following an operation in Spokane.

November 14, 1923
(Bozeman Courier)
James Harvey Boling, 16, son of Mrs. Nancy Boling of Manhattan was the first hunting fatality of the year when he was instantly killed by a shotgun in the hands of his young hunting companion, Howard Talbot.

The load of birdshot penetrated Boling's right temple and came out the left side of his head below the ear. The accident occurred on Spring Creek between Baker Creek and Camp Creek and about a quarter mile east of the F.T. Ulmer Ranch house.

Young Talbot ran to Manhattan where he told his mother about the terrible accident and Mrs. Mohra A. Talbot called the authorities. Coroner E.W. Harland decided not to hold an inquest because of the nature of the sad fatality.

According to the statement by the young Talbot boy, he had stayed Friday night, November 9 at the Boling residence so he and his buddy could leave early Saturday on a duck hunt. He said they had reached Spring Creek at an early hour when he saw a bunch of ducks and he pulled one of the triggers of his double-barreled shotgun, which brought down a number of birds.

When Talbot threw the shotgun into the crook of his left elbow as he was on his way to retrieve the ducks the other barrel exploded into the head of his companion who was at his side.

November 23, 1923
Fourteen-year-old Cecil Trusty of Somers died at the Sisters' Hospital in Kalispell from an accidental gunshot wound sustained while he was hunting near his home. Cecil had been hunting with his friend,

Chapter Two: KILLED BY THEIR COMPANION

Harry Joy on the hills west of Somers when Joy's 22-caliber rifle accidentally discharged, striking Trusty just forward of his ear.

Harry Joy tried to carry his wounded friend out of the hills by himself, but realizing he couldn't he made the boy as comfortable as possible and then ran to Somers.

The Joy boy notified his own parents as well as Mr. and Mrs. Howard Trusty and after Cecil Trusty was given first aid at Somers he was rushed to the hospital at Kalispell. At the Kalispell hospital the bullet was never recovered and he died a day later.

December 12, 1923
Peter Henningson, the 15-year-old son of Mr. and Mrs. Amos Henningson was accidentally shot and killed by his friend while they were hunting on the Henningson place about 3 miles north of Glasgow.

Peter was hunting with several boys when Jasper DeDobeleer, thinking his weapon was unloaded pointed his gun at Henningson and it accidentally discharged. The bullet struck the boy right over the heart, killing him instantly.

September 21, 1924
The 15-year-old son of Mrs. John Kaoski, Everett Kaoski of Stockett was accidentally shot and killed while he was rabbit hunting with his friends near the Cascade County mining town.

The four neighborhood boys, Everett Kaoski, Walter Rekonnen, William Lahto and his brother Victor had been given a new .22-caliber rifle by Henry Prooyen of Stockett, which he had won on a punchboard.

The boys took turns in shooting their brand new gun and at one point William Lahto was carrying the weapon and walking a few feet in front of Kaoski. Victor Lahto was in a nearby gully and he yelled to the others to come down.

The boys all turned and when Lahto swung the rifle it accidentally discharged into Kaoski's arm, missing the bones and pierced his heart. The boy reportedly collapsed without saying a word.

The other boys immediately ran to Stockett to notify the authorities and Mrs. Kaoski. It was reported that the entire town was shocked by the tragedy and an unusually large crowd from the mining town rushed to the scene.

Everett Kaoski was preceded in death by his father, John Kaoski who had been killed in a mining accident in June of 1923 Since Mr. Kaoski's death, the family had been supported by Mrs. Kaoski and her older children including Everett.

November 30, 1924
John Vanden-Wall, 28, from Holland was accidentally shot and killed while he was hunting on the Andrew Erickson Ranch a few miles southwest of Conrad.

Mr. Vanden-Wall was employed at the ranch and following the Thanksgiving dinner he joined Hans and Allen Erickson into the fields to do some jackrabbit hunting.

After driving into the fields Allen Erickson, the 16-year-old son of the rancher got out of the vehicle and fired at a rabbit with his 12-guage Remington pump shotgun.

While trying to eject the expended shell from his gun Erickson turned towards the vehicle where Vanden-Wall was seated and the weapon accidentally discharged into the car.

Chapter Two: KILLED BY THEIR COMPANION

Mr. Vanden-Wall was struck in the right eye with the full load of number 2 shot, which went straight through his skull, killing him instantly. The Hollander left a sister living in Washington state and a brother in Canada.

October 23, 1925
(Bozeman Courier)
Twenty-four-year-old Stanford native and popular student at Montana State College at Bozeman (now called MSU), <u>J.H. Waddell</u>, died at a Bozeman hospital from an accidental gunshot wound.

Waddell had been hunting with a classmate, Carl Albrecht in the mountains north of Pass Creek about 35 miles from Bozeman when they were tracking a deer they had wounded.

As the men were going down a mountainside the .35-caliber automatic rifle of Albrecht accidentally discharged. Waddell was so startled by the blast that he didn't realize he had been hit at first, and even asked Albrecht why he had fired.

Suddenly Waddell became weak and he fainted onto the trail. Albrecht immediately placed Waddell in a sheltered spot, covered him with his coat and then ran to the Moore Ranch, which was about two and a half miles away.

Finding no one at the Moore place he went another half a mile to the McBroom Ranch where he telephoned Bozeman for a doctor and additional help. Elmer Tilley returned with Albrecht to the scene of the accident and the other men soon met them to help transport Waddell down the narrow and steep trail to a logging road where an automobile was waiting to rush him to town.

Because of the poor condition of the road it took another three hours to reach Bozeman, making it seven hours total from the time of the accident to when Waddell was under medical care. By the time

Waddell had finally reached the hospital he was so weakened from loss of blood, shock and exposure that he died just 3 hours later.

Dr. J.F. Blair later reported that the heavy caliber bullet had entered Waddell's left thigh, fracturing the femur bone and destroyed a great deal of the muscle tissue. J.H. Waddell was buried at Stanford.

December 14, 1925
Fifteen-year-old Clifford Wesley Ofstie died at a Lewistown hospital a day after being accidentally shot in the chest with a shotgun while he was hunting rabbits north of town.

The son of Mr. and Mrs. Paul W. Ofstie had been hunting with 13-year-old Melvin Maury and the two boys had only one shotgun between them. After spotting a rabbit Ofstie called to Maury to take a shot and the younger boy missed the animal with his first shot.

As Maury was taking another shot at the running rabbit he struck Ofstie in the chest. Young Maury went to a neighboring house and Clifford Ofstie was rushed to the hospital where two physicians worked on the boy but he died the next morning.

September 17, 1926
(Anaconda Standard)
Farney L. Coles, 19, of Billings died in a local hospital four hours after being accidentally shot while he was duck hunting about a mile west of Molt Thursday by his 15-year-old companion, Edward Baumgardener.

While trying to break down his shotgun, Baumgardener inadvertently drew back the hammer and the weapon discharged into the back of Coles' head.

Farney Coles' accident was the first of the season in Stillwater County in 1926. Although the boy died in a Billings hospital, his death will be found listed in Stillwater County.

Chapter Two: KILLED BY THEIR COMPANION

September 17, 1927
<u>Huston C. Peters</u>, the proprietor of Peters' Pool Hall at Choteau was accidentally shot and killed while he was hunting about 12 miles southeast of the Teton County seat.

Mr. Peters and his longtime friend, William Emerick left Choteau early Friday morning on a duck hunting trip at the Cascade Ranch. Peters was walking in front of his companion while they were crossing an irrigation ditch on a board when Emerick slipped and fell. As Mr. Emerick's shotgun struck the ground it accidentally discharged into the back of Mr. Peters and he died instantly.

Huston Peters was a veteran of the Spanish-American War and the Chinese Boxer Rebellion where he was cited for bravery. Mr. Peters had lived in Choteau for about 20 years and he was survived by a wife and 5 children, the oldest being 18 years old. William Emerick had also resided in Choteau for about 20 years and he owned a photographic business at the time.

September 25, 1928
Eight-year-old <u>Carlton Whitsell</u> of Great Falls died at Deaconess Hospital from an accidental gunshot wound sustained while he was hunting with his family and a friend near Cascade.

Carlton and his parents, Mr. and Mrs. Joel A. Whitsell and 8-year-old Randall Tracey stopped near Telegraph Hill to hunt. The two boys ran ahead and when young Tracy tried to load his .410-guage shotgun it accidentally discharged into Carlton's abdomen. The boy was rushed to Great Falls but there was never any real hope of saving him, and he died at 4 o'clock the next morning.

October 13, 1928
Twelve-year-old <u>Olive Shaw</u> died at a Lewistown hospital after she was accidentally shot in the abdomen by her brother. The young boy had been shooting at prairie chickens on their parent's farm in Fergus County.

Chapter Two: KILLED BY THEIR COMPANION

November 17, 1928
<u>Sergeant Paul B. Portis</u>,
stationed at Fort Missoula was
accidentally shot and killed by
his hunting companion near St.
Regis.

November 25, 1929
<u>William Baumgartner</u>, the 19-
year-old son of Mr. and Mrs.
Mathias Baumgartner of Billings
was accidentally shot and killed
on the first day of the 5-day
pheasant-hunting season.

Mr. Baumgartner was hunting with four other men, 21 miles north of
Billings when he was accidentally shot in the chest by Phil Shaffer of
Billings.

November 2, 1932
(Bozeman Daily Courier)
<u>Lewis W. Maynard</u>, 15, of Stevensville was shot and killed in a
hunting accident near Stevensville some 30 miles south of Missoula.

The Maynard boy had been hiking with James Moore when they
spotted a deer along the Bitterroot River. The boys ran to the Liddel
Ranch house where they borrowed a .32-Caliber rifle and went after
the deer. The rifle accidentally discharged when Moore handed the
weapon over to Lewis Maynard, killing him instantly.

October 10, 1933
(Missoulian)
<u>Vincent Walcott</u>, 17, of St. Ignatius died in a local hospital two and a
half hours after being accidentally shot with a shotgun while he was
hunting.

Young Walcott was with some other men looking for a bee tree east of St Ignatius near the fish hatchery when they met the 12-year-old son of Chris Feuchet who was hunting in the area.

As the Feuchet boy approached the party of men his shotgun accidentally discharged and the blast struck Walcott who was reportedly about 50 feet away.

At first it was thought the wounds to his back and hips weren't serious but he was rushed to the hospital where he slipped into unconsciousness and died. Walcott's mother had died about 2 years earlier and his family had just moved to St. Ignatius where his father had opened a dental office.

October 19, 1933
<u>Walter L. Kulbeck</u>, 47, of Big Sandy was shot and killed by his brother, Ed Kulbeck while they were big game hunting west of Whitefish.

The two brothers were in a hunting party of 15 men from Havre and they were hunting in the Star Meadows area some 50 miles northwest of Kalispell.

Walter Kulbeck had wounded a deer and he was tracking the animal when Ed Kulbeck shot at and missed the same injured deer, striking his brother in the leg just above the knee. Walter only lived a few minutes after his brother had reached him.

The brush in the area was so thick that it took ten men six hours to carry Kulbeck's body a mile to the highway. A coroner's jury exonerated the grief stricken brother of any wrongdoing. The two brothers were both experienced hunters and they had hunted the same together area for many years.

Chapter Two: KILLED BY THEIR COMPANION

November 4, 1933
Twenty-two-year-old <u>Charles Midboe</u> died in a Glendive hospital from an accidental gunshot wound while he was hunting near Stipek.

Russell Osmundson of Richy, and a boyhood friend of the victim, shot Mr. Midboe while they were hunting in a thicket. Glendive-resident Charles Midboe was struck in the leg and his femoral artery was cut and he had lost a great deal of blood before reaching medical assistance.

October 14, 1936
(Missoulian)
<u>Clifford Smith</u>, 30, of Craig died at a Helena hospital after being shot through both legs with a high-powered rifle while he was coyote hunting.

Mr. Smith and Dan Anderson were cutting wood for their employer who had a large sheep ranch when they spotted a coyote. As Mr. Anderson was getting out of their truck his .30-30 rifle accidentally discharged into Smith's legs severing the arteries.

October 19, 1936
Fourteen-year-old <u>Aurel Tucker</u> of Lolo died in a Missoula hospital after being accidentally shot while he and his friends were preparing to go hunting in a field near their home.

While Tucker and 7-year-old Donald Doyle were riding ahead on a bicycle a .308-caliber Savage rifle accidentally discharged and the bullet grazed Doyle's neck, just missing his jugular vein before entering Tucker's back and passed through his abdomen and hand.

There were 3 different versions of how the rifle discharged, first that 15-year-old Warren Griffin had leaned it against a tree and it fell over and went off, second, Griffin had been playing around with the weapon when it accidentally discharged and finally that he had placed it on the porch and when another boy stepped over it the weapon fired.

Chapter Two: KILLED BY THEIR COMPANION

The authorities didn't place fault with anyone and they later determined that the boys didn't know the weapon was loaded and when Warren Griffin worked the action a shell entered the chamber. Griffin then placed the rifle down on the porch and he and another boy ran into the Doyle home to find some ammunition and either he or the other boy struck the weapon and it discharged.

November 30, 1936
George Reissing, 14, was killed in a hunting accident at Leavitte Gulch above Gibson Dam near Augusta. He had been hunting elk with four of his friends when he was accidentally shot in heavy timber by one of the other boys.

October 31, 1938
Carl Anderson, 19, of Geraldine was killed instantly while he and his friend were trying to kill a skunk. The two men had chased the skunk into a culvert and they were on their hands and knees when they decided to shoot the animal.

The .22-caliber rifle accidentally discharged as Wayne Nicol, also of Geraldine was handing it to Anderson. The bullet entered Carl Anderson's right side and then struck his heart.

November 22, 1938
Robert Felieous, 24, of Butte was killed instantly when he was accidentally shot on a hunting trip 23 miles east of the mining city.

Mr. Felieous was hunting with his brother-in-law, Pat Stretch when the latter man's rifle butt struck a tree and it accidentally discharged into Felieous' head.

November 23. 1938
(Missoulian)
Frank Seiller, 17, of Arlee was accidentally killed while he was hunting ducks about 10 miles west of Arlee. Seiller and his 19-year-

old brother, Floyd were both carrying .22-caliber rifles when they were climbing a bank through heavy brush with Frank in the lead.

Floyd later told the authorities that his rifle became entangles in the brush and a twig caught on the trigger, causing the rifle to accidentally discharge in to his brother's back. The bullet entered the boy's back and then it ranged upward through his abdomen.

Floyd ran for help and he and the others carried his wounded brother out with an improvised stretcher to a car and there he was taken to his parent's home in Arlee where he died 30 minutes later.

October 17, 1940
Grover C. Bryan, 54, of Big Timber died in a local hospital from a gunshot wound received while he was hunting in the Crazy Mountains northwest of Big Timber.

Mr. Bryan and three of his friends had returned to their cabin after a day of deer hunting when one of their rifles accidentally discharged while they were being cleaned.

Grover Bryan was struck in the right arm about one inch below his shoulder, shattering the bone and fragments of the bone had entered his chest. He was rushed to Big Timber where his arm was amputated but he died from shock and the loss of blood.

October 30, 1941
Hezekiah VanDorn, 62, of Missoula died at a local hospital of injuries suffered when he was shot while he was pheasant hunting near St. Ignatius.

A shotgun being carried by a member of the hunting party accidentally discharged into the calf of VanDorn's left leg.

Chapter Two: KILLED BY THEIR COMPANION

November 17, 1941
George W. Flamm, 58, of Billings died in a local hospital from a gunshot wound to his right leg he suffered while he was hunting.

Mr. Flamm and his son, Bryce had stopped south of Bridger to hunt pheasants when the trigger on the boy's .22-caliber rifle caught on the hammer of a 12-guage shotgun in the backseat and it accidentally discharged as he was removing it. George Flamm was standing on the other side of the vehicle when the bullet went through the rear door and hit him above the knee.

October 27, 1942
Elmer Buck, 28, of Kalispell died two days after being accidentally shot while he was hunting near Fielding. It was reported that Mr. Buck and his hunting companion, Shorty Harmon had both slipped and fell as they were walking down a steep hill and Harmon's gun accidentally discharged into Buck's abdomen.

November 10, 1942
Walter Grimes, 46, of Cascade died a day after being accidentally shot in the leg while he was hunting near Cascade with his son, Tom Grimes. The 11-year-old boy was in the process of placing his shotgun into the vehicle when it accidentally discharged into his father's right leg above the knee, severing the main artery and blowing away much of the man's muscle tissue.

Tommy Grimes immediately made a tourniquet for his dad out of rope and a screwdriver and he drove him to Cascade where friends of the family transported him to Great Falls. Initial reports from the Great Falls hospital stated that Grimes was in satisfactory condition but his status deteriorated quickly from the loss of blood.

October 17, 1945
J.H. Meiers of Polson became the first hunting fatality of the 1945 Big-Game Season when he was accidentally shot and killed by one of his hunting companion in Elks Park in northwestern Montana.

Chapter Two: KILLED BY THEIR COMPANION

One of the men in the party ran 4 miles through the rugged timber for help but Mr. Meiers reportedly died about an hour after being shot in his pelvis.

October 20, 1945
John William Redlingshafer, 32, of Kalispell was accidentally shot and killed by his father while they were hunting about 7 miles northwest of Kalispell. He died instantly after being struck by three bullets when his father was loading his .32-caliber Winchester rifle.

John Redlingshafer was a father of 3 children and was employed by the Wilson Brothers Produce Company

October 22, 1945
Creed R. Morgan, of Kellogg, Idaho died in a Missoula hospital after being treated for a gunshot wound as a result of a hunting accident in the Bitterroot National Forest near the Montana-Idaho border. Mr. Morgan was seriously injured in the right arm when he stepped into the line of fire as his companion was shooting at a bear.

One of the hunters in Morgan's party rode a horse to the Moose Creek Ranger Station where a rescue party was formed. After administering emergency first aid to the wounded hunter they marked the spot, which was on a ridge between Goat Creek and its southern tributary for a doctor to parachute in.

Renowned Army Paratroop doctor, Captain Amos Little of Marlboro, Massachusetts was flown from Great Falls to a remote landing strip in the wilderness south of Missoula where he boarded a tri-motor plane along with several smoke jumpers and they proceeded to the jump site.

Despite having sheer cliffs on both sides of the narrow ledge, Captain Little and the other jumpers successfully landed within 20 feet of the injured man.

Chapter Two: KILLED BY THEIR COMPANION

After the doctor stabilized Mr. Morgan the rescue party transported him to Missoula where he survived for a week before he died.

November 25, 1945
<u>Monty Leavitt</u>, 9, of Shelby was killed by his 11-year-old brother, Gary while they were hunting rabbits with their friend, Junior Ruhby near the old petroleum refinery near their home.

Apparently a rabbit had run in front of the boys and Monty was accidentally shot in the excitement.

October 29, 1947
<u>Charles Masker</u>, 19, of Stanford was shot and killed by his 15-year-old friend while they were rabbit hunting.

October 31, 1948
<u>Donald J. Bertoglio</u>, 15, of Butte was shot and killed by his friend, 16-year-old Frank Grebenc, while they were rabbit hunting about 13 miles east of the Mining City.

Frank Grebenc later told officials that his .22-caliber rifle accidentally discharged and it struck his friend. He said that Don Bertoglio cried out, "I'm shot!" Grebenc immediately ran for help but when he returned the young boy was already dead.

November 19, 1948
<u>Raymond Necklace</u>, a teenager from Brockton was fatally shot while he was preparing to go hunting with Rudolph Young of Poplar.

Rudolph Young was holding a 12-guage shotgun that he didn't think was loaded when it accidentally discharged into Raymond Necklace just below the ribs on his left side. The young boy died about four hours later.

Chapter Two: KILLED BY THEIR COMPANION

October 9, 1950
<u>Mrs. Sam (Caroline) J. Ullery</u>, 23, died in a Miles City hospital from an accidental gunshot wound she sustained in the kitchen of her home just one day after being married.

The day after they tied the knot, Mr. and Mrs. Sam Ullery got up and planned to go hunting. While Mrs. Ullery was washing the breakfast dishes her 21-year-old husband was cleaning their guns on the kitchen table. As he reached for a pistol it accidentally discharged into his wife's abdomen.

Although Mrs. Ullery's condition improved a couple of days later, she died at 11:30 on the morning of October 11. Mrs. Ullery left her husband and 3 children from a previous marriage.

Photo by Joyce Obland
(www.graves-r-us.com)

October 23, 1950
<u>Alvin Austin</u>, a teacher at the Plains High School was shot and killed in a hunting accident by his brother near Whitepine.

The two men had been tracking a wounded buck deer on a brushy hillside when George Austin accidentally shot his brother in the shoulder. Alvin Austin reportedly lived for about an hour and a half after being wounded.

November 15, 1950
<u>Robert Wesley Brown</u>, 17, of Missoula was accidentally killed in a hunting accident by his 18-year-old companion, Robert Chilcote while they were in the Grant Creek area about 10 miles north of Missoula.

The two boys along with another friend, 17-year-old Gary Larson, were getting up after resting from a hard climb, when Mr. Chilcote's .30-30-caliber rifle accidentally discharged into Brown's chest.

October 18, 1951
Fourteen-year-old <u>Edward Robinson</u> of Bainville was killed while he was deer hunting with three other youths in the wooded Missouri River bottom land on the farm of Glen Simard, which was about 5 miles from their home.

Edward had separated from his brother, Robert and their friends, Dennis Crusch and Robert Smith when they were stalking a deer. The boys later said that they had shot at and missed the deer and then went back to their pickup to wait for Edward to return. When he didn't show up they went looking for him and they located his body with a gunshot wound to the chest.

November 5, 1951
<u>Gerald Hays</u>, of Butte was accidentally shot and killed by a companion while they were hunting deer and elk in the Crippled Horse area about 27 miles northwest of Libby.

Mr. Hays' party was walking down a steep trail when Jack Dofflemire, who was behind Hays, saw a deer and he raised his rifle to take a shot when he stumbled and fell and his rifle accidentally discharged.

It was reported later that Dofflemire had been using a rifle that he wasn't very acquainted with. According to the coroner's report the bullet entered Hays' right shoulder and then came out the left side below the ribs, killing him instantly. After visiting the accident site, the coroner's jury cleared Mr. Dofflemire of any criminal responsibility in the death of Gerald Hays.

November 14, 1951
<u>Marvin H. Wagner</u>, 24, of Polson died from an accidental gunshot wound he received while he was hunting near Plains, Montana.

Chapter Two: KILLED BY THEIR COMPANION

Mr. Wagner was hunting with Lawrence Dresden when they spotted a deer on a logging road. Apparently when Dresden turned to speak to Wagner, his .30-30-caliber rifle discharged and struck Wagner in the chest at close range. Although Dresden rushed his friend to the Polson Hospital Wagner died the next day.

December 1, 1952
George Francis Delisle, 52, of Billings died shortly after arriving at the hospital from an accidental gunshot wound while he was hunting about 7 miles northeast of the Magic City.

Mr. Delisle was hunting with his 12-year-old son, Gerald and another boy from Billings, 19-year-old Russell Hein. While they were walking along a railroad embankment Hein tripped and fell, which accidentally discharged both barrels of his .12-guage shotgun into Mr. Delisle in the left side and armpit.

Ironically Delisle's son, who was walking between the other two hunters, was untouched by the blast of flying lead.

October 17, 1953
Edwin Charles Ham, 16, of Garrison, Montana died from a wound he received while he was hunting near his hometown with 18-year-old Louis Dwyer of Butte.

Dwyer later told the authorities that they were on their way back to their car when the Ham boy stopped to shoot a chipmunk. When Dwyer turned to watch, his own gun accidentally discharged into Edwin Ham's abdomen.

October 21, 1953
Thirty-two-year-old Al Kruzon of Saltese, Montana died in a hospital two days after being accidentally shot in the abdomen while he was hunting elk with two of his friends about 2 miles west of Saltese.

Chapter Two: KILLED BY THEIR COMPANION

According to accounts, Mr. Kruzon was shot through his liver while he was resting on a ridge and the officials had not determined who fired the fatal shot.

October 25, 1953
Francis Norquay, 55, of Whitefish died in a hospital 7 days after being accidentally shot by his son-in-law, Roy Simmons while they were hunting in the Dicky Lake area about 35 miles west of Whitefish.

Mr. Norquay had shot and wounded a deer and it ran towards Simmons. After seeing the deer coming his way, Simmons fired his rifle and the bullet missed the animal and it struck his father-in-law in the head.

November 8, 1953
Art Sanders, 16, of Roundup was accidentally shot in the temple by a friend while the two were hunting. The boys saw a deer while they were driving and Sanders was shot when they stopped.

October 28, 1954
(Missoulian)
Twenty-four-year-old David William Saltsman of Eureka died at a Whitefish hospital from a hunting accident at Sophie Lake about 8 miles north of Eureka.

Mr. Saltsman had been hunting ducks with a party of men when he was reportedly shot with a pistol in the hands of his best friend while the men were getting out of their vehicle. An inquest later determined that the fatal incident was totally accidental.

David Saltsman, was a former smoke jumper at Missoula and he was employed by J. Neils Lumber Company at Libby at the time of his death.

Chapter Two: KILLED BY THEIR COMPANION

November 15, 1954

<u>Ray Johns</u>, 49, of Ronan, Montana was accidentally shot and killed by his hunting companion while his 17-year-old son witnessed the accident.

The three men had been road hunting about 9 miles west of Ronan when Mr. Johns spotted a deer in the field on the right side of the road and pulled his car over.

Fred Miles of Hot Springs, riding in the back seat on the passenger side, got out of the car as it was coming to a stop. The deer began to cross the road ahead of the vehicle and Miles was following the animal through his riflescope. Mr. Johns opened his door and began to stand up just as Miles took his shot across the hood of the car, striking the victim in the back of the head.

November 20, 1955

Nineteen-year-old <u>Ross Nelson</u> of Toston, Montana was accidentally killed when he was struck in the head at close range with a shotgun while he was hunting one mile north of Townsend.

Mr. Nelson had been pheasant hunting with Marvin Doig and Jack Nash, both 17 and from Toston, when Nelson spotted some birds and stopped his car The other two boys began firing at a pheasant over the hood of the vehicle just as Nelson stepped out of the car.

The newspaper article didn't specify which hunter had fired the killing shot, but it reported that Marvin Doig was under a physician's care and suffering from shock.

November 6, 1956

<u>Jim Hankinson</u>, 25, of Superior died in a Missoula hospital 5 days after being accidentally shot in the back by his wife while they were hunting along Nemote Creek about 15 miles east of their home.

According to the authorities, Mr. Hankinson was wounded when his wife's weapon accidentally discharged while she was trying to close the safety on her rifle. Apparently her thumb had slipped and she accidentally pulled the trigger and the rifle fired into the back of her husband standing about 15 feet away.

November 7, 1956
Nine-year-old <u>Gary Mosback</u> of Livingston was accidentally shot and killed when he ran into his father's line of fire. The father and son were hunting with two other neighbor boys in the Shields Valley north of Livingston when the man took a shot at a target. The bullet entered the youngster's back and it came out of his neck.

October 28, 1957
<u>Frank West</u>, 48, of Livingston was killed while he was pheasant hunting on his brother-in-law's ranch about 6 miles south of Livingston. He had been hunting with 4 other hunters when some pheasants flushed and everyone started shooting at the birds.

Mr. West was later found slumped over with wounds in his chest, throat and face. He died about 4 hours later and it wasn't determined who had fired the fatal shot. The coroner's report stated that Frank West had died "by accident or misfortune."

November 4, 1957
<u>Albert Hardie</u>, 21, of Helena was accidentally killed while he was hunting with his brother near Marysville. After leaving his wife and another friend at his car, Albert and his 16-year-old brother, Maurice climbed a mountain near the Empire Mine.

Maurice later told the authorities that he and his brother had been walking along a steep hillside when he slipped and his .22-caliber rifle accidentally went off striking his brother in the back and piercing his lung.

Chapter Two: KILLED BY THEIR COMPANION

The boy ran down to the road where he stopped a group of hunters who helped him carry Albert from the mountain but he had died before they got to the road.

November 12, 1957
Walter B. Sokoloski Jr., 18, of Hamilton was shot to death while he was hunting on a mountainside in the rugged Sleeping Child country southeast of Hamilton.

Sokoloski had been climbing up a hill that was nearly perpendicular when his hunting partner, Bill Thomas slipped and he lost control of his .33-caliber rifle. The safety wasn't locked on Thomas' rifle and as it hit the ground it discharged into Sokoloski's chest just below the collarbone.

Inscribed on Walter Sokoloski's tombstone reads: "At Rest Among the Mountains I Loved." The incident was made even more tragic when a local mortician, John W. Dowling died of a heart attack while he was climbing the same mountainside to help recover the dead hunter's body.

November 13, 1957
Forty-year-old Elias Hoch of Wolf Point, Montana was accidentally shot and killed by his 14-year-old son, David while they were deer hunting in the Missouri Breaks about 40 miles northwest of Jordan.

The two hunters had been firing at a herd of deer; the boy was shooting from a standing position while his father was firing from one knee. Apparently Mr. Hoch had stood up to change his position just as his son fired a shot, which struck the back of his father's head

October 1, 1958
John Gust Anderson, 71, of Richland was accidentally shot and killed while he was hunting near Glendive. Mr. Anderson became the first

hunting fatality in 1958 when he was accidentally shot by a shotgun carried by 47-year-old Clifford Wilson of Nashua, Montana.

Mr. Wilson and another man from Nashua, 50-year-old Chet Glazier had been walking on opposite sides of a coulee while Anderson was going down the middle when Wilson shot a prairie chicken.

The shotgun Wilson was using was old and a second blast went off apparently from the recoil from the first shot. The second shot hit John Anderson with 91 pellets, one of which severed his aorta.

November 30, 1958
Fifteen-year-old <u>Reuben Gomke</u> of Kremlin, Montana was dead on arrival at a Havre hospital after being accidentally shot by his hunting companion.

The authorities reported that Mr. Gomke had been hunting 3 miles south of Kremlin with his 16-year-old cousin, Melvin Gomke and two other boys from Kremlin, Marvin Melby, 15, and 14-year-old David Melby.

The officials didn't immediately indicate how the .22-caliber rifle discharged but the bullet struck Reuben Gomke in the back of the head and it lodged in his brain.

January 30, 1959
<u>Dale Robinson</u>, 20, of Musselshell, Montana died in Roundup shortly after being accidentally shot by his 16-year-old brother Wade while they were hunting rabbits.

The two brothers had been hunting with 18-year-old John Sanner when Wade shot over the hood of the car just as his brother stood up on the other side of the vehicle.

Chapter Two: KILLED BY THEIR COMPANION

Dale Robinson, who had just returned home from taking semester exams at Rocky Mountain College in Billings was shot in the back of the head and became the state's first hunting fatality of 1959.

October 12, 1959
Westley P. Stace, 29, of Havre was accidentally shot and killed while he was bow hunting with 5 other Havre hunters about 33 miles south Chinook.

Apparently the Northern Montana College professor was accidentally shot in the chest by a pistol, which had been carried by one of his friends.

October 19, 1959
Robert Walker Smith, 32, of Great Falls was killed while he was hunting with Allen Thoreson on the 7,500-foot Mount Baldy about 5 miles from Hughesville.

Mr. Smith was an employee of the Anaconda Company at Great Falls, but while the union was on strike he found work at the mine of Myron J. Olson near Hughesville. On Sunday morning he decided to go hunting with Mr. Olson's stepson, Allen Thoreson.

The two men were crossing a slippery snow covered hillside when Thoreson slipped and his .22-caliber rifle accidentally discharged into Smith's chest, just below the heart killing him instantly.

Robert Smith was born in Bismarck, North Dakota and he moved to Billings with his mother when he was nine years old. He attended schools in Billings and he joined the Army from the Magic City.

Smith moved to Great Falls in 1953 where he became a furnace refinery worker at the Anaconda smelter. Robert Smith left behind his wife and two daughters.

Chapter Two: KILLED BY THEIR COMPANION

Robert Smith's tombstone was chosen for the cover of this book along with the marker of Fred Kent who also lost his life hunting just 8 days after Smith's death. Since their deaths occurred so close, and because they were both veterans of the Second World War they were buried side by side in the same Great Falls cemetery. Although these two men probably didn't know each other in life they were brought together in death by their love of hunting.

November 1, 1959
Seventeen-year-old high school senior, Gary Sorenson of Malta died from an accidental gunshot wound sustained while he was pheasant hunting with his friends about 2 miles north of his home.

Gary Sorenson had been hunting with Leland Winkle and Britton Winkle Jr. when Leland's shotgun accidentally discharged into Sorenson's thigh. Although the victim had lost a great deal of blood and he went into prolong shock his companions managed to get him quickly to a hospital.

A few days later gangrene developed in his wound and the doctors amputated his leg in an attempt to save his life. For a couple of days it appeared that the young man would survive the tragedy but he took a turn for the worse and died a day later.

October 24, 1960
Twenty-two-year-old Judith Marie Walker of Glasgow became the first hunting victim of 1960 when she was shot by her 22-year-old girl friend, Sarah Lou Arnold also of Glasgow.

Sarah Arnold's .244-rifle accidentally discharged into the back of Judith Walker's head as they were getting out of their car. Judith had only been married for a year to Airman James Walker who was stationed at the Glasgow Air Force Base.

Chapter Two: KILLED BY THEIR COMPANION

October 16, 1961
Thirty-four-year-old <u>Jack R. Burger</u> of Missoula was accidentally killed while he was deer hunting about 8 miles west of Superior by his 32-year-old brother-in-law, Alvin Breaster, also of Missoula.

When the two men were walking back to the car north of the Clark Fork River, Mr. Breaster began to unload his .30-30 lever action when it accidentally discharged into the back of the World War II veteran, Jack R. Burger.

October 24, 1961
<u>Michael Long-Tree</u>, 16, of Poplar was killed when he was accidentally shot in the head with a shotgun while he was bird hunting about two miles north of town. His hunting partner, 16-year-old John Bill Jr. was unloading his shotgun when it accidentally went off into Michael Long-Tree.

November 7, 1961
<u>Don Cattnach</u>, 46, of Austin, Minnesota was accidentally shot and killed by his 26-year-old son-in-law, Dick Anderson of Minneapolis.

The two men had been hunting about 7 miles north of Teigen in Petroleum County when they came across several deer and they began shooting at the animals. While sighting through his scope on a running deer, Anderson shot when Don Cattnach was in his line of fire.

October 19, 1964
Forty-two-year-old <u>Frank L. Anderson,</u> a Wilsall carpenter became the first hunting fatality of the 1964 Big Game Season when his hunting partner accidentally shot him while he was removing his firearm from their car.

Chapter Two: KILLED BY THEIR COMPANION

October 26, 1964
Larry Walla, 13, of Shawmut accidentally shot and killed his 6-year-old brother, Lindy Walla after they had returned from a hunt with their father Mr. Bjarne Walla. Larry was unloading his .30-30 rifle when it accidentally went off into his little brother.

January 15, 1965
Carl Martin, 23, of Shelby was accidentally shot on a hunting trip on January 4 and he later died at a Great Falls hospital. Martin had been rabbit hunting with David Dugan and Harvey Moore, both of Oilmont near Shelby.

The three men were in a pickup truck when they saw a fox near the road. Stopping the vehicle Dugan grabbed his rifle and slipped while he was stepping down out of the truck. The weapon accidentally discharged into the neck of Carl Martin.

November 2, 1965
Regan Hoyt, the 14-year-old son of Mr. and Mrs. Paul Hoyt of Red Lodge died 19 days after being accidentally shot by his companion, 14-year-old Larry Griffin while they were duck hunting on a private pond near town.

While the two boys were in a boat on the pond, Griffin began shooting at something in the water. At that point the boat apparently began to rock and Griffin lost his balance and his weapon accidentally discharged into Regan Hoyt.

November 7, 1965
Seventeen-year-old Daniel Allen Jewett of Virginia City was killed while he was on a hunting trip with two of his friends in the upper Ruby Country.

Dan Jewett was shot in the right side of his abdomen with a high-powered rifle when one of his teenage friends was putting his rifle into the trunk of their car.

Apparently when the weapon fell against another loaded rifle in the trunk it accidentally fired and the bullet went through the back seat just as Jewett was leaning over in the backseat to pick something up from the floorboard.

November 19, 1968
Pregnant 18-year-old <u>Amber Spence</u> of Libby, and previously from Great Falls, was killed when she was accidentally shot in the stomach. Her husband, Dennis had been cleaning his rifle after a hunting trip when it went off killing his wife and their unborn child.

October 5, 1969
<u>George R. Frank</u>, 22, of Missoula was accidentally shot to death by his 26-year-old hunting companion, James Baker also of Missoula. The two men had been elk hunting about 10 miles southeast of Lolo Hot Springs at the time of the tragedy.

November 13, 1969
<u>Norris Thompson</u>, 19, of Glasgow was pronounced dead on arrival at a Glasgow hospital after being accidentally shot by a friend while they were hunting in the Vandalia region about 22 miles northwest of Glasgow. Norris Thompson had been married for only two months at the time of his death.

October 24, 1970
Sixteen-year-old <u>Michael Fadness</u> of Bozeman was accidentally shot to death at close range by his twenty-year-old friend, Lem Love, also of Bozeman. The two men had been hunting in the rugged Deer Creek area some 40 miles south of Livingston.

Weeks later Lem Love was being held in connection with the shooting death of Michael Fadness and he was eventually committed to Warm Springs State Mental Hospital for the Killing.

Chapter Two: KILLED BY THEIR COMPANION

October 16, 1972
Mark Allen Lueder, 15, of Vaughn was accidentally shot and killed by his 16-year-old friend, Steve Quast while they were hunting ducks near a reservoir about 5 miles from their home.

Lueder and Quast and a third boy from Vaughn, 16-year-old Gary Knobf were all carrying .22-caliber rifles when one of them shot a duck, which fell into the water and they couldn't retrieve it.

While waiting for the duck to float to shore the boys decided to split up and do some more hunting. Just as Quast was shooting at another duck that had taken flight, Mark Lueder came over the top of the dirt dam about 100 yards away and took the slug to his heart.

November 21, 1972
Nadine J. Riedl, 20, of Billings was accidentally shot and killed while she was on a hunting trip about 6 miles north of Broadus. The young lady was shot in the left side of the chest while she was sitting in the cab of a pickup truck.

Three young men were climbing into the camper on the rear of the truck when one of their rifles accidentally discharged and the bullet passed through the wall of the camper and into the cab.

November 23, 1973
Eighteen-year-old Wade Drollinger of Kalispell was accidentally killed in a hunting accident just 10 days after his father had also died in a hunting incident.

Wade Drollinger had been hunting with a juvenile friend on River Road about 3 miles south of Kalispell when he was accidentally killed. Drollinger was getting out of the car on the passenger side just as his friend was shooting at a deer over the roof of the vehicle.

Chapter Two: KILLED BY THEIR COMPANION

October 12, 1976

A hunting companion accidentally shot and killed <u>Roger Lee Jorgenson</u>, 27, of Billings while they were in the Stillwater Country. Mr. Jorgenson was killed instantly when he was struck in the back of the head with a high-powered rifle bullet.

Roger Jorgenson was part of a 5-member hunting party that had spotted a herd of antelope and they pursued them into a field to get a better shot. The men got out and began shooting at the animals from both sides of the vehicle when Jorgensen stood up just as another man was firing over the hood of the car.

October 26, 1976

Twenty-seven-year-old <u>Mark S. Koefod</u> of Havre was accidentally shot and killed with his own rifle when it was being handled by a friend on a deer hunting trip about 33 miles northwest of Inverness, which is about 43 miles west of Havre

Mr. Koefod was with a party of friends when he asked Scott Patrick to get his rifle from their truck and the weapon accidentally discharged as he was picking it up. The 30-caliber round tore through the cab of the pickup and hit Koefod in the abdomen and he died a few minutes later.

October 2, 1977

<u>Lewis Paul "Skipper" Sprattler</u>, 22, of Great Falls was accidentally shot and killed by his 18-year-old brother, Mark while they were duck hunting at Freezeout Lake north of Fairfield on opening day of the 1977 season.

Louis Sprattler was shot in the head and neck at close range when Mark's shotgun accidentally discharged while he was reaching for a duck that he had just shot.

October 18, 1977
Jerry Scott Kroh of Laurel was accidentally shot and killed by a companion with a 12-gauge shotgun while they were hunting between Park City and Laurel. Mr. Kroll was only about 10 feet from the muzzle when the shotgun accidentally discharged.

October 29, 1979
(Daily Inter Lake)
Fifteen-year-old Jordan S. Sorenson of Whitefish was accidentally shot and killed by his 14-year-old companion as they were leaving their rural home to go hunting.

The unidentified 14 year old grabbed a 30-30 rifle off the wall and announced, "Lets go hunting," and the weapon accidental discharged into Sorenson's eye. The young boy was declared dead on arrival at North Valley Hospital.

December 1, 1980
Lee Faw, 15, of Big Timber was accidentally shot and killed outside the Grand Hotel after he and 15-year-old Roger Zimbar had finished eating dinner after their hunt.

When they returned to their vehicle Mr. Zimbar was moving a .243-caliber rifle in order to unlock the other door and it accidentally discharged into Lee Faw.

October 26, 1983
Twelve-year-old Deidra Broderick accidentally killed her 45-year-old father, Holis M. Broderick of Kalispell as they were hunting on the Floyd Blair Ranch about 6 miles east of Denton.

Chapter Two: KILLED BY THEIR COMPANION

They were returning from a hunt with Deidra's grandfather when Mr. Floyd Blair picked them up and give them a ride back to their vehicle in his pickup truck.

After arriving at their car, the girl and her father jumped out of the back of Mr. Blair's truck when her weapon accidentally discharged and struck her father in the heart.

January 2, 1987
(Havre Daily News)
Wade Otto Stuber of Havre was accidentally shot and killed by his partner while he was goose hunting along the Missouri River about 14 miles northeast Fort Benton.

Twenty-eight-year-old Wade Stuber and Steve Renaker had floated down the river when they landed their boat to walk along the shore. The men separated and when Stuber didn't return to the boat his partner reported his disappearance at Loma about 4 o'clock that afternoon.

The following morning the authorities found Stubers's body in the river, about 20 to 25 feet from the shore in about 5 feet of water some 1,500 yards from where the two men had separated. Obviously it was thought that Mr. Stubers had lost his life by drowning but it was later determined that his body ended up in the river after he had been accidentally shot by Renaker. Apparently Renaker didn't realize his partner was in his line of fire when he shot at some birds.

October 26, 1987
(Missoulian)
Kenneth M. Reinhart died at St. Patrick Hospital in Missoula after being accidentally shot by a .300-caliber rifle bullet while he was standing in the parking lot of a bar in Condon when another man was removing a rifle from his vehicle.

Chapter Two: KILLED BY THEIR COMPANION

Forty-eight-year-old Reinhart was struck near the shoulder as an unidentified man was removing his Remington rifle from the dashboard of his pickup truck. The rifle accidentally discharged through the front windshield and into Reinhart.

After being first treated by the Condon Quick Response Unit Reinhart was flown by helicopter to the hospital at Missoula. Kenneth Reinhart left a wife, two sons and two daughters.

October 30, 1987
(Miles City Star)
Thirty-two-year-old Custer County rancher, Kary Schanz was accidentally shot and killed while he was hunting with three other men in the eastern part of the county.

Custer County Sheriff Tony Harbaugh reported that three of the men were carrying out a deer when a rifle being carried by a 16-year-old Miles City youth accidentally discharged into Mr. Schanz's upper body.

Mr. Schanz had been a smoke jumper in Missoula and at West Yellowstone but he was recently ranching near Ismay. Kary Schanz left a wife and two children.

August 23, 1990
(Flathead Courier)
Eric Watson, 14, of St. Ignatius was pronounced dead on arrival at St. Patrick Hospital in Missoula after being accidentally shot while he was gopher hunting with two Missoula boys.

The three boys were hunting in St. Mary Canyon about 8 miles northeast of St. Ignatius when Watson reportedly stepped into the line of fire of one of the boys firing at a gopher. The .22-caliber bullet entered Eric Watson's right jaw and it exited near his left ear.

Chapter Two: KILLED BY THEIR COMPANION

After medical assistance was called to the sight the victim was transported to the Midway Store near Ravalli by ambulance and he was then flown to Missoula on a Life Flight Helicopter.

October 22, 1990
Thirty-five-year-old <u>Kay Fairservice</u> of Neihart was killed outside of her home while she was preparing to go hunting with her sister, Jacqueline Lynn Fairservice.

The two women had placed their rifles on the passenger side of the pickup when they noticed that one of the bolts was open. Lynn walked up and closed the action and the rifle accidentally discharged, killing Kay instantly.

November 19, 1991
<u>Mahlon Gunn Jr.</u>, 12, of Havre was killed when he was accidentally shot in the back while he was on a hunting trip on the Rocky Boy's Indian Reservation.

The boy had been walking along a trail when a 16-year-old boy behind him was carrying a rifle that accidentally discharged.

November 7, 1994
<u>Nathan Michael Cox</u>, 20, of Billings died in a local hospital after being accidentally shot by his 11-year-old brother while they were hunting near Belfry.

The two brothers and another friend had just parked to go hunting when the young boy's .22-caliber rifle accidentally discharged while he was getting out the car. The bullet struck his older brother in the back of his head. Nathan Cox was airlifted to Billings but he died the next day.

Chapter Two: KILLED BY THEIR COMPANION

November 30, 1994
(Billings Gazette) (Accident Report)
<u>Wendi LeAnne Weisgerber</u> of Bridger was accidentally shot and
killed while she was hunting with her husband and their friends in
Yellowstone County.

The 21-year-old Weisgerber was struck in the back with a .30-06-
caliber rifle bullet as she stepped into the line fire of her friend, 26-
year-old Theresa Ross just 30 feet from their vehicle.

The entire party including her husband, Dan witnessed the tragic
accident. In Wendi's obituary it was said that she had died doing one
of the things she loved most.

May 20, 1996
Eleven-year-old <u>Michael Glenn Privett</u> of Corvallis died at Marcus
Daly Hospital at Hamilton after being accidentally shot while he was
hunting with his father and 3 neighborhood boys near their home.

The authorities reported that one of the other boys was holding a 22-
caliber rifle, which accidentally discharged into Privett's chest.

Ironically Michael Privett and his family had just moved to Corvallis
two weeks earlier from the Sacramento, California area to escape the
increasing gang activity in that area.

December 23, 1997
<u>Christopher D. Weaver</u>, 14, of Kalispell was killed by an accidental
shotgun blast while he was duck hunting with David W. Hall in
Flathead County.

It was reported that Mr. Weaver was accidentally killed when Hall,
who was wearing heavy gloves, tried to un-cock his .12-guage shotgun
and it discharged into the victim's chest.

David Hall ran to a nearby house where a woman immediately called for help and then she went to the scene to try and assist the Weaver boy, but he was already died.

October 30, 2002
Thirty-nine-year-old <u>Thomas Asbridge</u> of Clinton was accidentally shot and killed by his wife while they were hunting northeast of Missoula near the Clearwater Junction.

The couple had been hunting earlier in the day and on their way back to their pickup they stopped to check the sights on the woman's rifle. They tacked some toilet paper to a tree for a target and after firing once at the tree she began reloading her rifle.

Mrs. Asbridge was having trouble forcing the bullet into the chamber while she was pointing the muzzle upward. She later said that she didn't know if her finger was on the trigger or not, but the rifle accidentally discharged just as her husband stepped in front of the barrel.

The woman ran about a mile back to the road and then she called for help from the convenience store at the Clearwater Junction.

November 19, 2002
(Billings Gazette)
<u>Chakay Ricker</u>, 12, of Poplar was accidentally shot and killed by a sixth-grade classmate at his home after a hunting trip.

It was reported that the unidentified 11-year-old shooter had recently completed a hunter safety course.

May 14, 2003
(Big Fork Eagle)
Twenty-two-year-old <u>Joshua N. Lee</u> of Ferndale was accidentally shot and killed in the driveway of his home after returning from a bear hunt with his friend, David Langlois.

Chapter Two: KILLED BY THEIR COMPANION

The boyhood friends were talking about their hunt that day when the 23-year-old Langlois removed the clip from a .40-caliber handgun, which unintentionally discharged into Lee's chest.

While the two men had been drinking before the incident, the authorities reported that Mr. Langlois' blood alcohol content was below the legal limit.

Chapter Three:
DYING AFTER BECOMING LOST OR MISSING

Cold and snow have always meant good hunting conditions, but they have also spelled death for many hunters who failed to be prepared. Hunters don't generally get lost because they have a poor sense of directions or that men don't like to ask for directions. Hunters get lost in areas that they are familiar with and we have recorded one case of a hunter dying after he had asked for directions.

While a hiker usually knows where they are and where they are going, hunters typically don't follow trails because big game animals rarely follow those routes. Also when a hunter wounds an animal they typically follow them without regard to their own physical condition and sense of direction into dense timber, deep snow or other treacherous terrain.

Experienced hunters suggest several precautions to divert a deadly disaster. A hunter should take the time to study the area that he will be hunting or he should tag along with someone who is familiar with the country. Always tell someone exactly where you are going and when you will be back. Even if you're going for a day hunt be prepared and equipped to spend the night. Take along every thing you would need if you were going to stay over night including food, water, shelter, matches, hatchet or saw, first aide supplies and a flashlight.

Lost hunters generally have an eight to ten-hour head start on the rescue party, and with an average walking gate of about two-miles-per-hour they can be anywhere in a 64-square-mile area when searchers get on the scene. Experts report that it generally takes between 8 to 14 hours to locate a person after the call is received.

When a hunter realizes they're lost, they often become anxious; the adrenaline kicks in; they get scared and they have even started to run. It's best to get over the initial fear and except the fact, stay calm and build a fire. Staying put is difficult for many hunters, but the fire becomes your friend and you won't feel alone with a nice fire. Stay by the fire or your vehicle and wait for the rescue team to find you.

Even with matches, sometimes its difficult to find something dry enough to light. Some survival experts suggest carrying cotton balls soaked in Vaseline or even Frito corn chips for fire starter. The popular snack chips are a good choice not just because of the fire starting ability but because eating helps keep the person warm and calm while waiting for the rescue party.

The hunter should next make a shelter by digging a snow cave or construct a pine-bough lean-two. Blowing a loud whistle regularly will help guide rescuers to your position and three gunshots in the air is another well-known emergency signal.

If your hunter is overdue, don't hesitate calling the authorities as soon as possible. Every minute is important. The longer people at home wait to call, the worse it is for the search teams. The victim can travel farther, scents deteriorate over time and tracks or articles can be covered by snow

Chapter Three: LOST OR MISSING

**Persons missing for 10 days or more are
considered "Missing and Presumed Dead."**

January 12, 1881
(Helena Daily Herald)
The frozen body of <u>Private Severance</u> of Captain Paul's Company "K" attached to Fort Assinniboine was found after becoming lost while hunting big game for the fort.

A group of soldiers and civilian hunters left the 2-year-old fort to find several hundred pounds of wild game, which had been cached by a hunter. When the cache of meat wasn't located the detachment decided to hunt for some game instead of returning to the fort empty handed.

Private Severance became lost when the men separated and his tracks indicated that he had become bewildered and he walked in a wide circle before he became exhausted and died from exhaustion.

February 5, 1881
(Helena Daily Herald)
<u>Calvin Bryon</u> was reportedly missing and presumed dead in the buffalo range in Custer County. Bryon had not been seen for two weeks since he had left his cabin near Ferry Point to hunt buffalo.

The winter of 1880-1881 was reportedly quite severe and it had moved a great deal of animals down from Canada. The buffalo in particular were reported in great numbers that winter and both the Indians and whites slaughtered many of them.

Large bands of Indians were making big killings near the Buffalo Rapids about 12 miles from Glendive, and it was reported that area white settlers were able to shoot the shaggy animals from the doorway of their cabins. The huge migrating herds of buffalo often slowed down and even stopped several stagecoaches that year.

July 11, 1884
(Weekly Missoulian)
Seth Whipple, reportedly the oldest buffalo hunter in the Upper
Missouri River Valley was presumed dead after he had been reported
missing since April from a hunting trip.

His friends reported that he had left his wood yard near Popular
Creek four months earlier and he hadn't been seen or heard from
since. Since the frontiersman was very familiar with the prairie his
neighbors believed that the Cree Indians might have killed him.

February 22, 1896
(Anaconda Standard)
The body of 55-year-old James Bingley was found near Blackfoot City
in present day Powell County after being missing for about two weeks
while hunting.

The single man had apparently gotten disoriented in the heavy
snowstorm and fell unconscious after he stopped to rest. Mr. Bingley
was found in a sitting position in the snow with his gun lying across
one of his arms and a jackrabbit he had shot by his side.

October 21, 1899
William Longstaff of Sauk Centre, Minnesota reportedly strayed
from his hunting party in the mountains of the North Fork Canyon
about 6 miles from the Beach Ranch, which was about 20 miles from
Augusta.

Five days later a search party found the hunter's rifle sticking about 3
inches out of the snow and the man was buried under a drift of snow
several feet deep.

June 15, 1901
George Reiter of Trail Creek was presumed dead after being missing
for two months while hunting bear in Gallatin County. Reiter was

last seen leaving for the mountains with his dogs in early April, and while two of his dogs had returned, the man never came back.

November 7, 1902
The superintendent of the Great Northern Railway, <u>Benjamin F. Egan</u> became lost and presumed dead between Coram and Belton while he was hunting deer with Dr. Hubert E. Houston and Dr. R. Houston.

On Tuesday, November 4, 1902 Mr. Egan and his secretary, H.J. Stoops along with the Houston brothers left the Kalispell railroad yards for the Coram area on Engine No. 1128 pulling the superintendent's personal car No. A-14. Along the way the men had dinner on the car, talked about previous hunts and then donned their hunting clothes and readied their gear.

The men left the car and did some target shooting while they waited for the westbound train, which took their car to Belton where it would be placed on a sidetrack until the hunters' return. The three men had planned to walk to Lake Five and then hunt towards Belton.

Since Mr. Stoops decided to stay at the car and get caught up on some paperwork, Mr. Egan elected to take Stoop's 30-30 Savage rifle because it was lighter than his personal 45-70.

Mr. Egan was dressed very warm, wearing a suit of heavy woolen underwear in addition to an extra undershirt, 2 pairs of socks, one woolen and one of cotton. He was wearing three-quarter inch felt lined hunting boots, heavy woolen pants and a vest along with an oil duck canvas coat. The gentleman topped off his ensemble with a slough hat and buckskin gloves. The superintendent also wore shawl straps, which he wrapped over the top of his boots to keep the snow out of them.

Along with his clothing Mr. Egan carried about 30 rounds of ammunition, a small pearl-handled pocketknife, a watch and a compass. The Houston brothers reported that Egan had two sandwiches but they were concerned that he may not have had matches.

Dr. H.E. Houston, who was the division surgeon for the Great Northern, described his friend, Mr. Egan, as a little man of about 35 years old and a die-hard railroad man who would never give up. Although he was unfamiliar with the area the doctor considered Mr. Egan as a seasoned hunter and an experienced outdoorsman. Egan had hunted throughout the western states and had recently hunted near Summit.

The three men walked together to the head of Lake Five where they all consulted Mr. Egan's compass and determined it to be accurate and they all knew the direction to Belton. Mr. Egan and H.E. Houston decided to walk the three and a half miles to Belton along the east side of the lake while the other Houston brother took the west side.

After traveling together for about 400 yards down to the head of Half Moon Lake, Mr. Egan veered left slightly while the doctor went right. That was the last time Mr. Egan was seen alive.

The hunters had planned to meet at the bottom of Lake Five and then walk together to the superintendent's car at Belton. Upon arriving at the lake the Houston brothers waited for Mr. Egan until dusk and then thinking their friend had gone ahead to Belton they walked on to the railroad car.

After arriving at Belton at about 6:30 p.m. in a snowstorm the two brothers only found Mr. Stoops waiting for them. The men waited supper until 7:30 for Mr. Egan and then they ate an uneasy meal. While the Houston's were very alarmed and wanted to notify the superintendent's office at Kalispell Mr. Stoops insisted that they wait for his boss. He argued that Mr. Egan would be furious if a fuss was made over his tardiness.

First thing in the morning, thinking that Mr. Egan had taken shelter in one of the surrounding cabins, the three men along with a couple of local fellows quickly searched the shelters. After not finding the lost hunter at the cabins Mr. Stoops returned to Belton and called the Kalispell office where a formal search was finally initiated. The Houston brothers along with others continued the search around Lake Five for Egan while Mr. Stoops was calling for help.

While small groups searched that next day, the main search party of about 150 men was organized, outfitted and sent to the scene but owing to the time and weather it wasn't dispatched until the following morning.

The preliminary searchers were encouraged when they found a deer near Half Moon Lake that had been shot and some of the meat taken, making them believe that Mr. Egan was safe and he was eating venison while waiting for his rescue.

Within a day of being notified the Great Northern Railroad had offered $500 to the person finding their superintendent and the Conrad National Bank of Kalispell matched it for a total reward of $1,000. These circulars reportedly attracted up to 400 additional searchers and later there became an ugly issue between the railroad, county officials and many of the local residents. A few officials had implied that some of the local woodsmen had already found Egan's body and they were holding it for the reward money.

After a week of financing the search including the feeding and housing of hundreds of men, the Great Northern Railroad sent everyone home except for an experienced tracker and hunter, Daniel Doody of Nyack and his hand-picked 9-man search party.

Dying to Hunt in Montana
Chapter Three: LOST OR MISSING

Mr. Doody along with John O'Brien, Jack Wise, Charles Buckley, Tom King, Jake Nickling, Charles E. Ramsey, Billy Lawrence, Ernest Christensen and Jack Rabideux were supplied and equipped to stay out for 10 days at a time. This party of experienced men was never able to locate the missing man.

Mr. Egan's wife and children were going to stay at the superintendent railcar at the scene but instead it was used by his family from Breckenridge, Minnesota and local friends who had continued the search.

By the end of November Mr. Egan was replaced as the superintendent by the railroad and the search for the missing hunter's body would have to wait until the spring of 1903.

In early April of 1903 Mr. Egan's brother, A.H. Egan, who was also a railroad superintendent out of Chicago came to Montana to organize another search for his lost brother. Dan Doody, the Houston brothers and a former sheriff of Flathead County, T.C. Hand were all brought in for the search.

While the Egan family had intended to finance the search, which was based out of Lake Five, the Great Northern insisted on covering all of the costs and they promised to continue the search until the body was found or all leads were exhausted. Because of the deep snow in the region the search for Egan's body didn't get started until mid May and after a week the effort was interrupted by another heavy spring snowstorm.

On June 1, 1903 a search party led by Charles Emmons located the body of Mr. Egan in the hilly timber about a mile from the Great Northern tracks. Mr. Egan had only gone about 2 miles from where he and Dr, Houston had separated near Crescent Lake.

When found, the body was on its stomach with his right arm doubled under his chest and his left hand was under his shoulder

118

indicating that he had fallen and had tried to catch himself. His head was resting on a dead log and there was a snag by his temple.

A very close examination showed that the body didn't have any other wound, which disproved the many rumors of possible foul play and a theory that Egan might have been shot by one of his hunting companions.

While his body was well preserved by his heavy clothing his head and face were badly decomposed and beyond recognition. Identification was made from his papers and an inscription found on his pocket watch. Besides his watch, a knife, matches and 28 cartridges were found on his body but his rifle and compass were not found at the scene.

The final coroner's jury report ruled that Benjamin Egan had tripped and fallen rendering him unconscious and he had died from exposure the night of November 4, 1902. Mr. Egan had reportedly carried $25,000 in life insurance.

Eleven years later in 1913 Dr. H.E. Houston was involved in another hunting tragedy when his wife was accidentally shot and killed with her own shotgun, while she was removing it from under the seat of their vehicle when they were hunting with friends.

November 21, 1903
(Missoulian)
The body of M.M. Johnson, a hunter and miner of Wallace, Idaho was found in the DeBorgia region after dying of exposure.

Johnson had shot a deer; dressed it out and he had drug the large carcass some 3 miles when the weather became bitterly cold and it started to snow. Eventually the man gave up dragging his deer and he placed the animal's liver in his game bag on his belt and he began walking out.

By overexerting himself in the cold weather, he had gotten sweaty and then when he abandoned the carcass he became chilled. Mr. Johnson was wearing a pair of gumboots and while fording a deep creek his boots became filled with water and his tired legs became chilled to the bone. Apparently he was in the act of cutting away one of his boots when he fell into his endless sleep.

August 3, 1905
While returning from Fish Lake near Eureka Dan Shea and Lew Babcock found the body of a trapper named Barnaby along a trail after he had been missing since the previous winter.

Deputy Rich of Lincoln County reported that Barnaby's body was found face down in the canyon about 300 yards off the trail. When found, Barnaby was wearing his snowshoes and his axe-handle walking stick was located near by. The large bruises on his shoulder and head indicated that he had apparently lost his balance and fell down the side of the canyon.

Searchers had passed over the same trail the previous year but a snow slide had covered the body and it wasn't exposed until the snow had melted during the summer. On his person was found a silver watch, a six-shooter and $14.30 in cash. No inquest was held and the remains were buried nearby.

October 25, 1908
Harry Heath, a well-known miner of Unionville, had been missing for 10 days when a search party was organized and sent to the Dearborn area to search for him.

The authorities had been notified by a man who had arrived at Heath's cabin on October 24, and found a note stating that the miner had treed a bear cub and he was going back to get the bruin. The note, dated October 13, went on to say he would be back in two days.

No trace of Heath was ever found and it was speculated that he was either killed by the mother bear or he perished in a raging snowstorm that was being experienced at the time.

October 26, 1909
(Republican Courier)
Central Park resident, E. Lund was never found after being reported missing while he was on a hunting trip in the Crazy Mountains during the first week of October of 1909.

Mr. Lund worked for a Mr. Charles White who was in the well drilling business and his four-man crew had gone to the Shields River country for a job. Lund decided to do some hunting while the crew was waiting for the supplies and equipment to be delivered.

The man was never seen again and the speculation ranged from death by accidental gunshot, falling from one of the many steep cliffs in the area to being attacked and eaten by bears.

It wasn't thought that Mr. Lund had skipped out because he was reportedly happily married with 2 children and he had at least $400 in wages coming to him from his employer.

November 14, 1910
(Fort Benton River Press)
The bodies of Walter Schultz, 14, and his 11-year-old brother, Amos Schultz were found on Sunday November 13 in the hills about 14 miles north of Fort Benton after being missing on a hunting trip on November 8.

While their father was in Fort Benton on business one of the boys had shot a prairie chicken in the morning near their dry-land farm and the two lads begged their mother to let them leave the ranch for more birds. Reluctantly the mother consented and as the two young boys were walking off a light snow began to fall.

Chapter Three: LOST OR MISSING

By that afternoon a blizzard had taken over the countryside and the youngsters apparently became disoriented and got lost in the storm. Walt and Amos probably became bewildered and exhausted that night when they were overcome with sleep from which they never awakened.

The Schultz family had just settled on their new farm near the Benton Sheep Company Ranch from Colfax, Washington and the two young hunters weren't adequately familiar with the area.

When the two youngsters failed to return home a search party was organized of the few settlers in the vicinity. Their grief-stricken father found the boys in each other's arms, and while their bodies were badly decomposed, the animals hadn't disturbed them.

October 10, 1912

The body of twenty-two-year-old Thomas "Dick" Stark was found in the deep snow after being missing overnight while hunting in the Big Belt Mountains about 15 miles southeast of Cascade. Apparently Stark had become exhausted and he died of exposure while he was searching for his lost brother.

Stark had been hunting with his brother, Blaine Stark and John Flannigan for several days when Flannigan returned to his ranch, which was about 7 miles from their hunting cabin. The two brothers left for another hunt and in an attempt to scare up some deer they split up with the intentions of meeting back at the hunting cabin that evening.

A terrible snowstorm hit the area and at about 5:30 a.m. the next morning Blaine Stark stumbled into the Flannigan Ranch house after losing his way to the hunting cabin in the blizzard. While tramping through the 2 feet of snow to safety Blaine Stark had froze both of his hands and feet.

John Flannigan immediately traveled to the hunting cabin where he found Dick Stark's frozen body several hundred feet from the shelter.

Chapter Three: LOST OR MISSING

Evidence indicated that Dick had found his way through the storm to the hunting cabin, started a fire and had waited for his brother. Eventually Dick left his rifle behind at the shelter and went searching for his lost brother.

While frantically looking for his brother Dick Stark probably over exerted himself and he was soon overtaken by exhaustion and he died of exposure.

November 23, 1912
The body of <u>Joe Waigel</u> was found after being missing for 2 weeks while on a hunt trip in the Wolf Creek country in the western part of Flathead County. The 26-man search party was made up of forest rangers, veteran hunters and woodsmen who were thoroughly familiar with that part of the state.

The evidence at the scene indicated that Waigel had gotten disoriented while stocking or chasing a wounded deer. Apparently the man realized he was lost after he finally killed the deer, which was found near the scene, and he tried but was unable to start a life saving fire. Waigel's brother-in-law, Dr. A. Houston had offered a $1,000 reward for the locating of Waigel dead or alive.

December 2, 1914
(Weekly Courier)
<u>Wallace Brown</u>, who had owned a hunting lodge on the state line near Yellowstone Park, about 80 miles from Monida along the Madison River was reported missing and presumed dead after not being seen for 3 weeks in the country between his lodge and the Henry's Lake Station.

On November 11, 1914 Mr. Brown said that he was going to Henry's Station and two days later his horse returned without a rider, and with Brown's rifle in its case. Mr. Brown was one of the best-known men in Southwestern Montana and his many friends started out immediately on the trail and they reportedly covered every foot of the area without finding a trace of the man.

About a month earlier Brown had complained of illness and he was reportedly out of his head for a time. Because he had been recently bed ridden Mr. Brown's friends feared that he may have had a relapse and that he may have been wandering through the woods delirious.

Mr. Brown was about 60 years old at the time and he had lived and worked in the area for many years. As a contractor he had built several railroad stations on the Oregon Short Line including the station where his hunting lodge was located. The man was about 5 feet 7 inches, of medium build and he weighed about 150 pounds. He was said to have worn no beard but he had a mustache.

October 21, 1915

The remains of trapper, <u>David A. Long</u> were found near the head of Bunker Creek, about 8 miles from the Spotted Bear Ranger Station after being lost since the fall of 1908.

Ora Reeves, Win Ainsworth and Valentine Neitzling discovered an old camp where they found a .38-55-caliber Marlin rifle, 3 watches, about 100 traps, a pair of gold bowed eyeglasses and various other camping equipment while they were hunting in the South Fork. About 100 feet from the main camp the men later found a skull and a few scattered bones.

The hunters brought the skull and all of the personal belongings back to Columbia Falls where they notified Flathead County authorities to establish the identification of the remains.

One of the watches was identified by jeweler, Frank Calbick as one that he had sold to Mr. Young in the fall of 1908. The skull still had 4 teeth remaining on the left jaw with silver fillings, which also helped in the identification of Mr. Young.

David Long was well known in Kalispell and he and his family had lived in the area for quite some time. He had left in the fall of 1908 to trap in the South Fork of the Flathead and he was never heard from again.

A search was made for him the following year and many folks at the believed that he had met with foul play. When David Long failed to return to his home in Kalispell his family left the area, some going to Iowa and Florida.

November 23, 1917

Frank Carlson was reported missing while he was hunting in the Highwood Mountains east of Belt and after 3 weeks it was presumed that he was dead

Frank lived at his father's ranch north of Belt and he went hunting in the hills with Elmer Warells, John Matlehn and Carlson's younger brother. After hunting for several miles the men separated and the younger boy went home.

There was a severe snowstorm in the area that evening and by morning it was feared that the man had gotten lost and had perished. While his family and friends continued to look for the remains of their family member many people believed that he might have skipped the country.

Carlson had reportedly been worried about the war in Europe and because he was of draft age, some people believed that he was afraid of being called up for service.

In July of 1918 the body of Frank Carlson was found in the Little Belt Mountains about 2 miles from the ranch of Alex Stone. Speculation continued that the young man had killed himself rather than join the service when his Marlin rifle, which had been fired, was located next to his body.

November 23, 1920

The body of Carl Osmand of Lemhi County, Idaho was found several days after being reported missing while he was big game hunting in the mountains on the Donovan Ranch near Dillon.

Mr. Osmand apparently became crazed after losing his way and wading through waist-deep snow for several miles before tossing his rifle and wandering senselessly until he died. At one point Osmand was within sight of the Donovan Ranch, but he turned around and retraced his trail before he became exhausted.

October 31, 1925
The frozen body of <u>Frank A. Matt</u> of Evaro was found near Frenchtown after being missing for two days while hunting.

Matt had been hunting with a friend when they became separated and he failed to return to his home at Evaro. A search party was organized the following day and 24 hours later his body was found.

November 19, 1926
Thirty-two-year-old Clinton area rancher, <u>John Ben Hougland</u> became lost from his hunting party in the mountains near his hometown. At the time of his disappearance his companions reported that Mr. Hougland was only wearing thin clothes and that he was poorly equipped to survive a winter night in the mountains.

At the time of his disappearance Hougland was on foot while his hunting companions, James House and Guy Ask were on horseback. The local authorities conducted a massive search of the area with bloodhounds and U.S. Army troops from Fort Missoula.

The citizens of Clinton raised and offered a $100 reward in order to stimulate the search for Mr. Hougland because his insurance carrier required definite proof that he had perished in the hills. Hougland was a veteran of the World War and he carried government insurance, which his aunt, with whom he had been living with was the beneficiary.

Ten years later in October of 1936 Blackfoot Valley rancher, Roy Willis found the remains of John Hougland about 6 miles from

Chapter Three: LOST OR MISSING

the west fork of Nelson Creek in the rugged Hellgate country near Missoula. Positive identification was made from a belt buckle, a .308-Savage rifle, a jackknife and a pocket watch, which were found near the few scattered bleached bones.

The articles were identified by Mr. Hougland's hunting companions on that tragic hunting trip, James House and Guy Ask, both of Clinton. John Hougland was last seen going over a ridge and he apparently lost his way in a blizzard and had died of exhaustion and exposure.

An interesting quirk in this incident was when Roy Willis found the Elgin pocket watch among the remains of the victim he had wound the piece out of habit and it began ticking. After 10 years the timepiece started right up after the lost hunter had fallen exhausted in the cold mountain air.

November 27, 1932
Forty-year-old Jack Carlisle was reported lost after being separated from his hunting companions, Everett Vaile, George Moken and Tom Fontaine while they were hunting near Cutbank.

His body was found a year later near Summit, west of Shelby by three Havre railroad workers while they were deer hunting in the area.

December 16, 1932
(Bozeman Daily Courier)
The frozen body of 52-year-old John Hinz was found about a mile and a quarter from his cabin near Gregson Spring after he had been reported missing on December 5.

A neighbor who had been hunting with Mr. Hinz was the last person to see him alive in the hills southeast of Anaconda, and Steve F. Karlock, an iceman from Anaconda and a friend of the victim found his body 10 days later.

Theories advanced at the time were that the lost prospector had become disoriented in a storm and he became exhausted in the deep snow and sub zero weather before he could reach his cabin.

Mr. Karloch found Hinz's rifle leaning against a tree, his pistol and belt on a stump, probably placed there by the lost hunter to lighten his load. Evidence indicated that Mr. Hinz had stumbled for several yards before he finally fell to his hands and knees and then fell dead in the snow.

Even in death the rugged hills and bitter cold didn't give up John Hinz's body easily. It took a full day and eleven men along with a horse to carry his body the 8 miles to the Clayton Ranch.

November 8, 1933
The body of 57-year-old George Armitage of Ennis was found in the mountains near Ennis after being reported missing while on an elk-hunting trip. The hunter apparently had gotten lost and he died from over exertion in the deep snow.

November 10, 1935
(Missoulian)
The frozen body of 69-year-old prospector, George Westfall was found about a mile from his cabin in the mountainous Lake Delmo region east of Butte. Mr. Westfall had been missing for a week after sub-zero weather had blanketed the area.

Mr. Westfall's gun was resting against a rock, and near his body was a pile of twigs, which he had apparently intended to light before he was overcome by exhaustion and died of exposure.

November 12, 1936
Albert Westberg, 28, of Straw, Montana was reported missing in the Castle Mountains near White Sulphur Springs while on a hunt. When the railroad worker failed to return from his planned one-day

Chapter Three: LOST OR MISSING

hunt his family and friends had first thought he might have stayed over with Joe Martino, the only remaining inhabitant of the old mining camp of Castle.

Albert's family became concerned when they didn't find him at Martino's place and the temperatures had dropped to 20 below and heavy snows had covered the area. Even though Albert was able to care for himself in the mountains he hadn't taken any supplies with him to spend a night out.

The brothers of Albert were afraid that he may have been injured in a fall in the rough mountain country and they continued the search for their brother for a week after his disappearance.

The body of Albert Westberg was eventually found about 15 miles from Ringling and the officials ruled that he had perished from hunger and exposure.

October 22, 1937
Twenty-one-year-old Alfonse Chourand of Glasgow was presumed dead after being missing for a week while he was hunting in the Missoula area.

October 19, 1938
(Missoulian)
Clarence Dorey, 25, of Florence was the subject of a widespread search after his disappearance in the mountainous Rock Creek area and he was given up for dead 11 days later. Mr. Dorey had become separated from his companion, Alfred Buss while they were hunting elk in the Eight Mile Creek area.

The two men had left Florence on Sunday morning to hunt in the woods near their hometown and Mr. Buss later said that they had decided to hunt separately and then meet at their car at 3 o'clock that afternoon. Buss returned to the vehicle early and he waited until after dark, and then he left the car for Dorey and he walked home.

When Dorey failed to return on Monday morning, Buss enlisted Walter Martin and Albert Adley of Florence to look for their lost friend. The men followed Dorey's tracks through about 18 inches of snow for about 15 miles before they lost his trail.

After camping over night near a ridge where they had lost Dorey's trail the three men made their way to the Finlen Ranch near Gilbert Creek in the Rock Creek area and notified the authorities nearly 48 hours after Dorey had disappeared.

Missoula County officers searched the Rock and Gilbert Creek area while Ravalli County and other volunteers helped Buss and his companions continue to search the Florence side of the mountain range but nothing was found.

Alfred Buss noted that Dorey's tracks were straight indicating that he had not lost his sense of direction. He told the authorities that Dorey was an experienced woodsman but he was thinly clad that day. Buss and his friends found another set of tracks and the remains of a small fire but it was later learned that another rescue party in the area had made them.

At first the authorities believed that Mr. Dorey had been injured and had been "hold up" waiting for his rescue, but he was later presumed dead and the search was concluded on October 26, 1938

On December 15, 1938 Clarence Dorey's wife gave birth to their only child, a baby boy. The people of Florence and other friends of Dorey in the Bitterroot offered a $100 reward for anyone finding the lost hunter's body.

October 21, 1938
(Missoulian)
Twenty-year-old Belt farmer, <u>William Hauskamaa</u>, was given up for dead after being missing for a week in the Yogo Creek area in the Little Belt Mountains near Stanford.

Chapter Three: LOST OR MISSING

Mr. Hauskamaa had been hunting with Otto and John Koskella of Belt and although he failed to return to their hunting camp his companions weren't very concerned because he was heavily attired and well equipped. After searching for their friend for 3 days the two men finally reported Hauskamaa missing.

Morrison Flying Service pilot, Glenn Grazier of Great Falls made an air search of about 30 square miles but Hauskamaa's tracks became lost at the top of the divide between Yogo Creek and at the head of Sage Creek.

The authorities reported that Hauskamaa was not in the best of health and they feared that he had perished in the snow-covered mountains.

November 14, 1938
(Missoulian)
George Mcleslie, 34, of Chinook was found frozen to death on a small island in a reservoir 16 miles southwest of Havre by a Blaine County sheriff's posse.

McLeslie's hunting companion, William Forsyth, also of Chinook was found nearby in serious condition suffering from shock, two frozen feet and exposure.

November 15, 1938
Dick Powell, 20, of Bozeman was reported missing while hunting in the rugged Squaw Creek region in the Gallatin Canyon south of Bozeman. He was last seen leaving the camp of some woodcutters on Squaw Creek and the men didn't report him missing for two days as they thought he had gone back to Bozeman.

A search plane along with about 200 Conservation Corps assisted the sheriff deputies in the search when Forest Ranger, Verne Edwards found the frozen body of Powell on November 16.

Dick Powell had stumbled and rolled 125 feet down a slope into the under brush where he apparently died of exhaustion and exposure. There were reportedly bruises on the man's body and one of his trouser legs was almost torn completely off.

November 9, 1940
(Missoulian)
Sixty-year-old Gus Stean of the Superior area had been missing while hunting near the Horning Mine on the upper Trout Creek since October 5 and the authorities of Mineral County announced a month later that the search would not be continued.

The disappearance of Mr. Stean was quite bizarre with many twists and turns. The Superior blacksmith and prospector had been known to frequently go into the backcountry for 2 or 3 weeks at a time, and therefore his friends weren't too concerned when he didn't return from his hunting trip.

An official search for Stean began after a week and it went on until it was reported that he had walked into a mining camp about 2 weeks after he had disappeared. The Mineral County authorities immediately called off the search and they naturally went on to other business.

Then about 2 weeks after the original search had been called off it was determined that it was not Gus Stean who had walked into the mining camp and that the man was still in fact missing. By that time it was implied that Gus Stean was presumed dead.

November 29, 1941
Seventy-year-old woodsman, James "Butch" McBride of Lupfer was reported missing and assumed dead after apparently becoming lost while hunting in the mountains of northwestern Montana.

The well-known old-timer had been staying alone at the cabin of Herbert Roskey and Olaf Gustafson while they were away on business.

When Mr. Gustafson returned from Idaho on November 17 he found McBride and a hunting rifle missing from the cabin and he assumed that the elderly man had gone hunting. After Mr. Roskey returned the two men made a search for the lost Mr. McBride and they located his tracks but they were soon obliterated by the fresh snowfall.

October 30, 1942
Klein area miner, Frank Pogacher was never found after becoming lost while hunting in the Little Snowy Mountains about 35 miles northwest of Roundup.

He became separated from his hunting companion, Clyde Scritchfield on Sunday, October 25 and he didn't return to their car.

The authorities made several searches for the lost hunter with large parties of men including area boy scouts and the Tri-County Sportsman's Association at Roundup had offered a $100 reward for the recovery of the man.

November 10, 1942
First World War veteran, Paul Praast of Missoula was given up for dead after being missing for 9 days while hunting in the wild upper Blackfoot River country north of Ovando.

Mr. Praast was considered an experienced woodsman but he was partially crippled from a war wound and the authorities believed that he might have become exhausted in battling the deep snow that had fallen in the area.

The skeletal remains of Paul Praast were eventually found by sheepherder, Pete Gudornson on September 3, 1943 in the Second Creek Basin about 3 miles northwest of the Arastra Creek Lookout Station.

Two days later Sheriff Valiton of Powell County led the 5-man search and recovery team that found only a few rags of clothing, which had been torn and scattered by the wild animals.

The sheriff reported that the remains indicated that the hunter must have gotten lost and apparently perished in a blizzard. The sheriff and his party walked in about 6 miles to the solemn scene and they used 2 horses to pack the remains out of the mountains.

November 21, 1944
Bryon C. Wilson, 54, of Essex was found dead from exposure after being lost while on an elk hunt. Wilson became separated from his hunting companion and he was located the next day in knee-deep snow, slumped against a tree.

November 10, 1945
Helena guide and packer, James Callaway, about 47, was presumed dead after being missing for 9 days in the rugged and dangerous country at the head of Falls Creek about 25 miles northwest of Lincoln.

Mr. Callaway was last seen on November 3 by his two hunting companions leaving his hunting camp with a 3-horse pack train of supplies and he was heading for another camp about 4 miles away.

Since Callaway had been very familiar with the area the authorities didn't believe the man was lost but may have met with an accident. The searchers located the 2 packhorses at the head of Tom's Gulch, but they feared that they would never find Callaway alive when his saddle horse showed up at the hunting camp a week later.

October 20, 1946
The body of Ed Bloodgood, a Park County trapper and hunter was found by searchers in the Crazy Mountain area about 35 miles northeast of Livingston. He became the object of a search in the rugged area when he hadn't been seen for about a week.

November 9, 1947
George Lofftus, 38, of Sleeping Child Springs failed to return from a day hunt and his wife reported that he hadn't taken any food with

him. After being missing for 2 days about 100 men were searching for Mr. Lofftus in the Bitterroot Mountains some 15 miles southeast of Hamilton.

Although more men were added to the search for the father of 4 children in the Sapphire Mountains heavy snows caused many postponements. After a week Mr. Andrew J. Lofftus offered a $500 reward for the recovery of the body of his son. The reward came with a stipulation that the body not be disturbed until the sheriff could investigate. Since Lofftus was so familiar with the area it was suspected that another hunter had shot him.

The search for George Lofftus was officially suspended in mid-November of 1947 after about 2 feet of new snow had covered the region. The following year the distraught father again renewed the $500 reward but nothing was found. Then almost two years after his son's disappearance the 67-year-old Andrew J. Lofftus died, some of his friends saying of a broken heart.

In September of 1952 Ted Vann of Darby found a rusty rifle near Sleeping Child Divide about 5 miles from Darby, which was later identified as George Lofftus' weapon. Ravalli County Sheriff F.O. Burrell led a search party in the area where they found parts of a skeleton and bits and pieces of the missing man's clothing.

The authorities in 1952 reported that the evidence at the site indicated that Lofftus might have accidentally shot himself after tripping over a large log. The remains were near such a log and there was a piece of clothing caught in the hammer of the rifle.

When the rifle, coat, a shoe and some bones including the skull of George Lofftus was found his family could finally have a funeral for their father in 1952. They reportedly buried a leg bone, pieces of 3 ribs, and the skull in a baby's casket in the Darby Cemetery.

Then nearly 54 years after the disappearance of George Lofftus, mushroom pickers in the Rye Creek area found a charred human jawbone in mid June of 2001.

The bone was located in the same general area on Forest Service land about 200 yards from the North Fork Rye Creek Road where other bones of the lost hunter were found 49 years earlier.

Lofftus' daughter, Shelley Oertli of Hamilton was a sophomore at Hamilton High School when her father disappeared in 1947 and she believes that he was accidentally shot and killed by other hunters in the area.

Oertli reported that as her mother was driving her 4 children to Hamilton that morning they were stopped by a party of drinking hunters for directions and then they proceeded to the same area that her father had gone hunting.

The next day as the Lofftus family and friends were searching for her father they met the same hunters that had stopped Mrs. Lofftus for directions the day earlier.

Shelley Oertli recalled that the men obviously didn't want to stop but finally did, but they wouldn't answer any questions about whether or not they had seen her father. Lofftus' daughter didn't know the hunters and because they left so quickly she couldn't catch their license plate number.

November 3, 1950
Mrs. Mary Winkley, 40, of Dillon was given up for dead after being missing for over 2 weeks while she was hunting deer in the heavily wooded area about 30 miles north of her home.

The 40-year-old woman was last seen leaving her husband's wood camp at the old Stinson Sawmill on her way into the Willow Creek of the Birch Creek district.

Chapter Three: LOST OR MISSING

While the large search for the lost woman was being carried out on foot, horseback and from the air, one of the would-be rescuers, 42-year-old Philip Krisk became lost himself and had to spent a night out before finding his way to the small town of Glen.

October 15, 1951
E.C. Humphrey, 85-year-old Lewistown rancher was reported missing while hunting on the neighboring N-Bar Ranch. After losing her husband, Mrs. Humphrey sold the property to the N-Bar, and she died in 1958.

Nine years later in 1960, some hunters found several bones and pieces of clothing of E.C. Humphtery on the N-Bar Ranch.

October 21, 1951
Twenty-one-year-old James Wishart of LaSalle was presumed dead after being missing while hunting in the Hungry Horse Dam area.

Mr. Wishart became separated from his hunting companions, Gary Thacker and Robert Teets Jr. on the rugged Doris Ridge. All hope of finding the lost hunter vanished after he had been missing for over a week and more than 2 feet of snow had covered the region.

October 8, 1953
Thirteen-year-old Donald Raymond Fain was last seen on October 3 leaving his ranch southwest of Norris carrying a rifle and going hunting.

After family members and neighbors were unable to locate the boy, the Madison County officials were notified.

The well-known searcher, George Talbot of Hamilton and his bloodhounds were also called to join in the search. Mr. Talbot and his dogs were used in many missing person cases in Montana.

Donald Fain was 5 foot 9 inches tall and he weighed 110 pounds; he had brown eyes and brown hair. When last seen he wore metal rimmed glasses and was wearing an overall jacket and overalls, a grayish blue cap and a dark blue shirt.

November 19, 1953
Ben Reimer, 45, of Kalispell was given up for dead after being missing for over a week while hunting in the Foys Lake area.

Reimer's jacket was found near the Foys Lake road and he was reportedly only wearing a black tee shirt, bib overalls and with no hat. Since the lost man's trail was 4 days old and recent rains had washed it, tracker George Talbot of Hamilton and his bloodhounds were unable to find Reimer's tracks.

Reimer was very familiar with the area and at first it was hoped that he had taken shelter in one of the many deserted cabins and other buildings in the area. The countryside was heavily searched and even about 40 Kalispell boy scouts and their leaders were involved in the search.

October 13, 1957
The body of Gerald Barney was found by his brother-in-law, Donald Metcalf in the snow swept Skalkaho Pass region about 40 miles west of Phillipsburg. Mr. Barney had been reported missing a week earlier while he was hunting in the Frog Pond area about 25 miles from Anaconda.

The 25-year-old Barney was from Phillipsburg and was said to have been very familiar with the area where he had perished.

The day after Barney was reported missing a 60-man search party found no trace of the man and the authorities later brought in government trapper and lion hunter, Frank Hakke of Hamilton with his dogs into the search. For a while two airplanes were also involved in the broad search for the Montana Power construction worker.

Mr. Barney was wearing cotton clothing with a hunting jacket, hat and gloves and he only had an apple to eat. Tracks indicated that he had walked about 25 miles after becoming lost and he didn't smoke and he wasn't carrying matches to start a fire.

It was determined that Barney had died of exposure about 30 hours after becoming separated from his hunting companions and he was found face down next to his rifle along a creek near Fish Lake.

Gerald Barney's body was brought out of the backcountry on horseback and his wife and 2 sons survived him.

October 23, 1958
The body of Clyde F. Williams, 74, of Belgrade was found several days after he was reported missing while hunting in the Broadus area.

Mr. Williams was hunting with his 58-year-old brother, Charles of Broadus when they were over taken by a savage snowstorm. Charles was able to make his way to safety but his brother didn't.

October 23, 1958
As Buster Dives-Backwards of Lame Deer was driving on a county road just beyond the "Crossroads" or "Four Corners" area about 12 miles south of Lame Deer he noticed some magpies circling the pile of snow along the road.

Buster then noticed a pair of shoes protruding out of the 3 feet of snow. Buster had found the frozen body of 28-year-old Robert Pittman about 20 feet from the junction of two roads and only about 2 miles from Vic Small's occupied line camp.

Pittman was reported missing while hunting in the mountainous area south of Lame Deer by his hunting partner, Lester C. Scott when they became separated in the primitive area when their truck skidded off the road during a heavy snowstorm.

Chapter Three: LOST OR MISSING

The late October snowstorm had blocked roads, knocked out power and telephone lines and stranded many people. While Scott went for help Pittman apparently also left the stalled vehicle to find shelter.

By the time Scott made it to Lame Deer he was snow blind and suffering from frostbite. When Pittman wasn't found near the men's vehicle an aerial search was initiated but it failed to find any sign of the missing man.

The following day 50 men along with bulldozers were looking for Pittman. Searchers from the air reported that some of the draws were filled with as much as 100 feet of snow and a few of the Powder River Country old timers said that the storm was the most vicious to hit the area in memory.

The 42-year-old Scott returned to the area to look for his friend and the searchers had renewed hopes of finding the lost hunter after they discovered traces of scraps of burned paper.

Airplanes, bulldozers and about 70 men on snowshoes continued to crisscross the snowbound terrain, but after an intensive 5-day search the officials called off the search. Two days later Dives-Backwards located Pittman's body.

Magpies also led searchers to the bodies of two more hunters lost in that terrible snowstorm of 1958 in the Powder River Country.

October 24, 1958
Searchers spotted the birds swarming around the boots of nineteen-year-old Clyde Escher, which were sticking out of the snow on the M.M. Crocker Ranch, a few miles north of the Wyoming border.

Chapter Three: LOST OR MISSING

The body of nineteen-year-old <u>Tony Stepanek</u> was then found in a snow filled draw about a mile from where Escher was found.

The two young men from Hopkins, Minnesota had been reported missing in the mountainous Northern Cheyenne Indian Reservation just north of the Wyoming line at the 7,000-foot level. They were hunting in the Powder River country when they were separated from their hunting party by the heavy snowstorm that struck the region.

Rescue parties conducted a search of all the area cabins and reported that they had found a hanging deer in one of them. The rope that was used to hang the animal up was identified as belonging to one of the missing lads, proving that they had been there but they apparently left the shelter to find their way out.

Four days after the boys' disappearance their parents and the original hunting party from Minnesota came to Montana to help search for the boys. It was reported that another 200 searchers from Minnesota were planning to come out to help but Montana Governor J. Hugo Aronson advised them to stay home.

Just as the family members from Minnesota were heading out to begin their search, word was received that the bodies of the two boys had been found about 80 miles south of Miles City.

It was reported that after getting cut off in a coulee by a huge snow drift, Clyde Escher apparently became panicky about dying from the cold and he shot himself in the head with his big-game rifle.

It was determined that Tony Stepanek had died of exposure and his body was spotted by a helicopter pilot flying over a snowy pasture about 50 miles southwest of Broadus. Both of the boys were lightly dressed and they only had light caps, trousers and they didn't have overshoes or gloves at the time.

The boys' family had often hunted for big game in Montana and Tony Stepanek's father had bought his son a brand new rifle to mark his first hunting trip in the "Big Sky Country." Another example of out-of-state hunters **"Dying to Hunt in Montana."**

October 27, 1959
The body of <u>Fred E. Kent</u>, 32, of Great Falls was found near Prospect Ridge in the Judith Basin area after being lost while was hunting in the Belt Mountains.

The grave markers of Fred Kent and Robert Smith at Great Falls, Montana used on the cover of "Dying to Hunt in Montana."

The authorities believed that Kent had shot and killed an elk because there was fresh blood on his clothing, and then got lost and died of exposure during a heavy snowstorm. His body was found about 20 miles southwest of the Yogo Lookout and about 10 miles off the highway.

Mr. Kent was born at Hinsdale, Montana and he attended schools there and at Neihart. He came to Great Falls after his service in the

Army where he found work as a sheet metal worker. Fred Kent left a wife, two daughters and a 6-month-old son.

Fred Kent's tombstone was chosen for the cover of this book along with the marker of Robert W. Smith who was killed by his companion just 8 days before Kent's death because of a sad coincidences.

Since their deaths occurred so close, and because they were both veterans of the Second World War, they were buried side by side in the same cemetery at Great Falls. Although these two men probably didn't know each other in life they were brought together in death by their love of hunting.

November 7, 1959
Clarence Trader, 29, of Glendive was presumed dead after being missing for over a week while hunting in the Hardin-Custer area,

November 17, 1959
The day after he was reported missing while hunting alone some 15 miles south of Bozeman, the frozen body of MSU student and former U.S. Navy pilot, Adrian Dick Joki was found about 4 miles from his vehicle by a logger.

It was reported that the Red Lodge native had left his dormitory to go hunting, but he didn't tell anyone where he was going or what he was hunting for. The rescue team wasn't able to concentrate their efforts and by the time they located Mr. Joki's vehicle the search had to be scheduled the next day.

November 28, 1959
Fifty-nine-year-old Kalispell motel owner, Arthur D. Jordan, was given up for dead after being missing for about 2 weeks in the Seeley Lake area northeast of Missoula.

Searchers located Jordan's hunting camp where they found his rifle and jacket in the cab of his truck along with a half an elk hanging from a nearby tree. The authorities reported that a large grizzly had been in the area and that Mr. Jordan might have attacked by the animal or he might have suffered a heart attack in the hills.

In September of 1961 the Flathead County sheriff appealed to hunters in the upper Swan River country to be on the lookout for the remains of Arthur Jordan and he stated that there was a $1,000 reward offered for information to the recovery of the man's body.

October 15, 1960
The skeletal remains of <u>Harvey E. Hewitt</u> were discovered in a coulee about 7 miles northwest of Wolf Point.

Hewitt was reported missing while on a hunting trip in October of 1954 and positive identification was determined when a billfold was found intact containing his identification papers and $100 in cash.

November 16, 1960
Sixty-five-year-old Missoula rancher, <u>Fritz Fry</u>, was reported missing while he was elk hunting with his son, Clifford between Lolo Hot Springs and Lothrop.

Fry was an experienced packer and he was familiar with the country that they had been hunting in. The search effort was hampered by waist-deep snow and it was eventually abandoned and Mr. Fry was presumed dead by the end of November.

In September of 1961 Joe Field of Missoula found a boot top near the remains of a dead elk while he was hunting in the mountains. The boot was identified by Clifford Fry as the type that his father had been wearing at the time of his disappearance the year before. The authorities believed that Fry had killed an elk and he may have been shot by another hunter or may have suffered a heart attack.

144

Chapter Three: LOST OR MISSING

Sheriff William J. Walker of Missoula County conducted another full-scale search in the remote area in September of 1962 but again no sign of Fritz Fry was ever found.

October 29, 1962

The body of 74-year-old <u>Fred Hamilton</u> of Cascade was located a day after he had been reported missing while he was hunting in the Swan Mountains about 10 miles west of Highway 200.

Only faint footsteps were found of Hamilton at the end of the day when he became separated from his 3-man hunting party while they were hunting in the Soup Creek area.

Even though Hamilton was reportedly dressed warmly, he apparently wasn't able to withstand the temperatures of the night and he died of exposure.

November 13, 1962

Fifteen-year-old <u>David Klien</u> of Swan Lake was reported missing while hunting east of Swan Lake in the Lost Creek area.

The next day his body was found about 3 miles up Jim Bond Canyon. The boy was reportedly not dressed properly for the heavy snow and that he had died of exhaustion and exposure.

November 2, 1963

<u>Victor Vermillion</u>, 25, of Bozeman was reported missing in the Bridger Canyon area about 20 miles northeast of Bozeman. He had been hunting with his brother-in-law, Jim Freese and another friend, Butch Olsen when they separated.

When Vermillion failed to return to their car, the other two hunters went back to search for their friend. When they couldn't locate Vermillion they went to town and reported the incident.

Two days later Vermillion's body was located from the air in the Middle Fork Ridge area of Bracket Creek. A partially cleaned out buck deer was found by the body along with his rifle.

November 24, 1965
<u>Larry Kruger</u>, 18, of Missoula was reported missing by his sixteen-year-old friend, Tommy Mattfeldt, who had made his way out of the backcountry after being lost for two days while on a hunting trip.

Tom Mattfeldt was suffering from exhaustion and was delirious but he was still able to describe the area to search for his lost friend. It appears that the two boys were together when they got lost, but for some reason Kruger didn't go with Mattfeldt. The survivor reported that Kruger had leaned his rifle against a tree and he sat down to wait for his friend to return with help.

Members of a 100-man search party located the snow-covered body of Larry Kruger in the West Fork of Twin Creek along the Montana-Idaho border about 5 miles from Bob Rutherford's ranch. The men found Kruger's rifle leaning up against a tree next to his body just like Mattfeldt had described.

It was later reported that health problems had prevented Larry Kruger from being able to keep up with his friend and to make his way out.

November 17, 1968
The body of <u>Tassie H. Farmer</u>, 41, of Tallahassee, Florida was found along a logging road after being lost overnight in the Woodward Creek area of the Swan River drainage.

Mr. Farmer was found without his rifle about 8 miles from where he had been hunting. Apparently after becoming lost the hunter panicked; dropped his rifle and he died of exposure after exhausting himself.

November 5, 1969
Clay Morris, 73, of Dillon was reported missing on opening day of the general big game hunting season on October 19, 1969. His body was found about 5 miles northwest of Dillon on November 12, 1969.

November 22, 1970
Annie Marie Hammond, 19, of St Ignatius was found frozen to death in the rugged Ferry Basin area about 15 miles northwest of Thompson Falls by a search team on snowmobiles. She had been hunting in the area with her stepfather, Ross DuPuis when the two got caught in a heavy snowstorm.

About seven days later the frozen body of 63-year-old Ross DuPuis was found a considerable distance from his truck in a small clearing on the Moss Ranch about 11 miles north of Dixon.

Since the first search party had found the rifles near the girl's body, the authorities speculated that the young woman stopped to rest while her father attempted to find their truck during the storm, which had dumped as much as 8 feet of snow.

October 26, 1972
Fred Hellman, 64, of Kalispell was presumed dead after he apparently became lost while he was on an elk hunt in the rugged mountains near the southern tip of the Hungry Horse Reservoir. The heavy snows in the area hampered the reported 75 searchers and the official search was called off on October 30.

November 1, 1973
Herman Skagen, 59, of Lewistown was reported missing after he and a hunting companion had split up and he didn't join up at the bottom of a ridge. When he failed to show up a search was started in the foothills of the Snowy Mountains about 25 miles from Lewistown.

The search was hampered by heavy snow but the body of Herman Skagen was located 27 days later.

November 8, 1973

The body <u>Thomas N. Chamberlain</u>, 48, of Spokane, Washington was found in about 2 feet of snow just west of Ovando.

Officials reported that Mr. Chamberlain apparently had died of exposure and fatigue after walking all night. He became lost while he was searching for another member of his hunting party who ironically had only strayed from the others for just a few minutes.

November 8, 1973

<u>Kenneth L. Fultz</u>, 54, of Woodlake, California was found dead by a search party in the fresh snow after being missing while hunting in the Bitterroot Mountains about 75 miles southwest of Hamilton.

November 8, 1974

The body of 37-year-old <u>Donald Ray Kimberlin</u>, was found by his hunting partner, Joe Daniels in the rugged Coeur d' Alene Mountains about 25 miles northwest of St. Regis.

The two Libby hunters were trying to locate two elk that they had killed when Kimberlin apparently lost his bearings and got lost. He died that night of exposure and exhaustion and his body was found the next morning near the junction of the Mount Bushnell and Cameron Peak trails on the 5,100-foot divide between Sanders and Mineral Counties.

The authorities said that 2 to 3 inches of new snow had fallen in the area and that the nighttime temperatures were below freezing.

November 25, 1974

<u>Louis Callender</u>, 62, of Anaconda was reported missing while he was hunting in the Sheephead and Watchtower Creek country southwest

of Darby. A search party located Callender's vehicle but there was no sign of the hunter.

Two days later the man's body was found by two Anaconda searchers in the Sheephead drainage of the West Fork of the Bitterroot River about 7 miles from his vehicle.

About 30 volunteers from the forest service and friends and relatives of Mr. Callender aided the Ravalli County Search and Rescue team that brought the body out of the rugged backcountry on horseback.

October 28, 1975
Donald Harper, a 50-year-old Los Angeles police officer was reported lost while he was hunting in the remote Big Creek region southwest of Livingston.

The search was started after Harper had failed to show up at a predetermined meeting spot on the trail in the Gallatin National Forest. It was reported that Mr. Harper had hunted the same area for the past 2 years with his friend, Lawrence Chapel of Livingston. The search for the lost man was called off just 3 days later when about 4 feet of snow fell in the region.

No sign of Harper was found in the spring of 1976 and it wasn't until 1981, six years later that the bones of Donald Harper were finally recovered. The authorities said that they didn't think the man had gotten lost but that he had probably died of exposure in the heavy snowfall.

November 26, 1975
Timothy Schock, a 22-year-old postal worker from Billings was reported missing in the Little Belt Mountains on the last day of the 1975-hunting season.

Chapter Three: LOST OR MISSING

A 30-man search party, half of them from Billings, was searching an area based on a report from a Great Falls hunter, Reed Larson who had actually spoken to Tim Schock several miles from the Jamison Trail on the day he became lost. Larson told the authorities that Schock had told him that he was lost and he wanted directions back to his camp on Dry Creek.

Larson gave the young man directions back to Dry Creek, but he also explained that it was getting quite late and that it would be dark soon. When Larson suggested that they go back to his vehicle and that he would drive him to his camp, Schock said that he wanted to make it back to his camp on his own. Mr. Larson was the last person to see Timothy Schock alive as he was walking up a hill on a logging trail.

Hampered by heavy snow, the search party began checking the cabins in the area between where Larson last spoke with Schock and his hunting camp in hopes that he had taken shelter in one of them.

After a week the coordinated search was called off because of the heavy snows and falling temperatures. The authorities didn't believe Schock could have survived even though he had been an outdoor counselor and he had taken several solo survival treks because he was dressed for a day hunt and not for spending the night.

The following summer the scattered remains of Timothy Schock were found in the upper tributary of the Smith River by the voluntary Mountain Patrol Search and Rescue Organization led by Dr. George Eusterman of Great Falls. Reed Larson, the last man to see Schock alive, also accompanied the recovery team.

November 27, 1976
The body of 27-year-old Richard Jacobson of Whitefish was found in the Shorty Creek drainage about 35 miles northwest of Whitefish after a 2-day search.

Chapter Three: LOST OR MISSING

Jacobson had been on a hunting trip in the Stryker region and he apparently died of exposure after becoming lost. About 55 searchers had joined in the search for the man who was reportedly skilled in skiing and in winter survival.

November 30, 1981
The bodies of <u>Wilbur H. Stedman,</u> 20, and his 19-year-old pregnant wife, <u>Vicki K. Stedman</u> were found about 33 miles north of Forsyth 4 days after they had set out on a hunting trip. The search wasn't initiated for three days because the couple hadn't informed anyone that they had gone hunting. They weren't reported missing until Wilbur Stedman failed to report to work at Colstrip.

Photo courtesy of Joyce Obland with "Graves-R-Us," of Colstrip, Montana 59323. (www.graves-r-us.com)

The Stedman's pickup truck was located about 10 miles from where the bodies were discovered, and they apparently left the vehicle after it had gotten stuck in a coulee and they later died of exposure.

Two area ranchers found the two bodies near the bank of Porcupine Creek while they were out hunting. The two men found a gate left open and they followed the tracks to the bodies. With temperatures of about 8 below, the young couple had tried to find shelter in some sagebrush and they were found huddled together.

Chapter Three: LOST OR MISSING

The authorities pointed out that the couple had died of exposure and if the search had been started sooner there might have been better results. Mr. and Mrs. Stedman had only lived in Forsyth for 3 months having come from Deer Lodge.

February 16, 1983
Tracy Cray, 25, of Billings was reported missing while he was on a special elk hunt with his father in the Absaroke-Beartooth Wilderness area north of Gardiner.

After about 5 days of searching for the missing hunter the authorities called a temporary halt to the search because of the bad weather. A week later the search was suspended after an air and ground search with dogs found no trace of the young man.

Another search for Cray's body was organized in June of 1983 between Eagle Creek and Little Trail Creek but it wasn't until seven years later, in the fall of 1990 when two elk hunters found the man's remains along with his driver's license, camera and hunting rifle in the remote back country.

November 1, 1984
Glenn Carr, 46, of San Marcos, California but formerly from Libby was reported missing in the Bob Marshall Wilderness while he was hunting.

Mr. Carr was last seen on October 25 leaving his hunting camp to retrieve a horse that he had left about thirty minutes away. The searchers found the man's horse alive in the No Name Creek drainage in the Spotted Bear Ranger District but Carr was never found.

While the lost hunter was reportedly warmly dressed the authorities theorized that the man may have suffered from hypothermia, which impaired his judgment and he began circling and became lost.

Chapter Three: LOST OR MISSING

After an eight-day intensive search including from the air with helicopters Glenn Carr was presumed dead and that his body was under a thick snow, which had been falling in the area every day.

November 17, 1987
Two Great Falls' hunters, John Doyle and James A. Steging, both 24-year-old Air Force personnel, were reported missing while they were hunting in the Lost Horse region southeast of Hamilton.

The authorities reported that about 8 inches of new snow had fallen in the area where the men's Chevy Blazer loaded with food and gear was located near a cabin in the Lost Horse Canyon. The authorities speculated that the men had spotted some elk, jumped out of their Blazer and had gotten lost while chasing after the animals deep into the backcountry.

After two weeks without any sign of the lost hunters, their wives still held out hope that their husbands would still be home for Thanksgiving. John Doyle had been an Eagle Scout and he had hunted for years with his father and he had taken other hunting trips in the Bitterroot Mountains with his wife. The officials reported that the two men had taken only their rifles with them when they headed up the Bailey Lake Trail Head.

Ravalli County Sheriff Printz said that hunters should always carry emergency gear with them because they often get tunnel vision when they spot elk, and end up getting lost chasing after them.

The sheriff explained that he had gotten lost himself in a blizzard while elk hunting in 1970 and that it was the worst feeling in the world to be lost over night. The sheriff went on to say that if it hadn't been for a fire he might have died.

Ron Garlick, president of Ravalli County Search and Rescue Association reportedly had seen Steging and Doyle just before they had become lost and he said that the two men were physically fit; they were well equipped and they had plenty of matches with them.

Mr. Garlick and his search and rescue organized conducted an organized search along with bloodhounds and about 150 volunteers from Malmstrom Air Force base at Great Falls for the bodies of the missing hunters in late June of 1988. The entire region was closed off to the public and nearly every square foot of the basin was covered but nothing was found.

John Doyle's mother and father each hired a psychic and neither were presented any background information of the incident and one of them, Aggi Spellman of Pennsylvania had insisted that the missing hunters would be found near a shelter. While the local searchers weren't confident of the psychic's information, they did check out all of the cabins, caves and mines in the region.

In July of 1988 the body of John Doyle was found in the Bitterroot Selway Wilderness by outfitter, Arthur Griffin about 20 miles from the Bailey Lake Trail Head. There was no sign of his hunting partner, James Steging. Doyle had walked some 20 miles from his vehicle and he probably died of exposure by the second night out.

Doyle's body was discovered under a rock outcropping along Cox Creek. Griffin found no sign of a fire at the location, but there were 11 spent cartridges from Doyle's rifle, which he apparently fired in an attempt to signal for help.

Arthur Griffin made another unpleasant discovery in October of 1988 when he found the remains of James Steging about a half a mile from where he had found Doyle's body in July of that same year. It appears that the two men had gotten lost near Bailey lake; walked all night and into the next day, and then separated, each dying alone of exhaustion and exposure.

October 4, 1990
Another victim of the Bitterroot-Selway Wilderness was 42-year-old Susan Adams of Austin, Texas when she was reported missing near the Montana-Idaho border.

Mrs. Adams had come to Montana with her husband on a hunting trip and they were camped near Battle Lake, which is about 20 air miles from Hamilton. Susan told the other members at the hunting camp that she was going on a bird watching hike to a meadow a couple of miles up the trail. She was last seen leaving the camp with her bird book and binoculars.

Search and rescue personnel located where the woman had left the trail about a mile and a half from the hunting camp, but her tracks became faint and later became covered by fresh snow. About 3 inches of snow fell on the first night of her disappearance and there was little hope that she would be found alive.

Mrs. Adams had little or no experience in the backcountry and she was only wearing jeans, T-shirt, a light flannel camouflage shirt and she had no food or matches.

To date, Susan Adams has never been found, and officials believe that the woman was injured and was unable to respond to the many searchers and had died of exposure.

In a terrible twist of fate, Mr. and Mrs. Adams were being guided by Arthur Griffin, the outfitter who had discovered the bodies of lost hunters, John Doyle and James Steging in 1988 in the same general area.

Because of his experience with the earlier tragedy he specifically cautioned all of his clients so that they wouldn't repeat the same fate of the two dead hunters. Griffin specifically told Mr. and Mrs. Adams to stay put if they ever became lost.

November 4, 1991
Livingston hunters, 41-year-old <u>Charles E. Miller</u> and <u>Tom E. McDaniel</u>, 44, were both found dead after being reported missing about 18 miles southwest of Livingston in the steep and heavily timbered backcountry.

The authorities said that the two hunters were on a one-day hunt and that they were caught unprepared by a snowstorm that hit the area. The search party found the bodies of the two men wearing light jackets just a short distance from their vehicle.

Evidence showed that the two elk hunters had first tried to start a fire but after failing they evidently split up. One man's body was found on top of a ridge where he had tried to start another fire before he died from exposure. The second body was located a few hundred yards away partially covered with snow.

December 12, 1991
The Madison County authorities found the body of <u>James Telegan</u>, 59, of Pacifica, California in the Warm Springs area west of Norris in southwestern Montana. Mr. Telegan had died of exposure 5 days before he was even reported missing by his family in California.

Telegan had been hunting during the Thanksgiving Day weekend with two other men from California but they had come to Montana in separate vehicles. Apparently the other two men had packed up and left camp earlier in their vehicle just as a bad winter storm was overtaking the region and Telegan's truck became disabled about 4 miles from their hunting camp.

Chapter Three: LOST OR MISSING

Being stranded in a heavy snow storm with near zero visibility and wind-chill temperatures of 20 below, Telegan made the fateful decision to try and return to the hunting camp.

Apparently the three men hadn't arranged to meet somewhere after leaving the mountains, and the first two hunters were on their way home safely as Telegan was dying of exposure and his frozen body was later found in a snow drift about 300 yards from his truck.

November 7, 1994
The body Ernest L. Houghton, 78, of Choteau was found on a ridge in the Deep Creek drainage about 25 miles west of Choteau after being missing for 4 days.

It was reported that the hunter wasn't dressed for the cold weather conditions and that he didn't have much experience in the outdoors. Mr. Houghton had left his wife at their cabin to hunt elk and he never returned.

Houghton's wife was stranded at their cabin for 3 days before she could make it to town to report her missing husband. After the report was made Mr. Houghton's body was discovered about a mile from his cabin.

December 11, 2001
Twelve-year-old Kodi Chapman of Whitefish died of hypothermia after becoming lost with his stepfather while they were hunting in Flathead County.

Kodi and his stepfather, Kelly Quinn, 27, had left their pickup truck about 7 miles up Stryker Ridge Road and they hiked some 5 miles during a snow storm.

Chapter Three: LOST OR MISSING

About 18 inches of snow had reportedly fallen in the area, which covered their tracks and they couldn't find their way back to the vehicle.

That evening Mrs. Quinn called the authorities and reported that her husband and son had not returned from their hunt. Mr. Quinn and young Kodi spent the night in a tree and in the morning Quinn left his exhausted stepson and he continued to look for his pickup.

The searchers found Quinn at about 3 o'clock that afternoon and a helicopter crew located the dead body of Kodi Chapman before sundown.

October 20, 2004
The body of 62-year-old Michael LaMere of Rocky boy was found after being missing for two days while he was hunting on Moses Mountain.

LaMere had gone hunting Sunday morning and he was reported missing that same afternoon when he had failed to return at a specific time. Searchers reported that the temperature in the mountains was about 30 degrees and that the hunter had died of hypothermia.

Chapter Four:

KILLED WHEN MISTAKEN FOR AN ANIMAL

Of all the fatal hunting accidents, probably the most disturbing and tragic are those involving a person mistaking another person for an animal in the field. The tragedy is naturally compounded when the victim is a relative or close friend of the shooter.

Although the number of fatalities have gone down drastically since the requirement to wear hunters orange went into effect in 1972, there was still a fatality as recent as 2004 when a 16-year-old boy was accidentally shot when he was mistaken for a deer.

After the turn of the twentieth century when the United States began keeping track of hunting fatalities, the shooting of a hunter, thinking he was a deer or some other game animal was the second most frequent accident of the sport, behind the careless handling of firearms.

While some sportsman organizations of Montana had recommended the passage of laws requiring hunters to wear red sweaters or coats as early as 1920, there wasn't a law passed in the state until the late 1950's.

The resistance to wearing bright and easily discernable colors by Montana hunters goes back to when concealment was crucial for the survival of the early-day hunters and trappers. To better evade hostile Indians, early hunters would wear earthy and natural colors and before it was determined that most game animals were colorblind the more modern hunters wore neutral colors so not to alarm their quarry.

Chapter Four: KILLED WHEN MISTAKEN FOR GAME

Over the years hunters have been excused for killing fellow hunters who were wearing these natural colors, for making noise like an animal, or for breaking through the brush or for not answering to warning shouts. A hunter was even forgiven in 1953 for killing a deaf man who couldn't hear his verbal warnings that he was about to shoot into the brush. The coroner's jury ruled that since there wasn't any evidence of criminal intent the incident it was ruled an accident.

The courts have gotten tougher on these negligent hunters and while few have received prison terms, they usually loose their hunting privilege and their right to possess firearms. While the restriction of firearm possession varied from case to case, in many of the cases the person gave up the sport after the accident and they never handled a weapon again.

Judges and the families of victim have often made statements that they felt that the hunter had suffered enough knowing that they had taken another person's life. While society and the people close to the tragedy may often forgive the hunter, they probably have not or will not ever forgive themselves.

There has never been, and never will be a good enough excuse for killing a person for thinking they are an animal. The only possible exception to this would be at night in grizzly bear country. It would be unwise for a silly prankster to sneak up on a hunting camp at night growling like a bear and swatting the tent.

CASES OF MISTAKEN FOR GAME

December 8, 1890

Harry Emery of Lake City, Minnesota was accidentally shot and killed by his father after he was mistaken for a deer on the upper Smith River about 40 miles southwest of Great Falls.

The younger Emery worked for the Jewell Nursery of Minnesota, and since he was originally from Montana, the firm placed him in charge of a shipment of trees for the city of Great Falls in 1890. After two or three weeks of working with the trees, Mr. Emery decided to go deer hunting with his father and two other Great Falls men.

After several days of hunting the men were packing up their gear to leave when they spotted a deer enter a thicket near their camp along Deep Creek. The Emery's, John Bridges and Joe Peeper decided to surround the thicket in order for one of them to get a shot at the animal. Harry Emery took his position up the creek and just a short distance from the thicket.

Becoming impatient to get a shot at the deer Harry moved silently into the underbrush of the thicket and he was undetected by his other hunting companions. When Mr. M.S. Emery observed the bushes part and saw what he thought was the deer he quickly fired. The shot struck the young man in the groin and it came out through his hip. The father was completely beside himself after he realized what he had done.

The wounded man was taken to a nearby cabin while Mr. Peeper drove their wagon back to Great Falls for medical help. On the way out of the backcountry it started to snow very hard, and by the time Peeper had gotten a fresh team and had picked up Dr. Gordon the weather had gotten worse with the snow drifting over the roads.

Chapter Four: KILLED WHEN MISTAKEN FOR GAME

Harry Emery suffered greatly and he had died well before Mr. Peeper and Doctor Gordon arrived. The men involved with the tragedy said that the boy's father had also suffered greatly. The following day the party returned to Great Falls where the victim was embalmed and he was sent to Minnesota on the Milwaukee Railroad.

February 9, 1898
(Missoulian)
M.C. Beach of St Regis was accidentally shot and killed when Charles Mase mistook him for a mountain lion while they were hunting together. The two men were the best of friends; both worked for the Goughnour's Mill, and they were in the habit of hunting in the nearby hills on their days off.

The men reportedly found the tracks of a mountain lion and Mr. Beach left the trail and he went uphill while Mase continued to follow the cat's tracks.

After a ways Mr. Mase saw something moving in the brush and he thought he had come across the lion. Mase fired into the brush, but the object kept moving and he fired again. Running up to the site he was horrified to find that he had just killed his best friend.

While M.C. Beach was taken to Missoula for burial, Charles Mace had become so distraught that he couldn't remain in St. Regis and he left the country.

September 19, 1902
Louis Gardape was accidentally shot and killed when he was mistaken for a wolf at night on Dry Fork about 5 miles southwest of Grass Range and about 40 miles from Lewistown.

Gardape and another Indian boy had set up a hunting camp up in the timber about a half a mile from the cabin of Louis Hovland, a Norwegian sheepherder working for Ole Vinegar. That evening the

Chapter Four: KILLED WHEN MISTAKEN FOR GAME

two boys decided to pay the old herder a visit and they began walking down the coulee when the herder's dog begin to bark.

Investigating the noise, Mr. Hovland noticed a form coming down the coulee and he said he fired at what he thought was a wolf. The bullet struck Louis Gardape in the stomach and then it ranged downward and shattered his backbone.

The injured boy was carried to the cabin but when his father arrived at the scene Louis Gardape insisted on dying at his own hunting camp. Unfortunately his last wish wasn't granted and he died en route to the boy's tent.

Louis Hovland was charged with manslaughter and he stated that in the dark of the night, Gardape's white shirt under his dark jacket gave the appearance of a wolf coming down the hill.

September 20, 1903
Jesse Hodges was the first fatality of the 1903 Deer Season in Fergus County when his best friend, Billy Baker mistook him for a deer in the Snowy Mountains.

Hodges, the two Baker brothers and Claude West were all hunting deer at the head of Cottonwood Canyon when they spotted 5 deer. While the other boys remained in the canyon Hodges went up on the mountain ridge to drive the animals down to the others.

After a short time Billy Baker saw the bushes moving and when he saw a grayish looking object emerge he thought it was a deer and he quickly fired. A man's scream followed Baker's shot and when he ran to the spot he found that he had shot Hodges.

Baker used a .30-30-caliber rifle with soft-nosed bullets, which expanded after they struck their target. The round that struck Hodges inflicted a terrible wound, entering the middle of his back just to the left of the spinal column, coming out his chest above his heart, and taking away a piece of his left arm.

Claude West quickly ran to the sawmill of Jim Pratt where he secured a horse to rush to Lewistown for help. Despite the muddy road conditions West made it to town within 2 hours after the accident.

The Baker brothers constructed a crude but comfortable litter and they carried the injured man down the icy and snow-covered trail two miles to their camp. They didn't reach camp until 5 o'clock and when they arrived Dr. Long was there to meet them.

The doctor immediately made an examination and he did everything possibly for the young man but the nature of his wounds made it impossible to save his life. Hodges was conscious the entire time and he reportedly suffered a great deal. Jesse Hodges died 24 hours after he had been shot.

It was reported that Jesse Hodges was about 25 years old and he was a hard working and upright young man. He had just gotten married and he had acquired a ranch on Upper Cottonwood Creek where he was working hard to build a permanent home for his bride.

It was ruled that because Hodges had been wearing a gray coat and cap he was mistaken for a deer in the snow-laden brush. It was said that Billy Baker was devastated by the death of his best friend and Jesse Hodges' new wife was reportedly bed ridden and her health was failing.

September 12, 1904
Charles Wiitala, 23, of Sand Coulee was accidentally shot and killed when he was mistaken for a deer along Sheep Creek about 40 miles from Neihart.

Mr. Wiitala had been hunting with Matt Sands, Abel Salo and N. Eastman when they camped on Sheep Creek. Apparently Mr. Wiitala had gotten up late at night to start a campfire and while he was collecting firewood his companions thought he was a deer going through the brush.

In those days, persons were permitted to hunt game 24 hours a day and Matt Sands fired his .30-30-caliber rifle at what he thought was a deer. The bullet struck Charles Wiitala behind the right ear and it came out the left side of his head.

The body of the single miner was taken to Neihart where an inquest was held and Judge Mayor ruled that the death was an accidental shooting.

September 5, 1905
Mrs. Coventry of Deadwood, South Dakota was accidentally shot and killed while her husband was hunting near Clyde Park, about 18 miles from Livingston.

Dr. Coventry, also known as Doctor Abbo, a traveling eye specialist of Deadwood was hunting bobcat while his wife was waiting at their vehicle. Mrs. Coventry apparently decided to join her husband and as she was making her way through the brush the man mistook her for a wild animal and he fired his .22-caliber rifle. The bullet entered the woman's head and she died instantly.

September 15, 1906
Creston area rancher, Aaron McGuire, 36, was accidentally shot and killed by his father-in-law, J.C. Eslock while they were hunting about 5 miles from the head of Swan Lake.

Mr. McGuire was hunting with Eslick and his two sons and a cousin when the men divided up to better cover the area. McGuire and his father-in-law were hunting together when Mr. Eslick began trailing a deer.

Mr. Eslick managed to jump the animal twice, but each time he missed an opportunity to take a shot at the deer. As he was cautiously proceeding, and expecting to jump the deer again, Mr. Eslick observed the bushes shake a few yards ahead of him.

Not wanting to miss a third chance at the deer, and not expecting anyone else to be in the area he fired at the moving object and he hit Aaron McGuire in the top of his head, killing him instantly.

The .30-30 bullet ripped part of McGuire's skull away and it shattered his brain. The 65-year-old Eslick was reportedly devastated by his carelessness. Aaron McGuire and his wife and 2 children had moved to Creston about two and a half years earlier from Iowa and he was buying into Mr. Eslick's ranch.

November 10, 1906
Fergus County area rancher, S.E. Wilson was fatally wounded when he was mistaken for a deer while he was hunting at the head of Rock Creek in Fergus County.

Mr. Wilson, who had a ranch a few miles from Lewistown on Beaver Creek, had been hunting for deer with his friend, Mr. Meir when the two men decided to separate and hunt alone. Although Mr. Meir was reportedly a great shot and a careful hunter he mistook Wilson for a deer and shot him.

After the shooting Mr. Meir immediately sent for a doctor at Lewistown but Wilson died before medical help could arrive. Wilson was a young man and he had reportedly just gotten married.

Chapter Four: KILLED WHEN MISTAKEN FOR GAME

December20, 1907
(Inter Lake)

Charles Robert "Bob" Peterson, a ranger with the Forest Service was accidentally shot and killed by his close friend, Major George E. Doll when he was mistaken for a deer while they were hunting near Trego.

The two men decided that the Major should take a stationary position on a ridge where deer were known to travel and Peterson was to work the draw. They agreed to meet after dark and then return to Kalispell.

Just before dark a deer appeared near Doll's position but he wasn't able to get a shot off before it disappeared into the timber. He watched for it to reappear and when he saw movement where he expected the deer to come out he fired 2 quick shots with his automatic rifle.

Mr. Doll was horrified to find that he had shot and killed Charles Peterson. No one knows for sure why Peterson came up the ridge when they were to meet in the draw. The first shot hit Peterson's gunstock and the second round struck the victim in the eye and it passed through his head.

George Doll was reportedly an old and experienced hunter and he was one of the last people anyone would expect to make such a terrible mistake.

December 19, 1908

Well known Troy rancher, Robert A. Taylor was accidentally shot and killed by his brother, Leland while the two were hunting.

The brothers separated and Leland later said that he saw an object in the dense timber, and thinking it was a deer he fired one shot and then he moved on.

167

After a while Leland Taylor went home and when his brother failed to return he led a party of searchers back to the hills. When the search party came to where Leland had taken his "pot shot" they found the badly bleeding body of Robert Taylor with a large wound in his leg.

Since it had been about 4 hours since he was wounded, Mr. Taylor died from loss of blood and from shock before they could get him to a nearby ranch house.

November 10, 1912
John Easlack of Libby was accidentally shot and killed when he was mistaken for a deer while he was hunting near Eureka on Sunday, November 3.

Mr. Easlack had killed and dressed out a small deer, and he was carrying it out over his shoulders when George Gordon, also of Libby who was at the top of the hill caught sight of the deer and he quickly fired. After rushing to the scene Mr. Gordon realized that he had killed a man and he immediately reported the incident with the authorities at Eureka.

John Easlack left a wife and 4 small children. The family had recently relocated to Montana from New Jersey. and Mr. Easlack was working at a Libby lumber mill.

George Gordon was placed in custody in Eureka on the day of the incident and he was later transferred to the Libby jail. He was later exonerated at the coroner's jury on November 8, 1912.

November 14, 1912
(Anaconda Standard)
Sixteen-year-old George Goss was accidentally shot and killed while he was hunting with two of his relatives near Ekalaka in Carter County.

After hunting together, the Goss boy became separated from his two companions. As he was making his way through the underbrush he was accidentally shot by one or both of the other hunters when they mistook him for an animal.

While an attempt was made to bring medical attention to the wounded victim, George Goss died before help arrived.

November 2, 1914
George Standiford, the youngest son of Mr. and Mrs. A.R. Standiford of Polson was accidentally shot and killed when he was mistaken for a deer while he was hunting in the hills near Libby.

Mr. Standiford and his two sons left camp early to hunt deer and he and his oldest son were to take the ridge tops while young George was to come up through the bottom.

While on the hilltop Mr. Standiford spotted a deer run into a clump of brush at the edge of the timber and he decided to wait for it to reappear. Instead of remaining in the draw as he was instructed, young George came up the hillside and he entered the same clump of bushes that his father was watching.

As the boy was coming out of the brush his father mistook him for a deer and he fired. The bullet struck the lad in the back and it came out near the center of his chest, killing him instantly. The fog, which was hanging over the mountains, was blamed for Mr. Standiford not seeing his target clearly that morning.

It was reported that the distraught father and his oldest son carried the boy's body the 35 miles to Libby, from there it was sent to Kalispell. From Kalispell the men escorted the body across the Flathead Lake to their home at Polson.

Chapter Four: KILLED WHEN MISTAKEN FOR GAME

Mrs. Standiford was in Missoula at the time, and although word of the tragedy had been sent, it never caught up with her, and she didn't learn about the death of her young son until she arrived home.

September 4, 1915
<u>Ernest B. Clark</u>, assistant forest ranger of the Cabinet Forest was accidentally shot and killed on September 3 when he was mistaken for a bear by two hunters about 3 miles from Thompson Falls.

Ranger Clark was placing a line through the thick brush and he came into a clearing when Frank Wineland of Drummond and L.C. Pine of Thompson Falls spotted him. Mr. Clark was reportedly dressed in a dark khaki suit and the two hunters said that the ranger was stooping as he was coming out of the brush.

The two men discussed how difficult it would be to kill the bear at such a range but Wineland took the long-distance shot anyway. The bullet struck Clark in the back and it came out of his neck near the collarbone, killing him instantly.

When the hunters discovered that they had killed a man instead of a bear they were horrified and they immediately turned themselves in to the sheriff at Thompson Falls.

Two forest service employees went to the tragic scene and stayed with the body until the coroner arrived. Volunteers from Thompson Falls cut a trail through the woods to allow a team of horses and wagon to return Mr. Clark's remains to town.

Ernest Clark had been with the forest service for about 8 years and he was well liked by his associates and the community. Mr. Clark left behind a wife and three children.

Chapter Four: KILLED WHEN MISTAKEN FOR GAME

May 17, 1916
(Weekly Courier)
<u>Samuel G. Massey</u> also known as Sam Conboy was accidentally shot and killed by his partner, E.O. Rolstad when he was mistaken for a black bear on Green Mountain.

Mr. Massey had worked for a couple of weeks on a farm owned by Rolstad and his brother-in-law, F.L. Sears near Green Mountain about 7 miles from Bozeman. On Thursday morning Rolstad and Massey scared up a bear and her cubs on the mountain and the two men began to beat the brush for the animals when they became separated.

They had previously agreed to keep track of each other's location by imitating the hoots of an owl, and about 10:45 a.m. Rolstad heard the signal from Massey but he misjudged his partner's location, and when he saw the bushes moving and a dark object coming out he fired his 3000-Savage rifle.

The bullet struck Massey in the left thigh and he was rushed to Bozeman where he was operated on at 9 o'clock Thursday night. Friday morning Massey appeared to be recovering but he failed quickly that afternoon and he died of shock just before 2 o'clock.

Sam Massey arrived at Gordon, Montana near Bozeman in November of 1915 and for some unknown reason he had changed his name to Conboy when he was in the area and he had been known to use several other names in his travels. When notified of his death, his two brothers in Idaho didn't show any willingness to receive his body and he was buried in Bozeman.

December 14, 1916
<u>Dan Murr</u> was accidentally shot and killed by Howard Stevens after being mistaken for a deer in the Fisher River country about 60 miles

from Kalispell. The incident took place in what was then Flathead County but is now part of Lincoln County.

According to reports from the state game warden, Stevens was hunting with Lew Redfern when he said he spotted a deer and he told Redfern to take the shot. Redfern couldn't see the animal and he said that Stevens became disgusted and he exclaimed that it was too late. A short time later Stevens saw what he thought was another deer and he fired, striking Mr. Murr in the neck.

Although a coroner's jury found that the killing of Dan Murr was an accident, Howard Stevens was later arrested by the Flathead County authorities for poaching. Evidently Stevens had more deer in his possession than he was allowed.

September 16, 1917
Twenty-five-year-old <u>Sullivan Berger</u> was accidentally killed when his 40-year-old brother-in-law, John Lafountain mistook him for a coyote about 4 miles from Armells in Fergus County.

While hunting for rabbits on the evening of September 15 Lafountain and Colin Daniels spotted what looked like a coyote across a small creek. With coyotes bringing in a valuable bounty, Lafountain took careful aim and fired. After crossing the stream they found the lifeless body of Sullivan Berger. Mr. Berger was reportedly stooped over taking a drink from the creek when the hunters spotted him.

October 23, 1919
<u>Captain William Strong</u> of Helena was accidentally shot and killed when he was mistaken for an elk about 47 miles north of Ovando.

Strong had been hunting with Hans M. DeLong, the chief clerk at the state treasurer's office and two other men when one of them killed a bull and the others were pursuing a cow elk.

DeLong saw what he though was an elk about 60 yards away and he fired, killing Mr. Strong. Captain William Strong had served in Europe with the 363rd U.S. infantry and before that he was the range master at Camp Lewis, Washington.

October 25, 1919

<u>Norman Winchell</u> of Trident was accidentally shot and killed when E.L. Ruegamer, a rancher from the Porcupine Creek area mistook him for an elk in the Gallatin Canyon.

Mr. Winchell was hunting with two other men when they sighted a herd of elk. Winchell was left to care for the horses while the other men tried to flank the animals. Ruegamer was hunting the same territory when he reportedly saw Winchell's fur coat in the thick timber and he fired, the bullet striking the victim in the chest.

November 3, 1919

<u>James McWhethey</u>, 27, of Helena was accidentally shot and killed when his friend, James Best mistook him for an elk just inside Powell County.

Mr. McWhethey was hunting with Best and G.B. VanCleve at the time of the shooting and he bled to death before his companions could get him medical aid.

December 1, 1920

Sixty-one-year-old <u>Ernest Balke</u> was accidentally shot and killed when he was mistaken for a deer while he was hunting near Egan northwest of Kalispell.

The elderly homesteader had asked his neighbor and friend, Otto Hoffman to help him get a deer before the season closed. Although Hoffman had already gotten a big buck the day before he agreed to help his friend.

Chapter Four: KILLED WHEN MISTAKEN FOR GAME

When the two hunters got into the woods they separated and they took different trails. After a while Hoffman picked up the trail of a wounded deer and he began following it.

Mr. Hoffman later said that he had seen something moving ahead of him and thinking it was the injured animal he fired, but he shot Ernest Balke instead. The bullet entered the man's left side just above the hipbone and it lodged in his body. Hoffman ran to a nearby woodcutter and together they carried the injured man to Egan where he died a few minutes later.

Ernest Balke was a bachelor and he lived alone on his homestead. Hoffman was also a homesteader near Egan, but he spent part of his time at Butte where he had been engaged in mining for 27 years.

On December 3, 1920 a coroner's jury while rendering a verdict that exonerated Otto Hoffman from criminal intent in the death of Ernest Balke, they seriously condemned anyone shooting without being absolutely certain what they were shooting at.

October 20, 1923
The body of Harold Wallinder was found in the heavily timbered mountains near Troy after he had failed to return from a hunt. The 18-year-old Havre youth had been hunting with Charles Purkett and some other friends from Havre when he failed to return to their hunting camp.

Harold Wallinder had been shot and it was believed by the authorities that he had been mistaken for a deer and accidentally killed by an unknown hunter.

November 11, 1927
Eden rancher, Kenneth Gardner was accidentally shot and killed when he was mistaken for a deer while he was hunting in the south fork of Dry Creek about 45 miles south of Great Falls.

Chapter Four: KILLED WHEN MISTAKEN FOR GAME

The 21-year-old Gardner was in one of the most inaccessible areas of Cascade County with his uncle, Ralph F. Cook and friends, Willis R. Major and Chester Lee.

Gardner and Major separated from the other two men and they began tracking a deer about 3 o'clock in the afternoon. When they reached the west slope of the south branch of Dry Creek they jumped a deer, which ran towards the rim rocks.

Willis Major sent the younger Gardner to the rim rocks to wait while he forced any other animals up his way. After giving Gardner enough time to take his position, Major started moving into the timber.

It didn't take long before Major observed what he thought was a deer jumping over a log and he fired from a distance of about 100 yards. Rushing to the spot he heard Kenneth Gardner scream out: "My God, I'm shot!"

The bullet had entered Gardner's left groin but he said that he wasn't in any kind of pain. Major placed his leather vest around the wounded man and began carrying him down the mountain.

The rugged terrain, which was covered with heavy timber and deadfalls made it almost impossible for Mr. Major to carry his burden. He quickly constructed a travois and with the crude device he hauled Gardner for about a mile.

Finally when he couldn't drag the wounded man any further Major placed Gardner in a dry location and he ran to their hunting camp for help. Finding the camp empty, Major rounded up the horses and he waited for the other two hunters to return.

When Cook and Lee returned to the camp the three men rode up to where Gardner was left but by that time he was dead. After bringing his body down from the hills the men finally arrived in Great Falls just before midnight.

The county coroner ruled that the death was purely accidental and he didn't hold an inquest. Little was known of Kenneth Gardner other than he was born in Iowa 20 years earlier and that he had operated a ranch about 7 miles east of Eden for several years.

December 11, 1929
The body of Frank Mayash was found shot in the head on the Rigler Ranch near Corwin Springs. The authorities reported that another hunter apparently shot the 57-year-old Mayash after mistaking him for an elk while he was checking his trap line.

Mr. Mayash was a carpenter by trade and he trapped during the winter months. He lived near Pray, Montana with his two sons, Frank and Tony.

November 11, 1931
Adolph A. Coverdell, 31, of Kalispell was accidentally shot and killed when another hunter mistook him for a deer in the Kila area.

Walter Colby Jr. reported that he had jumped several deer and he thought Mr. Coverdell was one of them at about 300 feet away. Colby's bullet struck Coverdell in the abdomen and he died before he could be taken from the hills.

Two days later a coroner's jury had decided that the death of Adolph Coverdell was accidental because he had been wearing clothing that resembled the color of a deer.

November 8, 1932
Orville Briner, 21, of Melville was accidentally shot and killed by his hunting companion when he was mistaken for a deer on Porcupine Butte near Big Timber.

Chapter Four: KILLED WHEN MISTAKEN FOR GAME

November 14, 1932
Twenty-year-old <u>Edgely Mills</u> was killed instantly and his father <u>Harvey H. Mills</u> died later after being accidentally shot while they were hunting elk in the southern part of Granite County.

The two Whitefish hunters were walking one behind the other when a bullet struck the younger Mills in the neck and then it struck the father in the neck as well. When Harvey Mills regained consciousness he came across other hunters who rushed him to Anaconda where he later died.

The next day expert trackers were called in to follow a faint trail near Elk Creek of the hunter who might have mistaken the 2 men for an elk and had accidentally shot them. The authorities later believed that there may have been 2 separate bullets involved in the deaths of the father and son.

November 6, 1933
<u>Homer Schuchmann</u> of Stevensville died while he was being brought out of the Burnt Fork area after suffering from an accidental gunshot wound he received when he was hunting with his friend, Albert Barrott.

The report stated Mr. Barrott had seen what he thought was a deer across the gully and he fired at it. Mr. Schuchmann took the hit above his left knee and he died as his friend and others were trying to carry him out to their car.

November 7, 1933
Thirty-year-old Virginia City area rancher, <u>Carl Burnston</u> was accidentally killed when he was shot in the back while he was dressing out a deer by his hunting partner, Ivan Winslow.

The two men had been hunting near Lyon in Madison County when Mr. Winslow reportedly shot at what he thought was a bear about 30 yards away feeding on a deer carcass.

Chapter Four: KILLED WHEN MISTAKEN FOR GAME

November 7, 1933
(The Missoulian)
Melvin Evenson, 54, of Whitefish died in a Kalispell hospital several days after being shot by his son in a hunting accident near Stryker Mountain. It was reported that the boy mistook his father for a deer that the hunting party had been tracking.

November 20, 1935
Wilbur Coe of Trego was accidentally shot and killed by a hunting companion when he was mistaken for a deer near Kalispell.

November 10, 1936
Thomas Weir, 45, of Deer Lodge died in a hospital a day after being accidentally shot in the abdomen by another hunter in the Hoover Creek area near Gold Creek.

It was later discovered that a 60-year-old sheepherder and trapper, George Huffman had mistakenly shot Mr. Weir for a coyote about 18 miles from Deer Lodge.

Judge R.E. McHugh later sentenced Mr. Huffman to a 3-year term in the state penitentiary after he had pled guilty to involuntary manslaughter in the shooting death of Thomas Weir.

November 10, 1936
Twenty-seven-year-old Bruce Schwenneker of Billings was killed instantly when he was accidentally shot by his father after being mistaken for a deer.

The father and son had been hunting in the Beartooth Mountains when Bruce wounded a deer and they were tracking the injured animal. The men separated, the younger man going down a small valley and the father taking the mountainside.

While following the deer Bruce started up the hillside and when his father noticed movement in the thick brush, and believing his son was still in the valley below, he fired, striking his son through the heart.

November 15, 1938
(Missoulian)
Howard V. Little, of Stevensville died at the Thorton Hospital in Missoula after being accidentally shot while he was hunting in the South Fork of Bear Creek in the Three Mile country.

Mr. Little, his son, Joe Little and Charles Dawson of Stevensville were hunting deer when they decided to separate. Joe Little and Dawson hunted together while the family dog accompanied Mr. Little.

Joe Little and Dawson reportedly saw a flash of white through the brush, which they later determined was probably the dog's tail. Both hunters fired at the movement and one of their bullets struck Mr. Little's rifle butt and then it entered his hip.

After realizing what they had done the boys immediately ripped off some of their clothing to wrap the injured man and then they packed his wound with snow.

While Joe Little remained with his father, Dawson ran the 2 miles to their car and then drove to the Patton Mill. Workers at the mill rushed to the accident scene while Dawson continued on to Stevensville where a rescue party was organized along with a physician.

A physician and an ambulance met the mill workers who had carried the wounded man with an improvised stretcher, but it was dark by the time the ambulance left for the hospital in Missoula. It was reported that Mr. Little never did lose consciousness during the entire ordeal.

November 30, 1939
Clarence Baker of Bozeman was accidentally shot and killed when another Bozeman hunter, Clarence Mason mistook him for an elk in the upper West Fork area of the Gallatin River.

October 8, 1940
(Missoulian)
Edward Duby, 28, of Wallace, Idaho died in a Missoula hospital after being accidentally shot by his hunting companion near the Powell Ranger Station in western Montana.

Ed Duby and 24-year-old Alvis Parmley were both miners at the Morning Mine at Wallace and they had hunted and fished together for about 5 years. On Sunday, October 4 the two friends went on a day hunt in the popular Powell Ranger District.

While their wives remained at the car the two men hunted for a while when they began following an elk. At about 3 o'clock in the afternoon the two men separated, Duby was going to return to the car, which was about 6 miles away while Parmley was gong to continue after the elk and then meet him later with their wives.

After initially leaving, Duby apparently decided to rejoin Parmley and while he was looking for his friend he had taken off his red jacket keeping only his red hunting cap on. Parmley later said that he saw what he thought was an elk and he fired at the target about 150 yards away.

After hearing his friend cry out, Parmley realized that he had struck Duby by mistake. The bullet passed through the butt of Duby's rifle and then the .32-caliber slug entered the man's abdomen.

Two other hunters joined Parmley and they made the injured man as comfortable as possible and then constructed a stretcher out of their shirts and started to carry him out of the mountains. The three men carried their burden for about a mile through the rough country before they became too exhausted to continue.

Parmley left the group to get more help and he returned with about ten men and Duby's wife. This larger rescue party carried Duby out to the road about a mile north of the Powell Ranger Station where they were met by an ambulance and a Missoula doctor.

Two blood transfusions were given Monday in the fight to save Mr. Duby, one by his wife and another by his brother but he died a little more than 24 hours after being shot by his friend.

During the week that Edward Duby was hunting near the Powell Ranger Station the Forest Service reported that about 525 hunters had been hunting in the area. One of those many hunters was an experienced woodsman from Missoula who later described an incident that same weekend.

The Missoula man said he was concerned for his safety because he wasn't wearing any red and he was in some good elk and moose country.

When he saw another hunter plodding through the brush with his rifle at the ready he whistled at him. The hunter apparently thought it was an elk and he swung his rifle in his direction and he was about to pull the trigger. The man said that he started to scream at the other hunter so that he wouldn't shoot.

The man relating the story said that fortunately the hunter didn't fire, but the incident certainly took the fun out of that day's hunting.

October 17, 1943
Eighteen-year-old <u>Albert Mora</u> of Great Falls was accidentally killed after being shot twice by members of another hunting party in the

Sun River country. Mr. Mora had been hunting with William Lehto about 30 miles from Augusta when he was shot in the body and the head.

Three men, Louis Berger, Jervals Demmings and Jim Lee later admitted that they had been hunting in the same area and that they had shot at an unknown object in the poor early-morning light.

A few days later the county attorney filed second-degree assault charges against 60-year-old Louis Berger of Sun River and the two boys, Demmings and Lee were turned over to the juvenile authorities for the gunshot death of Albert Mora.

Although the medical investigation revealed that Mr. Berger probably didn't fire the fatal shot the authorities charged him with the death because he was the only adult in his hunting party. Berger said that he didn't know why he had shot when he did, explaining that he hadn't seen anything to shoot at. He stated that the moonlight was very bright that morning, and when the others in the party started shooting across the coulee, he fired too.

October 16, 1948
Walter Laughfranere, 25, of Savage was accidentally shot and killed on opening day of the 1948 Big Game Hunting season in the Jardine area in Park County. It was later determined that he had been shot in the face with a .30-30 rifle fired by a member of his 6-man hunting party.

Mr. Laughfranere had been walking with Guy Howard when another member of the hunting party fired into the thick underbrush after hearing a noise. Howard reported that after Walter Laughfranere was shot in the face he walked a few steps and never did cry out.

Chapter Four: KILLED WHEN MISTAKEN FOR GAME

October 19, 1951
Lowell Webb of Butte was accidentally shot and killed when he was mistaken for an elk on a hunting trip up the West Fork of the Bitterroot River.

Mr. Webb had been hunting with four other men when Ernest Townsend Jr. of Darby shot him for an elk. Later that month Mr. Townsend was officially charged with involuntary manslaughter in the death of the hunter.

Records indicated that Lowell Web had been shot twice while he was wearing a red cap and coat.

October 28, 1951
Forty-year-old Guy Long of Whitefish was accidentally shot and killed and another hunter was injured from a single bullet when they were mistaken for an elk by another hunter on Knief Creek on the west side of Hungry Horse Reservoir.

Mr. Long had been walking with two of his companions along the newly cleared Hungry Horse Dam road when Baker Hagestad of Coram fired the fatal shot.

Wayne McCool of Columbia Falls was in the lead when he heard a bullet whiz past his head and strike Long who was next in line in the chest. Third in line was Don Doane of Columbia Falls and after passing through Long's body the bullet entered Doane's side, breaking a rib and then lodged next to his spine. Mr. Doane was able to walk out after the shot, and after surgery he reportedly recovered.

November 16, 1951
Charles Webber, 17, of Charlo was accidentally shot and killed by a member of his hunting party on the last day of the 1951-hunting season when he was apparently mistaken for a deer.

The five Charlo men had been hunting in the brushy country in the Fish Creek area when Mr. Webber was shot in the hip and he died before help could be reached.

Although Royal Marquardt admitted that he had fired at what he thought was a deer, the coroner jury ruled that the death was an accident under excusable circumstances.

October 18, 1952
The <u>Reverend Charles Bolin</u>, 35, of Big Sandy died from an accidental gunshot wound to the abdomen, which was fired by his companion while they were hunting on the South Fork of the Flathead River near Kalispell.

Twenty-four-year-old Reverend Bernard Lund, also of Big Sandy reported that he had accidentally shot Mr. Bolin when he shot at what he thought was an elk.

November 3, 1953
<u>Harry Howard</u>, 84, of Libby was accidentally shot and killed in the brush by a hunter who claimed that he had yelled four times before shooting at some noise.

The hunter, twenty-one-year-old Narven Osteen told the authorities that he saw a dark object moving in the brush and he shouted four times to determine if it was a man or animal. Getting no answer, Osteen fired and he hit the man about 75 feet from his cabin located about 12 miles south of Libby.

Mr. Howard had lived in Lincoln County since 1886 and he was reportedly totally deaf. When other hunters arrived to recover his body they found his dog standing guard over his fallen master. Lloyd Williamson had to lasso the dog and pull him away so that the medical personnel could reach Mr. Howard.

Chapter Four: KILLED WHEN MISTAKEN FOR GAME

At a coroner's jury the following day Mr. Osteen explained that he had shouted: "If there is a man in there, yell out, because I'm going to shoot." When there was no answer, Osteen shot and the bullet went through Howard's body severing his spinal cord. The jury found, "no evidence of criminal intent" in the accidental death of the Libby pioneer.

November 1, 1954
Twenty-one-year-old William Orr of Dillon was found dead by an unidentified hunter in the Blacktail Mountains near Dillon.

Apparently the young hunter was accidentally shot in the back when he was mistaken for an animal while he was dressing out an elk. The Sheriff's officers checked several hunters in the area in an effort to locate the shooter.

November 20, 1955
John Burvich, 19, of Butte was accidentally killed while he was hunting at Maiden Rock about 30 miles south of Butte after he was shot through the diaphragm just below the chest by Jim Rogers from another hunting party.

A veteran hunter, Mr. Rogers reported that he had been following fresh elk tracks during a blinding snowstorm when he shot at some movement ahead of him.

October 17, 1956
Thirty-two-year-old Ralph Younglove of Rea, Missouri was accidentally shot and killed by his hunting partner while they were hunting in the mountains southeast of Augusta.

Walter T. Burns of Dallas, Texas told the authorities that he had mistaken Ralph Younglove for an elk in the early morning light.

October 18, 1956
At first it was reported that an unidentified hunter had accidentally shot and killed 32-year-old Clarence Skaggs of Broadus in the May

Creek area and that the authorities had ordered roadblocks in the region to record hunters and their rifles in an effort to locate the shooter.

The following day thirty-nine-year-old Robert Frankfurter of Broadus was charged with involuntary manslaughter in the hunting death of Mr. Skaggs when he had admitted accidentally shooting the victim.

Mr. Frankfurter stated that he had been on the trail of an elk when he shot at what he said looked like an elk in the jack pines. After he fired the shot he heard a cry, and by the time he reached Clarence Skaggs he was already dead.

November 4, 1957
Robert C. Jennings, 17, of Hamilton died in a local hospital a day after being accidentally shot by his father near their farm in the Charlotte Heights southwest of Hamilton.

The father, Dale Jennings, told the officials that his son had been hunting ahead of him when he mistook him for an elk. The bullet reportedly entered the boy's left side and it came out of his neck.

October 19, 1959
Donald Marko, 26, of Great Falls was accidentally shot and killed while he was hunting on horseback in the Deep Creek area about 65 miles south of Great Falls.

Mr. Marko had been hunting with Darrell Loveland and Gary Anderson both of Great Falls while 49-year-old Archie Cummins and two other Wisconsin hunters were stalking elk in the same area.

Chapter Four: KILLED WHEN MISTAKEN FOR GAME

Mr. Cummins said he saw an elk going into the same area where the three horsemen were riding and he fired into them. One .30-caliber bullet entered Marko's back just above the belt and he died just moments later.

Marko was wearing a blue jacket with a large red patch sewn on the back, which extended across the shoulders, a red cap and there was red on the leather of his saddle. The authorities reported that Cummins had been about 400 yards away from the victim when he fired, and that there were no trees between them.

Immediately after the shooting Mr. Cummins had to be treated for shock in a Great Falls hospital and a few days later he was charged with involuntary manslaughter for being careless and negligent.

At his trial Archie Cummins stated that he had been standing near his truck when he saw several elk break from the trees into a clearing. He said he fired once and he saw the elk scatter; then he walked closer to see if he had hit one. As he got closer he saw the two other men standing over the body of Don Marko.

Archie Cummins of Madison, Wisconsin was given a 3-year suspended prison term after pleading guilty. The judge explained that nothing would be gained by sending him to prison and Mr. Marko's widow said that she believed that Cummins had already suffered enough.

The judge also ordered that Cummins not own, posses or use a firearm for three years. It was reported that Archie Cummins had hunted in the area before, and during the previous season he had shot and killed an elk in the same spot.

November 8, 1959
About 10 months after being accidentally shot, Wesley H. Elbert, 33, of Billings died from complications from the wound he received while hunting in the rugged mountains of the Wise River country.

Mr. Elbert was leading a horse through the tree-covered mountain area east of the Wise River when a bullet shattered the butt of his rifle; entered his left hip and then exited his right hip.

Twenty-four-year-old Donald Warner of Butte later told the authorities that he definitely thought the horse was an elk and that he fired once with his .30-06 rifle.

Wesley Elbert was evacuated from the backcountry by helicopter and taken to Butte. Donald Warner was found guilty of "Reckless Hunting" and given a 3-month suspended sentence, fined $250 and he lost his Montana hunting privileges for life.

November 22, 1959
Neil Christenson, 30, of Martin City was killed in a hunting accident near the Yaak Post Office about 35 miles west of Kalispell on U.S. Highway 2.

The officials reported that Mr. Christenson had been hunting with two other men along the Flathead-Lincoln County border when they spotted a deer crossing the road. The men split up, two of them going in one direction and the third took another route.

The lone hunter saw some movement ahead and he thought it was the deer and he fired. Neil Christenson was struck in the back and the bullet severed an artery in his abdomen.

November 22, 1959
Ernest Hammer, a man from Valier in his 40s was accidentally shot and killed by his 15-year-old-son, Dennis while they were deer hunting during a snowstorm in the mountainous region about 17 miles west of Dupuyer.

Apparently the two had wounded a deer near Split Mountain and they had split up to search for the animal in the dense timber. The man was killed instantly with one shot through the chest by the boy's .30-06 rifle.

Dennis Hammer reportedly went into shock after walking and running 3 miles for help and he was unable to talk about the incident.

November 20, 1960
<u>Walter Franke</u>, 52, of Thompson Falls died from an accidental gunshot wound to the chest after being shot by his 15-year-old son, Walter Franke Jr.

The boy later told authorities that he had seen a deer go into the brush and he shot at it, when he went to look for the animal he found his father fatally wounded.

October 21, 1961
Twenty-one-year-old <u>James Miller</u> of Fairview was dead on arrival at Memorial Hospital at Sidney after being mistaken for a deer and accidentally shot along the Yellowstone River.

Mr. Miller was hunting with two other Sidney hunters, Richard H. Christensen and Orvin Finsaas north of a bridge about 5 miles south of Sidney when they spotted a deer along the river. The men decided to split up and to advance to the river, walking a breast with James Miller in the middle.

Apparently Miller had easier going and he ended up being about 100 yards ahead of the other two hunters. Christensen heard and saw some movement ahead of him and he fired, wounding Miller.

After the shooting Christensen and Finsaas ran to a neighboring farmhouse where they called for an ambulance from Sidney. A handyman on the farm, Richard Riggs ran back to Miller and he covered him with his sheepskin coat and kept him company.

James Miller was born in Fairview on April 6, 1940 and graduated from high school there in 1958. Mr. Miller left behind a new wife of just 3 months, his parents, 6 brothers and 5 sisters.

October 22, 1961
Norman Glen Thrasher, a 21-year-old airman stationed at Malmstrom Air Force Base was accidentally shot and killed on the Kitchingman Ranch near the St. Peter's Mission about 25 miles north of Cascade.

Mr. Thrasher was wearing blue pants, a red hat and a maroon jacket, which may have been the reason why a fellow airman mistook him for a deer. Wilbur Davis Smith was later exonerated in the killing of Thrasher because the victim's apparel had contributed to his death.

November 5, 1961
Thirty-nine-year-old Thomas Kelsey of Libby died from an accidental gunshot wound just a few hours after he arrived at a hospital in Spokane, Washington. Mr. Kelsey was shot while he was dressing out an elk by Edward Peck, also of Libby, while the two men were hunting in the Little Wolf Creek area about 45 miles east of Libby.

About 9:30 in the morning Kelsey killed an elk and he had removed his red hunting cap and jacket before he began dressing out the animal. Mr. Peck said he saw the animal on the ground and detected movement through some brush and he fired his .30-06 rifle. When the heavy slug struck Kelsey in the midsection Peck immediately realized that he had shot his companion.

Another hunting companion, Dr. W.T. Mathews administered first aid and helped Peck carry the wounded man about 2 miles on an improvised stretcher while Richard Kelsey, the son of the victim and Richard Plass went ahead to bring up the car. The victim was flown by private plane to Spokane where he died about 4:35 p.m. that same afternoon.

Chapter Four: KILLED WHEN MISTAKEN FOR GAME

Ten days later a coroner's jury at Libby found that the hunting death of Thomas Kelsey, a foreman for J. Neils Lumber Company was not the result of criminal or inexcusable circumstances by Edward Peck, also a foreman at the same mill.

November 5, 1962
James Gibbons, 29, of Billings was accidentally shot and killed next to a deer he had just downed by his brother-in-law, Dean Coddington also of Billings. The hunters had been hunting near Hardin when Mr. Coddington apparently thought he was shooting at a deer.

October 4, 1965
William Townsend, 50, of Bozeman died from an accidental gunshot wound while he was on horseback and mistaken for an elk on a hunt in the upper Gallatin Canyon south of Bozeman.

The single bullet passed through Townsend's leg and then it went through his horse. The horse died immediately while Townsend died three hours later from massive bleeding and shock.

Mr. Townsend had been hunting with Leonard Kruger and he was reportedly wearing a red hat and an orange shirt while they were hunting in the Lightning Ridge area of Taylor Fork.

The next day, it was reported that Blaine Bolyard of Three Forks had jumped an elk and he was tracking the animal when he thought he saw it again and he fired. When he heard a man scream he ran over to find William Townsend shot.

October 9, 1965
Jeff Thomas, 50, from Grampian, Pennsylvania was accidentally shot and killed by members of his own hunting party from Pennsylvania.

The hunters had a base camp about 3 miles west of Indian Lake about 13 miles from the nearest road and about 48 miles southwest of Hamilton. Mr. Thomas was reportedly mistaken for an elk in the brush and he was struck in the stomach by one of at least 7 rounds fired in his direction.

November 8, 1965

Twenty-three-year-old Reino Nikula Jr. of Red Lodge was accidentally shot and killed by his 20-year-old companion while they were hunting at Town Point, which is about six and a half miles southwest of Red Lodge.

Mr. Nikula was reportedly wearing a white T-shirt under a black jacket and his friend thought he was shooting at a white tail deer in the brush.

September 21, 1969

Hans I. Ericksen, 52, of Escalon, California was accidentally shot and killed by Rudy Nuzzo of Verona, Pennsylvania while they were hunting in the remote Bob Marshall Wilderness.

It was reported that Mr. Nuzzo mistook Hans Erickson for a bear when they were hunting on the East Fork of Strawberry Creek.

October 7, 1969

Raymond Edward Rathie, a 41-year-old Missoula commercial guide and packer was accidentally shot and killed by a client he was guiding along the Montana-Idaho border.

Mr. Rathie and a doctor from New York were hunting when they separated and the Easterner thought he saw a bear in the brush. He later said he had called out to Rathie twice and when there was no answer he fired his 300-magnum at the target. Raymond Rathie was struck by the bullet and he only lived for about 15 minutes.

The New York man went into shock and he stayed alone with the dead man's body for another day and a half before walking out of the backcountry. When he came across another guide they reported the incident together at the West Fork Ranger Station.

November 7, 1969

Earl E. Talbert, 43, of Missoula was accidentally shot and killed by his 15-year-old son, Richard W. Talbert while they were deer hunting near the Clark Fork River midway between Paradise and St. Regis.

Mr. Talbert was reportedly wearing khaki coveralls and his son who had been hunting on a ridge mistook him for a deer in the shadows and brush.

November 28, 1971

Thirty-two-year-old Douglas Arthur Madigan of Victor was accidentally killed when he was shot through the abdomen by his friend and hunting companion while they were tracking elk about 3 miles west of Victor.

Mr. Madigan had been hunting with Leroy Smith and Gerald Martin when they came upon some elk and Madigan shot once and he followed after the elk. Martin said that he spotted another elk, shot at it, and followed it for about 150 yards. At that point Martin explained that he heard a noise and he saw movement about 50 yards away and he shot at it. He then said that he heard Doug Madigan calling his name and then moaning and yelling for help.

June 28, 1982

Twenty-eight-year-old Shannon Weatherly of Bozeman was accidentally shot in the head and died in her tent at the Eagle Creek area about 12 miles from Gardiner. The Montana State University student was in a yellow 2-man tent when two Livingston men, Steven Keys, 31 and Rodney Schultz, 28 said they mistook it for a bear.

The victim and her companion, 26-year-old Bill Hull of Bozeman had pitched their tent on the closed Forest Service road in the Eagle Creek Campground, which is between Gardiner and Jardine.

Chapter Four: KILLED WHEN MISTAKEN FOR GAME

Keys and Schultz were returning from a bear hunt about 10 o'clock at night when they saw an object on the road ahead of them. Keys said that they heard what they thought was growling noises and they couldn't make out the color of the tent in the darkness.

Both men had shot at the tent but it was Schultz's bullet that struck Weatherly and he was given a 3-year deferred sentence; fined $4,000, his rifle confiscated and sold at auction for $300 and he was not allowed to own a gun during his sentence.

A year later Rodney Schultz drowned in a boating accident near Mandan, North Dakota.

November 21, 1984
Daniel Michael Davy, 35, of Lolo was the first hunting fatality of the 1984 season when he was accidentally killed in the Fish Creek drainage north of Lolo Hot Springs while he was hunting with his very close friend.

Mr. Davy's partner later said the two men had wounded an elk earlier and he shot at an object in the brush that he thought was the injured animal. When the man realized that he had shot his friend in the thigh with his .338-caliber rifle he immediately applied a tourniquet to the wound to stop the bleeding and then went for help. Unfortunately Daniel Davy died before the help arrived.

September 15, 1995
A bow hunting expedition to Montana by four Wisconsin hunters turned into a tragedy when one of the men shot his partner with a hunting arrow.

Forty-one-year-old Ronald S. Molback of Kenosha, Wisconsin became the first bow-hunting fatality (excluding earlier Indian attacks) when he was pronounced dead on arrival at the Mountain View Medical Center at White Sulphur Springs.

Chapter Four: KILLED WHEN MISTAKEN FOR GAME

It was reported that 39-year-old Douglas Elfering, also of Kenosha, Wisconsin had accidentally shot his best friend in the neck.

The four hunters were all wearing camouflage-type clothing and they were hunting just after sunrise in the Atlantic Creek area northwest of White Sulphur Springs when Mr. Elfering mistook his friend for a mule deer.

In May of 1996 District Judge Roy Rodeghiero sentenced Douglas Elfering to a 6-year deferred prison term after he pled guilty to negligent homicide for the death of his friend Ron Molback. The judge also stipulated that Elfering could not possess or use any deadly weapon during the sentence period, and he ordered him to perform 250 hours of community service. There was no monetary restitution ordered because the victim's family didn't request any.

November 18, 1996
Randall Phillip Moses, 39, of Lakeside was accidentally shot and killed by his hunting partner while they were hunting on the west-shore of Flathead Lake.

Neither men were wearing the required hunter's orange, and the victim was wearing tan coveralls. Eighteen-year-old James Allan Wagner of Lakeside said he saw a deer about 75 feet away in the brush and he fired his 7-mm rifle. When he ran to the spot he found Randall Moses shot in the back.

By the time Wagner returned to the scene with help Randall Moses was dead. James Wagner was later charged with negligent endangerment and he was given a six-month suspended sentence and fined $120 for the accidental death of his hunting partner.

November 21, 1999
Thirty-six-year-old Roger Allen Wagner of Helena was accidentally shot and killed while he was hunting elk seven miles north of Avon and Highway 12 in the Snowshoe Creek drainage.

Mr. Wagner had been hunting with his brother, Jim Wagner when he wounded an elk and the two got separated while they were tracking the blood trail. Roger Wagner was in a thick stand of timber when his brother saw something brown moving through the brush and he fired his rifle.

Roger Wagner wasn't wearing blaze orange at the time and he died from a shot to his back with a high-powered rifle.

December 7, 2004
(Missoulian)
Sixteen year-old <u>Francis Carl Plante Jr.</u> of Arlee was accidentally shot and killed when he was mistaken for a deer while he was hunting on the Flathead Indian Reservation.

The Plante boy was hunting with a family member and a friend, all members of the Confederated Salish and Kootenai tribes at the top of North Couture Loop Road when the tragedy took place.

The Two Eagle River School sophomore was shot in the chest with a high-powered rifle and the authorities didn't identify the person responsible for the shooting.

DEATH DUE TO HEALTH REASONS

According to the Montana Heart Association, heart attacks kill far more hunters than gunshot wounds. With all the stresses on the heart from the excitement of the hunt, sloshing through marshes and snow, climbing over steep terrain and packing out animals it's a wonder that more fatalities don't occur.

The association has recommended that all hunters have a physical examination several weeks before going hunting, get into condition and train like an athlete would. Before the hunt let your body get used to the altitude, and when you're in the field know your limitations.

When you feel tired, rest as long as necessary; never attempt to drag an animal out by yourself; never hunt alone, and if you have a heart condition tell at least one of your companion about your medications.

The heart specialists also have offered tips on how to care for the hunter who is suffering a heart attack while on hunt. The stricken hunter should be kept absolutely still, and when ever possible get the doctor to the patient rather than getting the patient to the physician.

The victim should not be allowed to walk or ride a horse, and if he must be moved, use a litter. Loosen the person's clothing and keep him warm, but don't let him perspire. If the victim has meds and is able to swallow, administer the prescriptions in their proper dosages.

Health Related Deaths Over The Years.

Our research didn't turn up any health-related fatalities during the nineteenth century and very few at the turn of the next century. This would indicate that either the newspapers didn't report these cases as they do now or older persons didn't hunt as often or the sportsmen were in better condition.

While we don't know the facts in most of the cases of health related deaths we have found that 8 of the hunters suffered heart failure while they were shooting at or in pursuit of big game animals; 5 died while they were dressing out animals and 3 met their deaths by over exerting themselves pushing or chasing after their vehicles.

Although there is sadness in any death, health-related hunting fatalities are generally not as disturbing because of their nature. Except for the very young victims, most of these fatalities were the result of "natural causes" and were to be expected. Another reason why these cases aren't as tragic is the fact that the loss of life wasn't at the hands of another hunter. The vast majority of these fallen hunters died in the pursuit of a sport that they loved and they were usually with their family and friends during their last moments.

Chapter Five: FROM HEALTH REASONS

HUNTING DEATHS FROM HEART ATTACKS, OVER EXERTION, PNEUMONIA, APPENDICITIS AND COMPLICATIONS FROM DIABETES.

December 3, 1910
After failing to return from a day hunt, the frozen body of Ray Forcum was found by a search party about 2 miles from Essex in Flathead County.

The body of the popular young engineer for the Great Northern Railway was reportedly unmarked, and it was believed that Mr. Forcum had died from poor health. The authorities reported that the victim was susceptible to fainting spells, and while he was hunting alone there was no one to assist him.

Mr. Forcum had been running the helper engine on Essex Hill and he was considered one of the best engineers on the road. He left a young wife and 2 small children along with several other relatives in Whitefish.

October 29, 1914
(Silver State)
The body of young Roy Blow, the son of Harry Blow of Elliston was found dead face down on his gun in the foothills near his home. Roy had been grouse hunting with Lester Thompson when they separated and agreed to meet at a given point at a certain time.

Thompson arrived at the designated meeting place and after waiting for his friend for quite some time he concluded that Roy had forgotten about meeting and went home.

Upon returning to Elliston Thompson went to the Blow residence where he learned that his friend had not returned and he immediately returned to the hills with several other men. After going a short distance in the direction Roy had gone they found him dead.

Coroner Harry Peterson decided that an inquest wasn't necessary, as the young man had been in poor health for many years and his death was due to natural causes and exertion.

November 24, 1916
Geza Ottopal of Lewistown died of pneumonia while he was on a hunting trip with his friends in the badlands along the Missouri River about 40 miles from Roy.

A doctor was dispatched from Lewistown but his car broke down along the way and he wasn't able to reach the newly naturalized citizen before he had died at his hunting camp.

Mr. Ottopal was about 36 years old and was an unmarried native of Hungary. He was reportedly a man of wealth and refinement as well as being a former officer of the Hungarian Army. Mr. Ottopal was said to be a giant of a man and his friends thought he was invincible.

September 19, 1917
The decomposing body of Edward Leitner Volcour was found with his hunting rifle about 200 yards from his cabin in Lincoln County.

The 60-year-old single homesteader had reportedly been suffering from health problems and he apparently suffered from a heart attack as he started out on a hunt.

October 29, 1919
P.L. Woods, one of the best-known guides in the Flathead Valley died of acute appendicitis while he was at a hunting camp up the South Fork at Riverside.

Chapter Five: FROM HEALTH REASONS

Mr. Woods had taken a party of Eastern hunters into the backcountry when he was stricken and he was later brought out to the Spotted Bear Ranger Station.

The forest rangers there tried to take him out on a stretcher but he wasn't able to withstand the journey down the mountains and he died before a doctor could get to him.

November 2, 1919
Gallatin County hunter and trapper, Thomas C. Page died of bronchial pneumonia on the way to the McCurdy Ranch about 18 miles from Wilsall.

Mr. Page had been trapping coyotes with Tate McCurdy and F. Bean when the 65-year-old single man became very sick and he was taken to the ranch through the deep snow on a bobsled pulled by a team.

September 29, 1924
The body of Peter Irvine of Arlee was found about 7 miles from the old Jocko Agency nearly a week after he had been reported missing by his hunting companion. It was determined that Mr. Irvine had died of a heart attack.

November 15, 1925
(Missoulian)
Charles Donnally of Quartz and Superior died suddenly in his bunk of an apparent heart attack while he was at a hunting cabin in the Four-Acre region of Western Montana.

Mr. Donnally had been hunting with Philip Ray and another man for several days when he told his friends that he didn't feel well and he was going to stay near the camp. When the other men returned to the cabin from a hunt they found Charles Donnally dead in his bed.

Chapter Five: FROM HEALTH REASONS

October 3, 1931
The body of <u>Steve Chrisman</u> of Billings was found on an abandoned mountain road in the Bull Mountains northeast of the Magic City.

Area ranchers, Fred and E.F. Marsh found a rifle next to the body but Chrisman wasn't shot. According to the victim's sister, Steve Chrisman had been suffering from a weak heart.

November 14, 1933
After being reported missing for a week, the body of 63-year-old <u>Robert Harkness</u> was found about 3 miles from where he was last seen in the rugged Fish Creek area above Lolo Hot Springs. Apparently Mr. Harkness had died of a heart attack while he was drinking from Granite Creek.

Mr. Harkness had a large quantity of matches with him and his rifle was found leaning against a nearby tree. The former Missoula County under sheriff had been the subject of a mass search by an airplane and hundreds of men including 60 soldiers from Fort Missoula.

Harkness' hunting companions, his son, Chester Harkness and Robert Griffith were convinced from the start that he was not lost but either sick or injured because he was an expert woodsman and very familiar with the area.

September 30, 1934
Sixty-year-old Lewis and Clark County rancher, <u>Harry Hines</u> died of an apparent heart attack while he was running after a wounded deer.

Mr. Hines had been digging potatoes with his wife and David Hunter when a deer, which had been shot, ran past them. Apparently not wanting to miss out on some easy venison, Hines gave chase after the animal armed only with his digging tool. The rancher chased after the animal for quite a distance before he finally sat down from exhaustion. By the time his wife caught up with him he was dead.

October 24, 1935

The body of <u>William Powell</u>, 80, of Moore was found in the Belt Mountains after he had been reported missing while hunting deer. Apparently Mr. Powell became ill and had stopped to rest while his hunting party went on.

The old gentleman, who had reportedly said that deer hunting was his favorite sport, started a fire to warm himself. Evidently the old man suffered a heart attack and he fell onto his fire.

Although the body was badly burned the other hunters were still able to identify Mr. Powell and they notified Sheriff Black at Stanford, Montana.

October 22, 1937

Forty-two-year-old <u>Ed Cameron</u> of Livingston died of a heart attack while he was on a hunting trip about 50 miles north of White Sulphur Springs.

October 17, 1938

<u>James A. Parrish</u>, of Helena died of a heart attack while he was hunting ducks in the Helena Valley only a few miles north of his home.

November 4, 1938

(Missoulian)

Great Northern Railroad break-man, <u>Frank Thompson</u> of Whitefish died of a heart attack while he was hunting elk on the South Fork of the Flathead with his nephew, Newton H. Olson of Fort Peck.

The two hunters were setting up their camp on Dean Creek, which is about 17 miles from the Spotted Bear Ranger Station when Mr. Thompson suddenly fell to the ground. The attempts to revive him by Olson and two other hunters were futile.

November 11, 1940
(Missoulian)
Claude S. Averill, 54, of Alberton died of an apparent heart attack while he was hunting near Round Butte south of the Pablo Reservoir.

The Milwaukee Railway conductor had gone to the lower Flathead Valley with Alberton Postmaster, R.G. Nichols to hunt ducks and to scout out the area for pheasant season.

The hunters separated and when Mr. Averill failed to meet Nichols at their car a search was started. The body was found a short distance from where the two men had separated.

November 17, 1941
Seventy-year-old Oliver Gaston died of a heart attack at his hunting cabin after spending the day hunting near Kalispell.

November 5, 1942
Arthur S. Borden of Libby died of an apparent heart attack while he was hunting in the Fisher River Country.

Mr. Borden had been hunting with his son, Clair who was on leave from the Navy, and a friend, John Brooks. Mr. Borden and Brooks reportedly had left their hunting cabin to track deer, and they had only gone about a mile when Borden collapsed.

November 7, 1942
Alley C. McGilvrey, 78, of Kingston, Idaho died at the Powell Ranger Station of a sudden heart attack while he was hunting in the Lolo National Forest with his son.

November 1, 1943
Fifty-one-year-old Oscar Bye of Butte died of a heart attack while he was pheasant hunting with his friends near the Crow Agency.

November 9, 1943
Henry W. Bassett, 64, of Whitefish died of a heart attack while he was on a hunting trip near Fielding, which is not far from Essex.

October 5, 1945
William R. Reymerson, the 56-year-old production superintendent of the General Petroleum Corporation of Los Angeles dropped dead from an apparent heart attack while he was hunting elk about 35 miles southwest of Hamilton near the Montana-Idaho line.

Mr. Raymerson's hunting companion, Lawrence L. McCrea of Fullerton, California later told the authorities that they had arrived in Hamilton on Saturday, September 29 and they packed into the rugged country of the West Fork of the Bitterroot River on Monday.

On Tuesday the two men climbed a mountain and were hunting close together when McCrea killed an elk and while he was dressing the animal he heard Reymerson fire 2 shots. McCrea called out to his companion but there was no answer.

Thinking that Reymerson had left to track down a wounded elk, McCrea spent the remainder of the day taking his meat to their camp. When Reymerson failed to return to the camp Tuesday night, McCrea began searching for his fiend early Wednesday morning, and he found Reymerson's body lying on a slope just about where he was last seen the day before.

October 23, 1945
Vern Simaro, 35, of Kalispell reportedly died of natural causes while he was hunting in the Wolf Creek area northwest of Marion. The

recent World War II veteran had been hunting with his father-in-law and brother-in-law when he slumped over with severe cramps and he died soon afterwards.

November 14, 1945
(Dillon Examiner)
Fifty-one-year old <u>Henry Staffan</u> of Anaconda died of an apparent heart attack at his hunting camp north of Wisdom.

The well-known sportsman had been hunting with his friends, Joe Hill, Al Blaskovich and J. Anerson near the Jackson Ranch in the Big Hole Basin.

October 29, 1946
<u>John N. Thomas</u> of Cokefield, Wyoming died suddenly of a heart attack while he was on a hunting trip near Livingston.

October 8, 1947
The body of <u>Louis Camp,</u> a 66-year-old retired rancher from Burley, Idaho was brought out on packhorse after he had died of a heart attack while he was hunting in the Lost Horse Mountains west of Hamilton.

A week earlier he and his hunting companion, Robert C. Pallard had become sick from food poisoning at the camp and they were treated in the backcountry by a physician who had parachuted into the area.

Mr. Pallard later commented that he was worse off than Camp who had recovered nicely from the food poisoning before he was stricken by his heart ailment.

Mr. Camp wouldn't be the last hunter stricken by a heart attack in the Lost Horse Creek area in 1947.

Chapter Five: FROM HEALTH REASONS

October 9, 1947
Forty-seven-year-old <u>Ross Collins</u> of Modesto, California was also stricken with a heart attack in the Lost Horse Wilderness area.

Collins was the second big-game hunter to die of a heart attack in the remote area within a week. Mr. Collins had been brought out of the backcountry by horseback and he was rushed to Hamilton where he later died at the hospital.

October 12, 1947
<u>Robert Longnecker</u> of Arcanum, Ohio was found dead of a heart attack next to his tent at his hunting camp about 40 miles south of Hamilton. The man was only 39 years old and he was the third hunter to die of a heart attack in the Bitterroot area during a two-week period.

October 27, 1947
<u>Henry A. True</u>, 64, of Shelby died of a heart attack while he was pheasant hunting 12 miles northeast of Conrad with his friend, H.H. Bell of Cut Bank.

October 28, 1947
Forty-four-year-old <u>Benedict D. Perga</u> of Butte died of a heart attack while he was hunting ducks near Harrison.

November 16, 1947
<u>Robert A. Ryan</u>, 63, of Big Timber died of a heart attack while he was on a hunting trip.

November 16, 1947
<u>Ralph Adkins</u>, 57, of Drummond died of a heart attack while he was hunting.

Chapter Five: FROM HEALTH REASONS

November 16, 1947
Charles Brewster, 58, of Great Falls was stricken and died of a heart attack while he was hunting.

November 29, 1947
Fifty-five-year-old Girrald Eddy Townsend of Bozeman died of a heart attack while he was hunting on Thanksgiving Day near his country home.

November 1, 1948
Arne Haugse, 76, of Great Falls died suddenly of a heart attack while he was on a hunting trip near Fairfield.

Mr. Hauges and his hunting partner and good friend, Ole Lien had reached their hunting spot when he became ill, and as they were returning to their car Mr. Haugse dropped dead.

October 12, 1949
Floyd E. Stiles of Filer, Idaho died of a heart attack just one day before his fifty-fourth birthday while he was at his hunting camp near the Powell Ranger Station in the Bitterroot Mountains.

Mr. Stiles' son, Herbert and the rest of the hunting party had to fight through 16 inches of snow to take his body out of the backcountry.

October 12, 1949
Fred Jaqueth, 51, of St. Maries, Idaho died of heart failure while he was hunting near Kalispell.

October 12, 1949
Jesse L. Odelle, 64, of Great Falls died October 7 of a heart attack while he was hunting ducks west of Brady.

Chapter Five: FROM HEALTH REASONS

October 20, 1949
George L. Russell, 51, of Butte died in a hospital after suffering a heart attack while he was hunting with his wife near the Mining City.

September 27, 1950
Charles F. Maris died of a heart attack while he was hunting on the Gofferia Ranch just east of Roundup. Mr. Maris was found sitting by a tree near his vehicle with 2 grouse he had shot that day.

October 24, 1950
Sixty-four-year-old construction worker, William A. Olsen of Helena died of heart failure at the Legion Hot Plunge after hunting near Malta.

October 24, 1950
Oscar Butts, 59-year-old former hotel owner at Ronan suffered a heart attack and fell from his horse dead on October 17 after he had shot an elk about 3 miles above the Clearwater Crossing on Fish Creek.

November 17, 1950
Elmer A. Findall, 65, of Missoula died of a heart attack while he was hunting in the Blackfoot Valley northeast of the Garden City.

October 27, 1951
The state reported that by October 26, 1951 there had already been 4 gunshot fatalities during the young 1951 Hunting Season along with loosing the following 4 hunters to heart attacks.

Ernest Dubie of Dillon
John Heiland of Charlo Heights
Bernard V. Urich of Sweet Grass County
Rudolph B. Krutar of Anaconda

There would be many more heart-attack victims before that year was out.

Chapter Five: FROM HEALTH REASONS

November 1, 1951
Thirty-nine-year-old <u>Fred Anderson</u> of Lakeside died of heart failure while he was hunting in the Emry Creek area up the South Fork of the Flathead River.

Mr. Anderson was the fifth person to die of a heart attack while hunting since the big game season opened on October 15.

November 6, 1951
Five days later Fifty-three-year-old <u>Arthur Foster</u> of Gallatin Gateway was stricken while he was hunting with his 11-year-old son, Roy Foster on Sheep Rock Mountain in the Gallatin Canyon about 25 miles from Bozeman.

November 7, 1951
The next day <u>Thomas Edward McClure</u>, 65, of Billings died of a heart attack while he was hunting along the Stillwater River.

November 14, 1951
A week later <u>Roy Rush</u> of Creston became the last hunter to die of a heart attack in 1951 when he was stricken while hunting about 40 miles west of Kalispell.

October 20, 1952
<u>William F. Johnson</u>, 69, of the state of Ohio died in a helicopter en route to a Missoula hospital after suffering his heart attack while he was hunting near the Dearborn River.

October 21, 1952
Fifty-year-old <u>Frank Yale</u> of Whitefish died of a heart attack while he was hunting near Whitefish.

October 29, 1952

Another victim, <u>Alfred Sterner</u>, 70, of Missoula died of heart failure while he was hunting near Charlo.

Mr. Sterner was with his brother and a friend when he complained of a sudden pain in his chest and then collapsed.

October 17, 1953

Sixty-two-year-old <u>William Lowney</u> of Butte died from an apparent heart attack while he was hunting in the Mount Fleecer area just south of Butte.

November 8, 1953

<u>Bert Bailey</u>, 47, of Victor died of a heart attack while he was on a hunt east of Stevensville. He was hunting with two of his friends in the Rosemont Hills area when he collapsed while getting out of his car.

October 19, 1954

Thirty-nine-year-old <u>Leonard Richard Schmidt</u> of Roundup was found dead from a heart attack in the Bull Mountains south of Roundup.

October 19, 1954

<u>Charles Thomas Case</u>, 50, of Butte died of a heart attack while he was hunting in Beaverhead County.

November 1, 1954

<u>John Earl Murphy</u>, 63, of Helena died of a heart attack while he was hunting near Wolf Creek with his son-in-law, Thomas Stoll.

November 2, 1954
Seventy-year-old <u>John Synnes</u> of Helena reportedly died of a heart attack while he was hunting near the Capital City.

November 20, 1954
Another Helena man, 72-year-old <u>John H. Mueller</u> died of heart failure while he was on a duck-hunting trip in the Helena Valley. Mr. Mueller and two other Helena hunters were walking back to their car when he collapsed.

October 16, 1955
<u>Harry Luce</u>, 58, of Conrad died of a heart attack while he was hunting antelope south of Ulm.

October 16, 1955
Sixty-Six-year-old <u>Silas H. Jerome</u> of Missoula died of heart failure as he was loading his rifle before going hunting in the Blackfoot Valley.

He was found dead in his parked car with his rifle in one hand and a cartridge in the other.

October 19, 1955
<u>William N. Hughley</u>, 64, of Deer Lodge became the third hunter to suffer a fatal heart attack during the 1955-hunting season when he was stricken while dressing out a nice 2-point buck at Sandy Beach on the Missouri River northeast of Helena.

October 27, 1955
The fifth hunter reported to have died of heart failure that season was 55-year-old <u>Joseph K. Harbison</u> of Livingston. The authorities said that Mr. Harbison had just killed a deer and he was stricken while he was dressing the animal.

Chapter Five: FROM HEALTH REASONS

October 31, 1955
Rudolph Pries, 82, of Wibaux died of a heart attack while he was hunting north of his hometown.

He was with his friends when he saw a deer, and the other men said that he called out to them and then fell to the ground.

November 9, 1955
William Jones, 60, of Ennis also reportedly died of heart failure while he was on a hunting trip.

November 9, 1955
Henry J. Jondrow, a 78-year-old retired Livingston railroad engineer was the second man to die of a heart attack on November 8 when he was stricken while pheasant hunting east of Big Timber.

November 15, 1955
Thomas Melton, 47, of Missoula probably died of a heart attack while he was walking toward the Bitterroot River on a duck hunt.

October 18, 1956
William R. Clark, 56, of Seattle, Washington died of a heart attack while he was hunting in the Wise River area with his brother, Oliver Clark.

October 28, 1956
Sixty-one-year-old George Henry Mills of Hamilton died at a local hospital after he had over exerted himself on a big-game hunt in the southern part of the Bitterroot Valley.

October 29, 1956
Like Mr. Mills the day before, Herbert Goecks, 47, of Helena also died from overexertion while he was pheasant hunting near Townsend.

Chapter Five: FROM HEALTH REASONS

October 30, 1956
The very next day another pheasant hunter, <u>Pearl Herndon</u>, 63, of Milltown died of a heart attack while he was bird hunting with two of his friends about 2 miles from his home.

November 12, 1956
<u>June Cleveland Edmondson</u>, 69, of Miles City died of a heart attack while he was hunting on the Fort Keogh Reserve in Custer County.

November 13, 1956
The next day 50-year-old <u>Burton Davenport</u> of Thompson Falls died of a heart attack while he was hunting elk north of his home.

November 13, 1956
On the same day Mr. Davenport died, <u>John F. Detz</u>, 50, of Bozeman also died of a heart attack in the hills south of his hometown.

Like many other heart-attack victims, Mr. Detz was stricken while he was dressing out a deer in the mountains.

October 22, 1957
<u>Jack Kosola</u>, 48, of Georgetown Lake reportedly died of a heart attack while he was deer hunting with his wife in the Gold Coin Mine area about 16 miles west of Anaconda.

November 12, 1957
Sadly, a Hamilton mortician, <u>John W. Dowling</u> died of a heart attack while he was climbing a steep mountainside in the Bitterroot Mountains to help the authorities in recovering the body of Walter Sokolski who had been killed in a hunting accident.

Chapter Five: FROM HEALTH REASONS

November 16, 1957
Herb Martinich, 48, of Great Falls died of heart failure while he was
hunting with Morris Muzzana near Linshire in Meagher County.

After hunting for about 100 yards the two men were returning to
their jeep when Mr. Martinich complained about being dizzy and
then he collapsed.

October 24, 1958
John Stone, 75, of Columbia Falls died of a heart attack while he was
hunting up the Middle Fork of the Flathead River.

He and his son-in-law, Merle Greenland and three other men had
been camped near Spruce Park near Essex.

The other men in the party said that they had heard Mr. Stone
coughing in his sleeping bag and when they checked on him later he
was dead.

October 26, 1958
Ralph W. Harbaugh, 64, of Miles City reportedly died of a heart
attack while he was deer hunting in the Sandy Creek area about 12
miles east of Jordan.

October 28, 1958
Two days later Walter Lee Collins, 66, of John Day, Oregon died
of heart failure while he was hunting with his son, Lee Collins of
Thompson Falls.

The two men had been hunting about 15 miles up Prospect Creek
just south of Thompson Falls when the elder Collins was stricken.

November 10, 1958
Twenty-seven-year-old Ivan L. Gamett of Great Falls died of a heart
attack while he was hunting elk with two of his friends in the Lincoln
area.

Chapter Five: FROM HEALTH REASONS

Tim Potter and Stan Meyer, who worked with Gamett at KFBB TV, in Great Falls reported that Gamett had just shot an elk and he was running after it when he collapsed. Mr. Gamett reportedly died in the car on the way to Lincoln.

November 15, 1958
Another young hunter, <u>Robert C. Brewer</u>, 35, of Great Falls also died of a heart attack while he was hunting north of Fairfield.

Mr. Brewer was found dead in his car with his hunting dog, and sadly he wouldn't be the last young hunter to die of health reasons that year.

November 17, 1958
<u>Walter Talbot</u> of Butte was only 44 years old when he died of natural causes while he was hunting in the Silver Star area.

November 23, 1958
Forty-five-year-old <u>Clyde Jenkins</u> of Noxon died of a heart attack while he was hunting elk in the Prospect Creek area near Thompson Falls. A friend of the victim later reported that Jenkins had taken a shot at an elk just before he collapsed.

November 8, 1959
<u>John Andrew Robinson</u>, 47, of Warm Springs reportedly died of heart failure while he was hunting with his 13-year-old son, Kenneth and two other men from Helena.

The party had been hunting in the Little Creek area near Wolf Creek when Mr. Robinson became the fourteenth fatality of the 1959 Hunting Season.

November 11, 1959
<u>John B. Bourassa</u>, 64, of Helena died of a heart ailment while he was on a hunting trip about 14 miles northwest of Fort Logan. He and his wife had gotten their game and were on their way home when he was stricken.

Chapter Five: FROM HEALTH REASONS

November 14, 1959
Forty-four-year-old Joseph P. Jansen Jr. of Shelby died of a heart attack while he was on a pheasant-hunting trip south of town.

Mr. Jansen had been hunting with his 11-year-old son, Pete when their truck became stuck and he suffered the attack while he was trying to free the vehicle.

The man's young son walked about 3 miles to a nearby farmhouse to get help for his father but Mr. Jansen couldn't be saved.

November 22, 1959
Another heart attack victim of the 1959 hunting season was 50-year-old George Wood of Libby when he was stricken while hunting with his two brothers at the Pival Cabins near Lions Springs on Highway Number 2.

October 16, 1961
Kenneth Rawson of Kalispell died of a heart attack while he was hunting deer about 30 miles east of Fort Benton.

October 17, 1961
Emil L. Rozuoi, 51, of Merrimal, Wisconsin died of heart failure while he was carrying out a deer along Otter Creek near Ashland about 95 miles south of Miles City.

October 18, 1961
Fifty-eight-year-old Troy E. Thacker of Columbia Falls died of a heart attack while he was hunting along the North Fork of the Flathead River about 7 miles from his home.

October 18, 1961
Robert Zeuler, 52, of Billings reportedly died of a heart attack while he was on a hunting trip.

Chapter Five: FROM HEALTH REASONS

October 23, 1961
The body of 49-year-old Coffee Creek farmer, Egbert Zyp Jr. was found next to his pickup truck after being reported missing from his hunting trip. His death was believed to have been from an insulin reaction due to diabetes.

1962

While we found no reported incidents of hunters dying from heart attacks or other ailments in 1962, the following year continued with 4 more hunters stricken including one man who was only 42 years old.

September 21, 1963
Clifford M. Ware, 63, of Camden on Gauley, West Virginia was declared dead on arrival at a Sidney hospital from an apparent heart attack he had suffered while bird hunting north of Lambert.

It was reported that Mr. Ware had parked his car on a hill, and when the brakes failed it started to roll down the road. When the man gave chase after the run-away vehicle he collapsed.

October 18, 1963
Dr. Gunder O. Sweum, 62, of Eau Claire, Wisconsin died while on a hunting trip in the Miles City area.

November 13, 1963
Calvin L. Seeley, 42, of Billings died in a Lewistown hospital after suffering a heart attack while he was hunting on horse back in the Belt Mountains.

Mr. Seeley was hunting with his brother, Frank of Utica and Kenny Twifold when he had his attack and he fell from his horse.

Frank reported that he knew about his brother's heart condition, and said that he wouldn't have taken him along on the trip except that Calvin told him that he had a complete checkup and was in good health.

November 22, 1963
Robert A. Gruber, 68, of Townsend died of a heart attack while he was hunting with his 76-year-old brother, John about 12 miles southeast of Townsend along Dry Creek.

The older man reported that he had heard 3 signal shots from Bob, and after answering the signal with one shot; John followed the tracks to find his younger brother dead.

October 20, 1964
Earl James Gaw, 57, of Boothbay, Maine died of an apparent heart attack while he was deer hunting about 40 miles south of Miles City.

Mr. Gaw and Lewis Alexander, also of Boothbay had been hunting in the Volberg area when Alexander shot a deer first thing in the morning.

While his companion was field dressing his animal Mr. Gaw followed after some other deer over a hill. At about noon, Alexander started out after his friend and he found Earl Gaw's body after about 30 minutes.

This was the victim's first hunting trip to Montana although Mr. Alexander had hunted in eastern Montana every year since 1952.

November 2, 1964
Fifty-two-year-old Floyd Greenup of Helena died of a heart attack while he was hunting near Duck Creek Pass about 20 miles northeast of Townsend.

Chapter Five: FROM HEALTH REASONS

November 16, 1964
The last health related hunting fatality we've recorded in 1964 was that of 64-year-old Frank McCauley of Jefferson City who was found dead from a heart attack in Jefferson County.

October 5, 1965
Ward A. Staats Sr., of Great Falls was found dead from an apparent heart attack about 12 miles east of Lincoln where he had been hunting.

Mr. Staats was reported missing when he failed to return from his hunting trip and he was found the next morning by searchers using a helicopter.

October 26, 1965
Wallace Mack, 70, of Miles City died of a heart attack while he was hunting about 40 miles south of Miles City.

November 24, 1965
Forty-year-old Eugene E. Eggert of Libby died of a heart attack while he was hunting in the Fisher River drainage southeast of Libby.

October 25, 1966
Vern McKay, 50, of Butte died of a heart attack while he was hunting on Wisconsin Creek in Madison County.

October 26, 1966
The body of fifty-one-year-old Donald L. Kelly of Great Falls was found 15 miles southwest of Stanford in the Little Belt Mountains by Game Warden Bud Hubbard of Stanford.

Mr. Kelly had apparently died of heart failure while he was dressing out a deer about 200 feet from the summit of Taylor Mountain.

November 1, 1966
Lester R. Comstock, 58, of Missoula died of a heart attack while he was hunting with his son, Douglas about 7 miles west of Ovando.

Chapter Five: FROM HEALTH REASONS

November 15, 1966
Stewart White, 55, of Butte died of a heart attack while he was pushing his stalled pickup truck on a hill about 6 miles north of the 19-Mile Inn.

Mr. White and his wife had been hunting when they got stuck on a country road in Jefferson County.

November 21, 1966
Forty-eight-year-old George Vince Doherty of Havre died of a heart attack while he was hunting southeast of Havre.

October 24, 1967
Carl Willis, 66, of Kalispell was found dead from a heart attack while he was hunting in the Lost Prairie area, north of McGregor Lake near his hometown.

November 8, 1967
Peter R. "Speed" Lesofski, 44, of Helena died of a heart attack while he was hunting in the Cottonwood area on the Beartooth Ranch north of Helena.

November 24, 1968
Another 44-year-old hunter, Wayne E. Obert of Deer Lodge died of a heart attack while he was hunting near Brazil Creek about 2 miles north of US Highway 287 near Helmville.

Mr. Obert reportedly had only walked about 50 feet from his vehicle when he suddenly collapsed.

September 19, 1969
John A. McFarland, 73, of Missoula died of a heart attack while he was hunting grouse in the Moccasin Creek area just east of Clinton.

Chapter Five: FROM HEALTH REASONS

October 20, 1969
Thirty-five-year-old <u>Tech. Sergeant Gerald F. Thompson</u> of
Malmstrom Air Force Base at Great Falls died of a heart attack while
he was hunting in the Kirby Canyon area near Butte.

October 21, 1969
<u>William Lovell</u>, 63, of Augusta died of a heart attack while he was
climbing a steep slope while he was hunting in the Beaver Creek area
northwest of York.

Mr. Lovell had been hunting with his wife but when she couldn't
make it up the steep slope she stayed at their car.

When the couple didn't returned home the authorities were notified
and the searchers found the wife still waiting for her husband at the
car, and Mr. Lovell's body just up the slope.

October 1, 1970
<u>Carl Knutson</u> of Great Falls died of a heart attack while he was bird
hunting in the steep terrain of the Castle Mountain region about 25
miles northeast of Augusta.

October 20, 1970
<u>Morris C. Holton</u>, 52, of Padeeville, Wisconsin died of a heart attack
while he was hunting antelope north of Jordan.

Mr. Knutson's hunting partner said he was dressing out an antelope
when he heard Mr. Horton fire his rifle; then he fell to the ground
dead.

October 29, 1970
Fifty-five-year-old <u>William Dillabaugh</u> of Scoby died of heart failure
while he was hunting deer about 5 miles south of Redstone.

Chapter Five: FROM HEALTH REASONS

October 19, 1971
(Lewistown Daily News)
Leonard H. Strand, 68, of Sandstone, Minnesota died of a heart attack while he was riding in a van with a hunting party northeast of Roy.

October 19, 1971
(Lewistown Daily News)
Robert L. Marshall, 80, of Park Rapids, Minnesota died of heart failure while he was hunting in the Alaska Bench area of Fergus County.

Mr. Marshall had just dropped a group of hunters off and he was stricken while he was driving to the pickup point.

November 23, 1971
James B. Palmer, 54, of Missoula apparently died of a heart attack while he was hunting in the Rye Creek area about 25 miles south of Hamilton.

October 26, 1972
Merle Berggren, 50, of Forest Lake, Minnesota died of a heart attack while he was hunting in the Miles City area.

November 25, 1973
Paul D. Buck, 57, of Great Falls died of heart failure while he was hunting in the Alaska Bench area about 20 miles south of Lewistown.

Mr. Buck was hunting with Harold McElroy, and the two men had separated and agreed to meet for lunch at a designated point. After Mr. Buck failed to return, McElroy found his friend's body in a small coulee.

October 12, 1976
Ralph Steinberg, 66, of Superior died of heart failure in the Cohagen area northwest of Miles City while he was walking up to an antelope he had just killed.

Mr. Steinberg had been in poor health for about 2 years, but he died on his last hunt, which he shared with both his wife and son.

November 16, 1977
Fifty-four-year-old Paul S. Wininger of Sheridan died of heart failure while he was on an elk hunt in the Wisconsin Creek area near his hometown.

November 12, 1980
J.K. Bowling, 66, of Silver City, North Carolina died of an apparent heart attack while he was hunting near Lost Trail Pass south of Hamilton.

The victim had been with a party of hunters in the West Fork of the Bitterroot River drainage and he was getting on his horse when he reportedly slumped over and died.

October 26, 1981
James Hugh O'Neill, 64, of Great Falls died on opening day of the 1981 Hunting Season from an apparent heart attack.

After field dressing a deer about 4 miles southwest of Wolf Creek, Mr. O'Neill was stricken as he was dragging the animal to the Wolf Creek Road, where it joins Montana Highway No. 434.

October 26, 1981
Fifty-nine-year-old Harold Quarles Sr. of Butte died of an apparent heart attack while he and his friends were hunting on Mt. Fleecer near Divide.

November 2, 1982
Clyde C. Richardson, 79, of Havre reportedly died of natural causes on October 31 while hunting.

Chapter Five: FROM HEALTH REASONS

February 16, 1983
<u>William G. Nemeth</u>, 62,
of Missoula died of a heart
attack while he was hunting
in a special elk hunt north of
Gardiner.

November 2, 1987
(Miles City Star)
Forty-one-year-old <u>James Drury</u> of Troy died of a massive heart attack
while he was hunting in the China Basin near Libby.

Mr. Drury was reported missing by his wife after he had failed to
return from his day hunt. Libby search and rescue personnel found
James Drury's body the following morning.

October 26, 1988
The body of <u>Jack Love</u> of Swan Lake was found in the Lost Creek
region just south of his home after he was reported missing.

The 53-year-old Mr. Love had been hunting with his nephew when
they separated and he apparently died of natural causes. When the
older man didn't report to the designated meeting point his nephew
notified the authorities.

October 28, 1988
<u>Arthur L. Schmidt</u>, 57, of Mount Prospect, Illinois died from a heart
attack while he was hunting with his son near Kerlee Lake west of
Darby in the Selway Bitterroot Wilderness.

November 4, 1992
The body of 41-year-old <u>Herman C. Saari </u>was found in the Rock
Creek region after he had been missing for nine days.

It was determined that he had suffered a heart attack and had
collapsed face down on the trail about a mile from his vehicle.

Chapter Five: FROM HEALTH REASONS

November 10, 1992
Roger Allen English, 61, of Victor died from a heart attack while he was hunting in the Taylor-Hilgard area of the Lee Metcalf Wilderness.

Mr. English had been walking with his son to their hunting camp between Wolf Creek and Corral Creek when he began complaining of severe chest pains.

He reportedly sat down while his son went for their vehicle, and when the younger man returned he found his father lying dead in the snow.

November 26, 1996
Kieran Patrick Grant, 41, of Missoula died of a heart attack while he was bird hunting near Ronan. His body was found near his vehicle on Duck Road about 4 miles south of Ronan.

October 24, 2000
(Missoulian)
Fifty-year-old Daniel Ova of Colstrip died of an apparent heart attack while he was hunting in the Peterson Basin of the Centennial Valley, southeast of Dillon.

Mr. Ova had been hunting in the mountains with his family when they were separated and his body was found later in the rough terrain.

Chapter Six:

KILLED WHILE HUNTING ON OR NEAR THE WATER

Hunters and trappers using boats or pursuing game near the water suffer some of the highest fatality rates among sportsmen. The sportsmen should always be weather wise and be on constant lookout for any sudden wind shifts and storms, which may make the surface water choppy.

All hunters should tell someone where they plan to go, who is with them and when they will return. The boat should be thoroughly checked out to insure it is sea-worthy and that it contains the proper equipment, motor and fuel supply. Care should be taken not to overload the craft as it often leads to capsizing, which accounts for about 70 percent of boating fatalities.

The use of life jackets is always advisable because they will help the hunter remain afloat even with heavy clothing. It is crucial to get out of the water as soon as possible as cold water lowers body temperature 25 times faster than cold air. It should be pointed out that in water just above freezing, a person can become unconsciousness in just 15 minutes and death can occur within 30 minutes. Consequently the victim should be treated for hypothermia immediately upon reaching the shore.

While wading in rivers a hunter should use a sturdy stick or ski pole to maintain at least two points of contact with the streambed at all times. Before crossing the hunter should always survey the water way and plan for any possible escape route through shallow water in case of a mishap. They should never exceed their physical limits in strength, agility and endurance. A tired wader trying to make his way through rapid water over slick rocks is inviting a tragedy.

If the hunter is swept away, they should float on their back drawing their knees up to the chest with their feet pointing down streams. The sportsman's head can best be protected in that position while their arms can help steer him into the shallow or slower water. In deep water the person should swim diagonally and with the current. When in shallow waters the hunter should roll over and crawl to shore.

When hunting or trapping on ice remember to test the ice before going out on it. If the ice at the shoreline is cracked or slushy, stay off of it. Avoid the ice during periods of thaws and beware of thin, clear ice or when it is honeycombed. Small bodies of water are less prone to wind and wave action but avoid venturing on the ice in areas with currents and around bridges.

If you do fall through the ice, avoid panicking or trying to climb out, as you'll probably just break the ice again and go under. Lay both arms on the ice and kick your legs hard, which will help lift your body onto the ice. Once you are on the ice, don't try and stand but roll to safety.

While trying to help someone else out of the water lie down on the ice and if possible form a human chain to reach the victim with a pole, stick, branch or rope. After getting the victim out of the water, wiggle backwards to solid ice but don't try to stand up.

Other tips to remember while on the ice are if your feet are cold keep your head warm, as most of your body heat is lost through the head and neck. Dress in layers, wool, silk and certain synthetics are best; wear insulated and waterproof boots, gloves and have a windbreaker handy.

Always hunt with a partner; take along food and hot drinks; don't build a fire or gather in large groups on the ice. Don't drive your vehicle onto the ice but make sure there are blankets, extra clothing and a first aid kit in the trunk.

Chapter Six: WATER DEATHS

The following are real life stories of sportsman who lost their lives near or on the water, many of which hadn't followed the safety tips.

September 7, 1886
(Helena Daily Herald)
Robert Whipple of Helena drowned in Cooper's Lake about 70 miles northwest of the Capital City while he was retrieving a duck. Cooper's Lake was located in Lewis and Clark County at that time but it is presently in Powell County.

Mr. Whipple was a wallpaper hanger by trade, but during the summer he went to the hills in search of quartz. During the summer of 1886 Whipple was prospecting with his friend, Frank Vautour and they had made their camp on the shore of Cooper's Lake.

On the day they were packing up their gear to move to another location Mr. Vautour shot a duck as it passed overhead. The bird was killed but it fell into the lake about 30 to 40 feet from the shore. While Mr. Vautour was willing to abandon the bird and continue packing, Robert Whipple jumped on a raft and he started out after the bird.

Whipple quickly reached the bird and then he flipped the duck over towards his partner on the shore. Vautour said that he turned away for only a second, and when he looked back again he saw that Whipple was struggling in the vegetation and water trying to reach the raft.

Since Vautour couldn't swim he ran to a neighboring cabin where a strong swimmer ran to the water and dove in to save the man. Unfortunately Whipple had gotten exhausted and had disappeared for the last time before the man could reach him. While the small lake was dragged for three days his body didn't turn up until three weeks later.

Chapter Six: WATER DEATHS

May 20, 1893
(Livingston Enterprise)
Olof Olson of Great Falls drowned on May 11 in the Swan River when the raft he was riding capsized. Two other hunters were listed in serious condition from exposure after the accident.

Mr. Olson was a member of a bear hunting party of eight men, which had left Columbia Falls. When their raft struck a snag all eight men were thrown into the swift current. Along with the loss of life and injuries, the party lost 8 guns, 4 bear skins and all of their provisions.

May 20, 1893
(Livingston Enterprise)
Northwestern Montana hunting guide, Charles F. Foley drowned while he was attempting to ford Fisher Creek near Jennings, which is about 14 miles east of Libby. The 35-year-old guide was returning from a backcountry trip he had completed with a party of men in the St. Mary's country.

Mr. Foley had two horses with him at the time and as he was nearing the north bank of the stream his lariat tangled on a submerged tree and it pulled him and his horse under the water.

September 7, 1893
The body of Stanisloff Crelslenski was found on a sandbar near the McIver's Ranch along the Sun River about 6 miles from where it enters the Missouri. His cousin, Steve Crelslenski had dropped him off to hunt the day before, and his body was found about 500 yards from where he was last seen.

The 23-year-old smelter worker apparently drowned as he tried to wade across the river. Crelslenski was found without his pants and the authorities believed that he had taken them off in order to keep them dry. The victim's pants and his shotgun were not found at the scene.

Chapter Six: WATER DEATHS

Steve Crelslenski was at first held by the authorities but he was reportedly released immediately after it had been determined that his cousin's death had been accidental.

January 6, 1896
(Anaconda Standard)

Thirty-five-year-old <u>Walter Joy</u> drowned after breaking through the ice on the Flathead River while he was checking his trap line at the mouth of Elliott Creek.

When Mr. Joy didn't return that evening a search party began tracking the Columbia Falls rancher the following morning. The men tracked the man to the point where he had broken through the ice. There they found his cap frozen into the large patch of slush ice where the trapper had made a hard struggle for his life.

The search party tried to drag for the body through the hole in the ice without sucess, and Mr. Joy was found 2 days later by Henry Collins and Mr. Hall. It was reported that Walter Joy had been repeatedly warned by his friends not to venture onto the ice.

October 11, 1896

<u>LeGrand "Lee" S. Contalou</u> of Little Milwaukee, a suburb of Great Falls, drowned while he was hunting ducks on the Sun River near where the American Brewery once stood.

The 38-year-old Contalou and his friend, James Lopren had been recently laid off from the smelter and they decided to spend a few days hunting along the river. The men took along extra food and Contalou's hunting dog.

When the hunters reached the brewery they decided to cross over and hunt on the other side of the river. There was an old flatboat moored near the brewery and a man living nearby volunteered to take them across.

The wind was said to be blowing hard and by the time they were halfway across the river the water was coming over the sides of the overloaded craft. When it became evident that the boat was going to sink the men jumped overboard and they started to swim to shore.

While Lopren and the other man made it to the opposite shore Contalou fought in the water with a heavy overcoat filled with shotgun shells and he drowned in the deep water. His companions reached shore just in time to watch him go under for the last time.

Mr. Contalou's dog went back into the water and he retrieved his master's hat and returned it to shore and then laid down and guarded it. After the men returned to the site with the authorities they found the faithful animal still by his master's hat. Soon after the men returned the dog seemed to realize that something had happened to his master because he started to whine from time to time.

Sheriff Dwyer, T.P.A. Howe, Coroner Weitman and several other men began searching for the body with grappling hooks but they had to give up the search when it became dark. James Lopren was given the sad duty of informing Mrs. Contalou about her husband's death. The woman reportedly became so hysterical that it was all the men could do to prevent her from going out into the night in search for her dead husband's body.

The following day the searchers found the body of Lee Contalou not far from the spot where he was last seen. His unfortunate wife was left to care for their two small children.

November 8, 1903
<u>Max Wright</u> and <u>Bridge Williams</u> both of Granite, drowned in Georgetown Lake while they were hunting ducks in a steel boat.

Chapter Six: WATER DEATHS

The two men had been hunting on the big flats for several days before they were last seen leaving in their loaded down boat.

The boat was found floating upside down along with a decoy case and an oar. It was believed that the two men were gathering in ducks when their boat overturned. The weight of their heavy clothes along with the many ammunition belts they had strung over their shoulders probably took them to the bottom of the lake.

Large crowds of men searched the area for several days before the lake finally froze over. The bottom of the lake in that area was made up of deep and sticky mud, which didn't give up bodies easily. The crews intended on setting off dynamite to help raise the bodies but the waves on the lake were always too rough.

The 45-year-old Max Wright was a machinist by trade and he had lived in Anaconda for years before moving to Granite to work for the Bi-Metallic Company. While at Anaconda he had been a member of the local Rod and Gun Club where he was an expert marksman, winning the Klepetko and Brownlee medals several times in competition. He was married and had three children.

Bridge Williams was also a machinist and he was employed at a shop in Granite. Like Wright, Mr. Williams was also an excellent shot and he was once a member of the Butte Gun Club.

September 14, 1904
Forty-eight-year-old Sun River Valley rancher, Lucien A, Enders told his wife that he thought duck hunting would be good and that he was going down by the river to try his luck. As he was leaving he told her that he would be back by noon. That was the last time she saw her husband alive.

Chapter Six: WATER DEATHS

Mrs. Enders waited at their ranch on the south side of Sun River about 12 miles from Great Falls until about 8 o'clock that evening and then she ran the 2 miles to the river to look for her missing husband. She frantically searched for him all night and her desperate cries attracted the attention of many people across the river at Sunnyside.

By the time the neighbors reached Mrs. Enders she was suffering from exhaustion and hypothermia and she was rushed to a nearby ranch house to recover. Mr. Morgan of Sunnyside immediately organized a search of the countryside along both sides of the river. A call was also made to the sheriff's office and Deputy Hogan drove a team to Sun River to assist in the search.

Mrs. Enders believed that her husband might have had a fainting spell while he was retrieving a duck in the river and had drowned. Most of the locals didn't think the missing man had drowned because there weren't any real deep holes in the river. The stream was very low and the water so clear that the body would be easily detected. Most of the searchers thought that Mr. Enders had accidentally shot himself and he was somewhere in the brush.

Over the next 9 days more than a hundred men on foot and on horseback searched just about every square foot of a 10-mile area for the lost hunter. Every coulee between the Ender Ranch and Square Butte was searched as well as every building on the property including turning over all the hay in the barn and the stacks in the fields. All the reservoirs and the river it self were dragged and two of the organizations that Mr. Enders belonged to offered a $50 reward for the recovery of his body.

Nothing was ever found except for two freshly fired shotgun shells of the type Mr. Enders reportedly used. There were no footsteps found leading to or away from the empty shells and it couldn't be proved that the expended ammunition were in fact the missing hunter's.

Chapter Six: WATER DEATHS

Although the water in that area was quite shallow, the searchers still worked it over with the drag hooks primarily for the benefit of the man's stricken wife.

By September 21, 1904 the search had been abandoned and many theorized that Mr. Enders had left the country but no one could offer a plausible motive for his leaving. Mrs. Enders and her nearest neighbor Lee Monk still believed that Enders' body was still in the area and probably in the river.

Lee Monk dynamited the river on his own for about a mile up and down stream from where those two shotgun shells were found along the bank. After several days even Mr. Monk had become discouraged and he was about to give up. On September 22, 1904 after tossing his last charge of explosives into the river, he started to walk down stream when he happened to take another look. Suddenly he noticed something floating in the water near the opposite bank.

Excitedly Mr. Monk waded and finally swam out to find the body of Mr. Enders. Monk immediately notified Mrs. Enders, their friends and the county coroner. When the coroner arrived at the scene the body was still floating face down in the river.

Mr. Enders' body was recovered from a hole that had been earlier thoroughly dragged by searchers from Great Falls. Several times the dragging hooks, which were attached to a bar of iron had caught on something but easily disengaged, leaving the searchers to believe it was just a snag. The hooks had probably caught the man's rubber boots and then tore away.

The body was lifted to shore with ropes and the cold water had preserved the remains from decomposition. The only distortion was in the man's face, which had swollen considerably and was unrecognizable.

One of Mr. Enders' boots was missing and in the pockets of his overalls were 5 loaded shells that matched the empty ones found earlier on the bank. In the pockets of the Ender's hunting coat were a duck and a jackrabbit.

L.A. Enders had come to Montana from North Dakota and he had lived in Cascade County for 12 years. Up until 2 years earlier he had operated L.A. Enders & Company, a paint and wall paper business in Great Falls. His store was on Central Avenue across from the old Post Office and he was in partners with O.F. Wadsworth Jr. In 1902 the partnership was dissolved and Mr. Enders moved out on the Sun River.

October 21, 1907
Arthur Donegan, T. Stewart and James Brown were all reported missing and presumed drowned on Lake Hauser while they were hunting ducks.

William Muth of Helena discovered the tragedy when he found that the victims' boat had drifted back to shore, their shoes were left sitting on the dock and their horse and buggy in the stable with the animal being nearly famished.

It was later learned that the missing black men had rented the horse and buggy from a Helena liveryman and they said that they were going hunting on the lake. At the time it was said that this was the first drowning in Hauser Lake and that the men were intoxicated.

September 21, 1914
Robert W. Rheinackle, 19, of Spokane, Washington lost his life on Lake Francis near Valier while he was hunting ducks with his friends.

Mr. Rheinackle was hunting with Fred Nelson and another man by the name of Mr. Stanton and they didn't find any ducks near the shore of the lake. Rheinackle found an old boat and he began rowing out to where they had seen some birds on the lake.

Chapter Six: WATER DEATHS

The boat apparently began to fill with water faster than Rheinackle could bale and he finally jumped overboard and began swimming for shore. The icy water must have been too much for the young man and he began to swim back to the boat because it was closer than the shore.

Unable to stop the craft from sinking, Rheinackle once again had to swim to shore. This time the young man was overcome with exhaustion and he sank out of sight while his companions watched helplessly from the shore.

The drowning was reported in Valier and many of the townspeople went to the lake to help recover the boy's body. At first the flotilla of small boats couldn't find the body until someone came up with the idea of dragging the waters with strands of barbwire pulled by a team of horses on shore. Mr. Rheinackle's body was finally located in about 10 feet of water.

At the time of his death Robert Rheinackle was working for his uncle, Robert Wilson at Drake Drug, a pharmacy in Valier. The boy's body was shipped to Spokane for burial.

November 7, 1917
Fred H. Batts, 34, of Granite County drowned in Georgetown Lake while he was duck hunting. Mr. Batts had a homestead about a mile east of the Strom Ranch and within site of the Lake.

Georgetown Lake had frozen over except for the extreme center and the open water attracted many ducks. Although the ice was reportedly quite thin Batts apparently felt it would hold him since he was on skis. At one point his wife saw him moving about on the lake while she was working at their place.

When the hunter failed to return that evening she went to their neighbors for assistance. A search party found his tracks leading to the open water and later they located his hat and skis floating on the surface of the water.

The authorities ruled that Fred Batts probably broke through the ice while he was retrieving a bird and he couldn't pull himself out of the 10 to 30 feet of water.

November 15, 1917
Andrew Craig drowned in Hollings Lake while he was hunting and fishing with Arthur Halyean. The two men were fishing for turtles and hunting from a boat when Craig reached for his shotgun to take a shot at a duck, which reportedly capsized the craft.

The men were in the freezing water for about 30 minutes before their screams attracted the attention of a nearby farmer. Before the farmer was able to reach the distressed hunters in his boat, Craig had lost his hold and he had gone under. Mr. Halyean was virtually unconscious and it was lucky that he was revived.

October 23, 1918
Thirty-year-old Louie Hoop drowned in Sage Lake near Kremlin while he was duck hunting with another man who was eventually rescued.

October 26, 1918
John J. Robertson drowned while he was hunting on Madison Lake in Gallatin County.

September 22, 1921
Harry G. Hawkins, 25, of Great Falls drowned in Mission Lake about 18 miles from Cut Bank while he was hunting ducks.

Mr. Hawkins had been hunting with seven of his friends when they found an abandoned boat on the shore of the lake. The other men refused to accompany Hawkins in the leaky craft and he finally insisted on crossing the small lake on his own.

Although the empty boat drifted back to the shore about 2 hours later, Hawkins was never seen alive again. A few weeks later Hawkins' hat was found on the lakeshore and on October 19 his body was found floating in the lake by 2 other hunters. Harry Hawkins left a wife and a small child.

November 9, 1922
A triple tragedy took place at the Pablo Irrigation Reservoir 5 miles south of Polson when three brothers broke through the ice and drowned while they were hunting ducks and trapping muskrats.

William Combs, 23, Lyle Combs, 19, and 15-year-old Lee Combs, left the home of their parents, Mr. and Mrs. J.W. Combs about 6 miles east of Polson with a team of horses and a wagon to camp at the reservoir to hunt and trap.

Although there were no witnesses to the tragedy the authorities believed that it was a case of one or two of the brothers breaking through the ice and the others giving up their lives trying to save them.

A young man hunting near the dam heard a cry for help and he ran to the top of the dike just in time to see one of the young victims go under for the last time. The hunter ran to Pablo for help but they had to call Polson for a boat. A boat was rushed to the scene on a truck but it was too late to save the three brothers in the 7 to 8 foot of water.

The mother of the three boys became so hysterical that the doctors listed her condition as serious. The dead brothers were survived by an 8-year-old brother and sister twins, a sister in Washington and a brother in the East.

November 19, 1923
(Anaconda Standard)
While several men on the shore were frantically constructing a raft they could only watch fellow duck hunter, <u>Andrew Hakke</u> of Butte drown in Georgetown Lake.

Mr. Hakke and two companions were hunting along the shore when they spotted some ducks in the open water. It was said that Hakke was determined to get the birds and he had crawled out about 200 feet from the shore on the ice.

While he was lying on the weakened ice watching the ducks he suddenly broke through. After coming to the surface Mr. Hakke grasped the jagged edge of the ice sheet and he called for a knife in order to get a firmer hold on the ice.

Several other men on the shore heard the cries and they made an effort to assist the struggling man. While most of the men began collecting timbers to construct a raft others ventured out onto the ice to offer support for their friend.

Deputy Game Warden McCafferty came upon the scene in his automobile, and after realizing the situation he drove to the Knapp Boat House where he secured a boat, which he drug behind his vehicle to the scene of the tragedy.

Just moments before the rescue efforts were to begin Mr. Hakke made one last effort and he successfully pulled himself onto the surface of the ice. The effort took his last bit of strength and he slumped to a heap on the ice totally exhausted. Then as the men on the shore were watching, the ice broke away again, and the doomed hunter disappeared beneath the surface without a struggle.

The warden and several men in the boat recovered Hakke's body a few moments later and an effort was made to resuscitate him by a nurse for 30 minutes. Mr. Hakke had a powerful physique and he was a shoemaker and he owned the Champion Shoe Repair Shop in Butte. Andrew Hakke left a wife and a 10-year-old daughter.

November 26, 1923
Thirty-five-year-old Ted Ellis of 605 Eighth Avenue South, Great Falls drowned on Bynum Reservoir while he was hunting ducks with several other men from the city.

Mr. Ellis and S.G. Evens went out on the reservoir in search of ducks in a steel boat with air chambers while Louis Scharrer, C. Craft, Bill Parker and others remained on shore to eat their lunch.

By the time Ellis and Evens had gotten out about 300 yards from the shore the men on the beach heard Ellis shouting for help as their craft was taking on water. The water on the reservoir was reportedly very rough and the wind was blowing against the men in the boat.

The large waves had flowed over the craft and the boat soon filled with water and it started to submerge. While Mr. Evens was able to hold on to the boat, Ellis went under and was lost. After Mr. Evens was rescued he spent several hours recovering from his experience at the nearby Bailey Ranch. For several days searchers from Teton and Cascade Counties searched for Ellis' body but within a week the reservoir had frozen over and the search was suspended.

Ted Ellis was a black man who had been employed as a porter and a janitor at the Bee Hive, the Board-of-Trade Cigar Store, Edison Phonograph Company and the Den Hargrove Store. He was married and had a son and 2 daughters.

Chapter Six: WATER DEATHS

September 18, 1926
(Anaconda Standard)
The body of <u>James Keefe</u> was found in the shallow reeds next to his
overturned boat on Red Rock Lake near Dillon. The well-known
Butte businessman had been staying at a lodge near the lake with
several companions when he decided to go duck hunting by himself.

Apparently his small boat overturned when he fired his shotgun at a
flight of ducks and Mr. Keefe struck his forehead on the craft as he
went into the water. Mr. Keefe managed to get to shallow water with
the boat but he wasn't able to right the craft by himself.

While the elderly man was within shouting distance of nearby
hunters he never called out for assistant. His friends said that he
would have been too proud to ask for help and too sensitive to bother
strangers while they were hunting.

When Mr. Keefe failed to return from his hunt his companions
immediately started a search but his body wasn't discovered until
the following morning. Evidence showed that James Keefe had spent
several hours in the cold water trying to right his overturned boat,
and at one point he even had a cigarette before dying of exposure.

October 31, 1927
<u>Frank Balkovich</u>, 39, of Helena drowned in Helena Lake when his
boat capsized and he was thrown into the icy wind-swept waters. Mr.
Balkovich reportedly clung to the boat for at least 20 minutes until a
large wave washed him away.

Balkovich's 19-year-old companion, Andrew Sapolovich held onto the
stricken craft for more than 2 hours before it finally drifted to shore
and he was rescued. From the hospital where he was suffering from
exposure he stated that the unusually large waves and heavy winds
were responsible for the tragedy.

Chapter Six: WATER DEATHS

November 17, 1928
Twenty-year-old <u>Von Hartso</u> drowned on Fitzpatrick Lake near Kevin while he was hunting.

October 21, 1929
Two Great Falls duck hunters, 22-year-old <u>Clifford Harrison</u> and <u>Otto Garrison</u>, 35, were reported missing and presumed drowned on the Missouri River near Cascade.

Wilson Calvert had launched the two missing men and their canoe; then waited for them down stream at the Cascade Bridge. The three men had drawn straws to determine who would get to hunt from the canoe, and who would be left behind to meet the others with the automobile. Calvert became anxious when the hunters hadn't shown up by late afternoon and he notified the authorities.

A fisherman later found a paddle of their canoe floating along the bank about 40 rods above the Cascade Bridge. Although the men's canoe and its contents of shotguns and other equipment were found on the river bottom, the bodies of the two men were not located.

October 23, 1929
<u>Evert Applegate</u>, 34, of Great Falls was drowned when he was carried away by the Missouri River after the riverbank collapsed under him while he was hunting ducks about a mile and a half from Cascade. Mr. Applegate was hunting with several others, including some of the men who had been searching in the same area for the bodies of two other missing hunters, Clifford Harrison and Otto Garrison.

Applegate and Jack Kelly were walking together on the bank when it went out from under them. Kelly managed to make it to shore but Applegate, who was wearing chest-waders, went under quickly.

Mr. Kelly removed his waders and risked his own life by trying to save his friend but it was in vain. Evert Applegate's body was found two days later about a mile and a half from Cascade in a very deep hole.

Chapter Six: WATER DEATHS

November 19, 1929

<u>Andrew Kola</u>, 40, of Butte fell through the thin ice on Georgetown Lake and drowned while he was hunting ducks. Mr. Kola was hunting with Henry Karkanen and George Myllynaki both of Butte when he broke through the ice.

Both of Kola's friends ran out onto the ice to help him but they stopped when the ice began to crack under their feet. Former deep-sea diver, Gene Burris was called in to help recover the body.

November 24, 1930

The body of 38-year-old Great Falls barber, <u>Andrew J. Marouthas</u> was found in about 10-feet of quiet water after he had drowned while he was duck hunting on the Missouri River near Cascade.

Mr. Marouthas left Great Falls with Louis Scharrer and Sam Laymon to hunt near the Beecher Ranch about 3 miles down stream from Cascade. Sam Laymon remained on the shore while Marouthas and Scharrer were on the river in a steel boat.

Apparently the craft began taking on water and it started to sink quickly leaving the two men in the icy water. Mr. Marouthas was unable to swim and he reportedly sank immediately while Scharrer swam the 100 yards to shore with his heavy hunting boots. Scharrer had intended to swim back out with a rope to where his friend went down, but he was totally exhausted by the time he reached the shore.

Andrew Marouthas had come from Greece, and he had lived in Great Falls for about 17 years where he had operated the Olympia Barber Shop for several years.

October 15, 1933

(Missoulian)

After nearly drowning while he was duck hunting on Priest Lake, 30-year-old <u>Ford R. Lake</u> of Great Falls eventually died of exhaustion on the shore of the lake. Mr. Lake had gone to the small lake about 4 miles from Choteau to hunt ducks with his brother-in-law, 20-year-old Donald Roth of Sun River.

The two men were in the middle of the lake in a tin, flat-bottom boat when an unexpected windstorm hit the area. Although the body of water was only about a half a mile across, the water became very rough and the wind and waves were breaking over the sides of the craft. The men were frantically bailing but the huge waves eventually swamped and sank the boat, forcing them to swim for the shore.

Within 100 feet of the shoreline Mr. Lake had given up and his brother-in-law drug him through the shallow water, weeds and the mud to the shore. Roth later reported that Ford Lake was exhausted but they agreed that the younger man should go to the car and return with help. By the time Roth had gotten back with help his brother-in-law had died.

November 7, 1935
Hugo Benedetti, 35, of Black Eagle was drowned while he was on a duck-hunting trip on the Missouri River about 12 miles south of Great Falls. The searchers found his car and the hunter's tracks to a break in the ice on the river.

Ten days later the body of the Great Falls smelterman was found with the use of grappling hooks on the north side of the river near the Henry Dick Ranch

Shortly after Bendetti's disappearance Mr. Dick reported that he had heard cries for help, but by the time he reached the river the calls had ceased. Sheriff Palagi, his deputies and more than 30 friends of the missing hunter were involved in the search.

Chapter Six: WATER DEATHS

October 23, 1937
The body of <u>George T. Westover</u> of Glasgow was recovered from the Nelson Reservoir where he drowned trying to recover a goose he had shot. George Westover was hunting with Ed O'Brien of Saco and J.H. Brown of Glasgow at the time of the incident.

October 5, 1940
(Missoulian)
Forty-two-year-old <u>George Eckelberry</u> of Kalispell drowned while he was duck hunting at Percy's Lake, which is about 6 miles northeast of his home. Mr. Eckelberry was hunting with Joe Leaf and Clem Zook when he waded out into the small lake to retrieve a duck he had dropped. The waters of the lake were shallow but he stepped into a hole about 10 feet deep and sank.

His companions reported that their friend had surfaced once and complained that his clothing and shoes were weighting him down before he sank out of sight. The incident occurred about 4 o'clock in the afternoon and Flathead County authorities recovered George Eckelberry's body about 7:30 that evening.

November 13, 1945
<u>Clifford Courtney</u>, 44, of Billings and his 15-year-old son, <u>Emmett Courtney</u> were reported missing and believed drowned while they were duck hunting on the Yellowstone River below Huntley.

The men's rubber raft was found stranded on a small sandbar in the river with a gapping hole in its bottom. A double-barreled shotgun was found with a ruptured barrel indicating that the missing hunters may have been killed or injured before slipping into the raging river.

The father and son had left the East Bridge near Billings and were going to be picked up by Mrs. Courtney about 35 miles downstream at Pompeys Pillar but they failed to show up. Searchers continued to drag the river for several days but the bodies hadn't turned up.

Chapter Six: WATER DEATHS

October 28, 1946

Jack E. Parmillee of Los Angeles, California and G.A. Zink of West Yellowstone were both drowned in Hebgen Lake, just north of the western entrance of Yellowstone National Park.

The two duck hunters were in a small boat trying to cross an arm of the lake when they were caught in some rough water and their craft was capsized. Three witnesses immediately went to the scene by boat but they were never able to locate the men in the water. Deputies later found the bodies of the 2 men with the use of grappling hooks.

November 21, 1946

Richard Busler of Polson was reported missing and believed drowned while he was duck hunting along Flathead Lake during a snowstorm. A neighbor was last to see Mr. Busler along the lake and he later reported hearing two shotgun blasts.

The authorities believed that Richard Busler might have tried to retrieve a fallen duck from the lake and he was swept away and drowned.

November 25, 1946

Twenty-three-year-old Robert Rodine of Missoula was missing and presumed drown when the makeshift raft that he and his 27-year-old brother-in-law, Steve Hoepfner were on overturned on the Clark Fork River while they were duck hunting.

Mr. Hoepfner was able to swim through the icy current to the bank and then make his way through snowdrifts for help. When he last saw Rodine he was in waist deep water and hanging onto a tree branch. When Hoepfner returned with help Robert Rodine was gone.

October 16, 1947

Two deer hunters, 42-year-old Clifford G Hogan of Missoula and Albert Lewis Richardson, 29, of Frenchtown were both drowned trying to cross the Clark Fork River on horseback.

The two men were knocked off their mounts when another horse in the party was swept off of its feet in the strong current.

Two other hunters in the party, Henry Lavoie of Frenchtown and Dan Rose of Huson were able to cross the river at the McDonald Ranch about 15 miles from Missoula.

The four men were packing into the mountains on the first day of hunting season and they were advised at the McDonald Ranch not to try to ford the river at that particular spot.

Five days later the body of Albert Richardson was found lying in shallow water near a sandbar about a mile and a half downstream from where he had entered the river.

The body of Clifford Hogan was found 18 days later in the river about 5 miles from the ford he had attempted to cross.

October 18, 1949
Charles Kirby, 52, of Lewistown failed to return from a hunting and fishing trip and was presumed drowned in Fisher's Bottom about 45 miles northeast of Roy, Montana.

October 24, 1950
The Reverend Horace H. Snider of Havre drowned in a reservoir near Dodson on October 6 when he tried to reach his struggling hunting dog.

Chapter Six: WATER DEATHS

October 15, 1954
Sixteen-year-old Jackie Shandy of Joliet drowned while he was duck hunting in Cooney Dam about 13 miles southwest of Joliet.

The victim and three other hunters had been in a boat that capsized. Jackie Shandy reportedly went under immediately while two of the other men swam to shore and another was rescued by another boat.

November 6, 1961
William John Batten, 26, of Butte fell through the ice and he drowned while he was retrieving ducks. His two companions could only watch him go under at the reservoir near Pony.

December, 16, 1962
The bodies of Kenneth H. Fraser, 31, of Columbia Falls and 29-year-old Floyd F. Knopes of Helena were recovered in Shallow Slough between Columbia Falls and Kalispell after failing to return from a duck hunting trip. Fraser's parked car was found near the 150-acre slough, which was about 4 to 6 feet deep.

The two men had left early on Saturday, December 15 and members of the Flathead Rescue and Life Saving Association who located the bodies reported that they believed the victims had drowned early that day.

Although the details of the accident were never known for sure, both men were wearing heavy clothes and the water was very cold, which would make swimming virtually impossible. The men's canoe and weapons weren't found until months later.

Ken Fraser was a native of Butte and the son of the late Kenneth B. Fraser, an officer of the Anaconda Company for many years. The younger Fraser had graduated from Flathead High School and after receiving an engineering degree from Montana State at Bozeman he worked for the Anaconda Aluminum Company at Columbia Falls. Floyd Knopes was employed by International Business Machines at Helena.

October 10, 1966
Richard Ertz, 24, of Kalispell drowned when the boat he was in capsized on Flathead Lake. He was duck hunting near McGovern Cove near Somers with Richard Austin.

October 8, 1967
Fifteen-year-old George Kapp of Cut Bank drowned while he was attempting to retrieve a downed duck in a reservoir on the Bill McAlpine Ranch west of Sweetgrass.

The young Kapp boy had been duck hunting with his brother and an uncle at the time of his death. The young man was reportedly a good swimmer and he wasn't wearing hip boots at the time.

October 20, 1968
Albert Haglund, 52, of Helena was reported missing from his cabin on Canyon Ferry Lake by his relatives and he was presumed drowned. His pickup truck was parked at the cabin but his boat and shotgun were missing.

Apparently Mr. Haglund had gone fishing and goose hunting on the lake and he fell into the lake as he tried to disentangle his fishing line from the boat motor.

The next day searchers located Albert Haglund's boat in a cove on the west shore of the lake with his fishing pole and shotgun in it. Although his wife reported that her husband couldn't swim and that he was deathly afraid of water he never wore a life jacket.

Chapter Six: WATER DEATHS

October 18, 1971
Erland Bruce Whaley, 48, of Trout Creek drowned when he waded into the rapids of Noxon Reservoir to retrieve a duck he had shot. His hunting companion, Gene Rhoutt said Mr. Whaley disappeared when he stepped off a ledge into about 10 feet of water.

October 31, 1971
Gerald W. Giesick, 33, of Billings was reported missing and presumed drowned when he disappeared into the Yellowstone River while he was duck hunting with his brother, John and their friend, William Dunlap about 2 miles west of Pompey's Pillar.

The two brothers left Dunlap on an island and they were circling it when their boat hit a tree in the water. Both men grabbed a branch when they were thrown from the boat. John later reported that he saw his brother fall into the river and he never resurfaced.

November 19, 1972
Sixty-two-year-old Louis Burrell, drowned in about 10 feet of water in a private pond on his ranch about 4 miles northwest of Libby while he was duck hunting with his dog in a canoe. The search of the pond was initiated when the overturned canoe and a floating hat were found.

October 29, 1973
Butte goose hunters, 23-year-old Gary Lawrence Palmer, and 21-year-old Steve Bullock were reported missing and presumed drowned on Meadow Lake near Ennis.

Local residents had reported that there was a bad storm on the lake the day of the men's disappearance. The body of Palmer and their empty boat were located in the middle of the lake but Bullock's body wasn't found.

Chapter Six: WATER DEATHS

November 1, 1973
<u>Dr. Charles McJilton</u>, 77, of Helena was reported missing and feared drowned in the Missouri River where it enters Canyon Ferry Lake. He was last seen duck hunting in the delta area where there are swift flowing and weed-choked channels.

November 24, 1973
Forty-year-old <u>Gordon Dressel</u> of Mora, Minnesota was presumed drowned in the Yellowstone River about 15 miles north of Yellowstone National Park while he was hunting.

The missing hunter was seen trying to wade across the turbulent river by a party of hunters who were watching from across the stream. They reported that Mr. Dressel had spotted an elk on the other bank and while he was crossing the river he lost his footing and disappeared in the current.

October 10, 1988
<u>Randy Lee Anderson</u>, 17, of Great Falls drowned when he waded into a pond to retrieve a duck that he had just killed. Anderson had been hunting with his relatives near the private pond east of Roy when he apparently got tangled in the weeds and he drowned.

November 4, 1992
<u>James Burrell</u> of Whitehall was reported missing and was believed drowned when the canoe he was hunting from capsized on the Jefferson River on October 30.

November 19, 1993
Forty-two-year-old <u>Lamar Rasmussen</u> of Kalispell died when he fell through the ice and drowned in Fickens Slough while he was duck hunting north of Somers. At first the searchers found his shotgun propped against a log; a hole in the ice and then they found his body 3 hours later.

Chapter Seven:
Fatal Animal Encounters

While an attack by an enraged grizzly bear is generally the first thing that comes to mind concerning fatal animal encounters, deer have probably killed more people than any other species as they cross the highways of our country.

Horse Encounters
Horses and other domestic animals have also caused the demise of many more persons than wild animals. Horses are probably the most dangerous animals that a hunter will be confronted with while hunting, as will as the most dangerous means of transportation.

While the automobile has been compared unfavorably today to air travel and a person in the military is said to have a better chance of survival in battle than he does on our nation's highways, compared to a horse the automobile is very safe.

While speed and reckless driving have killed millions of people, very few fatalities have occurred getting in and out or just walking around a parked car. Just try putting something into a horse's trunk and you will see what I mean.

Since thousands of Montanans were seriously injured or killed during the nineteenth century by merely riding to and from town or working on their farm, its only natural to believe that hundreds of hunters were probably seriously injured and many killed while they hunted on horseback. Most of these incidents were only reported as accidents in the hills, fields, while crossing rivers and streams or on their way home or to some other destination.

Chapter Seven: KILLED BY ANIMALS

Besides bear attacks, there have been other deadly encounters with wild animals such as the one found in 1920 between a bull moose and an unknown hunter. A workman who was building a trail through Glacier Park found and photographed the two skeletons on Divide Creek. Eventually the photograph became the property of T.J. Hileman of Kalispell.

The man's stockless muzzle-loader rifle was found, but there was no clothing found at the site except for the soles of his boots. Considering the evidence at the site and the type of weapon found the fatal battle probably took place in the 1870's.

Since the moose had a bullet hole in it's skull, the theory was that the man had wounded the animal but he was trampled to death before he could reload his weapon and the giant beast died during the fatal charge.

Bear Attacks
Since hunters don't often stay on the normal trails and because they are usually focusing intently on their quarry there is always the opportunity for an encounter with a bear. Although there have been many attacks on hunters over the years, there have only been a small handful of fatal confrontations.

In November of 1908 two hunters, J. Glenn and Tom McDonald found the bleached bones of an unidentified man and a large grizzly bear side by side while they were wandering in the Flathead Indian Reservation near Dixon. An old-fashioned gun with a twisted barrel found at the scene indicated that the two enemies went down fighting.

The bear was described as being one of the largest ever seen in the area and a tooth of the animal measured nearly 5 inches in length. Both Mr. Glenn and McDonald took a number of the bear's teeth as trophies and then took the old gun barrel and one of the teeth to the Dixon railroad section house were they were put on display.

The authorities predicted that the mortal combat probably occurred 30 to 35 years earlier on account of the style of the weapon, the condition of the remains, and because the wooden stock of the rifle had completely rotted away.

Another case of a fight-to-the-death between a man and a bear was found in August of 1924 on top of the Selway Divide near the Montana-Idaho border. A fire fighter named Alex Donnelly found the bones of a man and a large bear along with an old cap and ball pistol while working in the mountains. Mr. Donnelly turned the rifle over to Pat Pasley of 725 Holmes Street in Missoula for safekeeping that same year.[1]

Like the earlier case in 1908, it was believed that this mighty struggle for life had probably taken place well before 1900 because of the condition of the bones and because the old .36-caliber pistol had been manufactured before the Civil War.

These reports are supported by actual documented cases that are quite similar. First in 1905 the badly mangled body of Simon "Blondy" Clark, an old soldier and well-known plainsman and hunter was found beside the bodies of two dead grizzly bears that he had killed in the Big Horn Country of Wyoming.

Secondly, in October of 1958 the remains of Sam Adams of Missoula were found along with his broken hunting rifle in the mountains near Ovando and the evidence at the scene led the authorities to believe he too had lost a battle with a grizzly. The bear most certainly died as the result of the battle but it had apparently crawled off before it succumbed to its wounds.

To Help Avoid Conflicts With Bears, Hunters Should Follow These Precautions:

While Camping

Store all food including pop, beer along with flavored toiletries such as toothpaste and lip balm at least 10 feet off the ground and away from your camp.

While Hunting

Hunters on horseback generally have fewer problems with bears than those on foot, but everyone should carry pepper spray.

Avoid hunting alone and travel in pairs whenever possible in bear country. Be particularly cautious in dense timber or brush along creeks and rivers.

Learn to recognize bear sign and avoid areas with fresh scat, diggings, tracks and carcasses.

If you see an animal carcass or gut pile avoid getting close to it. Always remain alert, especially at the end of a long day of hunting.

After the Kill

Dress out the animal and remove the carcass from the area as soon as possible being alert to your surroundings while you work.

If you have to leave the carcass overnight, hang it up at least 10 feet off the ground. If the carcass is at least a half a mile from a trail or your sleeping area, you can leave it on the ground, but you still risk losing the meat to the bears.

Always leave the carcass where you can see it from a distance while approaching it upwind. Some hunters leave an article of their clothing around the carcass to help discourage predators.

Chapter Seven: KILLED BY ANIMALS

Encounters

Keep calm, back away slowly, avoid direct eye contact and speak in a soft monotone voice. Never turn your back, run or kneel down to the bear. Most bear encounters end up with the animal running off.

Don't try climbing a tree unless you are sure you can get at least 10 feet off the ground by the time the bear can get to you. When you get up in the tree, be sure to hold on tight because some large grizzlies have been known to slam so hard into trees that they were able to knock the man from the tree.

If the bear does charge, stand your ground because bears often "bluff charge" or run past the hunter. They may make several of these charges before they finally leave the area.

Shooting a charging bear should be your last resort because it's a difficult shot under ideal conditions and a large animal will usually live long enough to maul the hunter.

A logger was attacked by a medium sized black bear as he walked from his pickup to his trailer in Flathead County. The animal knocked the man down and then started jumping on his back and biting him on the shoulders and arms.

After being treated and released from the local hospital the next morning the man drove home where he was obviously expecting the worst. As he stepped from his pickup he placed his hand on his holstered handgun and he carefully surveyed the area as he walked cautiously to his house.

Within a couple of steps from the front door the same bear leaped from the bushes, knocked the man to the ground and once again began jumping on his back and biting him. All the logger could do while on his stomach with a bear on his back was to pull his weapon out and shoot towards the bushes.

After the explosive shot the marauding bear left immediately and never did return, but the young man had to drive himself back to the hospital to have his fresh bites treated. One can only imagine the reactions from the hospital staff when they saw him come back on the same day he was released.

This encounter not only proves the quickness of a bear, it also illustrates how little reaction time there is, even when trouble is anticipated.

Repellent
Bear repellent has been proven to be very effective against charging bears and it is available at most sporting goods stores.

As a last resort, play dead. Curl up into a ball, protecting your midsection with your knees, and guard your head and neck with your hands and arms.

The Fish and Game or Forest Service would like to know about all bear encounters to help prevent future events.

ACTUAL DOCUMENTED CASES OF FATAL ANIMAL ENCOUNTERS

(KILLED BY A CINNAMON BEAR)
September 10, 1881
(Helena Daily Herald)
<u>Peter Helstrom</u> died at the Sister's Hospital in Deer Lodge after being mauled by a cinnamon bear near the banks of Warm Springs Creek.

The big bear had harassed the area's livestock for about a yearand the local ranchers had offered a $100 reward for the predator.
Peter Helstrom had only been in the United States for about two months at the time of his death, and he wanted to use the reward money to help buy a ranch in Montana so that he could send for his sweetheart in Sweden.

Helstrom enlisted two other Swedish men, Christian Jorgenson and Andrew Peterson to help him take down the giant bear. The men found the bear's track in a large pasture known as Peterson's Field and Helstrom shot the animal as it was going into the brush.

The young man followed the bruin into the thicket where he shot the animal again, but before he could reload, the bear turned on him. With one swipe the big bear sliced off the man's nose and his upper lip. By the time the other men could take a safe shot and kill the bear, the bruin had scalped Mr. Helstrom and had bitten through his skull behind the ears.

Helstrom's friends quickly got the bear off of his back; constructed a stretcher from branches and their clothing and then carried him to Warm Springs. When they found that the local doctor was gone they commandeered a wagon and team and rushed the dying man to Deer Lodge.

All that Doctors Mitchell and Mussigbrod were able to do was to clean the wounds and Helstrom died about 15 minutes later. Before he passed, Helstrom whispered to Dr. Mitchell: "Am I going to die?" Dr. Mitchell leaned over the young man and quietly told him he was indeed going to die, and that he should just rest. Peter Helstrom then reportedly said: "Well, I killed the bear anyhow."

(KILLED BY A BEAR)
(Billings Gazette)
1894, Reported on 12/7/1897
The remains of an <u>Unknown Hunter</u> killed in 1894 were found in the Boulder River country three years later. While the article didn't mention the man's name it was implied that his identity was known and the authorities knew when he was reported missing.

(KILLED BY A GRIZZLY BEAR)
May 5, 1912
Long time Park County resident and hunter, <u>John Austin</u> was attacked and killed by a grizzly bear while he was hunting on Crevasse Mountain near Jardine, Montana.

According to Adolph Hagerman, who had heard the man's cries and went to the aid of the victim, Mr. Austin had encountered the huge grizzly in a dense timbered area and he apparently didn't see the bear until it was a few feet away.

Mr. Austin fired a shot into the bear, but it wasn't hit fatally and the man didn't have time for a second shot. The bear bit down on the man's head, crushing his jaw and skull and it was on top of the victim when Hagerman arrived at the scene.

Mr. Hagerman shot and killed the bear, and after rolling the animal off of the victim he cared for the man the best he could before running to Gardiner for help. In the two hours it took to return with a doctor John Austin had died.

(KILLED BY A HORSE)
October 18, 1937
(Missoulian)
Twenty-three year-old Ninemile area rancher, <u>Ralph Longpre</u> was killed while he was on a hunting trip about 18 miles southwest of Alberton when a horse kicked him in the head.

Mr. Longpre had been hunting in the Fish Creek region with his brother-in-law George Moen and he was packing an elk to the Edgewater camp at the time of the accident. Longpre was removing a hindquarter from the pack load when he lost his footing and he fell to the ground. The unexpected movement startled the packhorse and it kicked the man in the head, fracturing his skull.

Ralph Longpre's body was taken out of the mountains by Dr. W. J. Doyle of Superior and his brothers, William Longpre of Nine Mile and Dan Longpre, who was the under sheriff of Mineral County stationed at Superior.

The young victim left his widow and 2 children, his parents of Nine Mile, 4 brothers and 3 sisters. Ralph Longpre's death was the first hunting death reported during the 1937 season.

(KILLED BY A WOUNDED DEER)
November 3, 1938
(Missoulian)
<u>Grover Pace</u>, 44, of Sunburst was killed near Plains in a most unusual manner by his own rifle when a dying deer he had just shot apparently kicked the weapon. The high-powered rifle discharged into Pace's groin and he quickly bled to death.

Mr. Pace and Olie Hanson of Kevin were hunting in the Thompson River country and they were staying in a cabin on the river near Rock Creek about 40 miles north of Plains.

Mr. Hanson had been suffering from rheumatism and he stayed at the cabin while Pace went hunting alone. At about 8:30 that morning Hanson reportedly heard two shots and he naturally thought that his partner had gotten a deer.

Mr. Hanson became alarmed when Grover Pace didn't return that evening but because he was unfamiliar with the area and he was afraid to venture out alone at night and he waited until morning to look for his friend. The next day Hanson found Mr. Pace's body near Rock Creek along side the dead deer and his rifle near the feet of the animal.

(PROBABLY KILLED BY A BEAR)
November 19, 1940

Fifty-year-old Frank Howell of Kalispell was reported missing while he was on an elk hunting trip in the North Fork of the Flathead River country. The experienced woodsman and trapper had gone into the remote backcountry in November to spend the winter trapping with his partner, C.R. Hudsen.

When Mr. Howell didn't return to their camp Hudsen made his way out of the mountains and reported the incident to the authorities, but because of the deep snow, no search could be made until the spring of 1941.

In July of 1941, Frank Howell's brother, Edward and a Flathead County sheriff deputy found a large part of his brother's clothing and a few bones in a small spring. In November of that year searchers found the skull and other bones of Howell and they ruled that bears had devoured his body. Frank Howell was probably killed and eaten by a bear, as the trapper was very familiar with the area.

Chapter Seven: KILLED BY ANIMALS

(KILLED BY A HORSE)
November 16, 1941
<u>Charles McElroy</u>, 49, of Kalispell died of injuries he received when his horse fell on top of him while he was packing out a deer in Pleasant Valley near Kalispell. His hunting companion, J.C. Ellis told the authorities that he looked back and saw Mr. McElroy and his horse on the ground.

McElroy's hunting knife or the saddle horn had pierced an artery in his abdomen and he bled to death while Ellis and Mrs. McElroy were driving him to a Kalispell hospital.

(KILLED BY A HORSE)
November 6, 1947
<u>George Danford Mason</u> of Baker had been dead for about 2 weeks by the time his body was discovered by his nephew near his Valley County ranch. Mason was apparently seriously injured by a horse while he was hunting and he wasn't able to seek medical assistance. With no help available, the severly injured man apparently killed himself with his own shotgun.

Before taking his own life he left a note stating: "get rid of that sorrel horse, he's a man killer and he damned near killed me."

(KILLED BY A GRIZZLY BEAR)
October 22, 1956
Former Fort Benton star athlete, <u>William Kenneth Scott</u>, 29, of Loma was mauled to death by a wounded grizzly bear while he was elk hunting in the Bob Marshall Wilderness about 40 miles west of Augusta.

Scott's hunting partner, Vic Squires of Fort Benton was clawed in the foot during the struggle and he reported that the huge bear had jumped them as they were looking for elk. The bear attacked Squires who tripped on some brush and he went down to the ground as the bear was clawing at his boot.

As Mr. Squire was kicking at the animal it reared up when Mr. Scott yelled at the bear. Standing on a knoll, Scott shot the bear twice with his .30-06 rifle and the bear ran off into the nearby brush.

When Scott reached Squire they decided to track down and kill the wounded bear before it came across one of the other hunters in their party. With Squire in the lead, the men tracked the bear for about four hours through the brush.

When they again spotted the animal, Squire emptied his .30-30 into the giant bear but before Squire could reload his rifle the bear began to charge.

As Squire was retreating, Scott fired 2 more rounds into the bear and he shouted at Squire to run for it. Vic Squire started to run and he assumed that Scott was running behind him but apparently he remained to cover Squire's retreat.

Squire ran all the way to their hunting camp to muster the other 6 hunters in the party and they quickly returned to the scene where they found Scott severely injured and the bear was gone. Scott had suffered several scalp, facial and throat lacerations as well as vicious bites on his hands and arms.

The hunters carried their wounded friend to a riverbank to treat him when the bear attacked them again. Even with a campfire blazing nearby the wounded man, the raging animal appeared to have gone once more at the injured Scott. This time however the bear was killed by the hunting party but not until it had gotten within 10 feet of the wounded man.

Chapter Seven: KILLED BY ANIMALS

Members of the party drove into Augusta to get help and Dr. C.E. Magnor was flown into the backcountry to give emergency treatment to the injured hunter. Unfortunately, the former prized athlete died about five minutes before the doctor arrived at the camp.

Some of the men remained at the scene to skin out the 800-pound grizzly and the skin was later made into a rug and it was sold at auction and the proceeds went to Scott's widow.

Following a community movement in Fort Benton, the high school athletic field was dedicated to Kenneth Scott on October 12, 1957. Scott was the school's all-time athletic hero who had been a standout basketball player, star fullback and the captain of the 1944 championship football team. He was regarded throughout Montana as a one-man track team, having scored 23 of the team's 31 points for the 1945 championship.

Two years later a grizzly bear would kill another brave hunter in western Montana.

(KILLED BY A GRIZZLY BEAR)
October 31, 1958
Thirty-nine-year-old Samuel Adams of Missoula was reported missing since October 27 while he was hunting in the Chamberlain Mountains north of Ovando.

The World War II veteran had been hunting with friends, Ed Hodges, 40, and 52-year-old Calvin Trusty, both of Missoula when the men split up and Sam wasn't seen alive again. When Adams failed to return to their base camp on Chamberlain Creek, Hodges and Trusty went for help but the deep snow and bad weather ended the long search in the fall of 1958.

The following summer Adams' two hunting companions returned to the Blackfoot country to search for the remains of their lost friend and on July 13, 1959 his body was found.

Chapter Seven: KILLED BY ANIMALS

Mr. Hodges and Trusty located the grisly scene of Adams' untimely death near a mountain meadow about 65 miles northeast of Missoula. They found Adams' rifle, which was broken into three pieces, two empty cartridges, his shoes, which had been chewed by bear teeth, a knife and some pieces of clothing all indicating that the hunter had been killed and eaten by a bear after a brutal fight.

The following day they returned with officials from both Missoula and Powell Counties along with Charles Schmiedeke the leader of the Missoula County Search and Rescue Association. This expanded search party found additional evidence at the scene, which indicated positively, that Sam Adams had been killed and eaten by a bear, probably a grizzly. Adams' wallet, human bone; flesh, hair and clothing were all located in nearby bear dung.

The evidence at the sight suggested that Mr. Adams may have wounded the bear and the raging animal attacked him; then the animal left the scene. The injured man apparently crawled to a log where he removed the shoestrings from his shoes, probably to use as a tourniquet and then built a fire for warmth.

The officials said that the badly wounded Adams then fired his last two bullets to signal for help as they found the cartridges by the log and remnants of the fire. Some time later, probably that evening the bear returned and without ammunition, the gutsy man used his empty rifle as a club, breaking it over the attacking animal before he was finally killed.

Mr. Schmiedeke explained that the bear had either devoured Adams' body, bones and all, or it had dragged the skull and the larger bones away and buried them. The experienced outdoorsman said that grizzly bears had been reported in the area recently and that they commonly bury bones and other indigestible remains.

(KILLED BY A HORSE)
October 23, 1969
Roswel L. Breakus, 50, of Sidney died in a Bozeman hospital several hours after being dragged by a horse while he was on a hunting trip with his son.

The two men were hunting about 60 miles south of Bozeman in the Wapita Creek region when Mr. Breakus' horse stumbled and fell. The horse became spooked and the man was dragged after his foot got entangled in the rope on the saddle.

(KILLED BY A HORSE)
November 10, 1987
Twenty-two-year-old Alan K. Kitchel was found dead by searchers after being missing for two days. The young guide and outfitter reportedly died as a result of multiple traumas after being thrown and dragged by his horse.

At the time of the accident Alan Kitchel was riding alone to his hunting camp on Cherry Creek on the Shelton Ranch in the Spanish Peaks Wilderness about 18 miles south of Montana Highway 84.

(KILLED BY A GRIZZLY BEAR)
November 1, 2001
Timothy A. "Omar" Hilston, 50, of Great Falls was killed by a female grizzly bear with two cubs while he was dressing out an elk in the Blackfoot-Clearwater Game Range between Ovando and Seeley Lake.

Mr. Hilston left Great Falls alone about 4:30 a.m. in the morning and he drove to the management range where he was scheduled to meet his brother-in-law, Tom Sidor there later that afternoon.

Hilston killed an elk about 400 yards from his vehicle when the 350-pound grizzly, which had probably followed the blood trail of the injured elk, attacked him from behind as he was dressing out the downed elk.

After the bear and her 2 cubs fed on the elk carcass they buried what was left and they apparently left the area. Mr. Hilston must have regained consciousness and he tried to make his way back to his truck but he died about 150 yards from the vehicle.

When Tom Sidor arrived that afternoon he waited at Hilston's truck until that evening and then he reported him missing with the authorities. The next morning a large search party was at the scene with a dog, which soon discovered Hilston's body, the partially buried elk carcass and then they pieced together the death scene.

The local game warden immediately closed about 35 square miles of the management area north of Highway 200 and they began notifying the other 50-some hunters who had special elk permits in the area that it was closed until the man-killing bear was destroyed.

Since bears usually returned to their cached kills seven federal and state wildlife officers set 5 traps and snares for the grizzlies. Two days later the female grizzly and one cub were snared while the second cub was hanging around the area. The female bear and both of her 125-pound cubs were destroyed and removed from the area.

The female bear had never been in trouble before but it had been captured and collared by the Department of Fish, Wildlife and Parks in the spring of 1999 on the Two Creek Ranch and moved to the wildlife management area. The FWP tracked her movements into the North Fork of the Blackfoot River and she denned up in the Bob Marshall Wilderness area and her collar went dead in the fall of 2000.

A study by an interagency grizzly bear study team tracked radio-collared bears and they had documented that many bears, particularly males leave remote areas to find gut piles left by hunters. The state and federal biologists said that grizzlies seem to know when elk hunting season begins the same way they know when the salmon are going to run up the streams at certain times of the year.

It was also found that the bears might be actually attracted to gunshots to guide them to the food sources. These studies appeared to backup what bear managers and experienced hunters and outfitters had been saying for a long time: When the elk started to bugle and people began setting up their hunting camps the bears realized the time was right.

Game officials estimate that hunters leave about 370 tons of guts and discarded meat in the field every year. For the grizzly bears desperate to put on fat before a long winter's sleep this food source is too tempting, and it has changed their travel and how they react to people in the woods. Where as twenty years earlier outfitters and guides considered it a rarity to sight a grizzly in the mountains, presently the animals are even following hunters to the meat.

Mr. Hilston was born and raised in Ohio but he had fallen in love with Montana after being stationed at Malmstrom Air Force base at Great Falls. Although he was later transferred from Montana he returned to his adopted state when he was discharged in 1983.

After being discharged Timothy Hilston worked his way back to Montana and he lived in Missoula and Billings before finally settling again at Great Falls in 1998. Hilston was an X-Ray service engineer and he spent most of his free time in what he loved best, hunting, fishing and hiking in the mountains.

Tim's body was found in a beautiful location, a lightly timbered area not far from a grassy meadow.

(Endnotes)
[1] Great Falls Tribune, 8/1/1924, p5

Chapter Eight:

KILLED BY OTHER CAUSES

While they are as deadly and sad as the others hunting fatalities in this book, the tragic incidents in this chapter are by far the most interesting. There are accounts of early beaver trappers being killed by Indians shortly after the Lewis and Clark Expedition and another man who died in 1940, some sixty years after suffering wounds as a child at the hands of Indians when his parents were killed while hunting on the prairie.

A tragic poaching affair in 1908 left five men dead over a $1 hunting permit and their principles. Twenty-eight U.S. Army soldiers froze to death in the single largest hunting accident while another group of hunters left one of their own to freeze. The vast majority of hunters have died alone like the young man that was killed when he fell in front of a car along a dirt road.

There have been other men who have died falling from cliffs, from trees and from the sky in airplanes while hunting game in Montana. Hunters have died of suffocation, blood poisoning and carbon monoxide and even a case of the bubonic plague.

Stray bullets, ricochets and falling trees have killed several hunters while few others have died in bear and deer traps and on a bicycle.

Chapter Eight: DEATH BY OTHER CAUSES

(KILLED BY INDIANS)
Fall of 1808
("History and Stories of Nebraska" by Addison Erwin Sheldon and other histories)
Two of the earliest hunting related fatalities in what later became the state of Montana were those of 32-year-old trapper, John Potts and an unknown Blackfeet Warrior in what is now Madison County in the fall of 1808.

Potts had been trapping on the Beaverhead River near Point of Rocks, now known as Beaverhead Rock about 11 miles southeast of today's Twin Bridges with John Colter. Potts and Colter along with George Drouillard were all members of the Lewis and Clark expedition who returned to the headwaters of the Missouri in 1807 when the rest of the Corps of Discovery returned to the East.

The three veterans of the famous Corps of Discovery accompanied Manuel Lisa back up the Missouri River on an expedition to establish trading posts to trade with the Indians and to trap beavers.

At the Montana/North Dakota boundary the crew went down the Yellowstone River and they built Fort Manual Lisa near the mouth of the Big Horn River where they spent the winter.

The following fall Manuel Lisa returned to St. Louis to organize another mission while he sent Colter and Potts to the headwaters of the Missouri to trap beaver in the heart of Blackfeet Indian country.

The two white trappers knew first hand that the Blackfeet Indians were still furious about loosing two of their young warriors to the Lewis and Clark expedition when they tried to steal horses from members of the corp in northern Montana and for that reason they set their traps at night, took them in early in the morning and hid and skinned their catch during the day.

Chapter Eight: DEATH BY OTHER CAUSES

Even with the extra precautions the two white trappers were eventually discovered by a larges band of Indians. As the story goes, the two men were in a canoe when Colter thought he heard the horses of Indians and wanted to hide but the older Potts thought the noise was from a herd of buffalo and they continued.

When confronted by the Indians, Potts knew that the Blackfeet would dismember their bodies and he refused to surrender with Colter. John Potts reportedly yelled out that he would kill at least one of them, and he was shot full of arrows after he killed one of the Indians.

The Indians immediately tore Potts' body apart and threw many of his organs at Colter. The relatives of the dead Indian wanted to kill Colter but the leader of the band gave the trapper a chance to run for his life. This was when Colter made his historical escape from the Indians and his epic 200-mile walk back to Fort Raymond with only a blanket.

(KILLED BY INDIANS)
April 10, 1810
(From "Montana's Fur Trade Era" by F. Lee Graves)
(The Lewis and Clark Rediscovery Project)
Another original members of the Lewis and Clark Expedition met his death at the hands of the Blackfeet while trapping in the country that he loved.

The fierce Blackfeet Indians killed <u>George Drouillard</u> and another <u>Two Trappers</u> while they were trapping on the Jefferson River near present day Three Forks.

Drouillard had been an interpreter and the favorite hunter of the Corps of Discovery and he soon became Manuel Lisa's right-hand man in the wilderness that later would become Montana. Lisa and his newly organized Missouri Fur Company including George

Drouillard returned to the Yellowstone River to trap and establish trading posts as soon as the ice broke in the spring 1809.

The company spent the winter at Fort Manuel Lisa during the winter and in the spring of 1810 a group of trappers guided by John Colter crossed over the famous Bozeman Pass to the headwaters of the Missouri River. In April they built Fort Henry or Three Forks Post on the strip of land between the Jefferson and Madison Rivers.

The company normally trapped in large groups for security purposes but after a couple of weeks the 33-year-old Drouillard went out alone with two Delaware Indian trappers and they were attacked by a large group of Blackfeet. When the three trappers failed to return, a search party went out and the bodies of the men were found not far from the stockade.

The Indians apparently took extra pains in mutilating George Drouillard's body, and many people believed it was retribution for his and Meriwether Lewis' deadly encounter with the young Blackfeet warriors on the Marias River in 1806.

(KILLED BY INDIANS)
April 12, 1810
(1810 Report by Pierre Menard)
("Montana's Fur Trade Era" by F. Lee Graves)
Two days after the Blackfeet had killed George Drouillard and the two Delaware Indian trappers the large band Indians killed James Cheeks and four other trappers named, Hull, Ayres, Rucker and Freehearty near the Three Forks of the Missouri. During that encounter the Indians lost at least one unknown Blackfeet Warrior and at least one more critically wounded.

It was suspected that the English, who were supplying the Blackfeet with arms and ammunition, were in fact paying the Indians to kill off the Americans in the western territories. Although the company of men at the Three Forks had been able to keep the large band of Blackfeet at bay, as they rarely were willing to fight in an even battle against the whites, the trappers were being picked off while they were working their traps in small groups.

One such group of 11 Missouri River Fur Company trappers was detached from the fort with 7 horses and a large amount of gear. On the morning of April 12, 1810 most of the party were out trapping when the Blackfeet pounced on Cheeks and Ayers at their camp. It was here that Cheeks apparently killed the one Indian and possibly another before he was hacked to pieces in the usual Blackfeet fashion.

The party of Indians then tracked down each of the other trappers working their traps alone and killed Hull, Rucker and Freehearty. Michael Immel and the other five trappers including one by the name of Valle escaped and they made their way back to the main party. Returning to the scene, the party buried what was left of Cheeks and Ayers but they never did find the remains of the other three men.

The enraged trappers immediately went after the Blackfeet in force and the retreating Indians abandoned 44 traps and three of the horses that they had stolen from their victims. After the terrible loss of men, gear, horses, guns, traps and pelts the company began sending out teams of 14 to 16 men with only 3 traps each, but the moral of the company had become so demoralized that they finally abandoned the post and relocated.

(KILLED BY INDIANS)
May 4, 1823
(From "Montana's Fur Trade Era" by F. Lee Graves)
<u>Four Trappers</u> of William Ashley's Rocky Mountain Fur Company were killed by the Blackfeet Indians near the mouth of the Smith River on the Missouri River between Great Falls and Ulm.

The surviving seven trappers of the troop led by Ashley's partner, Andrew Henry abandoned their traps and returned to the mouth of the Yellowstone River.

Chapter Eight: DEATH BY OTHER CAUSES

Andrew Henry and his trappers continued to trap the many
tributaries along the Yellowstone River with success but he returned
to St. Louis in August of 1824 and he never returned. He later said
that a fortune could have been made in the Missouri and Yellowstone
country if it hadn't been for the Indians.

(KILLED BY INDIANS)
May 31, 1823
(From "Montana's Fur Trade Era" by F. Lee Graves)
(The Yellowstone Genealogy Forum on Indian Rock)
The Blackfeet Indians massacred another group of trappers in May of
1823, this time near the mouth of Alkali Creek on the Yellowstone
River near present day Billings. Michael Immel, Robert Jones and
Five other Trappers were killed and four others were wounded.

After this terrible loss of life and over $15,000 worth of furs, horses,
guns, traps and other supplies the Missouri Fur Company pulled the
rest of their trappers and traders from the area.

Near the site of the massacre there was a huge chunk of sandstone
that jutted out of the ground and it reportedly appeared to have
fallen off the nearby cliffs dove into the ground. For years this stone
was referred to as the "Indian Rock" and was near several Indian
trails, one being a trail leading to Big Porcupine and the Blackfeet
Nation.

It was said that the rock had hieroglyphics on its base, which
supposedly portrayed an ancient Indian battle, but they apparently
weren't significant to the early Billings residents at the turn of the
twentieth century and the rock was destroyed to make way for further
development of the city.

As the construction crew was excavating the site behind the rock
they reportedly uncovered the skulls of 7 white men. There were
no Indian artifacts found in the area and because the skulls have

disappeared over the years, it may never be known if they were in fact the remains of Immel, Jones and the other 5 trappers killed near the site in 1823.

(KILLED BY INDIANS)
January 30, 1832
(John Work's Journal; 8/18/1831-7/27/1832)
The Hudson Bay Company also had their share of troubles with the Blackfeet Indians in Montana.

John Work reported that after losing several of their trappers to the Piegans during the winter of 1831 between the Hell Gate Canyon at present day Missoula and Monture Creek near what is today Ovando, their main party was attacked by some 300 Blackfeet near their encampment at what is today Dillon on January 30, 1832.

During the 6-hour battle the Blackfeet and Gros Ventres Indians managed to kill a <u>Flathead Indian Trapper</u> and wounded 8 other men of the company.

(KILLED BY INDIANS)
October 14, 1832
("Adventures of Captain Bonneville" Washington Irving)
("Montana's Fur Trade Era" by F. Lee Graves)
<u>Henry Vanderburgh</u> and another trapper, a Frenchman named <u>Monsieur Pilou</u> of the American Fur Company were killed when a band of 100 Blackfeet Indians attacked their small band of white trappers.

Also killed in the short battle along the Ruby River near present day Sheridan in Madison County was an unknown <u>Blackfeet Warrior</u> who was reportedly killed by Vanderburgh.

In the spring of 1832 Henry Vanderburgh and Andrew Drips of the American Fur Company decided to divide their forces in order to cover more trapping grounds. Soon after they had separated, Vanderburgh and his 50 men received word from their scouts that they had come across the recent hunting camp of the Blackfeet.

The scouts reported that there were buffalo carcasses and campfires, which were still smoking indicating that the Indians had made a hastened retreat.

After Vanderburgh and 9 other trappers had investigated the camp they went in pursuit of the Indians. Vanderburgh had always been known to be wary and on the alert, but on this day he fell for the common tactic used by the Indians, which was to first retreat and then ambush with an over whelming force.

As the white men entered a wooded ravine some of the Blackfeet warriors jumped from their hiding places waving buffalo robes to frighten the horses while others were shooting at the enemy from behind the trees and from the steep cliffs. Vanderburgh's horse was reportedly shot and killed quickly and it pinned its rider to the ground.

As Vanderburgh was crying out for help, his French friend, Pilou quickly ran to his aid but he was shot down and scalped just a few feet away. Seeing that they were badly out numbered and their leader down, the other seven trappers made a quick retreat.

Although Vanderburgh was immobile, he was still armed with his long rifle and two pistols in his belt. As the Indians rushed in to dispatch the pinned rider, Vanderburgh killed one of the warriors with his rifle but before he could go for his pistols he was hacked to death by tomahawks.

The remains of the French trapper were buried where he had fallen but even though the Company had offered a reward for the remains of Henry Vanderburgh they were never located. About a year later at Fort Union, a Blackfeet chief displayed a pair of pistols, which were presumably Vanderburgh's.

(KILLED BY INDIANS)
Early in 1833
(Contribution to the Mont. Hist. Soc., Vol 8 and other sources)
One of the most famous mountain men of the era, Hugh Glass was killed by Indians along with his friend, Edward Rose and another man named Menard while they were trapping in what later became Yellowstone County early in 1833.

Hugh Glass was best known for his legendary encounter with a wounded grizzly, which chewed and mauled him so badly that his companions left him for dead. He lived on and he crawled some 200 miles to safety.

Ed Rose was born in Kentucky, the son of a white trader and a mother who was black and Cherokee. Rose had lived for many years among the Cherokee, Arikara and Crow tribes. Rose took a Crow wife and it was said that he was also a chief of the tribe.

Nothing is known of Menard, but he may have been related to Pierre Menard of the earlier Missouri Fur Company. Nor is there much known about the exact site where the three trappers were killed by the Arikara Indians near present day Billings.

According to the writings of Bonneville's Adventures the three trappers had been working out of Fort Cass near the mouth of the Big Horn River when the Indians surrounded them. The trappers resisted heroically before the Arikars started a prairie fire and rushed over their position under the cover of the smoke.

As a rescue party from the fort was nearing the scene they reportedly heard a loud explosion at the fight scene. The party then found the remains of the three trappers and an unknown number of Indians badly burned and disfigured by the explosion. It was presumed that when the trappers realized that their position was lost they ignited a keg of gunpowder in order to kill themselves along with as many of the Indians as possible.

(KILLED BY INDIANS)
Fall of 1866
(Contributions to the Montana Historical Society, Vol 8, 1917)
Charles Carofel, an old trapper and hunter was killed by the Blackfeet at Pablo's Island on the Missouri River near the present day Judith Landing Recreation Area.

Mr. Carofel had been in the west since 1826 and at the time of his death he was reportedly preparing ingredients to cure his hides and skins.

(FROZE TO DEATH WHILE HUNTING)
February 1874
(The Meagher Republic)
Twenty eight (28) United States Soldiers, under the command of General Frost froze to death while they were hunting buffalo along the old Fort Benton-Helena stage line above Vaughn in February of 1874. This event was referred to for years as the Frozen Hill Massacre.

A party of 70 soldiers left their fort on foot accompanied by several army wagons and mules with their camping outfit, supplies and whiskey to secure meet for their command.

On the third day, while the men were scattered over the prairie killing buffalo, antelope and other game animal they were overcome by a deadly blizzard and the temperatures dropped to 50 below zero. The survivors made it to the Robert Vaughn Ranch where many of them later lost hands and feet to frostbite.

Chapter Eight: DEATH BY OTHER CAUSES

(KILLED BY INDIANS)
4/2/1874
(Helena Weekly Herald)
A man named <u>Rock</u> was shot and killed by about 10 Northern
Blackfeet Indians while he was goose hunting near the mouth of the
Sun River.

The young man and his brother were hunting, one on each side of
the Sun River, when the Canadian band of Indians passed by on
their way to the border with some horses they had stolen from the
Crows.

Even after being mortally wounded, Rock reportedly raised up to
a sitting position and fired both barrels of his shotgun while his
brother commenced firing from the other side of the river.

(KILLED BY INDIANS)
Just days after Custer's Last Stand in June of 1876
(From an article written by Lone Eagle for an issue of "Adventure
Magazine" in 1925, portions reprinted in the Tribune)

In 1925 Lone Eagle, a Sioux Indian was living in the newly formed
Petroleum County where he owned and operated the Eagle Bar
Ranch near Winnett. According to Lone Eagle, the Sioux murdered
a white buffalo hunter by the name of <u>Jim Fowler</u> on their way to
Canada just days after the Indians had destroyed Custer and his
troops on June 25, 1876.

Jim Fowler was said to be in his forties when he was captured along
with his young partner, Walter John Winnett [1]during the fall of 1874
while they were hunting and trapping on the Yellowstone River in
southern Montana.

Over time the two white men settled into their captivity both taking
Indian wives and assuming Sioux names; Fowler was called Ishta-
Tanka, or Big Eye and Winnett was known as Eagle Eye.

As Custer was approaching the Indian encampment on the twenty-fifth of June, Fowler was in the camp near the Little Big Horn River about 13 miles southeast of present day Harlem, and Winnett was off in the hills hunting with four other Sioux Indians.

When Custer's men attacked the Indian village on that fateful day, Fowler was said to have rode towards the battle scene with the Sioux Indians and he reportedly observed the demise of the white soldiers. Although Winnett and his Indian companions heard the gunfire from their location, they were too far away to witness the battle.

The next morning while the Sioux were frantically packing up their camp for a quick escape to Canada, young Winnett made his escape in all the excitement. Walter Winnett eventually settled in Fergus County where he owned one of the largest ranches. The town of Winnett, which eventually became the county seat of Petroleum County was built on part of his ranch and named for the frontiersman.

Things didn't go quite so well for Mr. Fowler. After Winnett's escape, the Sioux feared that Fowler would also attempt to gain his freedom and guide the white soldiers to destroy them. The Indians considered additional guards to watch the white man but in the end they decided to silence him forever. It was said that Rain-In-The-Face of the Hunkpapa Sioux killed Fowler somewhere near the Canadian border and his body was buried in a shallow grave.

Lone Eagle learned this story from his foster father, Big Elk who had taken part in the battle with Custer and he was present when Jim Fowler was killed in 1876. In 1925 Lone Eagle had many mementos of the famous Bighorn Battle that Big Elk had given him including weapons, uniform buttons and even a scalp.

Chapter Eight: DEATH BY OTHER CAUSES

(KILLED BY INDIANS)
February 11, 1881
(Helena Daily Herald)
Indians reportedly murdered <u>Jonathan Erickson</u> while he was returning from a hunt in Custer County with a man named Williams. Erickson had become lame while they were hunting and Williams ran ahead to their cabin to start a fire.

When Erickson didn't get in that night Williams organized a search party the next morning, which soon found the body. The searchers discovered that Erickson had been shot several times and there were fresh Indian pony tracks circling the dead man's body.

(KILLED BY LIGHTNING)
September 1, 1894
(Livingston Enterprise)
Livingston guide <u>B.T. "Curly" Rogers</u> was killed by lightning while he was near an edge of a 300-foot cliff near his hunting camp in the upper Gallatin country in Park County.

Mr. Rogers, his wife and son had all been guiding wealthy New York merchant, John Claflin and several of his friends in the backcountry when the incident occurred.

This trip was the eleventh such Montana hunting trip that the hunter, trapper and guide, "Curly" Rogers had guided the New York sportsman when he was struck by the bolt of lightning and fell several hundred feet into a deep ravine.

A team of men reached Rogers' body by being lowered by ropes over 300 feet to the base of the cliff. The effects of the electric current had discolored the victim's breast down to his left leg.

(KILLED WHILE PLAYING WITH A WEAPON)
January 11, 1896
(Anaconda Standard)

Eleven-year-old <u>Charlie Housman</u> of Deer Lodge was accidentally shot and killed while he was looking down the barrel of a weapon as he was returning from a jackrabbit hunt in the foothills near town.

Emery Schoonover, 14, had left alone to go hunting when the Housman boy joined him as he was entering the city dump. After amusing themselves at the dump by setting a pile of boxes on fire they went on to hunt rabbits at Peter Valiton's meadows.

Having no luck at hunting rabbits, the boys decided to rest beside a haystack before returning to their homes on the east end of Deer Lodge. Charlie reportedly picked up the loaded needle gun by the barrel and laid it down in Schoonover's lap.

Still holding the weapon by the barrel Housman's boyish curiosity got the best of him and he peered down the bore. As he was adjusting the barrel to look straight down it accidentally discharged into his left eye and blew the back of his head off.

Young Schoonover ran back to town and told his father and then they notified Justice of the Peace Haertwell. The judge immediately organized a coroner's jury and the group of men recovered Housman's body and returned it to town.

The jury returned a verdict that Charles Housman had come to his death while carelessly looking into a barrel and they exonerated Schoonover from all blame in the incident. It was reported in the paper that it was hoped that the tragedy might be a warning to the other young boys in the area to be careful with firearms. Although we haven't recorded any other such incidents near Deer Lodge, many other children have met their deaths by playing with firearms.

(KILLED WHILE STRUGGLING OVER GAME BIRDS)
October 20, 1896
William W. White of Little Milwaukee, a suburb of Great Falls
died of blood poisoning in the Columbus Hospital after he was
accidentally shot while struggling with another man over some prairie
chickens.

Apparently an Italian by the name of James Minnea or Mane had
accused White's friend of stealing his game birds and the two men
started the struggle when White was shot in the shoulder.

At first it was thought that the bullet had only gone through White's
shoulder but in fact it had glanced off of a bone and entered his
lung. His condition worsened rapidly and he died within a week.
The funeral for William White at the St. Ann's Church and attended
by the local smelterman's union was reportedly the largest ever held
in Great Falls at the time.

After initially running after the incident, Minnea was arrested at
Cora and brought back to Great Falls where he faced manslaughter
charges.

(KILLED WHEN QUARRELING WHILE HUNTING)
May 6, 1899
Fifteen-year-old John Wills of Lewistown was killed by his 16-year-old
friend, Odilon Ouelette during a quarrel while they were hunting
ducks near their home.

While hunting, the two boys had sat down to smoke cigarettes when
they began quarrelling over some trivial matter and that is when
the fatal bullet was fired. The round went through Wills' lungs and
kidney and he died 12 hours later. Ouelette was immediately arrested
and he was charged with manslaughter for the death of John Wills.

(KILLED BY A LOADED WEAPON IN A MOVING BUGGY)
May 10, 1899

<u>Hugh W. Hutchinson</u> of Monarch died several hours after being accidentally shot while he was goose hunting near Stanford. The 26-year-old Hutchinson was riding in a buggy with Chauncey Stubbs near the Stubbs Ranch at the time of the accident.

After the hunters had traveled down to the creek Hugh reportedly left the buggy to do some shooting. On his return he placed his shotgun between himself and young Stubbs with the butt on the floor and the muzzle under his left arm.

Minutes later as they drove through an irrigation ditch the shotgun accidentally discharged directly into Hutchinson's chest just under his arm. Young Stubbs immediately took the reigns and drove to Lee Bain's place, and there, Mr. Bain helped transport the injured man to the Stubbs Ranch.

Chauncey then left for Stanford to bring back a doctor but he only got as far as Coyote Creek before he was forced to return to the ranch because of darkness and a terrible snowstorm.

Hutchinson died at 9:30 that evening after he reportedly suffered horribly. Because of the bad weather the news of the death didn't get out for another day when J.C. Hutchinson of Monarch received the telegraph reporting his brother's death.

Hugh Hutchinson was buried at the Lower Cemetery at Stanford where it was said that: "there was, there is, no gentler, stronger, manlier man than Mr. Hutchinson."

(DIED IN A STEEL TRAP HE HAD SET FOR A BEAR)
February 10, 1900

(The Glendive Independent)

The remains of a man believed to be <u>George Humphrey</u>, missing for 2 years, was found in the mountains of Madison County with both of his hands locked inside the steel jaws of a bear trap.

Chapter Eight: DEATH BY OTHER CAUSES

These large steel leg-hold traps utilized double springs to operate the 9 to 11 inch teeth-clad jaws. It took both hands of a powerful man to compress each spring, and after securing the first spring with a clamp or wire, the second was pressed down.

After the second spring was compressed, the jaws were set with the trigger. With the trigger set and held by the pressure from the second spring, the first spring was released.

If a trapper was caught by only one hand, he wouldn't be able to release himself from the trap but he could probably free the chain from the stake or tree and go for help, trap and all. But if the trap was secured to a stake or tree, and if both of his hands were caught in the jaws, he wood certainly be doom as was our George Humphrey in 1900.

(FROZE TO DEATH IN HIS TRAPPING CABIN)
February 17, 1900
Robert Waddell was found froze to death by his trapping partner, Ben Hale in their cabin at the head of Birch Creek about 15 miles west of the Summit just inside of Flathead County.

The two men had been running traps in the area and when Hale returned to the cabin from checking his traps he found his partner dead. Apparently Waddell had let the cabin fire die down and didn't awaken from hypothermia. Hale walked to Dupuyer where he reported the death and enlisted help with carrying out the body.

Waddell was from London, England and he had come to Montana from the Northwest Territories where he reportedly owned a ranch near Medicine Hat.

(KILLED WHILE PLAYING WITH A WEAPON)
August 23, 1900
August Lerch of Flathead County was accidentally shot and killed while he was hunting ducks with Edward Turn and another lad.

The boys had been using an unsafe shotgun, which had a hammer that was hard to cock and a hair trigger. The lads had successfully shot a duck, retrieved it from the pond and then they sat on a log.

Edward Turn was smoking while the dangerous gun was lying across his lap pointing toward Lerch. When Lerch reached over to snatch the pipe away from his friend, Turn leaned backward and the gun slipped and it discharged into the body of Lerch. August Lerch was rushed to his house but nothing could be done for him and he died the next morning.

(KILLED WHILE PLAYING WITH A WEAPON)
May 16, 1902
Although we don't normally list small children who have killed themselves or others while playing with firearms, the accidental death of a 5-year-old at an Indian hunting camp qualified because of certain circumstances. Since the incident occurred in a wolf-hunting camp, and because loaded weapons were readily available, this tragic case has been included.

The 5-year-old son of a Canadian half-breed, Henry Kyolle was accidentally shot and killed while he was at a wolfing camp around the East Butte of the Sweet Grass Hills. The Indians had been camped for a couple of weeks on Bear Gulch, which was about 4 miles east of the Whitlash Post office near the Canadian border. Whitlash is located along a gravel road north of Chester in Liberty County.

On the day of the incident, Henry Kyolle and his oldest son were getting ready to leave camp and the latter left his .22-caliber Winchester rifle against the wagon. While the two men were getting their gear together the women were attending the horses while the smaller children were eating their breakfast.

Since the adults were occupied with their work, none of them noticed Kyolle's second son, a 7-year-old, pick up the Winchester and go into the tent where his 5-year-old brother was eating his breakfast.

Chapter Eight: DEATH BY OTHER CAUSES

Because of the hustle and bustle in the camp it was said that no one even heard the shot inside the tent, but the small boy screamed in pain, and then he staggered out of the tent; walked about 15 feet and then fell dead over the wagon tongue.

The small but lethal 22-caliber bullet had entered the boy's left side, went through the heart and then left his body just inside the shoulder blade. Apparently the 7-year-old boy had playfully pointed the rifle at his little brother as he pulled the trigger.

(KILLED BY A STRAY BULLET)
May 30, 1902
A young Chipewa Indian lad named White-Boy died about two weeks after being struck in the side by a stray bullet while he and his friends were crossing the Milk River Bridge.

No one on the bridge heard the shot and it was never learned who had fired the deadly bullet. White-Boy was the son of Little-Bird, a sub-chief among the Cree Indians. White-Boy was buried at dusk in the Indian burial ground located on the Trochee Ranch in Hill County.

(UNKNOWN CAUSES)
December 30, 1903
Gallatin County farmer, G.W. Bowen was accidentally shot and killed while he was hunting with four of his neighbors. Mr. Bowen was married with 4 children the youngest was only a few days old.

(KILLED WHILE PLAYING WITH A WEAPON)
March 16, 1908
Ray Lefebvre, the 12-year-old son of Mr. and Mrs. Zoel Lefebvre was killed by the accidental discharge of a 22-caliber rifle while he was hunting with his 9-year-old brother, Lorin.

On Sunday about 2 o'clock the two boys left their home, which was about 3 miles southwest of St. Peter's Mission, to hunt jackrabbits.

Ray had a shotgun and Lorin was carrying a 22-caliber rifle when the boys sat down on a hillside for a rest.

While they were lying down with their weapons by their sides the two boys began to joke and kid one another. The two boys began to wrestle and when they rolled over the rifle the weapon discharged and the 22-caliber slug entered Ray's head near his left ear, which killed him instantly.

Lorin immediately ran the half-mile to his home with the sad news and a neighbor and his wife carried Ray's body to the families' home.

(KILLED IN A POACHING INCIDENT)
October 21, 1908

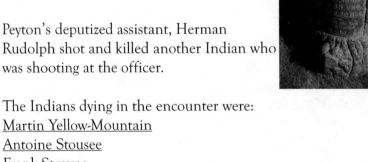

Montana State Assistant Game Warden, Charles B. Peyton reportedly died from a gunshot wound after he had killed 3 Indians while he was arresting one of them for hunting deer without a license in the Swan River country about 65 miles northwest of Ovando.

Peyton's deputized assistant, Herman Rudolph shot and killed another Indian who was shooting at the officer.

The Indians dying in the encounter were:
Martin Yellow-Mountain
Antoine Stousee
Frank Stousee
Camille Paul

By law all Montana residents in 1908, including Indians, were required to purchase a $1 hunting and fishing license to hunt deer and they were allowed to take 3 animals a year. Related tribes of the Flathead Reservation from Canada and Idaho would often hunt in

Montana and claim they were from the Flathead agency and therefore were charged resident fees.

Many Indians however never did purchase hunting licenses and they were also decimating wild game populations throughout the states of Montana and Wyoming at the time. The Indians would often get permission to travel to another reservation and while they were en route they would hunt for deer and other game. They reportedly searched riverbeds with sometimes 50 men abreast with dogs and they would kill every animal or bird they came across.

While bringing in three white forest rangers into Missoula for poaching deer, Warden Peyton received reports of a group of Indians poaching in the Swan Valley. Peyton was reportedly one of the bravest officers in the Fish and Game Department and on the night before his death he walked straight into the Indian camp about 3 miles from the Ben Holland Ranch.

It was determined that the four Indian men at the camp only had three licenses between them. While the Indians claimed that the oldest member of their camp was just a cook, he carried a rifle and he had accompanied them on their hunts.

While Peyton was telling the Indians that they would have to stop killing deer without a license one of the men pulled a rifle. Peyton was too quick and he had his 6-shooter in the Indian's face before he could raise the rifle. The man dropped the weapon and a squaw picked it up and was about to use it when Peyton jumped her and disarmed the woman. Peyton left the camp with a final warning to the Indians to clear out or he would arrest them the following day.

Peyton stayed at the Waldbillig Ranch that night and he was accompanied by Herman Rudolph when he returned to the Indian camp the next morning. As they approached the camp Peyton ordered Rudolph to stay back as it was official business and his duty.

According to Rudolph, Peyton walked into camp where he shot one Indian with his 6-shooter who drew down on him and then shots began to fly. Peyton was shot once in the abdomen but managed to kill two more of the attackers before he went down from his wound. As Rudolph advance to help the officer he started getting fired upon by the Indian women who had run into the woods when the shooting began. Rudolph managed to kill the last Indian and then mounted his horse and rode to the Waldbillig Ranch.

When Joe Waldbillig and Rudolph returned to the scene within 30 minutes and they found the dead warden and the 4 Indians in the same condition. The squaws later went to another Indian camp and got some men to help them move the dead Indians.

The violent encounter on Holland's Prairie lives on even today from both the Warden Peyton perspective and from the Indian position. The Indians on the Flathead Reservation have mounted a successful campaign to paint the fallen deputy warden as a racist and many whites have judged his law enforcement tactics, which were legal and customary in 1908 by the strict and sanitized techniques of today.

Some time ago many game wardens of the Montana Fish Wildlife and Parks Department petitioned for Peyton's name to be added to the Montana Law Enforcement Memorial but the department would not sponsor the action.

(KILLED IN A FALL)
December 4, 1908
Alexander MacAulay, a prominent businessman and legislator of Butte was killed in a fall from the high peaks of the Teton Mountains while he was hunting sheep near Midvale, present day East Glacier, in a remote and wild area of what was Teton County, now Glacier County.

Mr. MacAulay's body might have never been found if it weren't for his faithful dog, which remained by his master's body until it was located. MacAulay was an ardent sportsman and on Tuesday he and another hunter disregarded the warnings of the local mountaineers and ventured high among the dangerous cliffs at that time of year that they were the most treacherous.

The two men became separated in the cliffs and when MacAulay didn't rendezvous as scheduled his companion began searching for him. After a day and a half, MacAulay's companion heard the barking dog and he found the partial snow-covered corpse at the base of a steep cliff.

Mr. MacAulay was about 50 years old at the time of his death and he was a native of Scotland but he had lived in Butte for a number of years where he was engaged in the manufacture of tents and awnings. He was heavily involved in the Republican Party and he had served in the state legislature. He also supported local sports and was a leader of the Scots of Butte and their sport of curling.

(KILLED IN A FALL)
January 23, 1912
The body of Leon Stevenson, a well-known hunter of Bridger was found at the base of a cliff after being the object of a month long search after failing to return from a rabbit hunt.

Stevenson apparently fell off the cliff during a blinding snowstorm and then he crawled some 30 yards in a vain effort to reach shelter before he died.

(KILLED BY A FALLING WEAPON)
September 3, 1913
Mrs. James Morris of Havre was killed instantly while she was hunting on Beaver Creek about 20 miles south of town. Mr. and Mrs. Morris and her sister and husband, Mr. and Mrs. Robert Langford had hired liveryman, Harry Willets to drive them out to Beaver Creek.

After an hour or two of bird hunting and fishing the party gathered around the automobile to pose for a group photograph. The game birds were arranged in front of the car and two of the shotguns were placed across the hood of the vehicle.

The two sisters were standing on the running boards, one on each side of the car, and as Mr. and Mrs. Langford was settling into position for the picture the car shook slightly and one of the guns slipped off of the hood and fell to the ground. The sudden blast was deafening and Mrs. Morris received the full charge in the head and she died instantly.

(KILLED IN A FALL)
October 5, 1913
J. Dulen of Libby fell to his death while he was hunting Rocky Mountain Goats in the Cabinet Mountains. He had been hunting with several companions along the high and rocky ridges of the range, which is about 20 miles south of Libby.

Witnesses reported that Mr. Dulen fell about 125 feet onto a rock ledge, bounced off and then dropped another 300 feet to the bottom of the cliff. His body was taken out to Libby the following day.

(DIED FROM BLOOD POISONING FROM
A GUNSHOT WOUND)
July 29, 1914
Thirty-two-year-old Millegan rancher, Ervin M. Hilton, died of blood poisoning at the Deaconess Hospital in Great Falls after a long battle for his life from an accidental gunshot wound he sustained at his ranch house.

Although Mr. Hilton wasn't hunting at the time of the accident it was the result of an unsafe habit of keeping a loaded weapon at the ready for the purpose of hunting and shooting animals on his place.

Hilton kept the loaded shotgun hanging on the wall next to his outside door for easy access but on this fateful day the weapon fell to the floor as he closed the door. The shot struck him in the left leg inflicting a terrible wound to his ankle. Mr. Hilton left a wife and two children.

(KILLED BY A LOADED WEAPON IN A MOWING MACHINE)
September 22, 1914

Carl Pearson, the 12-year-old son of Mr. and Mrs. Ola Pearson, was killed instantly with a shotgun that he was carrying on a mowing machine as it was being pulled by a team of horses.

The child was driving the mowing machine for his father and he had taken the gun along "just in case he saw a rabbit." The weapon apparently slipped from the machine and it accidentally discharged into the boy's neck and chest and he fell between the rig and the team of horses.

The lad's father and a hired man were working near by and they ran to the scene when they heard the shot. The well-trained team of horses stopped immediately and they didn't pull the mower over the boy's body but he was dead by the time the men reached him.

His parents and an older brother and sister survived the boy. The Pearson family had come from Litchfield, Minnesota and they had recently settled on the C.H. Campbell Ranch in the Sun River Valley.

(KILLED IN A DEER TRAP)
November 21, 1915

Twenty-one-year-old Henry Divis was fatally wounded by a shotgun blast in a deer trap on a road 6 miles northwest of Troy in Lincoln County.

A neighbor of the Divis Ranch, Granville Boyd had set up the deer trap, which consisted of two shotguns about 150 feet across from each other and rigged by trip wire. These traps were often set up on game trails and they were designed to shoot deer or other game as they frequented the path.

Chapter Eight: DEATH BY OTHER CAUSES

Henry Divis was returning to his home on horseback on the evening of November 19 when his horse tripped the first shotgun and it was struck in the side. Divis dismounted his wounded horse and he began leading it to the Boyd Ranch for help when he ran into the second trip wire and he was shot in the groin.

Mr. Boyd heard the shots, ran to the scene and carried the wounded young man back to his house. Boyd then rushed to Troy for a doctor but Divis still died from his wounds at midnight. Henry Divis was single and he was living with his parents at the time of his death. As for Mr. Boyd, he was arrested and charged with manslaughter.

(KILLED IN AN AVALANCHE)
December 16, 1916
Thirty-three-year-old Park County rancher, Ernest Carlisle was killed on December 5, 1916 while he was hunting elk when an avalanche of snow buried him in the Miner Basin country.

(KILLED IN AN AVALANCHE)
December 20, 1916
(Weekly Courier)
Nick Carr, a Cooke City miner was killed while he was hunting near the Wyoming border on December 6, 1916 by a snow slide.

This was the fourth fatal avalanche in the area, one killing a soldier the previous winter at Mammoth Hot Springs in Yellowstone Park, several school children and their teacher were killed in an another, and days earlier another hunter, Ernest Carlisle was killed.

(ABANDONED BY HIS HUNTING COMPANIONS)
October 29, 1917
The frozen body of Adelore Lafrinire was found in the hills near Potomac in the Blackfoot Valley after being caught in a terrible blizzard while he was on a hunting trip with his friends.

Fifteen-year-old Lafrinire was with several of his companions when they were suddenly engulfed in a blizzard. Lafrinire reportedly collapsed from exhaustion as the party was rushing out of the mountains to safety. He was carried as far as possible, but he was finally left behind with the intentions of returning to him with help.

This story is similar to the one about the doomed Carlan hunting party that had ventured into the Clearwater country along the Montana-Idaho border in the 1890s. In that story the party of hunters left a camp cook behind, and he was also later found dead.

(KILLED WHILE PLAYING WITH A WEAPON)
December 6, 1917
Eleven-year-old <u>James Donald Ashe</u> of Devon died at a hospital at Conrad after being accidentally shot by one of his friends. The tragedy was the result of playing around with what was presumed as an unloaded weapon after returning from a hunt.

Shortly after returning home, which was between Chester and Shelby, an older boy playfully pointed his weapon at Ashe and the trigger was pulled and the victim was struck in the hip joint. James The Ashe boy was hurried to the hospital and where everything possible was done to save his life but infection set in and he eventually died.

(KILLED BY A LOADED WEAPON IN A MOVING WAGON)
September 21, 1919
Nineteen-year-old <u>Clyde Fryer</u>, the son of Livingston businessman, Alderson John Fryer was killed in an unusual hunting accident while he was riding in a spring wagon near McLeod about 12 miles south of Springdale.

Fryer and his companions, Charles Mendenhall and John Carney had been standing behind the wagon seat while they were traveling down a road on their way home from hunting. Clyde Fryer was apparently leaning over his loaded double-barrel shotgun when the wagon struck a rock on the road, which caused the young man's head to move over the muzzle at the same time the weapon accidentally discharged. Both barrels of the shotgun struck Fryer in the face tearing away the right side of his head.

(KILLED BY A LOADED GUN IN A VEHICLE)
October 2, 1921
<u>Floyd Lewis,</u> a 28-year-old farm hand on the Goetz Ranch near
Cascade died at the Columbus Hospital at Great Falls from an
accidental gunshot wound while he was returning from duck
hunting.

Mr. Lewis was crossing a creek near the ranch house in a light
roadster when the vehicle began to spin out on the slippery rocks in
the stream. The loaded shotgun at his side slid out of the open door
and it discharged when it struck the running board. The shotgun
blast struck Lewis in the right leg just above the knee and some of the
shot struck him in the chest and face.

The wounded man was immediately taken to the ranch house and a
physician was called. The doctor and the others drove Lewis to Great
Falls at 4 o'clock the next morning and his right leg was amputated
and several pieces of shot were removed from his eye leaving him
blind. Unfortunately the doctors weren't able to save the young man
and he died that evening at 5 p.m.

(KILLED BY A FALLING WEAPON)
September 27, 1923
Assistant car foreman for the Great Northern Railway, <u>Fred Mock</u>
of Cut Bank was accidentally killed and Miss Lora Ricards narrowly
escaped death while they and others were hunting at Rock Coulee
about 5 miles north of the W.P. Yunk Ranch and 18 miles from Cut
Bank.

Mr. Mock had been duck hunting with Ernest Crerar and Joe
Anderson and Lora Richards, Dorothea Halvorson and Della Leech
accompanied them.

Crerar went off in one direction while Mock and Anderson went
hunting in another area as the ladies remained at their car. Crerar
returned to the vehicle with a duck and he and the women drove up
the road to pick up the other two men.

Chapter Eight: DEATH BY OTHER CAUSES

After informing Mock and Anderson of his trophy, Crerar opened up the trunk to show them the duck. When the two hunters set their shotguns against the automobile and leaned over the vehicle Mock's weapon accidentally discharged. The hammer of the old-fashioned double-barrel shotgun apparently hit the running board and discharged into Mock's chest and lightly peppered Miss Richards' face.

Fred Mock was taken to a hospital in Cutbank where he received medical attention by Drs. Neraal and Nelson but he died shortly afterward.

(KILLED BY A DOG STEPPING ON A LOADED WEAPON)
October 28, 1924
The 6-year-old son of Mr. and Mrs. Luman Cavyell died from injuries he received from an unusual hunting accident in McCone County.

The boy and his older brother were shooting black birds in a cornfield on their parent's farm, which was about 3 miles south of Wolf Point. The older boy had laid the cocked .22-caliber rifle on a clump of weeds while he and his little brother ran after a wounded bird.

As the boys were running down the bird their dog also gave chase and as it ran to the boys it stepped on the trigger of the rifle and the bullet hit the boy in the abdomen. The child reportedly died before his father could return from town with a doctor.

(KILLED BY A FALLING WEAPON)
December 2, 1924
Hunt Coy, the young nephew of Mrs. R.E. Coy of Laurel was accidentally shot and killed while he was hunting rabbits on the Schauer Ranch about two and a half miles from town.

Hunt Coy and his school friend, Russell Ward had decided to go hunting after school and they went to a pile of lumber near where an oil derrick had blown over recently.

Apparently Hunt Coy had set his gun against the pile of lumber and while he was crouched over checking for rabbits the weapon fell over and discharged. The round entered the right side of his chest and then it went into his abdomen.

(KILLED BY A RICOCHET)
October 27, 1925

Pleasant Valley rancher, <u>H.E. Betts</u> died in a Kalispell hospital after being struck by a ricochet bullet while he was hunting on the E.G. Ranch about 60 miles from Kalispell.

Mr. Betts was hunting with Kalispell attorney, David Ross when he shot and killed a deer. While Betts was dressing out his animal Ross fired at another deer and his shot missed the animal and the bullet ricocheted off a rock and struck Betts' right arm and it pierced his lungs.

Hunting guide, James Whilt happened by with a horse and he assisted Mr. Ross to carry Betts the 4 miles to the E.G. Ranch house. Dr. Conway of Kalispell arrived at the ranch at about 7:30 pm that evening but they didn't transport the wounded man to the hospital until the next morning.

(UNKNOWN CAUSES)
November 1, 1926

A boot containing the skeletal foot of an unknown <u>Buffalo Hunter</u> and his Sharps rifle were plowed up on Big Island near Sidney. Frank Garsage discovered the relics as he was breaking ground near an old stump on his land.

The rifle was an "Old Reliable" model of the Sharps Arms Company of Bridgeport, Connecticut. This weapon had an octagonal barrel, weighed 16 pounds and it had one hammer governed by 2 triggers, one being referred to as a "set trigger." Except for the warped stock and despite all the rust, the rifle was said to be in pretty good condition.

Richland County Sheriff O'Brien was born and raised within 4 miles of the location and he estimated that the remains had been buried for at least 50 years.

Under Sheriff Obgerfell recalled that 25 years earlier when he was just a boy, he and his brother found the other boot and the man's skull in the same spot while they were collecting firewood.

Another set of remains, which were also probably of a buffalo hunter, were found in December of 1920 in the badlands east of Ekalaka in Carter County. Two boys found several human bones including a jaw containing several teeth while they were hunting in the bluffs near Horse Creek. Sheriff Boggs and a number of other people from Ekalaka later visited the area where the remains were discovered.

Further investigation proved that the body had been buried on a slope and the bones were brought to the surface after many years of erosion from rains and snow cover. The grave was found near two ancient dugouts and a fireplace, which were described as obviously fashioned by white men.

The Carter County sheriff and his deputies surmised that the victim had probably been a buffalo hunter because of the evidence at the scene including remnants of a pair of boots and empty large caliber cartridges.

(KILLED IN A DEER TRAP)
November 20, 1925

James Geer was accidentally killed by a set gun or a gun trap he had set for deer near the Stillwater River about 10 miles west of Whitefish.

Mr. Geer's partner, C.O. Yocum later told the authorities that the two men had been trapping and that they had planned to spend the winter in the cabin of C.W. Koontz.

Yocum reported that Geer had borrowed his Winchester .30-30 rifle to go hunting near the river. After about an hour Yocum said he heard a shot and then Geer's calls for help. Geer was alive when Yocum found him but by the time he returned with help he had bled to death.

The coroner's jury later ruled that Mr. Geer came to his death from a gun set by his own hand. The rifle was attached to a board, which was nailed to a tree and course black threat was used as the trip wire, which was attached to the trigger of the weapon.

Geer had set the trap, took a detour to another sight and he apparently lost his bearings in the thick brush and he accidentally tripped the rifle himself, which struck him in the right hip.

A spool of the black threat was found in Geer's pocket and Yocum testified that he had seen the victim with the board that was used to attach the rifle to. Very little was known of James Geer other than he was of middle age and had come to Montana from Minnesota.

(KILLED BY A FALLING WEAPON)
September 17, 1926
(Anaconda Standard)
After surviving 13 months of combat without an injury in France during World War I. Richard "Dixie" Driscoll, 27, of Butte was accidentally shot and killed while he was hunting ducks at Piedmont Lake, about 2 miles from Whitehall.

Richard Driscoll had been working for Richard Bray for several days on his farm when the two men decided to join the other duck hunters on opening day. After shooting a couple of ducks they were heading to the Bray Ranch when they met Barney Cook in a nearby duck blind.

When they reached the blind Mr. Bray leaned his double-barrel shotgun up against the shelter as they were talking. The weapon slipped to the ground and it accidentally discharged into Driscoll's back and he was dead within 5 minutes. An inquest was held by an acting coroner from Whitehall and it was determined that the death was purely accidental with no blame attached to Richard Bray.

(KILLED BY A LOADED GUN IN A VEHICLE)
November 14, 1926
James Royan died at a hospital in Williston, North Dakota after being accidentally shot while he was hunting at Smoke Creek about 9 miles north of the Logan Walker Ranch near Froid in Roosevelt County.

Mr. Royan was hunting coyotes with Allan Purves when they tried to drive their light vehicle across Smoke Creek. While they were trying to make it up the steep bank their engine stalled and the car slid backward and rolled into creek.

During the rollover a rifle in the car accidentally discharged and the bullet entered Royan's abdomen and it came out through his back above the kidneys.

As Purves was trying to get Royan out of the vehicle Logan Walker and Joe Obershaw came by with a load of coal for Froid. They took Mr. Royan to Froid and from there he was rushed to Williston where he died the next day. James Royan left a wife and a 13-year-old daughter and a son about 7 years old.

(KILLED BY A FALLING WEAPON)
October 17, 1928
Henry L. Houston, 54, of Great Falls died at the Columbus Hospital from an accidental gunshot wound while he was hunting deer in the Little Belt Mountains.

Mr. Houston left Great Falls with Ernest Steel and they had breakfast with their guides Sidney O'Connor and his son, Jack at Niehart. The party then drove 16 miles out of the mining town near the cabin of Jack Tripp.

Chapter Eight: DEATH BY OTHER CAUSES

Shortly after the men had separated Mr. Steel said he heard a shot followed by Mr. Houston shouting for help. It took about 20 minutes for Steel to locate his friend lying over a log with a gunshot wound. After firing 3 times to signal their companions, Steel administered first aid to the injured man.

Henry Houston was conscious and he explained that he had laid the rifle on a windfall and it had slipped off and accidentally discharged into him while he was sitting down resting. The bullet struck him in the hip and then it traveled through his back. Another factor in the accident was that Houston had borrowed the rifle from a friend and therefore not familiar with its operation.

The younger O'Connor was first on the scene and he and Mr. Steel tried to carry the wounded man, but they found that he was too heavy. Meantime the elder O'Connor met Jack Trip coming up the mountain with 2 horses to pack out some game he had shot. Sidney O'Connor took one of the horses to the accident scene and Mr. Houston was placed on the animal while another member rode behind and held onto him.

It took about 3 hours for the party to make their way down the two miles to their car. From there they hurried to the little hospital at Niehart where Mr. Houston was given additional aid before he was taken to Great Falls.

When Houston was first admitted to the Columbus Hospital at 6 o'clock that evening his condition wasn't considered fatal and he was reported as resting comfortably. Then shortly after 9 p.m. he suddenly grew worse and he was dead an hour later.

Mr. Houston had worked for the Armour Company for 22 years and he had managed both the Billings and Great Falls branches. Henry Houston left a wife and a son and daughter.

Chapter Eight: DEATH BY OTHER CAUSES

(KILLED BY A RICOCHET)
December 31, 1928
Leroy Jensen, the 16-year-old son of Mr. and Mrs. Nels Jensen of Lindsay was accidentally shot and killed while he was hunting on Christmas Day.

Leroy had gone rabbit hunting in their car with his brother, Milo Jensen and neighbor boys, Walter and Robert Schoengarth. Milo's rifle reportedly accidentally discharged and the bullet struck a nearby boulder and then ricochet into his brother's right cheek, killing him instantly. The untimely funeral for young Leroy Jensen was held in the family home near Lindsay in Dawson County.

(KILLED IN A FALL)
November 2, 1929
(Livingston Enterprise)
The body of 35-year-old Alva Williams of Big Timber was found frozen stiff in about 3 feet of snow on the Chester Martin Ranch near Hubbel in the Absaroka Mountains about 50 miles south of Big Timber.

Apparently Mr. Williams had broken his shoulder in a fall while he was hunting alone on Elk Creek, a tributary of the East Boulder River. Williams was found 2-days later on Thursday October 31 by a search party led by Sweet Grass County Sheriff, Ed Brannan.

Mr. Williams' body was in a clump of bushes at the base of a hill and it probably would never have been found if it weren't for a bear. A fresh snow had covered Williams' tracks but a bear had apparently walked to the dead body and after sniffing the man it left the scene. After losing the tracks of the missing man the searchers followed the bear tracks and they lead them to the body.

Alva Williams worked on ranches in the Big Timber area, and in the fall and winter he hunted and trapped predatory animals. He was on such a hunting and trapping trip when he failed to return and his friends initiated the search.

After investigating the body of the experienced mountaineer the authorities discovered a shoulder had been broken and bruised indicating that the man had apparently lost his footing and had fallen down a steep mountainside.

The position of the dead man's body indicated that he had crawled on his back for a considerable distance to find shelter in the clump of bushes. Empty rifle cartridges at the scene proved that Williams had fired all of his ammunition in an attempt to attract help. Further evidence showed that he had also tried to build a fire but failed.

(KILLED BY A LOADED GUN IN A VEHICLE)
November 29, 1932
Eleven-year-old Everett Hoar died from a shotgun blast to the face while he was sitting in a car with some of his friends. The shotgun accidentally discharged as it was being passed around in the vehicle.

The boys had returned from hunting and Everett Hoar had gotten in the back seat with two other young boys while the others got into the front with the loaded weapon.

The other two boys in the rear seat were also injured when the shotgun was passed back from the front of the car.

(KILLED BY A FALLING WEAPON)
October 31, 1933
James Vernon Booth, 40, of Missoula died in a local hospital from a shotgun wound he received while on a pheasant hunt with three of his friends.

Mr. Booth and another man had gone to a farmhouse to ask permission to hunt while the third man stayed in the vehicle. While the men were visiting with the farmer, one of the shotguns, which was leaning up in the porch fell over and went off. James Booth was struck by the blast, shattering the bone in his leg.

(KILLED BY A STRAY BULLET)
October 29, 1934
(Missoulian)

Emmitt Claire Watters, 24, of Missoula died in a hospital about 20 hours after he had been struck with a stray bullet while he was deer hunting near Drummond with his brother, Billy.

After the bullet entered Watters' left side and was lodged in his shoulder he was driven 8 miles to Drummond where emergency first aid was administered before he was transported to Missoula.

The wounded man was admitted into a Missoula hospital about 10:30 p.m. Saturday night where he gradually grew weaker until he died at 11:30 a.m. on Sunday morning.

(KILLED BY A STRAY BULLET)
December 19, 1937
(Missoulian)

Well-known Upper Yellowstone Valley rancher, Herman Merene died in a Livingston hospital hours after being shot while he was elk hunting in the "Firing Line" country in southern Park County.

A stray bullet from the rifle of an unknown hunter struck the 35-year-old Merene in the chest and his companions rushed him to the local hospital. There were reportedly about one hundred hunters in the area at the time of the tragedy. Herman Merene left his widow and a one-year-old daughter.

(KILLED BY A LOADED GUN IN A VEHICLE)
September 13, 1938
(Missoulian)
The body of <u>Vernon Ward</u> of Missoula was found in his pickup truck
at the junction of Stephens Avenue and the Bitterroot Road by his
stepson, Alfred Tracy after being missing. The vehicle was in a ditch
with the ignition on and a .30-caliber Winchester rifle in the cab with
the victim.

The official version of Ward's death was that the truck had run off
the highway causing the rifle to accidentally discharge into his head.
Mr. Ward had told his friends that he was going to the Lolo area. His
family and friends said that Vernon Ward frequently went to that
area looking for wood and he usually took his rifle along with him on
the trips in case he spotted game.

(UNKNOWN CAUSES)
November 18, 1938
<u>Dan Mitchell</u> of Shelby was reportedly shot and killed while he was
on a hunting trip. No other details were available.

(UNKNOWN CAUSES)
November 18, 1938
<u>John J. Marshall</u>, 35, of Helena was accidentally shot and killed while
he was hunting. No other details were available.

(KILLED BY A FALLING WEAPON)
October 5, 1939
<u>William Lloyd Wyrick</u>, 27, of Billings was killed when the shotgun he
had leaned against his car fell over and it accidentally discharged. Mr.
Wyrick was struck in his right side and he died minutes later.

(KILLED BY A FALLING WEAPON)
October 9, 1939
Fifteen-year-old <u>Wesley Burger Coley</u> of Billings was shot and killed
while he was hunting rabbits near his home. The .22-caliber rifle he

had leaned against his bicycle fell to the ground and it accidentally discharged into his head.

(DIED FROM AN OLD WOUND SUSTAINED DURING AN EARLIER INDIAN ATTACK)
August 29, 1940
Charles VanBolene Lambert, 67, of Frazer died from complications from a wound he had received 60 years earlier when Indians attacked and killed his family while they were hunting.

In 1880 the 7-year-old Charles was shot twice while his parents and others in the hunting party were killed by a band of Crow Indians. Left for dead, Charles was later found by his aunt who adopted him.

Lambert's aunt had treated a bone injury over the years that never did heal and it eventually brought on his death in 1940. The circumstance of Mr. Lambert's birth was almost as unusual as his death. He was reportedly born on the Missouri River Boat "Josephine" during the trip from St. Louis and Fort Benton.

(KILLED BY A STRAY BULLET)
October 21, 1940
A stray bullet killed 37-year-old Don P. Knapp of Missoula while he was hunting about 30 miles east of the Garden City and just 3 miles north of Ravenna.

The truck driver for the Missoula Mercantile Company was hunting with Harry Larson near Willis Park when they decided to have lunch.

Larson later told the authorities that they were sitting by a tree eating when he heard a shot and turned to Knapp to speak to him about the close gunfire and he noticed that he was dead.

Larson shouted out: "Who's shooting? You killed my partner," and then crawled behind the tree for his own protection. A few minutes later Eno Hill and Ernest Lizotte of Miltown joined Larson behind the tree. They had heard the shot themselves and they had run towards Larson because of his shouts.

The three men went to Missoula and reported the tragedy and said that they had heard about 17 high-powered rifle shots in the area between Ryan and Cramer Creeks.

(KILLED BY A LOADED GUN IN A VEHICLE)
December 3, 1940
Thirty-six-year-old Benjamin Mahr of Billings died at a local hospital from an accidental gunshot wound sustained a week early while he was hunting Chinese pheasants near Custer.

Apparently a .410-guage shotgun in the trunk accidentally discharged into the vehicle in which Mr. Mahr and others were riding. The full charge struck the victim in the buttocks and then penetrated his abdomen.

(KILLED IN A FALL)
November 15, 1945
(Missoulian)
Charles White, a 27-year-old Yellowstone Park Ranger was killed in a fall from a cliff while he was deer hunting near Electric, Montana, just north of the park boundary.

(KILLED BY A STRAY BULLET)
October 18, 1946
Thirty-nine-year-old Frank Meyers of Madison, Wisconsin died in a local hospital 6 days after being shot in the right leg in a hunting accident about 50 miles south of Bozeman.

It was later determined that Robert Fliehas Jr. of Gordon, South Dakota, who was himself wounded in the leg in the Philippines during the war had fired the shot that had struck Mr. Meyers. Mr. Fliehas told the authorities that he had shot at a bull elk from horseback and he apparently missed the animal and hit the hunter by mistake.

When Mr. Fliehas dismounted to take another shot he heard a man shouting for help. Frank Meyers was rushed to Bozeman where his leg was amputated but his condition still deteriorated.

(KILLED BY A STRAY BULLET)
October 24, 1946
George Johnson, about 30, of Butte, was killed in a hunting accident near Sheep Rock Hill, about 14 miles northeast of the mining city.

After being shot by a stray bullet Mr. Johnson was carried to the Frank Sologub Ranch on a litter, which his companions made of shirts and jackets. Although Johnson made it to the Sologub Ranch, he died before medical help could arrive.

The victim had been shot in the chest by a bullet, which the officials later determined was fired by rancher, Frank Sologub while he was hunting on his property.

(KILLED BY A LOADED GUN IN A VEHICLE)
October 12, 1948
Freddy Pitsch, 14, of Garrison was killed instantly after being shot through the heart while he was hunting near Hardin. Freddy had been riding in a small truck with his older brother, Reuben, when a .22-caliber rifle in the front seat between the two boys accidentally discharged when the truck lurched forward.

(KILLED BY A STRAY BULLET)
October 30, 1955
Sixty-five-year-old Clair C. Hood of Sidney, Montana was accidentally shot and killed by an unidentified hunter while he was hunting 4 miles southeast of Savage.

The high-powered rifle round struck Mr. Hood below and to the right of his breast bone and the authorities never did determine who had fired the fatal shot because there were about a dozen hunters shooting in the area at the time.

Mr. Hood's son-in-law, James Lang of Sidney reported that Hood had gone down after several shots had been fired at a deer about 75 to 100 yards away. Lang said that they had been standing in the open, and at first he thought his father-in-law had just "hit the dirt" because of all the shooting.

The victim had been wearing a fluorescent red jacket at the time, and the coroner's jury found that a hunter firing a rifle "in a careless and thoughtless manner" had caused his death.

(KILLED BY A LOADED GUN IN A VEHICLE)
November 12, 1955
Mrs. Robert Pulse, 19, of Eureka was shot and killed on a recent hunting trip with her husband Ted and their friend, Leland Smith. The party was returning home from their hunting trip when a rifle accidentally discharged in the vehicle and the .270-cailiber bullet struck her breastbone and then went through her neck.

(KILLED BY A STRAY BULLET)
October 22, 1956
Clark Russell Lane, 10, of Whitehall died two hours after being struck by a ricocheting bullet while he was rabbit hunting with his brother.

It was reported that 13-year-old Gary Lane had fired at a rabbit, and the bullet killed the animal and then glanced off a rock and hit his brother in the head. Gary carried his little brother down Pump Hill at the edge of Whitehall and then ran for help.

Chapter Eight: DEATH BY OTHER CAUSES

(KILLED IN A VEHICLE CRASH WHILE HUNTING)
October 28, 1957
Kenneth Schmidt, 28, of Butte was killed in a rollover while he was driving off the road while hunting near Shennon Creek in Beaverhead County.

Mr. Schmidt and his two companions were road hunting along a primitive logging road when they came across a slide, which obstructed the trail. While the other two hunters decided to get out of the vehicle and walk across the obstruction, Schmidt attempted to drive across.

As Mr. Schmidt was crossing the slide area the vehicle slid down and it rolled over him. Kenneth Schmidt left a wife and 2 children.

(KILLED BY A STRAY BULLET)
October 19, 1959
Sixteen-year-old James Farstad of Glendive was killed by a stray bullet to the head while he was hunting in the Frenchman Creek area just over the Phillips County line about 65 miles northwest of Glasgow.

The young Farstad boy had been hunting in the brushy country with his father, James Farstad and Nick Harshenko and his 2 sons. The authorities investigating the incident later said that it was unlikely that a member of Farstad's party had fired the fatal shot.

(KILLED BY A FALLING TREE)
October 26, 1959
James Garey, 64, of Kalispell was killed in the Bob Marshall Wilderness area when a large snag fell on him while he slept in his hunting camp. Mr. Garey had been hunting on Gorge Creek, a tributary of Bunker Creek about 25 miles above Spotted Bear.

Chapter Eight: DEATH BY OTHER CAUSES

(KILLED IN AN AIRPLANE CRASH WHILE HUNTING)
September 11, 1962

Duayne Murray, 29, of Lewiston and 27-year-old Ben Peterson Jr. of Buffalo were killed in their Piper Super Cub on a flight from Lewistown to Stanford when they apparently decided to shoot coyotes from their plane.

Their aircraft crashed nose first into the ground about 15 miles west of Lewistown but it never did catch fire. Witnesses reported that the plane made several low passes along the Judith River bottom about 2 miles west of the town of Ross Fork and they heard what sounded like shotgun shots before they saw the plane dive into the river bottom. These accounts were substantiated when a smashed up shotgun was found in the wreckage.

Harold Shankle, a Great Northern section foreman, was the first witness on the scene and he reported the incident to the authorities. Fergus County Sheriff George Stephens and Coroner Jack Newton and an FAA official worked for more than an hour to remove the bodies from the twisted wreckage.

The officials speculated that the flyers may have sighted a coyote and had made a low pass at a slow speed in order to take some shots at the animal and the plane stalled and they were too low for a recovery dive.

The plane belonged to Central Air Service of Lewistown and it was equipped with oversized tires for landing on rough terrain. Duayne Murray was a commercial pilot for Central Air Service and his widow who was expecting their first child survived him. Ben Peterson was himself a private pilot as well as a rancher in the Buffalo area and he left a widow and 4 children.

(KILLED WHILE HUNTING FROM A MOVING VEHICLE)
September 19, 1962

At first the death of 54-year-old Burton O. Burrell of Trego had been attributed to a car accident on a backwoods road about 16 miles southwest of Stryker in Lincoln County on September 14, but an autopsy later revealed that the man's death was caused by a single gunshot wound to the head.

Initially the county coroner had theorized that Mr. Burrell had been riding on the front fender of a moving vehicle while he was hunting grouse, and that he had either jumped or had fallon off and was run over by the car.

Apparently while Burrell and his cousin Robert Burrell were riding on the fenders of the car, which was being driven by one of their wives with their two children in the back seat, one of their rifles accidentally discharged and struck Burton Burrell in the head. After falling from the vehicle the man was then struck by the rear tire.

(KILLED IN A FALL)
October 2, 1962
After being missing for two days, the body of John Higgins, 47, of Kellogg, Idaho was found by a 25-man search party about 50 miles southeast of Missoula behind Lolo Peak.

Once separated from his hunting party, Mr. Higgins had apparently slipped on some ice and he went off a cliff, falling to his death. It took the search party a couple of days to recover the body from the rocky terrain.

(KILLED IN A VEHICLE CRASH WHILE HUNTING)
October 30, 1962
Kenneth Lynnes, the teenage son of Norman Lynnes of Havre died of injuries from a jeep accident Sunday, October 28 while he was hunting south of Lloyd. The jeep he was riding in rolled down a 30-foot embankment and he was crushed.

The young man had been hunting with his father and a neighbor who were following him in their car when they witnessed the accident. Ken Lynnes was first rushed to a hospital in Chinook and he died en route to the hospital at Havre.

Chapter Eight: DEATH BY OTHER CAUSES

(KILLED IN A FALL)
November 12, 1962
Richard Austad, 17, of Fairfield died in a fall from a high ledge about 20 miles west of Augusta in the Willow Creek Gorge area. He had been hunting with two or three other men including his brother who reportedly witnessed the tragic fall.

(KILLED IN A VEHICLE CRASH WHILE HUNTING)
November 12, 1962
Dennis Eaton, 42, of Laurel and Leo B. Johnson of Billings were both killed when their Jeep Wagoneer overturned on Iron Mountain while they were road hunting.

(KILLED BY A RICOCHET)
November 25, 1962
Eleven-year-old Steve Annas of Helena was shot and killed when he was struck in the back by a ricocheting .22-caliber bullet. One of his friends was shooting at a bird when a rounds struck a rock or tree and then it struck the young boy.

(KILLED BY A LOADED GUN IN A VEHICLE)
December 2, 1962
Joe Bernard Cowdry, 20, of Havre was accidentally shot and killed while he was a passenger of a car about 2 miles west of his home.

Cowdry was returning home from hunting rabbits with his friends when he was struck in the back with a high-powered rifle that was accidentally discharged in the back seat. It was reported that the victim's cousin, Allen Cowdry also of Havre, was sitting directly behind him at the time of the incident.

(DIED FROM SUFFOCATION OR ASPHYXIATION) **October 22, 1964**
Albert Altman, 52, of Laurel apparently died of suffocation while he was heating a pot of coffee in a trailer camper. Mr. Altman was found dead in his 2-wheel trailer, which was parked in the Gallatin Canyon on Wapiti Creek about 65 miles south of Bozeman.

The authorities believe that Albert Altman had gotten up to start his coffee and then he apparently fell back to sleep with all the windows closed.

(KILLED BY A ROCK AVALANCHE)
November 22, 1966
Leonard Gilbertson, 38, of Westhope, North Dakota was killed in a rock avalanche while he was on horse back along the Big George Point in the Gibson Reservoir area.

A portion of the trail he was on gave way and Mr. Gilbertson was struck in the head and he fell more than 100 feet down a cliff. It was believed that the rocks had been loosened by mountain sheep and by heavy rains.

(KILLED BY A STRAY BULLET)
November 11, 1967
Robert Michael Barnes, 17, of Missoula was killed in a hunting accident about 45 miles southwest of the Garden City.

Bob Barnes was a passenger in a car with 6 other young men along a creek near the Missoula-Mineral County line when a bullet entered the vehicle just missing Rod Sanderson who was sitting next to Barnes.

The bullet then hit a gun rack in the vehicle and then it struck Barnes in the back. Sanderson reported that right after the car was stopped an unidentified man came running up to the vehicle saying he had just shot an elk.

(KILLED BY A LOADED GUN IN A VEHICLE)
November 19, 1968
John E. Anderson, 41, of Anaconda died from a gunshot wound suffered on November 3 in a hunting accident near Deer Lodge.

Mr. Anderson had been hunting with his brothers and a Deer Lodge man when a loaded weapon fell from a gun rack in the truck and it accidentally discharged. The bullet went through Anderson's left hand and then into the left side of his head.

(KILLED BY VEHICLE WHILE HUNTING)
March 31, 1969
Fourteen-year-old <u>Gary Raunig</u> of Stockett died Sunday afternoon after he fell under a pickup truck while he was hunting gophers with his father and relatives about 10 miles northeast of Augusta along the Sun River.

Gary Raunig was apparently walking on the shoulder of a road when he accidentally lost his footing as a pickup truck was passing by. The rear wheel of the vehicle rolled over the boy's body and he died about 3:30 o'clock that afternoon.

(UNKNOWN CAUSES)
October 29, 1969
<u>Robert L. Kleist</u>, 50, of Prarie DuSac, Wisconsin died while he was hunting with a group on the Wilson Ranch about 12 miles southwest of Broadus.

(KILLED IN AN AIRPLANE CRASH WHILE EN ROUTE)
November 2, 1970
Minneapolis area hunters, 56-year-old <u>Howard H. Hanifl</u> and <u>Charles W. Fuller Jr.</u>, in his 40's were killed in an airplane crash near Carlyle, Montana near the North Dakota border.

Wibaux County authorities reported that the two Minnesota men were apparently coming to Montana for a hunting trip when their light plane developed engine trouble and it plunged to earth just as it crossed the state line.

Chapter Eight: DEATH BY OTHER CAUSES

(KILLED BY A STRAY BULLET)
November 4, 1970
Forty-nine-year-old outfitter and guide, Eugene Chapman was killed instantly by a stray bullet while he was on a hunt in the Lolo National Forest about 30 miles west of Superior. While it was not confirmed at the time, a member of Chapman's own hunting party may have fired the fatal stray bullet.

(KILLED IN A FALL)
November 5, 1971
Dennis A. Steffes, 29, of Illinois died in a fall while he was deer hunting near Big Timber. Mr. Steffes' body was found at the bottom of a 100-foot cliff in the Green Mountain area about 26 miles south of Big Timber.

Mr. Steffes had been hunting with his brother, Terry and Mike Holmberg, both of Illinois. Apparently Dennis Steffes had shot a deer and he approached the edge of the cliff to look over it and he fell to his death.

(DIED FROM SUFFOCATION OR ASPHYXIATION)
November 21, 1971
The bodies of four hunters from Malmstrom Air Force Base who had died of carbon monoxide were found in a suburban pickup in the middle of the Smith River at the crossing to Deep Creek Park.

The dead were Lieutenant Charles Guin, 24; Chief Master Sergeant Dickie Grisham, 41; Master Sergeant Erle Webster, 48 and his 14-year-old son, Larry Webster.

The bodies were found at about 11 o'clock on Saturday morning by two other hunters from the Great Falls air base. They reported that the motor of the suburban was running where it had gotten stuck while attempting to ford the river.

Chapter Eight: DEATH BY OTHER CAUSES

The four men had died about 4 a.m. that morning and the incident was reported about noon from the nearest telephone at Hound Creek.

The doomed men had been heading to their hunting camp near Deep Creek when their 2-wheel drive vehicle skidded off the regular crossing and got stuck in the loose gravel of the stream. The men apparently decided to wait until daybreak before attempting to get their vehicle out of the river.

The authorities said that Sergeant Webster's suburban was resting in about 2 feet of water, which would have normally stalled the motor but apparently the side panel on the vehicle had caused an air pocket that allowed the tailpipe to remain free of water. Although the air pocket had allowed the engine of the truck to run it also caused the exhaust fumes to enter the vehicle even though one of the windows was open 6 inches.

Sergeant Webster was reportedly found holding a flashlight in his hand, which he apparently was using to check his fuel gauge from time to time in the dark. His body and his son's were found in the front seat and those of the other two men were in the rear section.

When found all four bodies were in natural positions as if they had all fallen asleep while waiting for daybreak.

(DIED FROM SUFFOCATION OR ASPHYXIATION)
November 3, 1972
Revie W. Luce, 42, of Frewsburg, New York and 38-year-old Richard S. Rusidak of Cheektowogo, New York were found dead in their pickup camper from apparent asphyxiation. The two New Yorkers had been hunting in the Columbus area.

(KILLED BY A FALLING WEAPON)
October 23, 1973
Kenneth Harvey, 44, of Lewistown was the first fatality of the 1973 Big Game Hunting Season when a hunting rifle, which had been

propped up in the back of a pickup truck fell over and it accidentally discharged.

The rifle discharged just as Harvey was reaching for something in the cab of the truck and the .243-caliber round struck him in the upper back and it came out beneath his chin.

Mr. Harvey's 15-year-old son and two other friends were at the scene and witnessed his death near the head of Waite Creek in the Little Belt Mountains southeast of Lewistown.

(KILLED BY A STRAY BULLET)
November 8, 1973
David Nelson, 41, of Missoula was accidentally shot to death in the Sapphire Range about 25 miles southeast of Darby. Mr. Nelson was a passenger in a 4-wheel-drive vehicle when a bullet came through the passenger window and it struck him in the head.

After the shooting the driver, William Knuckle immediately started down the road on the East Fork of the Bitterroot when they met another vehicle. The person in the other car said that he had just shot at an elk.

(UNKNOWN CAUSES)
November 24, 1974
Thirteen-year-old Don Harkin of Bozeman was killed in a hunting accident in the northern portion of the Gallatin Canyon. He was shot in the stomach, and no other details were available.

(KILLED BY A STRAY BULLET)
October 22, 1975
Linda Palbykin, 25, of Plymouth, Indiana was killed near Nelson Reservoir between Malta and Glasgow when a stray high-powered-rifle bullet struck her in the back.

The Indiana woman was in a party of hunters after game birds and the authorities determined that a deer hunter had fired the bullet that killed her. After a search of the area no other hunter was ever found.

(KILLED BY A LOADED GUN IN A VEHICLE)
March 30, 1976
Kenneth Ray Barner, 17-year-old Choteau High School sophomore was accidentally shot and killed after returning from a gopher hunt with his friend, 16-year-old Mark Baker.

The two boys had just returned from hunting when they parked along side of another car of their friends near the museum at the edge of town. While they were talking a .22-caliber rifle "somehow accidentally discharged" in their vehicle and the slug struck Barner in the head, killing him instantly.

Teton County Coroner Lee Zwerneman ruled the shooting purely accidental, and it appeared to be another classic case of "not thinking the weapon was loaded."

(KILLED BY A LOADED GUN IN A VEHICLE)
October 9, 1976
Sixteen-year-old Barry Drake of Hysham became the first hunting fatality of the 1976-Hunting Season when he was accidentally shot and killed while he was bird hunting along the Yellowstone River.

A shotgun blast struck the Drake boy below his chin as he and his older brother, Roger and a classmate, Mark VanHale were riding home on a small tractor. Barry Drake reportedly dropped the shotgun and it discharged when it struck the draw bar on the tractor.

(KILLED BY A LOADED GUN IN A VEHICLE)
October 25, 1976
Max Clayton Hoff, 33, of Worden was killed with his own rifle in a freak accident while he was attempting to free his vehicle out of a ditch along a country road.

Mr. Hoff's auto had gone out of control and it rolled down a 10-foot embankment and it landed back on its wheels. The tire marks indicated that Mr. Hoff had tried at least four times to drive the 4-wheel-drive vehicle back up the bank when his 7-MM rifle, which was on the passenger side apparently accidentally discharged into his chest.

(KILLED IN AN AIRPLANE CRASH WHILE HUNTING)
November 22, 1976
Edward W. Langford, 67, of Lewistown was killed in a 2-seat Bellanca aircraft when it crashed during a coyote hunt in Fergus County.

The pilot of the plane, Douglas M. Norman, a 24-year-old nephew of Mr. Langford was attempting to land the plane to retrieve a coyote the men had just shot when one of the wings apparently hit something on the ground and the light plane flipped over and caught fire.

Douglas Norman survived the crash with a broken leg and he suffered severe burns while trying to free his uncle from the aircraft.

(KILLED BY A HUNTING KNIFE)
October 23, 1978
Richard McGillis, 24, of Great Falls died after falling on a hunting knife during a combination hunting and fishing trip.

Mr. McGillis was reportedly fishing with Jack Jarvey while Jose Guzman was hunting deer along the east side of the Missouri River. When they all spotted a deer, the two men stopped fishing to help flush the deer out of the brush toward Guzman.

Richard McGillis borrowed Guzman's hunting knife and he started running through the brush about 30 feet from the other men when he tripped and fell onto the sharp knife, which pierced his heart.

(KILLED IN A FALL)
October 26, 1978
James Boor, 30, of Glasgow died from a fall while he was on a hunting trip with his brother-in-law, Darwin Paden of Libby. While the men were hunting in the Cabinet Wilderness area Mr. Boor slipped and fell 200 feet off of a rocky ledge.

Mr. Boor had survived the fall but during the tumble his .30-06 rifle discharged and the bullet struck him in the right arm. Mr. Paden administered first aid on Boor's injuries and then he left for assistance.

More bad luck struck the ill-faded trip when Paden's flashlight gave out and he couldn't find his way in the dark of the night. At first light Paden went for help but James Boor had died before his brother-in-law returned with help.

(DIED FROM SUFFOCATION OR ASPHYXIATION)
November 3, 1978
Stanley Wood, 38, of Anoka, Minnesota and 42-year-old Earnest A. Hahnert of Brainerd, Minnesota were both found asphyxiated in their hunting tent on Blizzard Mountain about 18 miles east of Deer Lodge.

The two men had a small wood stove in their nylon tent and sometime during a storm the stovepipe came loose inside the shelter. A hunting companion who had driven out from Deer Lodge to accompany them discovered their bodies.

(KILLED IN A VEHICLE CRASH
WHILE EN ROUTE TO A HUNT)
October 22, 1979
Mitchell Kelley, 22, and 21-year-old Darcy Satterfield, both of Powell, Wyoming were killed in an automobile accident while they were on their way to a hunt in Montana.

Chapter Eight: DEATH BY OTHER CAUSES

The highway patrol reported that the two Wyoming men died when the jeep Satterfield was driving went out of control and rolled on U.S. 310 about 5 miles south of Bridger.

(UNKNOWN CAUSES)
October 23, 1979
James Wayne Jackson, 13, of Frazer died from an accidental gunshot wound while he was hunting near Frazer Lake.

(KILLED BY HIS OWN HUNTING KNIFE)
November 30, 1979
Seventeen-year-old Rodney McKenzie of Thompson Falls bled to death after falling onto his knife while on a hunting trip. McKenzie's father, Larry McKenzie and his brother, Randy found his body in the Deep Creek area northwest of Thomson Falls.

Rodney McKenzie had been reported missing when he failed to return from a hunt with his friends. The boy had almost severed his wrist after falling on his hunting knife and he wasn't able to stop the bleeding and went into shock.

(KILLED IN A FALL)
November 11, 1985
Leslie O'Neill, 27, of Butte died after undergoing surgery for an injury she received in the mountains while she was hunting south of Fairmont Hot Springs between Butte and Anaconda.

The woman had been dropped off to hunt in the German and American Gulch area where she fell down a deep embankment and suffered internal injuries. O'Neill was later found very cold and semi-conscious and she was air lifted by helicopter out of the Spring Creek drainage.

Chapter Eight: DEATH BY OTHER CAUSES

(KILLED WHILE HUNTING BEAR FROM A BICYCLE)
May 28, 1990
(Missoulian)

Seventeen-year-old <u>Ryan Voerman</u> was killed in one of the strangest hunting accidents while he and a friend were hunting bear about 35 miles south of Hungry Horse on the South Fork of the Flathead River.

The two young men were riding their bikes in the Wheeler Creek drainage looking for bear when they collided and Voerman went down on his rifle. Ryan Voerman was killed from blunt trauma when the barrel of his rifle penetrated his skull.

(DIED FROM SOFFOCATION OR ASPHYXIATION)
November 9, 1990

<u>Merle D. Wood</u>, 65, of Great Falls was reported dead from accidental asphyxiation and carbon monoxide poisoning in his camper near Lincoln while he was on a hunting trip. The authorities said that an unventilated propane stove burner was left on while the man was sleeping.

(KILLED BY A LOADED GUN IN A VEHICLE)
November 11, 1991

<u>Dana M. Fallsdown</u>, 15, of Lodge Grass was accidentally killed while he was hunting with three other men near the southern edge of the Crow Indian Reservation near Wyola.

The boy had been riding in a vehicle when a .223-caliber rifle accidentally discharged and struck him in the chest.

(KILLED BY BUBONIC PLAGUE)
November 8, 1992

<u>Mike Dahl</u>, 34, of Sheridan, Wyoming died at Deaconess Medical Center in Billings of pneumonic plague, an advanced form of the bubonic plague. Mr. Dahl contracted the highly infectious disease through small cuts on his hands while he skinned a bobcat that had been killed in southeastern Montana.

326

Chapter Eight: DEATH BY OTHER CAUSES

Gary Halverson, Ron Anderson and Dan Amende, all of Wyoming had shot a bobcat on October 31 on the Crow Indian Reservation about 2 miles below the Diamond Cross Ranch in Montana. The hunters took the animal back to Sheridan, Wyoming where Mike Dahl along with Dave Selig and Mike Dailey skinned the animal.

On November 4, 1992 Mike Dahl checked in to Memorial Hospital at Sheridan in "septic shock," where he was treated by local doctors and then he was flown to Billings. At the same time the bobcat carcass was being tested at the Federal Centers for Disease Control and Prevention laboratory at Fort Collins, Colorado.

The plague was spread to this country from Mainland Asia in the 1800's and it primarily affects animals. It usually is spread by fleas or from animal bites. The animal may also contract the disease by eating an infected animal.

The disease affects prairie dogs, rabbits, deer, antelope and wild as well as domestic cats. Earlier in 1992 a deer in Wyoming and an antelope in Montana tested positive for the plague. The bobcat in this case was probably affected by entering infected burrows or by eating diseased animals.

People can become infected if they are bitten by fleas or come in contact with a diseased animal. In 1987 a Montana hunter survived a case of bubonic plague that he had contracted from an antelope he had shot in Wheatland County, and a 31-year-old Arizona man died in 1992 from the disease after being sneezed on by a domestic cat. If the disease remains localized in a person, it is called the bubonic plague, but when it has spread throughout the blood stream and settles in the victim's lungs, it is referred to as pneumonic plague and is very deadly.

By the time Mike Dahl had gone to the hospital he had the symptoms of pneumonic plague including sores on his hands and congested lungs. One of the other men who had handled the skinned animal had symptoms of the disease and another man was also admitted to the hospital as a precaution. Everyone who was exposed to the bobcat was monitored and given antibiotics.

(DIED FROM SOFFOCATION OR ASPHYXIATION)
November 8, 1992
Stanley Andrzejek, 49, of Great Falls died in a vehicle fire while he was parked at a turnout on Highway 89 about 3 miles north of Neihart.

Apparently the physical therapist at the Columbus Hospital had gotten tired while he was driving to his hunting spot and he was in the habit of lighting a can of sterno to heat the cab of his pickup. The canned fuel must have tipped over and ignited parts of the cab and Mr. Andrzejek died of carbon monoxide poisoning and smoke inhalation.

(UNKNOWN CAUSES)
October 5, 1994
Sixteen-year-old Michael Keith Bonko of Garryowen, Montana died after surgery at a Billings hospital after being accidentally shot while he was hunting south of Crow Agency. Mike Bonko was fatally wounded while he and two of his friends were trying to fix a small-caliber gun, which had reportedly jammed.

(KILLED BY A RICOCHE)
July 19, 1995
Chad R. Haugen, an 11-year-old Chinook boy died at the Columbus Hospital in Great Falls a day after being accidentally shot while he was gopher hunting.

The young Haugen boy was struck in the head when a .22-caliber bullet fired by his brother William ricocheted off the water of a small reservoir. The young victim was flown to Great Falls directly from his family's farm south of Chinook.

Chapter Eight: DEATH BY OTHER CAUSES

(KILLED IN AN AVALANCHE)
November 17, 1998

The body of <u>Scott Bettle</u>, 36, of Butte was found south of Dillon after he was killed in an avalanche while he was hunting in the Lima Peaks region in Beaverhead County. His body was located in about 5 feet of snow in a saddle between the Middle Fork and Sawmill Creek.

(UNKNOWN)
November 23, 1998

<u>Stephen Wesley Hoscheid</u>, 36, of Anaconda was accidentally killed in a hunting accident in the Lone Pine Ridge region southwest of Philipsburg and south of the Skalkaho pass in Granite County.

(KILLED IN A FALL FROM A TREE)
November 29, 1998

<u>Robert Torgrimson</u>, 38, of Lewistown died from a 30-foot fall from a tree he had apparently climbed to scan the area. Mr. Torgrimson had been hunting with a party of men in the Cottonwood Creek area near Lewistown when he probably slipped on the wet branches.

The coroner reported that Bob Torgrimson actually died of asphyxiation when his windpipe was pinched in the fall leaving him unable to breath.

(KILLED IN A FALL)
October 25, 2000
(Montana Standard)

The body of 50-year-old <u>Dale Gummer</u> of Butte was found at the base of a 60-foot cliff in the Long Tom Creek area about 5 miles northeast of Wise River. Mr. Gummer apparently dropped a piece of his equipment and he slipped and fell while he was trying to retrieve the item.

(KILLED BY A MALFUNCTIONING WEAPON)
October 26, 2000

Nine-year-old <u>Gus Barber</u>, of Amsterdam died of an accidental gunshot wound to his abdomen from a malfunctioning .243-caliber hunting rifle in the hands of his mother while they were on their annual hunting trip.

While Barbara Barber was unloading the rifle the weapon discharged and the round traveled through an open door of the family's horse trailer and through the other side and struck her son who was standing on the other side of the trailer.

The family immediately called 911 and then rushed the boy towards Ennis. They were met at Cameron by an ambulance, which took them on to the Madison Valley Hospital. An emergency helicopter was called but Gus died before its arrival.

The parents of Gus Barber conducted a campaign to force the gun manufacturer to recall the defective weapon as a tribute to their son. The Barbers pointed out that the design of the rifle required Mrs. Barber to release the safety in order to unload the magazine. When she released the safety on the rifle the weapon discharged even without touching the trigger. The family researched that particular firearm and found that several other incidents had occurred, some fatal.

In March of 2002 the Remington Arms Company offered to modify all Remington bolt-action rifles manufactured before 1982. The company said that the program was initiated in part because of the death of Gus Barber.

(KILLED BY A STRAY BULLET)
November 13, 2000
(Billings Gazette)
Raymond A. LaRoche died in a hospital in Poplar from a single gunshot wound to the chest that he sustained 10 days earlier while he was hunting deer with his friends in northwestern Richland County.

The authorities said that the 20-year-old LaRoche had been walking in a ravine insight of his hunting companions when he was shot.

Ray LaRoche's companions later reported that they had heard the shot from an unknown hunter and then saw their friend fall to the ground.

(KILLED IN AN AIRPLANE CRASH WHILE HUNTING)
February 21, 2003

Thirty-three-year-old Jeff Puente of Hardin died at St. Vincent Hospital in Billings after the small plane he was piloting crashed in the Crow Indian Reservation. He was flying with Paul Garrison of Xavier when they were illegally hunting coyotes for some Hardin area landowners.

The two men had taken off from the Hardin Airport and they reportedly crashed about 20 minutes later while trying to chase down a particular coyote. The single-engine Piper Tri-Pacer crashed into some rugged terrain about 6 miles west of Garryowen just inside the boundary of the Crow Indian reservation.

Mr. Garrison later said that when he regained consciousness he discovered he had been thrown from the plane and he was suffering from a broken arm and leg. Garrison crawled back to the wreckage where he activated the plane's emergency locator, which was picked up at the airport at Hardin.

The Bighorn County coroner, who was also a pilot, flew over the sight and he determined the coordinates of the crash and directed a ground rescue crew in their 4-wheel-drive vehicle to the site.

Although Jeff Puente paid with his life, Paul Garrison was charged with illegal hunting from an airplane, which was a misdemeanor. Hunting coyotes and other predators from an airplane was legal in Montana with a proper permit from the Montana State Department of Livestock but the licenses are only given out to pilots who have met certain criteria, and are only for a specific area.

(DIED FROM CARBON MONOXIDE POISONING)
November 6, 2003

Robert Paul Rasmusson, 48, of Libby died from carbon monoxide poisoning from a propane heater at his hunting camp south of Dillon. Mr. Rasmusson was sleeping in the camper with his hunting partner from Libby, Mel Smith who managed to stagger out of the pickup camper also suffering from the effects of the poison.

When he was unable to wake up his friend, Mr. Smith went for help but they were unable to save Bob Rasmusson. Beaverhead County Sheriff Bill Briggs said that campers using propane heaters should always leave a window open and he also recommended they purchase of a carbon monoxide detector.

(KILLED IN A VEHICLE CRASH
WHILE EN ROUTE FROM A HUNT)
December 3, 2003
(Montana Standard)

Forty-five-year-old Robert Simonich of Clancy was killed in an automobile accident while he was returning home from a hunting trip.

Rob was a proud member of the Chippewa-Cree Indian tribe and his tribal name was Four-Star-Big-Bear, or Neo Asak Askeema Ska. The avid outdoorsman crafted knives and he was a gifted Indian pipe maker.

(Endnotes)
[1] While Winnett in later years played down the capture, his story confirms the rest of the story including his Indian name and the disappearance of Jim Fowler.

Table One:

HOW THEY MET THEIR DEATHS

REMOVING A WEAPON FROM A VEHICLE.

Killed or fatally wounded by an accidental discharge of a firearm while removing it from a car, truck, boat, buggy or wagon.

DATE	VICTIM	AGE
September 3, 1913	Mrs. Dr. H.E. Houston	
October 10, 1919	Alexander Stronach	
November 23, 1921	Archie Blair	
November 22, 1931	John C. Holland	
November 10, 1933	Donald Campbell	
October 29, 1934	Charles Jacobs	33
November 4, 1935	Lawrence Dean	34
November 6,1935	Lawrence Carmack	33
November 27, 1935	Philip Satterlee Terrio	19
October 22, 1936	Edward Neuman	33
November 10, 1936	Elmer E. Stockman Jr.	35
November 16, 1936	Ray V. Doney	35
October 23, 1938	Mark Kaulbach	19
November 1, 1938	Forrest Smurr	22
November 8, 1941	Riley Ray	56
October 14, 1944	Orit T. Forbes	40
October 17, 1949	William Patterson	27
October 24, 1950	Frederick Portman Jr.	43
November 4, 1952	Kenneth Newton	17
October 13, 1953	Clarence Sivertson	20
October 23, 1953	William Syblon	37
November 1, 1954	Dean Williams	18
October 7, 1957	Arthur Shoberg	15
November 13, 1962	Edward Olson	
October 24, 1966	William Allen Young	32
November 18, 1967	Clarence Stokes	57
September 30, 1986	Jeff Thomson	24
October 2, 1986	Mark Lowell Burgett	12

Table One: How They Killed Themselves

(Removing weapon from vehicle continued)

December 27, 1987	Taylor Buck	25
April 23, 1988	Gerald B. Jensen	48
October 31, 1990	Anthony "Tony" Kar Tuss	44
November 29, 2004	Joseph Holzapfel	44
February 3, 2005	Bruce J. King	53

PLACING A WEAPON INTO A VEHICLE

November 5, 1902	John Malloy	
November 15, 1909	George Clarence Beckman	14
November 29, 1932	Robert M. Bell	45
November 15, 1936	Arthur T. Ridgway	45
November 3, 1939	Chauncey Bowdin	
October 27, 1951	Raymond A. Kuaffman	16
November 20, 1964	William Popish	48
October 29, 1980	Walter Campbell	58
October 24, 1990	Scott L. Jorgenson	36

HANDLING A WEAPON BY THE BARREL

April 30, 1881	John Brown	
August 4, 1901	George E. Hailey	60
October 26, 1908	Andrew J. Martin	17
November 5, 1920	Thomas A. Towery	56
September 30, 1923	John Szasv	33
November 16, 1926	William Lawrence	
October 17, 1927	Joseph J. Kosena	16
December 11, 1927	Anton Schafer	15
November 4, 1928	Walter Griesbach	30
November 12, 1928	Herschel A. Dockery	18
October 26, 1931	Hollis B. Wiggin	
October 11, 1936	Edgar Hicks	16
November 10, 1936	Albert Booth	27
September 23, 1938	Earl Lyght	20
November 15, 1943	Gilbert John Pochervina	14
November 18, 1959	Aloysius Racine	14
November 12, 1973	Wesley Drollinger	42

Table One: How They Killed Themselves

THEIR WEAPON DISCHARGED IN A FALL

November 22, 1904	Percey Glenn	13
May 7, 1912	Floyd Ritch	22
November 26, 1912	Harrison Allan	23
September 25, 1926	Samuel B. Clark	17
November 6, 1928	Bozo Masanovich	
November 13, 1931	Floyd Marble	31
October 16, 1946	William Kercher Jr.	17
November 24, 1958	Harold T. Farron	57
October 24, 1977	William J. Pierson	13
November 5, 1979	David Wade Christianson	17
November 5, 1991	James M. Jackson	29
May 7, 2000	William Everett Cantrell	76
October 31, 2001	Dennis R. Nelson	45
November 7, 2003	Gary Lee Truax	55
June 4, 2004	Zachary W. Mienk	21

KILLED WHILE GOING THROUGH A FENCE

September 9, 1893	Eli Paulin	16
September 19, 1903	Nick Simon Jr.	13
October 8, 1908	Louis Deckerville	50
September 29, 1912	Richard Jones	
October 1, 1924	Larcey M. Lakar	15
September 28, 1930	Charles Montgomery	39
October 4, 1932	Clarence E. Fahlgren	
November 2, 1932	Oliver M. Johnson	45
November 8, 1935	Sam Kahl	17
October 4, 1936	John Fink	18
November 23, 1937	Berton Thompson	50
October 16, 1939	Robert Phoenix	21
October 11, 1952	Orville Clancy	17
November 14, 1963	Charles Nelson	63
October 18, 1991	Donald B. Hambrick	43
December 20, 1991	Harry D. "Tubby" Hilyard	52

Table One: How They Killed Themselves

WEAPON DISCHARGED AFTER BEING DROPPED

November 26, 1920	Charles L. Torrence	27
November 9, 1921	Knute Knuteson	27
September 2, 1923	Ralph Ryan	11
December 3, 1938	Fred Grinde	23
October 20, 1940	Robert Reesman	12
November 1, 1948	Jerry Brown	24
October 15, 1963	Theodore Haynes	19
October 25, 1990	Anita Louise Greenlee	34

GOING OVER, UNDER AND THROUGH OBSTRUCTIONS

Killed while improperly carrying their weapons through brush, timber and rocks; crossing creeks and streams; making their way over or under logs.

November 2, 1901	James Gamble	
October 5, 1902	Arthur Sharpe	16
August 15, 1904	William Malard	18
December 10, 1916	Joseph A. Stuesse	
October 26, 1918	Jack Smith	
January 2, 1932	William B. Burkhart	43
October 23, 1951	Curtis Westrum	31
October 16, 1967	Roy F. Warwood	18

USING THE WEAPON AS A CLUB

Their firearm accidentally discharged while they were swinging at wounded birds and other small game as well as using the butt of their weapon to even break ice.

January 5, 1902	William Stuart	16
September 2, 1905	Frank Gonsior	17
September 27, 1907	William Powell	
October 2, 1912	Martin McGraw	
August 7, 1922	Andrew Lubardo	31
November 1, 1943	James Bowden	11

Table One: How They Killed Themselves

KILLED WHILE CLEANING THEIR WEAPONS
Killed while cleaning their rifles, handguns and shotguns while at home, hunting camp or in the field.

November 30, 1911	Walter B. Munroe	38
November 10, 1931	Wallace Stone	23
October 4, 1940	Dennis F. Kohner	
November 8, 1947	Ralph T. Grosswiler	40
September 27, 1963	Billy Johnson	15
October 20, 1975	Robert Wright	23

KILLED WHILE THEY WERE LOADING, UNLOADING OR CLEARING THE ACTION OF THE WEAPON

September 9, 1912	John Sagar	15
November 18, 1940	Carl Shepka	13
November 22, 1940	James Brice	14

LEAVING FOR, OR RETURNING FROM A HUNT
Packing or unpacking their firearms and while carrying loaded weapons in backpacks.

October 24, 1918	M.F. Stoughton	48
September 30, 1927	Burr W. Clark	42
October 1, 1967	Michael P. Milelich	22
October 26, 1969	David Lee Schonenbach	16
October 18, 1974	Richard L. Middleton	17

ALCOHOL AND CARELESSNESS

November 26, 1990	Troy S. Goldston	18

Table One: How They Killed Themselves

NOT SPECIFIED

October 15, 1884	David Austin	50
December 29, 1895	John Whiting	
September 10, 1902	Rev. Leslie E. Armitage	26
September 5, 1913	Leslie Dodds	14
October 12, 1916	Ralph Belgrade	
October 8, 1924	Walter Wersall	15
November 15, 1927	Rex Roberts	16
November 16, 1927	George Kennedy	
November 25, 1929	Richard Allen	25
August 2, 1936	Harry Ernest Stradtzeck	12
October 17, 1936	Ruth Fraunhofer	18
July 13, 1937	Andrew Danielson	69
October 20, 1939	William Smith	21
November 7, 1942	John Eichstadt	54
October 22, 1952	Richard W. Gilber	60
October 17, 1956	Miles Spaich	41
October 18, 1956	Raymond H. White	42
October 20, 1958	Howard Gleason	77
November 22, 1958	LeRoy Tucker	41
November 1, 1959	John Edward Grady	44
November 1, 1960	John R. Dahl	41
October 2, 1961	James Gregory	17
November 24, 1962	Kenneth Eickoff	13
September 27, 1963	Charles William West	53
October 11, 1965	Egon Wagerer	38
October 30, 1968	Raymond Rebich	17
October 26, 1969	Daniel Herron	42
October 23, 1974	Sam McDonald	22
November 6, 1986	Raymond C. Eagle	29
November 1, 1991	Lucas Johnson	13
November 23, 1997	Todd Slauson	29

Table Two:

COMPANION
RELATIONSHIPS

Relationship abbreviations are found at the bottom of this table.

DATE	Victim	Reportedly Killed By	and Relationship
9/23/1893	Tom Tregoning	Jim Williams	Friend
12/28/1895	Paul Zias	not reported	Friend
8/11/1897	William Keogh	Alex Capewell	Friend
9/2/1901	Henry C. Love	L. Herbolsheimer	Friend
12/8/1901	Frank Swingley	Douglas Swingley	Brther
8/5/1903	Eddie Collins	not reported	Brther
9/9/1904	Iverson Vaughn	H.A. Johnson	Friend
11/17/1904	Warren Hulbert	Earl Hardman	Friend
11/14/1904	Harry Nagard	George Nagard	Brther
12/19/1904	Carroll E. Brooks	not reported	Friend
8/26/1906	Miss Ruth Bean	Edward Lunger	Assoc.
7/13/1908	A.F. Moody	S.T. Crum	Friend
1/1/1909	Otto Roll	Ottis Roll	Uncle
10/5/1909	Mike Friel	not reported	Friend
9/17/1912	Edward Michaels	not reported	Friend
12/29/1912	George Goss	not reported	Friend
12/2/1914	Fred E. Woodworth	Albert Florin	Friend
10/7/1916	Joseph F. House	John Delatt	Friend
10/13/1916	Oswald K. Sellar	Clarence Napper	Friend
12/16/1916	Wilbert Shipman	William Philo Pace	Cousin
9/27/1917	Gladys Bradley	Joe Collins	Friend
4/12/1919	Elijah Linn	Raymond Linn	Brther
10/2/1919	Leroy S. Tupper	O.E. Bolon	Partner
11/4/1921	James Pullman	Bert Schlogel	Friend
11/13/1921	Andrew Brae	Fred Jamison	Friend
12/9/1922	Paul Russell	Paul Boothman	Friend
11/14/1923	James H. Boling	Howard Talbot	Friend

Table Two: Companion Relationship

11/23/1923	Cecil Trusty	Harry Joy	Friend
12/12/1923	Peter Henningson	Jasper DeDobeleer	Friend
9/21/1924	Everett Kaoski	William Lahto	Friend
11/30/1924	John Vanden-Wall	Allen Erickson	Assoc.
10/23/1925	J.H. Waddell	Carl Albrecht	Friend
12/14/1925	Clifford W. Ofstie	Melvin Maury	Friend
9/17/1926	Farney L. Coles	Ed Baumgardener	Friend
9/17/1927	Huston C. Peters	William Emerick	Friend
9/25/1928	Carlton Whitsell	Randall Tracey	Friend
10/13/1928	Olive Shaw	not reported	Brther
11/17/1928	Sgt. Paul B. Portis	not reported	Friend
11/25/1929	Wm Baumgartner	Phil Shaffer	Friend
11/2/1932	Lewis W. Maynard	James Moore	Friend
10/10/1933	Vincent Walcott	Master Feuchet	Friend
10/19/1933	Walter L. Kulbeck	Ed Kulbeck	Brther
11/4/1933	Charles Midboe	not reported	Friend
10/14/1936	Clifford Smith	Dan Anderson	Assoc.
10/19/1936	Aurel Tucker	Warren Griffin	Friend
11/30/1936	George Reissing	not reported	Friend
10/31/1938	Carl Anderson	Wayne Nicol	Friend
11/22/1938	Robert Felieous	Pat Stretch	In-law
11/23/1938	Frank Seiller	Floyd Seiller	Brther
10/17/1940	Grover C. Bryan	not reported	Friend
10/30/1941	Hezekiah VanDorn	not reported	Friend
11/17/1941	George W. Flamm	Bryce Flamm	Son
10/27/1942	Elmer Buck	Shorty Harmon	Friend
11/10/1942	Walter Grimes	Tom Grimes	Son
10/17/1945	J.H. Meiers	not reported	Friend
10/20/1945	John Redlingshafer	Mr. Redlingshafer	Father
10/22/1945	Greed R. Morgan	not reported	Friend
11/25/1945	Monty Leavitt	Gary Leavitt	Brther
10/29/1947	Charles Masker	not reported	Friend
10/31/1948	Donald J. Bertoglio	Frank Grebenc	Friend
11/19/1948	Raymond Necklace	Rudolph Young	Friend
10/9/1950	Caroline J. Ullery	Sam Ullery	Hsbnd
10/23/1950	Alvin Austin	George Austin	Brther

Table Two: Companion Relationship

11/15/1950	Robert W. Brown	Robert Chilcote	Friend
10/18/1951	Edward Robinson	not reported	Friend
11/5/1951	Gerald Hays	Jack Dofflemire	Friend
11/14/1951	Marvin H. Wagner	Lawrence Dresden	Friend
12/1/1952	George F. Delisle	Russel Hein	Friend
10/17/1953	Edwin Charles Ham	Louis Dwyer	Friend
10/21/1953	Al Kruzon	not reported	Friend
10/25/1953	Francis Norquay	Roy Simmons	In-law
11/8/1953	Art Sanders	not reported	Friend
11/28/1954	David W. Saltsman	not reported	Friend
11/15/1954	Ray Johns	Fred Miles	Friend
11/20/1955	Ross Nelson	not reported	Friend
11/6/1956	Jim Hankinson	Mrs. Hankinson	Wife
11/7/1956	Gary Mosback	Mr. Mosback	Father
10/28/1957	Frank West	not reported	Friend
11/4/1957	Albert Hardie	Maurice Hardie	Brther
11/12/1957	Walt B. Sokoloski Jr.	Bill Thomas	Friend
11/13/1957	Elias Hoch	David Hoch	Son
10/1/1958	John G. Anderson	Clifford Wilson	Friend
11/30/1958	Reuben Gomke	not reported	unkwn
1/30/1959	Dale Robinson	Wade Robinson	Brther
10/12/1959	Westley P. Stace	not reported	Friend
10/19/1959	Robert W. Smith	Allen Thoreson	Friend
11/1/1959	Gary Sorenson	Leland Winkle	Friend
10/24/1960	Judith M. Walker	Sarah Lou Arnold	Friend
10/16/1961	Jack R. Burger	Alvin Breaster	In-law
10/24/1961	Michael Long-Tree	John Bill Jr.	Friend
11/7/1961	Don Cattnach	Dick Anderson	In-law
10/19/1964	Frank L. Anderson	not reported	Friend
10/26/1964	Lindy Walla	Larry Walla	Brther
1/15/1965	Carl Martin	David Dugan	Friend
11/2/1965	Regan Hoyt	Larry Griffin	Friend
11/7/1965	Daniel A. Jewett	not reported	Friend
11/19/1968	Amber Spence	Dennis Spence	Hsbnd
10/5/1969	George R. Frank	James Baker	Friend
11/13/1969	Norris Thompson	not reported	Friend

Dying to Hunt in Montana
Table Two: Companion Relationship

10/24/1970	Michael Fadness	Lem Love	Friend
10/16/1972	Mark Allen Lueder	Steve Quast	Friend
11/21/1972	Nadine J. Riedl	not reported	Friend
11/23/1973	Wade Drollinger	not reported	Friend
10/12/1976	Roger L. Jorgenson	not reported	Friend
10/26/1976	Mark S. Koefod	Scott Patrick	Friend
10/2/1977	Lewis Paul Sprattler	Mark Sprattler	Brther
10/18/1977	Jerry Scott Kroh	not reported	Friend
10/29/1977	Jordan S. Sorenson	not reported	Friend
12/1/1980	Lee Faw	Roger Zimbar	Relatv
10/26/1983	Holis M. Broderick	Deidra Broderick	Dghter
1/2/1987	Wade Otto Stubber	Steve Renaker	Friend
10/26/1987	Kenneth Reinhart	not reported	
10/30/1987	Kary Schanz	not reported	Friend
8/23/1990	Eric Watson	not reported	Friend
10/22/1990	Kay Fairservice	Jacq. Fairservice	Sister
11/19/1991	Mahlon Gunn Jr.	not reported	Friend
11/7/1994	Nathan M. Cox	not reported	Brther
11/30/1994	Wendi Weisgerber	Theresa Ross	Friend
5/20/1996	Michael G. Privett	not report	Friend
12/23/1997	Christopher Weaver	David W. Hall	Friend
10/30/2002	Thomas Asbridge	Mrs. Asbridge	Wife
11/19/2002	Chaskay Ricker	Not reported	Friend
5/14/2003	Joshua N. Lee	David Langlois	Friend

Abbreviations Used

Brther: (Brother)   Brther: (Brother)   Dghter: (Daughter)
Relatv: (Relative)   Unkwn: (Unknown)
Assoc. (Associate or co-worker)

Table Three:

TYPE OF COMPANION ACCIDENTS

Weapon Accidentally Discharged While Working the Weapon's Action

Pointing the Weapon in an Unsafe Direction While Loading, Unloading, Breaking the Action, Closing the Bolt, Clearing a Jammed Round etc.

Date	Victim	Reportedly Killed By
9/2/1901	Henry C. Love	Leonard Herbolsheimer
9/9/1904	Iverson Vaughn	H.A. Johnson
8/26/1906	Miss Ruth Bean	Edward Lunger
10/7/1916	Joseph F. House	John Delatt
11/30/1924	John Vanden-Wall	Carl Albrecht
9/17/1926	Farney L. Coles	Edward Baumgardner
10/20/1945	John Redlingshafer	Mr. Redlingshafer
10/16/1961	Jack R. Burger	Alvin Breaster
10/24/1961	Michael Long-Tree	John Bill Jr.
10/26/1964	Lindy Walla	Larry Walla

In The Line Of Fire
(Not being sure of the Target and Beyond)

8/5/1903	Eddie Collins	not reported
7/13/1908	A.F. Moody	S.T. Crum
1/1/1909	Otto Roll	Ottis Roll
10/5/1909	Mike Friel	not reported
12/2/1914	Fred E. Woodworth	Albert Florin
10/2/1919	Leroy S. Tupper	O.E. Bolon

Table Three: Type of Companion Accidents

(In the Line of Fire Continued)

12/14/1925	Clifford Ofstie	Melvin Maury
10/19/1933	Walter L. Kulbeck	Ed Kulbeck
10/22/1945	Greed R. Morgan	not reported
10/18/1951	Edward Robinson	not reported
10/25/1953	Francis Norquay	Roy Simmons
11/7/1956	Gary Mosback	Mr. Mosback
10/28/1957	Frank West	not reported
11/13/1957	Elias Hoch	David Hoch
11/7/1961	Don Cattnach	Dick Anderson
11/2/1965	Regan Hoyt	Larry Griffin
10/16/1972	Mark Allen Lueder	Steve Quast
1/2/1987	Wade Otto Stubber	Steve Renaker
8/23/1990	Eric Watson	not Reported
11/30/1994	Wendi Weisgerber	Theresa Ross

Pointing the Weapon in a Unsafe Direction

9/23/1893	Tom Tregoning	Jim Williams
12/28/1895	Paul Zias	not reported
12/19/1904	Carrol E. Brooks	not reported
9/17/1912	Edward Michaels	Not reported
11/14/1923	James H. Boling	Howard Talbot
12/12/1923	Peter Henningson	Jasper DeDobeleer
9/21/1924	Everett Kaoski	William Lahto
10/23/1925	J.H. Waddell	Carl Albrecht
9/25/1928	Carlton Whitsell	Randall Tracey
10/10/1933	Vincent Walcott	Master Feuchet
11/22/1938	Robert Felieous	Pat Stretch
11/23/1938	Frank Seiller	Floyd Seiller
10/30/1941	Hezekiah VanDorn	not reported
10/31/1948	Donald J. Bertoglio	Frank Grebenc
11/19/1948	Raymond Necklace	Rudolph Young
11/15/1950	Robert W. Brown	Robert Chilcote
11/14/1951	Marvin H. Wagner	Lawrence Dresden
10/17/1953	Edwin Charles Ham	Louis Dwyer
11/6/1956	Jim Hankinson	Mrs. Hankinson

Table Three: Type of Companion Accidents

(Pointing Weapon Unsafely Continued)

10/1/1958	John Gust Anderson	Clifford Wilson
11/1/1959	Gary Sorenson	Leland Winkle
10/2/1977	Lewis Paul Sprattler	Mark Splattler
10/18/1977	Jerry Scott Kroh	not reported
10/29/1979	Jordan S. Sorenson	not reported
11/19/1991	Mahlon Gunn Jr.	not reported
5/20/1996	Michael G. Privett	not reported
12/23/1997	Christopher Weaver	David W. Hall
10/30/2002	Thomas Asbridge	Mrs. Asbridge
5/14/2003	Joshua N. Lee	David N. Lee

While Removing or Placing a Weapon Into a Vehicle

8/11/1897	William Keogh	Alex Capewell
10/13/1916	Oswald K. Sellar	Clarence Napper
10/14/1936	Clifford Smith	Dan Anderson
11/17/1941	George W. Flamm	Bryce Flamm
11/10/1942	Walter Grimes	Tom Grimes
11/28/1954	David W. Saltsman	not reported
10/24/1960	Judith Marie Walker	Sarah Lou Arnold
10/19/1964	Frank L. Anderson	not reported
1/15/1965	Carl Martin	David Dugan
11/7/1965	Daniel Allen Jewett	not reported
11/21/1972	Nadine J. Riedel	not reported
10/26/1976	Mark S. Koefod	Scott Patrick
12/1/1980	Lee Faw	Roger Zimbar
10/26/1983	Holis M. Broderick	Deidra Broderick
10/26/1987	Kenneth Reinhart	not reported
10/22/1990	Kay Fairservice	Jacqueline Fairservice
11/7/1994	Nathan M. Cox	not reported

Shooting From or Over the Top of the Vehicle

11/8/1953	Art Sanders	not reported
11/15/1954	Ray Johns	Fred Miles
11/20/1955	Ross Nelson	not reported

Table Three: Type of Companion Accidents

(Shooting Over Vehicle Continued)

1/30/1959	Dale Robinson	Wade Robinson
11/23/1973	Wade Drollinger	not reported
10/12/1976	Roger L. Jorgenson	not reported

Weapon Discharged During a Slip, Trip or a Fall

12/16/1916	Wibert Shipman	William Philo Pace
9/17/1927	Huston C. Peters	William Emerick
10/27/1942	Elmer Buck	Shorty Harmon
11/5/1951	Gerald Hays	Jack Dofflemire
12/1/1952	George F. Delisle	Russel Hein
11/4/1957	Albert Hardie	Maurice Hardie
11/12/1957	Walter B. Sokoloski	Bill Thomas
10/19/1959	Robert W. Smith	Allen Thoreson

Discharged While Cleaning

12/8/1901	Frank Swingley	Douglas Swingley
10/17/1940	Grover C. Bryan	not reported
10/9/1950	Caroline J. Ullery	Sam Ullery
11/19/1968	Amber Spence	Dennis Spence

Unknown Reasons

11/7/1904	Warren Hulbert	Earl Hardman
12/29/1912	George Goss	not reported
9/27/1917	Gladys Bradley	Joe Collins
11/4/1921	James Pullman	Bert Schlogel
12/9/1922	Paul Russell	Paul Boothman
11/23/1923	Cecil Trusty	Harry Joy
10/13/1928	Olive Shaw	not reported
11/17/1928	Sgt. Paul B. Portis	not reported
11/25/1929	Wm Baumgartner	Phil Shaffer
11/4/1933	Charles Midboe	not reported
10/19/1936	Aurel Tucker	Warren Griffin
11/30/1936	George Reissing	not reported

Table Three: Type of Companion Accidents

(Unknown Reasons Continued)

10/17/1945	J.H. Meiers	not reported
11/25/1945	Monty Leavitt	Gary Leavitt
10/29/1947	Charles Masker	not reported
10/23/1950	Alvin Austin	George Austin
10/21/1953	Al Kruzon	not reported
11/30/1958	Reuben Gomke	not reported
10/12/1959	Westley P. Stace	not reported
10/5/1969	George R. Frank	James Baker
11/13/1969	Norris Thompson	not reported
10/24/1970	Michael Fadness	Lem Love
10/30/1987	Kary Schanz	not reported
11/19/2002	Chaskay Ricker	not Reported

Unsafe Passing off of a Firearm

11/14/1904	Harry Nagard	George Nagard
11/2/1932	Lewis W. Maynard	James Moore
10/31/1938	Carl Anderson	Wayne Nicol

Discharged While Going Through a Fence or Gate

4/12/1919	Elijah Linn	Raymond Linn

Discharged After Dropping

11/13/1921	Andrew Brae	Fred Jamison

WHERE THEY BECAME LOST OR MISSING

DATE	VICTIM	LOCATION	COUNTY
1881			
1/12	Private Severance	Fort Assinniboine	Hill County
2/5	Calvin Bryon	Near Glendive	Custer County
1884			
7/11	Seth Whipple	Upper Missouri	Roosevelt Co.
1896			
2/22	James Bingley	Near Blackfoot City	Powell County
1899			
10/21	William Longstaff	North Fork Canyon	Lewis & Clark
1901			
6/15	George Reiter		Gallatin Co.
1902			
11/7	B.F. Egan	Lake Five area	Flathead Co.
1903			
11/21	M.M. Johnson	DeBorgia region	Mineral Co.
1905			
8/3	Mr. Barnaby	near Fish Lake	Lincoln Co.
1908			
10/25	Harry Heath	Dearborn area	Lewis & Clark
1909			
10/26	E. Lund	Crazy Mountains	Park County
1910			
11/14	Amos Schultz	Fort Benton area	Chouteau Co.
11/14	Walter Schultz	Fort Benton area	Chouteau Co.
1912			
10/10	Thomas Stark	Big Belt Mountains	Cascade Co.
11/23	Joe Waigel	Wolf Creek	Flathead Co.
1914			
12/2	Wallace Brown	Henry Lake's Station	Beaverhead

Dying to Hunt in Montana
Table Four: Where They Became Lost or Missing

1915
10/21 David A. Long   Bunker Creek area   Flathead Co.
1917
11/23 Frank Carlson   Highwood Mts.   Cascade Co.
1920
11/23 Carl Osmand   Donovan Ranch   Beaverhead
1925
10/31 Frank A. Matt   Frenchtown area   Missoula Co.
1926
11/19 John Ben Hougland   Nelson Creek area   Missoula Co.
1932
11/27 Jack Carlisle   Summit area   Glacier Co.
12/16 John Hinz   Gregson Spring area   Deer Lodge
1933
11/8   George Armitage   Ennis area   Madison Co.
1935
11/10 George Westfall   Lake Delmo area   Silver Bow Co.
1936
11/12 Albert Westberg   Castle Mountains   Meagher Co.
1937
10/22 Alfonse Chourand   Missoula area   Missoula Co.
1938
10/19 Clarence Dorey   Rocky Creek area   Missoula Co.
10/21 William Hauskamaa   Little Belt Mts   Judith Basin
11/14 George Mcleslie   Havre area   Hill County
11/15 Dick Powell   Squaw Creek area   Gallatin Co.
1940
11/9   Gus Stean   Upper Trout Creek   Mineral Co.
1941
11/29 James McBride   Lincoln Co.
1942
10/30 Frank Pogacher   Little Snowy Mts.   Musselshell
11/10 Paul Praast   Second Creek area   Powell County
1944
11/21 Bryon C. Wilson   Flathead Co.

Table Four: Where They Became Lost or Missing

1945

11/10	James Callaway	Falls Creek area	Lewis & Clark

1946

| 10/20 | Ed Bloodgood | Crazy Mountains | Park County |

1947

| 11/9 | George Lofftus | Sapphire Mountains | Ravalli County |

1950

| 11/3 | Mrs. Mary Winkley | Willow Creek area | Beaverhead |

1951

| 10/15 | E.C. Humphrey | N-Bar Ranch | Fergus County |
| 10/21 | James Wishart | Hungry Horse area | Flathead Co. |

1953

| 10/8/ | Donald R. Fain | Norris area | Madison Co. |
| 11/19 | Ben Reimer | Foys Lake region | Flathead Co. |

1957

| 10/13 | Gerald Barney | Frog Pond area | Granite Co. |

1958

10/23	Clyde F. Williams	Broadus area	Powder River
10/23	Robert Pittman	4-Cnrs/Lame Deer	Rosebud Co.
10/24	Clyde Escher	MM Crocker Ranch	Powder River
10/24	Tony Stepanek	MM Crocker Ranch	Powder River

1959

10/27	Fred E. Kent	Yogo Peak Road	Judith Basin
11/7	Clarence Trader	Hardin area	Big Horn Co.
11/17	Adrian Dick Joki	Bozeman area	Gallatin Co.
11/28	Arthur D. Jordan	Seeley Lake area	Missoula Co.

1960

| 10/15 | Harvey E. Hewitt | Wolf Point area | Roosevelt Co. |
| 11/16 | Fritz Fry | Lothrop area | Missoula Co. |

1962

| 10/29 | Fred Hamilton | Soup Creek area | Lake County |
| 11/13 | David Klien | Jim Bond Canyon | Lake County |

1963

| 11/2 | Victor Vermillion | Bracket Creek area | Gallatin Co. |

1965

| 11/24 | Larry Kruger | Twin Creek area | Mineral Co. |

Table Four: Where They Became Lost or Missing

1968

11/17	Tassie H. Farmer	Woodward Ck area	Lake County

1969

11/5	Clay Morris	Dillon area	Beaverhead

1970

11/22	Annie M. Hammond	Ferry Basin region	Sanders Co.
11/22	Ross DuPuis	Moss Ranch	Sanders Co.

1972

10/26	Fred Hellman	Hungry Horse area	Flathead Co.

1973

11/1	Herman Skagen	Snowy Mountains	Fergus County
11/8	Tom Chamberlain	Ovando area	Powell County
11/8	Kenneth L. Fultz	Bitterroot Mts	Ravalli County

1974

11/8	Donald R. Kimberlin	Cr d' Alene Mts.	Mineral Co.
11/25	Louis Callender	Sheephead Ck area	Ravalli County

1975

10/28	Donald Harper	Big Creek region	Park County
11/26	Timothy Schock	Little Belt Mts	Cascade Co.

1976

11/27	Richard Jacobson	Shorty Creek area	Flathead Co.

1981

11/30	Vicki K. Stedman	Porcupine Creek	Rosebud Co.
11/30	Wilbur H. Stedman	Porcupine Creek	Rosebud Co.

1983

2/16	Tracy Cray	Eagle Creek	Park County

1984

11/1	Glenn Carr	Bob Marshall Wilderness	

1987

11/17	John Doyle	Cox Creek area	Ravalli County
11/17	James A. Steging	Cox Creek area	Ravalli County

1990

10/4	Susan Adams	Battle Creek area	Ravalli County

1991

11/4	Charles E. Miller	Livingston area	Park County
11/4	Tom E. McDaniel	Livingston area	Park County

Table Four: Where They Became Lost or Missing

1991 (continued)

12/12	James Telgan	Warm Springs area	Madison Co.
1994			
11/7	Ernest L. Houghton	Deep Creek area	Teton County
2001			
12/11	Kodi Chapman	Stryker Ridge Road	Flathead Co.
2004			
10/20	Michael LaMere	Moses Mountain	Hill County

CAUSES OF MISTAKEN IDENTIFICATION

Appreviations used in this section are found at the end of this table.

Mistaken for Game by <u>Movements</u> in the timber, brush, because of darkness or low visibility.

Date	Victim	Reportedly Killed By	Relationship
12/8/1890	Harry Emery	M.S. Emery	Father
2/9/1898	M.C. Beach	Charles Mase	Friend
9/19/1902	Louis Gardape	Louis Hovland	Stranger
9/20/1903	Jesse Hodges	Billy Baker	Friend
9/5/1905	Mrs. Coventry	Mr. Coventry	Husbnd
9/15/1906	Aaron McGuire	J.C. Eslock	F-in-Lw
12/20/1907	Charles Peterson	Mjr. George E. Doll	Friend
12/9/1908	Robert A. Taylor	Leland Taylor	Brother
11/14/1914	George Goss	not reported	Friend
11/2/1914	George Standiford	Mr. Standiford	Father
5/17/1916	Samuel G. Massey	E.O. Rolstad	Friend
12/17/1916	Dan Murr	Howard Stevens	Stranger
9/16/1917	Sullivan Berger	John Lafountain	B-in-Lw
10/23/1919	Cpt. William Strong	Hans M. DeLong	Friend
12/1/1920	Ernest Balke	Otto Hoffman	Friend
11/11/1927	Kenneth Gardner	Willis Major	Friend
11/6/1933	Homer Schuchmann	Albert Barrott	Friend
11/10/1936	Bruce Schwenneker	Mr. Schwenneker	Father
11/15/1938	Howard V. Little	not reported	Friend
10/17/1943	Albert Mora	Louis Berger	Stranger
10/18/1952	Rev. Charles Bolin	Rev. Bernard Lund	Friend

(Mistaken by Movement Continued)

11/20/1955	John Burvich	Jim Rogers	Stranger
10/17/1956	Ralph Younglove	Walter T. Burns	Stranger
10/18/1956	Clarence Skaggs	Robert Frankfurter	Stranger
11/4/1957	Robert C. Jennings	Dale Jennings	Father
11/8/1959	Wesley H. Elbert	Donald Warner	Stranger
11/22/1959	Neil Christenson	not reported	Friend
11/20/1960	Walter Franke	Walter Franke Jr.	Son
10/4/1965	William Townsend	Blaine Bolyard	Stranger
10/9/1965	Jeff Thomas	not reported	Friend
10/7/1969	Raymond E. Rathie	doctor from NY	Client
6/28/1982	Shannon Weatherly	Rodney Schultz	Stranger
11/21/1984	Daniel M. Davy	not reported	Friend

Mistaken for Game by <u>Sounds</u> in the timber, brush, darkness or low visibility.

9/12/1904	Charles Wiitala	Matt Sands	Friend
10/16/1948	Walter Laughfranere	not reported	Friend
11/3/1953	Harry Howard	Narven Osteen	Stranger
10/21/1961	James Miller	R. H. Christensen	Friend
11/28/1971	Douglas A. Madigan	Gerald Martin	Friend

Mistaken for Game by their <u>Appearance</u>, either by their clothing, actions or by the carrying of an animal.

11/10/1912	John Easlack	George Gordon	Stranger
9/4/1915	Ernest B. Clark	Frank Wineland	Stranger
10/25/1919	Norman Winchell	E.L. Ruegamer	Stranger
11/11/1931	Adolph A. Coverdell	Walter Colby Jr.	Stranger
10/8/1940	Edward Duby	Alvis Parmley	Friend
11/1/1954	William Orr	unknown	Stranger

Table Five: Causes of Mistaken Identification

(Mistaken By Appearance Continued)

10/22/1961	Norm G. Thrasher	Wilbur D. Smith	Stranger
11/5/1961	Thomas Kelsey	Edward Peck	Stranger
11/7/1969	Earl E. Talbert	Richard W. Talbert	Son
9/15/1995	Ronald S. Molback	Douglas Elfering	Friend
11/18/1996	Randall P. Moses	James A. Wagner	Friend
11/21/1999	Roger A. Wagner	Jim Wagner	Brother

Mistaken for Game by <u>Undetermined</u> reasons.

11/10/1906	S.E. Wilson	Mr. Meir	Friend
11/3/1919	James McWhethey	James Best	Friend
10/20/1923	Harold Wallinder	unknown	Stranger
12/11/1929	Frank Mayash	unknown	Stranger
11/8/1932	Orville Briner	not reported	Friend
11/14/1932	Edgely Mills	unknown	Stranger
11/14/1932	Harvey Mills	unknown	Stranger
11/7/1933	Melvin Evenson	not reported	Son-Fd
11/20/1935	Wilbur Coe	not reported	Friend
11/10/1936	Thomas Weir	Thomas Huffman	Stranger
11/30/1939	Clarence Baker	Clarence Mason	Stranger
10/19/1951	Lowell Webb	Ernest Townsend	Stranger
10/28/1951	Guy Long	Baker Hagestad	Stranger
11/16/1951	Charles Webber	Royal Marquardt	Friend
10/19/1959	Donald Marko	Archie Cummins	Stranger
11/5/1962	James Gibbons	Dean Coddington	B-in-Lw
9/21/1969	Hans I. Erickson	Ruddy Nuzzo	Friend
12/7/2004	Francis C. Plante	not reported	Fd-Rel.

Apreviations:

F-in-Lw	Father-in-law
B-in-Lw	Brother-in-law
Son-Fd	either a son or a friend
Fd-Rel	either a friend or a relative

CATEGORIES OF FATAL ANIMAL ENCOUNTERS

Killed in BEAR ATTACKS

September 10, 1881	Peter Helstrom	Deer Lodge Co.
1894 (reported 1897)	Unknown Hunter	Park County
May 5, 1912	John Austin	Park County
November 19, 1940	Frank Howell	Flathead Co.
October 22, 1956	William Kenneth Scott	Bob Marshall
October 31, 1958	Samuel Adams	Powell County
November 1, 2001	Timothy A. "Omar" Hilston	Powell County

Killed by a wounded DEER

November 3, 1938	Grover Pace	Sanders County

Killed by a HORSE

October 18, 1937	Ralph Longpre	Mineral County
November 16, 1941	Charles McElroy	Flathead Co.
November 6, 1947	George Danford Mason	Valley County
October 23, 1969	Roswel L. Breakus	Gallatin Co.
November 10, 1987	Alan K. Kitchel	Gallatin Co.

LOCATION OF WATER DEATHS

By Chronological Order

DATE	VICTIM	LOCATION
9/7/1886	Robert Whipple	Cooper's Lake
5/20/1893	Olof Olson	Swan River
5/20/1893	Charles F. Foley	Fisher Creek
9/7/1893	Stanisloff Crelslenski	Sun River
1/6/1896	Walter Joy	Flathead River
10/11/1896	LeGrand S. Contalou	Sun River
11/8/1903	Bridge Williams	Georgetown Lake
11/8/1903	Max Wright	Georgetown Lake
9/14/1904	Lucien A. Enders	Sun River
10/21/1907	T. Stewart	Hauser Lake
10/21/1907	Arthur Donegan	Hauser Lake
10/21/1907	James Brown	Hauser Lake
9/21/1914	Robert Rheinackle	Lake Francis
11/7/1917	Fred H. Batts	Georgetown Lake
11/15/1917	Andrew Craig	Hollings Lake
10/23/1918	Louie Hoop	Sage Lake
10/26/1918	John J. Robertson	Madison Lake
9/22/1922	Harry G. Hawkins	Mission Lake
11/9/1922	Lee Combs	Pablo Reservoir
11/9/1922	Lyle Combs	Pablo Reservoir
11/9/1922	William Combs	Pablo Reservoir
11/19/1923	Andrew Hakke	Georgetown Lake
11/26/1923	Ted Ellis	Bynum Reservoir
9/18/1926	James Keefe	Red Rock Lake
10/31/1927	Frank Balkovich	Lake Helena
11/17/1928	Von Hartso	Fitzpatrick Lake
10/21/1929	Clifford Harrison	Missouri River
10/21/1929	Otto Garrison	Missouri River
10/23/1929	Evert Applegate	Missouri River

Table Seven: Location of Water Deaths

11/19/1929	Andrew Kola	Georgetown Lake
11/24/1930	Andrew J. Marouthas	Missouri River
10/15/1933	Ford R. Lake	Priest Lake
11/7/1935	Hugo Benedetti	Missouri River
10/23/1937	George T. Westover	Nelson Reservoir
10/5/1940	George Eckelberry	Percy's Lake
11/13/1945	Clifford Courtney	Yellowstone River
11/13/1945	Emmett Courtney	Yellowstone River
10/28/1946	Jack E. Parmillee	Hebgen Lake
10/28/1946	G.A. Zink	Hebgen Lake
11/21/1946	Richard Busler	Flathead Lake
11/25/1946	Robert Rodine	Clarkfork River
10/16/1947	Clifford G. Hogan	Clarkfork River
10/16/1947	Albert Lewis Richardson	Clarkfork River
10/18/1949	Charles Kirby	Fishers Bottom
10/24/1950	Horace H. Snider	Reservoir by Dodson
10/15/1954	Jackie Shandy	Cooney Dam
11/6/1961	William John Batten	Reservoir by Pony
12/16/1962	Kenneth H. Fraser	small Flathead slough
12/16/1962	Floyd F. Knopes	small Flathead slough
10/10/1966	Richard Ertz	Flathead Lake
10/8/1967	George Kapp	McAlpine Ranch
10/20/1968	Albert Haglund	Canyon Ferry Lake
10/18/1971	Erland Bruce Whaley	Noxon Reservoir
10/31/1971	Gerald W. Giesick	Yellowstone River
11/19/1972	Louis Burrell	pond near Libby
10/29/1973	Gary L. Palmer	Meadow Lake
10/29/1973	Steve Bullock	Meadow Lake
11/1/1973	Dr. Charles McJilton	Canyon Ferry Lake
11/24/1973	Gordon Dressel	Yellowstone County
10/10/1988	Randy Lee Anderson	a pond near Roy
11/4/1992	James Burrell	Jefferson River
11/19/1993	Lamar Rasmussen	Fickens Slough

WATER DEATHS BY COUNTIES

Listed by the most deadliest waters.

FLATHEAD AND LAKE COUNTIES

Date	Victim	Age	Hometown
Flathead Lake			
11/21/1946	Richard Busler		Polson
10/10/1966	Richard Ertz	24	Kalispell
Flathead River			
1/6/1896	Walter Joy	35	Columbia Falls
Pablo Reservoir			
11/9/1922	Lee Combs	15	Polson
11/9/1922	Lyle Combs	19	Polson
11/9/1922	William Combs	23	Polson
Small slough between Columbia Falls and Kalispell			
12/16/1962	Kenneth H. Fraser	31	Columbia Falls
12/16/1962	Floyd F. Knopes	29	Helena
Fickens Slough			
11/19/1993	Lamar Rasmussen	42	Kalispell
Percy's Lake			
10/5/1940	George Eckelberry	42	Kalispell
Swan River			
5/20/1893	Olof Olson		Great Falls

CASCADE COUNTY

Date	Victim	Age	Hometown
The Missouri River			
10/21/1929	Clifford Harrison	22	Great Falls
10/21/1929	Otto Garrison	35	Great Falls
10/23/1929	Everett Applegate	34	Great Falls
11/24/1930	Andrew J. Marouthas	38	Great Falls

Table Eight: Water Deaths by Counties

(Cascade County, Missouri River continued)

11/7/1935	Hugo Benedetti	35	Great Falls

The Sun River

9/14/1904	Lucien A. Enders	48	Sun River Val.

Pond near Roy

10/10/1988	Randy Lee Anderson	17	Great Falls

LEWIS & CLARK COUNTY

Date	Victim	Age	Hometown
Hauser Lake			
10/21/1907	T. Stewart		Helena
10/21/1907	Arthur Donegan		Helena
10/21/1907	James Brown		Helena
Lake Helena			
10/31/1927	Frank Balkovich	39	Helena
Canyon Ferry Lake			
10/20/1968	Albert Haglund	52	Helena
11/1/1973	Dr. Charles McJilton	77	Helena

PARK AND YELLOWSTONE COUNTIES

Date	Victim	Age	Hometown
Yellowstone River			
11/13/1945	Clifford Courtney	44	Billings
11/13/1945	Emmett Courtney	15	Billings
10/31/1971	Gerald W. Giesick	33	Billing
11/24/1973	Gordon Dressel	40	Billings
Hollings Lake			
11/15/1917	Andrew Craig		Unknown

DEER LODGE and GRANITE COUNTIES

Date	Victim	Age	Hometown
Georgetown Lake			
11/8/1903	Bridge Williams		Granite
11/8/1903	Max Wright	45	Granite
11/7/1917	Fred H. Batts	34	Granite County

Dying to Hunt in Montana
Table Eight: Water Deaths by Counties

(Deer Lodge and Granite Counties, Georgetown Lake continued)

Date	Victim	Age	Hometown
11/19/1923	Andrew Hakke		Butte
11/19/1929	Andrew Kola	40	Butte

MADISON COUNTY

Date	Victim	Age	Hometown
Meadow Lake			
10/29/1973	Steve Bullock	21	Butte
10/29/1973	Gary L. Palmer	23	Butte
Nelson Reservoir			
10/23/1937	George T. Westover		Glasgow
Reservoir near Pony			
11/6/1961	William John Batten	26	Butte

GALLATIN COUNTY

Date	Victim	Age	Hometown
Hebgen Lake			
10/28/1946	Jack E. Parmillee		Los Angeles
10/28/1946	G.A. Zink		W. Yellowstone
Madison Lake			
10/26/1918	John J. Robertson		Unknown

MISSOULA COUNTY

Date	Victim	Age	Hometown
Clarkfork River			
11/25/1946	Robert Rodine	23	Missoula
10/16/1947	Clifford G. Hogan	42	Missoula
10/16/1947	Albert Lewis Richardson	29	Missoula

TETON COUNTY

Age	Victim	Age	Hometown
Bynum Reservoir			
11/26/1923	Ted Ellis	35	Great Falls
Priest Lake			
10/15/1933	Ford R. Lake	30	Great Falls

FERGUS COUNTY

Date	Victim	Age	Hometown
Fishers Bottom			
10/18/1949	Charles Kirby	52	Lewistown
McAlpine Ranch Pond			
10/8/1967	George Kapp	15	Cut Bank

OTHER MONTANA WATERS

Date	Victim	Age	Hometown
Cooney Dam, (Carbon County)			
10/15/1954	Jackie Shandy	16	Joliet
Cooper's Lake (Powell County)			
9/7/1886	Robert Whipple		Helena
Reservoir near Dodson, (Phillips County)			
10/24/1950	Horace H. Snider		Havre
Fisher Creek (Lincoln County)			
5/20/1893	Charles F. Foley	35	Unknown
Fitzpatrick Lake, (Toole County)			
11/17/1928	Von Hartso	20	Unknown
Lake Francis, (Pondera County)			
9/21/1914	Robert Rheinackle	19	Spokane, WA.
Jefferson River, (Jefferson County)			
11/4/1992	James Burrell		Whitehall
Noxon Reservoir, (Sanders County)			
10/18/1971	Erland Bruce Whaley	48	Trout Creek
Pond near Libby (Lincoln County)			
11/19/1972	Louis Burrell	62	Unknown
Mission Lake, (Glacier County)			
9/22/1922	Harry G. Hawkins	25	Great Falls
Red Rock Lake, (Beaverhead County)			
9/18/1926	James Keefe		Butte
Sage Lake, (Hill County)			
10/23/1918	Louie Hoop	30	Kremlin

HUNTING DEATHS DUE TO HEALTH REASONS

Date	Victim	Age	Cause of Death
12/3/1910	Ray Forcum		Poor Health
10/29/1914	Roy Blow		Poor Health
11/24/1916	Geza Ottopal	36	Pneumonia
9/19/1917	Edward L. Volcour	60	Heart Attack
10/29/1919	P.L. Woods		Appendicitis
11/2/1919	Thomas C. Page	65	Pneumonia
9/29/1924	Peter Irvine		Heart Attack
11/15/1925	Charles Donally		Heart Attack
10/3/1931	Steve Chrisman		Weak Heart
11/14/1933	Robert Harkness	63	Heart Attack
9/30/1934	Harry Hines	60	Heart Attack
10/24/1935	William Powell	80	Heart Attack
10/22/1937	Ed Cameron	42	Heart Attack
10/17/1938	James A. Parrish		Heart Attack
11/4/1938	Frank Thompson		Heart Attack
11/11/1940	Claude S. Averill	54	Heart Attack
11/17/1941	Oliver Gaston	70	Heart Attack
11/5/1942	Arthur S. Borden		Heart Attack
11/7/1942	Alley C. McGilvrey	78	Heart Attack
11/1/1943	Oscar Bye	51	Heart Attack
11/9/1943	Henry W. Bassett	64	Heart Attack
10/5/1945	Wm R. Reymerson	56	Heart Attack
10/20/1945	J. W. Redlingshafer	32	Heart Attack
10/23/1945	Vern Simaro	35	Natural Causes
11/14/1945	Henry Staffan	51	Heart Attack
10/29/1946	John N. Thomas		Heart Attack
10/8/1947	Louis Camp	66	Heart Attack
10/9/1947	Ross Collins	47	Heart Attack
10/12/1947	Robert Longnecker	39	Heart Attack
10/27/1947	Henry A. True	64	Heart Attack
10/28/1947	Benedict D. Perga	44	Heart Attack
11/16/1947	Robert A. Ryan	63	Heart Attack

Table Nine: Health Related Deaths by Category

11/16/1947	Ralph Adkins	57	Heart Attack
11/16/1947	Charles M. Brewster	58	Heart Attack
11/29/1947	Girrald E. Townsend	55	Heart Attack
11/1/1948	Arne Haugse	76	Heart Attack
10/12/1949	Floyd E. Stiles	54	Heart Attack
10/12/1949	Fred Jaqueth	51	Heart Attack
10/12/1949	Jesse L. Odelle	64	Heart Attack
10/20/1949	George L. Russell	51	Heart Attack
9/27/1950	Charles F. Maris		Heart Attack
10/24/1950	William A. Olsen	64	Heart Attack
10/24/1950	Oscar Butts	59	Heart Attack
11/17/1950	Elmer A. Findall	65	Heart Attack
10/27/1951	Rudolph B. Krutar		Heart Attack
10/27/1951	Bernard V. Urich		Heart Attack
10/27/1951	John Heiland		Heart Attack
10/27/1951	Ernest Dubie		Heart Attack
11/1/1951	Fred Anderson	39	Heart Attack
11/6/1951	Arthur Foster	53	Heart Attack
11/7/1951	Thomas E. McClure	65	Heart Attack
11/14/1951	Roy Rush		Heart Attack
10/20/1952	William F. Johnson	69	Heart Attack
10/21/1952	Frank Yale	50	Heart Attack
10/29/1952	Alfred Sterner	70	Heart Attack
10/17/1953	William Lowney	62	Heart Attack
11/8/1953	Bert Bailey	47	Heart Attack
10/19/1954	Leonard R. Schmidt	39	Heart Attack
10/19/1954	Charles T. Case	50	Heart Attack
11/1/1954	John Earl Murphy	63	Heart Attack
11/2/1954	John Synnes	70	Heart Attack
11/20/1954	John H. Mueller	72	Heart Attack
10/16/1955	Harry Luce	58	Heart Attack
10/16/1955	Silas H. Jerome	66	Heart Attack
10/19/1955	William N. Hughley	64	Heart Attack
10/27/1955	Joseph K. Harbison	55	Heart Attack
10/31/1955	Rudolph Pries	82	Heart Attack
11/9/1955	William Jones	60	Heart Attack
11/9/1955	Henry J. Jondrow	78	Heart Attack

Table Nine: Health Related Deaths by Category

11/15/1955	Thomas Melton	47	Heart Attack
10/18/1956	William R. Clark	56	Heart Attack
10/28/1956	George Henry Mills	61	Over Exertion
10/29/1956	Herbert Goecks	47	Over Exertion
10/30/1956	Pearl Herndon	63	Heart Attack
11/12/1956	June Edmondson	69	Heart Attack
11/13/1956	Burton Davenport	50	Heart Attack
11/13/1956	John F. Detz	50	Heart Attack
10/22/1957	Jack Kosola	48	Heart Attack
11/12/1957	John W. Dowling		Heart Attack
11/16/1957	Herb Martinich	48	Heart Attack
10/24/1958	John Stone	75	Heart Attack
10/26/1958	Ralph Hardbaugh	64	Heart Attack
10/28/1958	Walter Lee Collins	66	Heart Attack
11/10/1958	Ivan L. Gamett	27	Heart Attack
11/15/1958	Robert C. Brewer	35	Heart Attack
11/17/1958	Walter Talbot	44	Natural Causes
11/23/1958	Clyde Jenkins	45	Heart Attack
11/8/1959	John A. Robinson	47	Heart Attack
11/11/1959	John B. Bourassa	64	Heart Attack
11/14/1959	Joseph P. Jansen Jr.	44	Heart Attack
11/22/1959	George Wood	50	Heart Attack
10/16/1961	Kenneth Rawson		Heart Attack
10/17/1961	Emil L. Rozuoi	51	Heart Attack
10/18/1961	Troy E. Thacker	58	Heart Attack
10/18/1961	Robert Zeuler	52	Heart Attack
10/23/1961	Egbert Zyp Jr.	49	Diabetes
9/21/1963	Clifford M. Ware	63	Heart Attack
10/18/1963	Dr. G. O. Sweum	62	Unknown
11/13/1963	Calvin L. Seeley	42	Heart Attack
11/22/1963	Robert A. Gruber	68	Heart Attack
10/10/1964	Earl James Gaw	57	Heart Attack
11/2/1964	Floyd Greenup	52	Heart Attack
11/16/1964	Frank McCauley	48	Heart Attack
10/5/1965	Ward A. Staats		Heart Attack
10/26/1965	Wallace Mack	70	Heart Attack
11/24/1965	Eugene E. Eggert	40	Heart Attack

Table Nine: Health Related Deaths by Category

10/25/1966	Vern McKay	50	Heart Attack
10/26/1966	Donald L. Kelly	51	Heart Attack
11/1/1966	Lester R. Comstock	58	Heart Attack
11/15/1966	Stewart White	55	Heart Attack
11/21/1966	George V. Doherty	48	Heart Attack
10/24/1967	Carl Willis	66	Heart Attack
11/8/1967	Peter R. Lesofski	44	Heart Attack
11/24/1968	Wayne E. Obert	44	Heart Attack
9/19/1969	John A. McFarland	73	Heart Attack
10/20/1969	Gerald F. Thompson	35	Heart Attack
10/21/1969	William Lovell	63	Heart Attack
10/1/1970	Carl Knutson		Heart Attack
10/20/1970	Morris C. Holton	52	Heart Attack
10/29/1970	William Dillabaugh	55	Heart Attack
10/19/1971	Leonard H. Strand	68	Heart Attack
10/19/1971	Robert L. Marshall	80	Heart Attack
11/23/1971	James B. Palmer	54	Heart Attack
10/26/1972	Merle Berggren	50	Heart Attack
11/25/1973	Paul D. Buck	57	Heart Attack
10/12/1976	Ralph Steinberg	66	Heart Attack
11/16/1977	Paul S. Wininger	54	Heart Attack
11/12/1980	J.K. Bowling	66	Heart Attack
10/26/1981	James H. O'Neill	64	Heart Attack
10/26/1981	Harold Quarles	59	Heart Attack
11/2/1982	Clyde C. Richardson	79	Natural Causes
2/16/1983	William G. Nemeth	62	Heart Attack
11/2/1987	James Drury	41	Heart Attack
10/26/1988	Jack Love	53	Natural Causes
10/28/1988	Arthur L. Schmidt	57	Heart Attack
11/4/1992	Herman C. Saari	41	Heart Attack
11/10/1992	Roger A. English	61	Heart Attack
11/26/1996	Kieran Patrick Grant	41	Heart Attack
10/23/2000	Daniel Ova	50	Heart Attack

Dying to Hunt in Montana
Table Ten:

CATEGORIES OF DEATHS "BY OTHER CAUSES"

Listed in alphabetical order and not by frequency.

ABANDONED by his Companions
| 10/29/1917 | Adelore Lafrinire | Missoula County |

Killed in an AIRPLANE CRASH while en route
| 11/2/1970 | Charles W. Fuller Jr. | Wibaux County |
| 11/2/1970 | Howard H. Hanifl | Wibaux County |

Killed in an AIRPLANE CRASH while hunting
9/11/1962	Duayne Murray	Fergus County
11/22/1976	Edward W. Langford	Fergus County
2/21/2003	Jeff Puente	Big Horn County

Killed while ATTACKING Hunters or Trappers
Fall of 1808	Unknown Blackfeet Indian	Madison County
4/12/1810	Unknown Blackfeet Indian	Gallatin County
10/14/1832	Unknown Blackfeet Indian	Madison County

Died in a steel-jaw BEAR TRAP
| 2/10/1900 | George Humphrey | Madison County |

367

Table Ten: Categories of Deaths by Other Causes

Killed in a <u>BICYCLE ACCIDENT</u> while hunting bear
5/28/1990   Ryan Voerman   Flathead County

Died of <u>BLOOD POISONING</u>
from an accidental gunshot wound
7/29/1914   Ervin M. Hilton   Cascade County

Killed by the BUBONIC PLAGUE
11/8/1992   Mike Dahl   Big Horn County

Killed in a <u>DEER TRAP or SET GUN</u>
11/21/1915   Henry Divis   Lincoln County
11/20/1925   James Geer   Flathead County

Killed when a <u>DOG</u> stepped on a weapon
10/28/1924   Cavyell 6-year-old boy   McCone County

Killed in a <u>FALL</u> from a cliff
12/4/1908   Alexander MacAulay   Glacier County
1/23/1912   Leon Stevenson   Carbon County
10/5/1913   J. Dulen   Lincoln County
11/2/1929   Alva Williams   Sweet Grass County
11/15/1945   Charles White   Park County
10/2/1962   John Higgins   Missoula County
11/12/1962   Richard Austad   Lewis & Clark County
11/5/1971   Dennis A. Steffes   Sweet Grass County
10/26/1978   James Boor   Lincoln County
11/11/1985   Leslie O'Neill   Silver Bow County
10/25/2000   Dale Gummer   Silver Bow County

Dying to Hunt in Montana
Table Ten: Categories of Deaths by Other Causes

Died from a FALL FROM TREE
11/29/1998   Robert Torgrimson   Fergus County

Killed by a FALLING TREE
10/26/1959   James Garey   Bob Marshall

Killed by a FALLING WEAPON

Date	Name	County
9/3/1913	Mrs. James Morris	Hill County
9/27/1923	Fred Mock	Glacier County
12/2/1924	Hunt Coy	Yellowstone County
9/17/1926	Richard "Dixie" Driscoll	Jefferson County
10/17/1928	Henry L. Houston	Cascade County
10/31/1933	James Vern Booth	Missoula County
10/5/1939	William Lloyd Wyrick	Yellowstone County
10/9/1939	Wesley Burger Coley	Yellowstone County
10/23/1973	Kenneth Harvey	Fergus County

FROZE TO DEATH while hunting
Feb. 1874   28 U.S. Army Soldiers   Cascade County

FROZE TO DEATH while trapping
2/17/1900   Robert Waddell   Flathead County

Killed by INDIANS while hunting or trapping

Date	Name	County
Fall of 1808	John Potts	Madison County
4/10/1810	George Drouillard	Gallatin County
4/10/1810	Delaware Indian Trapper	Gallatin County
4/10/1810	Delaware Indian Trapper	Gallatin County
4/12/1810	James Cheeks	Gallatin County

Table Ten: Categories of Deaths by Other Causes

(Killed by Indians Continued)

4/12/1810	Ayers	Gallatin County
4/12/1810	Freehearty	Gallatin County
4/12/1810	Hull	Gallatin County
4/12/1810	Rucker	Gallatin County
5/4/1823	Unknown Trapper	Cascade County
5/4/1823	Unknown Trapper	Cascade County
5/4/1823	Unknown Trapper	Cascade County
5/4/1823	Unknown Trapper	Cascade County
5/31/1823	Michael Immel	Yellowstone County
5/31/1823	Robert Jones	Yellowstone County
5/31/1823	Unknown Trapper	Yellowstone County
5/31/1823	Unknown Trapper	Yellowstone County
5/31/1823	Unknown Trapper	Yellowstone County
5/31/1823	Unknown Trapper	Yellowstone County
5/31/1823	Unknown Trapper	Yellowstone County
1/30/1832	Flathead Indian Trapper	Beaverhead County
10/14/1832	Henry Vanderburgh	Madison County
10/14/1832	Monsieur Pilou	Madison County
Early 1833	Hugh Glass	Yellowstone County
Early 1833	Edward Rose	Yellowstone County
Early 1833	Menard	Yellowstone County
Fall 1866	Charles Carofel	Chouteau County
4/2/1874	Rock	Cascade County
June 1876	Jim Fowler	Northern Montana
2/11/1881	Jonathan Erickson	Custer County

Killed by a Hunting <u>KNIFE</u> in the field

10/23/1978	Richard McGillis	Cascade County
11/30/1979	Rodney McKenzie	Sanders County

Killed by a <u>LIGHTNING STRIKE</u>

9/1/1894	B.T. "Curly" Rogers	Park County

Table Ten: Categories of Deaths by Other Causes

Killed by a <u>LOADED GUN</u> "IN" or "ON" a VEHICLE
(wagons, automobiles, trucks etc.)

5/10/1899	Hugh W. Hutchinson	Judith Basin County
9/22/1914	Carl Pearson	Cascade County
9/2/1919	Clyde Fryer	Park County
10/2/1921	Floyd Lewis	Cascade County
11/14/1926	James Royan	Roosevelt County
11/29/1932	Everett Hoar	Silver Bow County
9/13/1938	Vernon Ward	Missoula County
12/3/1940	Benjamin Mahr	Yellowstone County
10/12/1948	Freddy Pitsch	Big Horn County
11/12/1955	Mrs. Robert Pulse	Lincoln County
9/19/1962	Burton O. Burrell	Lincoln County
12/2/1962	Joe Bernard Cowdrey	Hill County
11/19/1968	John E. Anderson	Powell County
3/30/1976	Kenneth Ray Barner	Teton County
10/9/1976	Barry Drake	Treasure County
10/25/1976	Max Clayton Hoff	Yellowstone County
11/11/1991	Dana M. Fallsdown	Big Horn County

Killed by a <u>MALFUNCTIONING</u> weapon

10/26/2000	Gus Barber	Madison County

Died from an <u>OLD WOUND</u> sustained in an earlier Indian Attack.

8/29/1940	Charles VanBolene Lambert	Valley County

Killed while <u>PLAYING WITH A WEAPON</u> during a hunt

1/11/1896	Charlie Housman	Powell County
8/23/1900	August Lerch	Flathead County
5/16/1902	5-yr-old Kyolle boy	Liberty County

(Killed while playing with weapons continued)

3/16/1908	Ray Lefebvre	Cascade County
12/6/1917	James Donald Ashe	Toole County

Killed in a <u>POACHING INCIDENT</u>

10/21/1908	Charles B. Peyton	Missoula County
10/21/1908	Camille Paul	Missoula County
10/21/1908	Antoine Stousee	Missoula County
10/21/1908	Frank Stousee	Missoula County
10/21/1908	Martin Yellow-Mountain	Missoula County

Killed while <u>QUARRELING</u> during a hunt

5/6/1899	John Wills	Fergus County

Killed by a <u>RICOCHETING BULLET</u>

10/27/1925	H.E. Betts	Flathead County
12/31/1928	Leroy Jensen	Dawson County
11/25/1962	Steve Annas	Lewis & Clark County
7/19/1995	Chad R. Haugen	Blaine County

Killed in a <u>ROCK AVALANCHE</u>

11/22/1966	Leonard Gilbertson	Teton County

Killed in a <u>SNOW AVALANCE</u>

12/16/1916	Ernest Carlisle	Park County
12/20/1916	Nick Carr	Park County
11/17/1998	Scott Bettle	Beaverhead County

Killed by a <u>STRAY BULLET</u>

5/30/1902	White-Boy	Hill County
10/29/1934	Emmitt Claire Watters	Granite County
12/19/1937	Herman Merene	Park County
10/21/1940	Donald P. Knapp	Missoula County
10/18/1946	Frank Meyers	Gallatin County
10/24/1946	George Johnson	Silver Bow County
10/30/1955	Clair C. Hood	Richland County
10/22/1956	Clark Russell Lane	Jefferson County
10/19/1959	James Farstad	Phillips County
11/11/1967	Robert Michael Barnes	Missoula County
11/4/1970	Eugene Chapman	Missoula County
11/8/1973	David Nelson	Ravalli County
10/22/1975	Linda Palbykin	Madison County
11/13/2000	Raymond A. LaRoche	Richland County

Killed while <u>STRUGGLING OVER</u> game

10/27/1896	William W. White	Cascade County

SUFFOCATION or ASPHYXIATION or CARBON MONOXIDE POISONING

10/22/1964	Albert Altman	Gallatin County
11/21/1971	Lieutenant Charles Guin	Cascade County
11/21/1971	Chf Mstr Sgt Dickie Grisham	Cascade County
11/21/1971	Master Sgt Erle Webster	Cascade County
11/21/1971	Larry Webster	Cascade County
11/3/1972	Revie W. Luce	Stillwater County
11/3/1972	Richard S. Rusidak	Stillwater County
11/3/1978	Stanley Wood	Powell County
11/3/1978	Earnest A. Hahnert	Powell County
11/9/1990	Merle D. Wood	Lewis & Clark County
11/8/1992	Stanley Andrzejek	Cascade County
11/6/2003	Robert Paul Rasmusson	Beaverhead County

Table Ten: Categories of Deaths by Other Causes

UNKNOWN CAUSES

12/30/1903	G.W. Bowen	Gallatin County
11/1/1926	unknown Buffalo Hunter	Richland County
11/18/1938	Dan Mitchell	Toole County
11/18/1938	John J. Marshall	Granite County
10/29/1969	Robert L. Kleist	Powder River County
11/24/1974	Don Harkin	Gallatin County
10/23/1979	James Wayne Jackson	Valley County
10/5/1994	Michael Keith Bonko	Big Horn County
11/23/1998	Stephen Wesley Hoscheid	Granite County

Hit by a VEHICLE while hunting

3/31/1969	Gary Raunig	Lewis & Clark County

Killed in a VEHICLE CRASH
while hunting or en route to or from.

While there have probably been hundreds of other hunters killed in vehicle accidents going to and returning from hunts, these are recorded incidents of deaths while en route to and from and while hunting.

10/28/1957	Kenneth Schmidt	Beaverhead County
10/30/1962	Kenneth Lynnes	Blaine County
11/12/1962	Dennis Eaton	Park County
11/12/1962	Leo B. Johnson	Park County
10/22/1979	Mitchell Kelley	Carbon County
10/22/1979	Darcy Satterfield	Carbon County
12/3/2003	Robert Simonich	Lewis & Clark County

Montana Hunting Fatalities By Year

Date	Victim	Age	Cause	Location
1808				
Fall	John Potts	32	Other Causes	Madison Co.
Fall	Blackfeet Warrior[1]		Other Causes	Madison Co.
1810				
4/10	George Drouillard	33	Other Causes	Gallatin Co.
4/10	Del. Indian Trapper[2]		Other Causes	Gallatin Co.
4/10	Del. Indian Trapper[3]		Other Causes	Gallatin Co.
4/12	James Cheeks		Other Causes	Gallatin Co.
4/12	Ayers		Other Causes	Gallatin Co.
4/12	Freehearty		Other Causes	Gallatin Co.
4/12	Hull		Other Causes	Gallatin Co.
4/12	Rucker		Other Causes	Gallatin Co.
4/12	Blackfeet Warrior[4]		Other Causes	Gallatin Co.
1823				
5/4	Unknown Trapper		Other Causes	Cascade Co.
5/4	Unknown Trapper		Other Causes	Cascade Co.
5/4	Unknown Trapper		Other Causes	Cascade Co.
5/4	Unknown Causes		Other Causes	Cascade Co.
5/31	Michael Immel		Other Causes	Yellowstone Co
5/31	Robert Jones		Other Causes	Yellowstone Co
5/31	Unknown Trapper		Other Causes	Yellowstone Co
5/31	Unknown Trapper		Other Causes	Yellowstone Co
5/31	Unknown Trapper		Other Causes	Yellowstone Co
5/31	Unknown Trapper		Other Causes	Yellowstone Co
5/31	Unknown Trapper		Other Causes	Yellowstone Co

Montana Hunting Fatalities By Year

1832

1/30	Flathead Indian Trapper		Other Causes	Beaverhead Co.
10/14	Henry Vanderburgh		Other Causes	Madison Co.
10/14	Monsieur Pilou		Other Causes	Madison Co.
10/14	Blackfeet Warrior[5]		Other Causes	Madison Co.

1833

Early	Hugh Glass		Other Causes	Yellowstone C
Early	Edward Rose		Other Causes	Yellowstone Co
Early	Menard		Other Causes	Yellowstone Co

1866

Fall	Charles Carofel		Other Causes	Chouteau Co.

1874

Feb.	28 U.S. Soldiers		Other Causes	Cascade Co.
4/2	Rock		Other Causes	Cascade Co.

1876

June	Jim Fowler	40's	Other Causes	Northern MT.

1881

1/12	Private Severance		Lost/Missing	Hill County
2/5	Calvin Bryon		Lost/Missing	Custer County
2/11	Jonathan Erickson		Other Causes	Custer County
4/30	John Brown		Own Neg.	Teton County
9/10	Peter Helstrom		By Animal	Deer Lodge Co.

1884

7/11	Seth Whipple		Lost/Missing	Roosevelt Co.
10/15	David Austin	50	Own Neg.	Missoula Co.

1886

9/7	Robert Whipple		Water Death	Powell County

Montana Hunting Fatalities By Year

1890

12/8	Harry Emery		Mistaken Id.	Cascade Co.

1893

5/20	Olof Olson		Water Death	Flathead Co.
5/20	Charles F. Foley		Water Death	Lincoln County
9/7	Stanisloff Crelslenski	23	Water Death	Cascade Co.
9/9	Eli Paulin	16	Own Neg.	Missoula Co.
9/23	Tom Tregoning		Companion	Broadwater Co.

1894

9/1	B.T. "Curly" Rogers		Other Causes	Park County

(Reported in 1897)

1894	Unknown Hunter	cc	By Animal	Park County

1895

12/28	Paul Zias		Companion	Cascade Co.
12/29	John Whiting		Own Neg.	Granite County

1896

1/6/	Walter Joy	35	Water Death	Flathead Co.
1/11	Charlie Housman	11	Other Causes	Powell County
2/22	James Bingley	55	Lost/Missing	Powell County
10/11	LeGrand Contalou	38	Water Death	Cascade Co.
10/27	William W. White		Other Causes	Cascade Co.

1897

8/11	William Keogh	30	Companion	Cascade Co.

1898

2/9	M.C. Beach		Mistaken Id.	Mineral County

1899

5/6	John Wills	15	Other Causes	Fergus County
5/10	Hugh Hutchinson	26	Other Causes	Judith Basin Co
10/21	William Longstaff		Lost/Missing	Lewis & Clark

Montana Hunting Fatalities By Year

1900

2/10	George Humphrey		Other Causes	Madison Co.
2/17	Robert Waddell		Other Causes	Flathead Co.
8/23	August Lerch		Other Causes	Flathead Co.

1901

6/15	George Reiter		Lost/Missing	Gallatin Co.
8/4	George E. Hailey	60	Own Neg.	Meagher Co.
9/2	Henry C. Love	40	Companion	Cascade Co.
11/2	James Gamble		Own Neg.	Blaine County
12/8	Frank Swingley	15	Companion	Cascade Co.

1902

1/5	William Stuart	16	Own Neg.	Ravalli County
5/16	son of Henry Kyolle	5	Other Causes	Liberty County
5/30	White-Boy		Other Causes	Hill County
9/10	Rev. L.E. Armitage	26	Own Neg.	Meagher Co.
9/19	Louis Gardape		Mistaken Id.	Fergus County
10/5	Arthur Sharpe	16	Own Neg.	Cascade Co.
11/5	John Malloy		Own Neg.	Flathead Co.
11/7	Benjamin F. Egan	35	Lost/Missing	Flathead Co.

1903

8/5	Eddie Collins	6	Companion	Flathead Co.
9/19	Nick Simons Jr.	13	Own Neg.	Madison Co.
9/20	Jesse Hodges	25	Mistaken Id.	Fergus County
11/8	Bridge Williams		Water Death	Granite County
11/8	Max Wright	45	Water Death	Granite County
11/21	M.M. Johnson		Lost/Missing	Mineral County
12/30	G.W. Bowen		Other Causes	Gallatin Co.

1904

8/15	William Malard	18	Own Neg.	Phillips County
9/9	Iverson Vaughn	25	Companion	Cascade Co.
9/12	Charles Wiitala	23	Mistaken Id.	Cascade Co.
9/14	Lucien A. Enders	48	Water Death	Cascade Co.

1904 (continued)

11/17	Warren Hulbert		Companion	Sanders County
11/19	Harry Nagard	10	Companion	Gallatin Co.
11/22	Percy Glenn	13	Own Neg.	Fergus County
12/19	Carroll E. Brooks		Companion	Missoula Co.

1905

8/3	Mr. Barnaby		Lost/Missing	Lincoln County
9/2	Frank Gonsior	17	Own Neg.	Cascade Co.
9/5	Mrs. Coventry		Mistaken Id.	Park County

1906

8/26	Miss Ruth Bean		Companion	Beaverhead Co.
9/15	Aaron McGuire	36	Mistaken Id.	Flathead Co.
11/10	S.E. Wilson		Mistaken Id.	Fergus County

1907

9/27	William Powell		Own Neg.	Chouteau Co.
10/21	T. Stewart		Water Death	Lewis & Clark
10/21	Arthur Donegan		Water Death	Lewis & Clark
10/21	James Brown		Water Death	Lewis & Clark
12/20	Charles R. Peterson		Mistaken Id.	Flathead Co.

1908

3/16	Ray Lefebvre	12	Other Causes	Cascade Co.
7/13	A.F. Moody	37	Companion	Madison Co.
10/8	Louis Deckerville	50	Own Neg.	Lewis & Clark
10/20	Charles B. Peyton	34	Other Causes	Missoula Co.
10/20	Camille Paul	45	Other Causes	Missoula Co.
10/20	Antoine Stousee	49	Other Causes	Missoula Co.
10/20	Frank Stousee	14	Other Causes	Missoula Co.
10/20	M. Yellow-Mountain	70's	Other Causes	Missoula Co.
10/25	Harry Heath		Lost/Missing	Lewis & Clark
10/26	Andrew J. Martin	17	Own Neg.	Cascade Co.
12/4	Alexander MacAulay	50	Other Causes	Glacier County
12/19	Robert A. Taylor		Mistaken Id.	Lincoln County

Montana Hunting Fatalities By Year

1909

1/1	Otto Roll	12	Companion	Gallatin Co.
10/5	Mike Friel		Companion	Silver Bow Co.
10/26	E. Lund		Lost/Missing	Park County
11/15	George C. Beckman	14	Own Neg.	Cascade Co.

1910

11/14	Amos Schultz	11	Lost/Missing	Chouteau Co.
11/14	Walter Schultz	14	Lost/Missing	Chouteau Co.
12/3	Ray Forcum		Health	Flathead Co.

1911

11/30	Walter B. Munroe	38	Own Neg.	Flathead Co.

1912

1/23	Leon Stevenson		Other Causes	Carbon County
5/5	John Austin		By Animal	Park County
5/7	Floyd Ritch	22	Own Neg.	Fergus County
9/9	John Sagar	15	Own Neg.	Silver Bow Co.
9/17	Edward Michaels	24	Companion	Jefferson Co.
9/29	Richard Jones		Own Neg.	Lewis & Clark
10/2	Martin McGraw		Own Neg.	Cascade Co.
10/10	Thomas Stark	22	Lost/Missing	Cascade Co.
11/10	John Easlack		Mistaken Id.	Lincoln County
11/14	George Goss		Mistaken Id.	Carter County
11/23	Joe Waigel		Lost/Missing	Flathead Co.
11/26	Harrison Allan	23	Own Neg.	Park County

1913

9/3	Mrs. H. E. Houston		Own Neg.	Flathead Co.
9/5	Leslie Dodds	14	Own Neg.	Beaverhead Co.
10/2	Mrs. James Morris		Other Causes	Hill County
10/5	J. Dulen		Other Causes	Lincoln County

Montana Hunting Fatalities By Year

1914
7/29	Ervin M. Hilton	32	Other Causes	Cascade Co.
9/21	Robert Rheinackle	19	Water Death	Pondera Co.
9/22	Carl Pearson	12	Other Causes	Cascade Co.
10/29	Roy Blow		Health	Powell County
11/2	George Standiford		Mistaken Id.	Lincoln County
12/2	Fred E. Woodworth		Companion	Sanders County
12/2	Wallace Brown	60	Lost/Missing	Beaverhead Co.

1915
9/4	Ernest B. Clark		Mistaken Id.	Sanders County
10/21	David A. Long		Lost/Missing	Flathead Co.
11/21	Henry Divis	21	Other Causes	Lincoln County

1916
5/17	Samuel G. Massey		Mistaken Id.	Gallatin Co.
10/7	Joseph F. House	42	Companion	Cascade Co.
10/12	Ralph Belgrade		Own Neg.	Cascade Co.
10/13	Oswald K. Sellar	35	Companion	Fergus County
11/24	Geza Ottopal	36	Health	Fergus County
12/10	Joseph A. Stuesse		Own Neg.	Lewis & Clark
12/14	Dan Murr		Mistaken Id.	Lincoln County
12/16	Wilbert Shipman	18	Companion	Gallatin Co.
12/16	Ernest Carlisle	33	Other Causes	Park County
12/20	Nick Carr		Other Causes	Park County

1917
9/16	Sullivan Berger	25	Mistaken Id.	Fergus County
9/19	Edward L. Volcour	60	Health	Lincoln County
9/27	Gladys Bradley	12	Companion	Beaverhead Co.
10/29	Adelore Lafrinire	15	Other Causes	Missoula Co.
11/7	Fred H. Batts	34	Water Death	Granite County
11/15	Andrew Craig		Water Death	Yellowstone Co
11/23	Frank Carlson		Lost/Missing	Cascade Co.
12/6	James Donald Ashe	11	Other Causes	Toole County

Montana Hunting Fatalities By Year

1918

10/23	Louie Hoop	30	Water Death	Hill County
10/24	M.F. Stoughton	48	Own Neg.	Chouteau Co.
10/26	Jack Smith		Own Neg.	Flathead Co.
10/26	John J. Robertson		Water Death	Gallatin Co.

1919

4/12	Elijah Linn	17	Companion	Musselshell Co.
9/21	Clyde Fryer	19	Other Causes	Park County
10/2	Leroy S. Tupper		Companion	Flathead Co.
10/10	Alexander Stronach		Own Neg.	Liberty County
10/23	Captain W. Strong		Mistaken Id.	Powell County
10/25	Norman Winchell		Mistaken Id.	Gallatin Co.
10/29	P.L. Woods		Heath	Flathead Co.
11/2	Thomas C. Page	65	Health	Gallatin Co.
11/3	James McWhethey	27	Mistaken Id.	Powell County

1920

11/5	Thomas A. Towery	56	Own Neg.	Gallatin Co.
11/23	Carl Osmand		Lost/Missing	Beaverhead Co.
11/26	Charles L. Torrence	27	Own Neg.	Teton County
12/1	Ernest Balke	61	Mistaken Id.	Flathead Co.

1921

9/22	Harry G. Hawkins	25	Water Death	Glacier County
10/2	Floyd Lewis	28	Other Causes	Cascade Co.
11/4	James Pullman	35	Companion	Flathead Co.
11/9	Knute Knuteson	27	Own Neg.	Silver Bow Co.
11/13	Andrew Brae	16	Companion	Missoula Co.
11/23	Archie Blair		Own Neg.	Hill County

1922

8/7	Andrew Lubardo	31	Own Neg.	Carbon Co.
11/9	Lee Combs	15	Water Death	Lake County
11/9	Lyle Combs	19	Water Death	Lake County
11/9	William Combs	23	Water Death	Lake County
12/9	Paul Russell	18	Companion	Lincoln County

Montana Hunting Fatalities By Year

1923

9/2	Ralph Ryan	11	Own Neg.	Silver Bow Co.
9/27	Fred Mock		Other Causes	Glacier County
9/30	John Szasv	33	Own Neg.	Broadwater Co.
10/20	Harold Wallinder	18	Mistaken Id.	Lincoln County
11/14	James Harvey Boling	16	Companion	Gallatin Co.
11/19	Andrew Hakke		Water Death	Granite County
11/23	Cecil Trusty	14	Companion	Flathead Co.
11/26	Ted Ellis	35	Water Death	Teton County
12/12	Peter Henningson	15	Companion	Valley County

1924

9/21	Everett Kaoski	15	Companion	Cascade Co.
9/29	Peter Irvine		Health	Lake County
10/1	Larcey M. Lakar	15	Own Neg.	Carbon County
10/8	Walter Wersall	15	Own Neg.	Yellowstone Co
10/28	Cavyell boy	6	Other Causes	McCone Co.
11/30	John Vanden-Wall	28	Companion	Pondera Co.
12/2	Hunt Coy		Other Causes	Yellowstone Co

1925

10/23	J.H. Waddell	24	Companion	Gallatin Co.
10/27	H.F. Betts		Other Causes	Flathead Co.
10/31	Frank A. Matt		Lost/Missing	Missoula Co.
11/15	Charles Donally		Health	Mineral Co.
11/20	James Geer		Other Causes	Flathead Co.
12/14	Clifford W. Ofstie	15	Companion	Fergus County

1926

9/17	Farney L. Coles	19	Companion	Stillwater Co.
9/17	Richard Driscoll	27	Other Causes	Jefferson Co.
9/18	James Keefe		Water Death	Beaverhead Co.
9/25	Samuel B. Clark	17	Own Neg.	Missoula Co.
11/1	Buffalo Hunter		Other Causes	Richland Co.
11/14	James Royan		Other Causes	Roosevelt Co.
11/16	William Lawrence		Own Neg.	Meagher Co.

1926 (continued)

11/19	John Ben Hougland	32	Lost/Missing	Missoula Co.

1927

9/17	Huston C. Peters		Companion	Teton County
9/30	Burr W. Clark	42	Own Neg.	Broadwater Co.
10/17	Joseph J. Kosena	16	Own Neg.	Deer Lodge Co.
10/31	Frank Balkovich	39	Water Death	Lewis & Clark
11/11	Kenneth Gardner	21	Mistaken Id.	Cascade Co.
11/15	Rex Roberts	16	Own Neg.	Ravalli County
11/16	George Kennedy		Own Neg.	Flathead Co.
12/11	Anton Schafer	15	Own Neg.	Judith Basin Co

1928

9/25	Carlton Whitsell	8	Companion	Cascade Co.
10/13	Olive Shaw	12	Companion	Fergus County
10/17	Henry L. Houston	54	Other Causes	Cascade Co.
11/4	Walter Griesbach	30	Own Neg.	Chouteau Co.
11/6	Bozo Masanovich		Own Neg.	Lewis & Clark
11/12	Herschel A. Dockery	18	Own Neg.	Cascade Co.
11/17	Sgt Paul B. Portis		Companion	Mineral County
11/17	Von Hartso	20	Water Death	Toole County
12/31	Leroy Jensen	16	Other Causes	Dawson Co.

1929

10/21	Clifford Harrison	22	Water Death	Cascade Co.
10/21	Otto Garrison	35	Water Death	Cascade Co.
10/23	Evert Applegate	34	Water Death	Cascade Co.
11/2	Alva Williams	35	Other Causes	Sweet Grass Co
11/19	Andrew Kola	40	Water Death	Deer Lodge Co.
11/25	Wlm Baumgartner	19	Companion	Yellowstone Co
11/25	Richard Allen	25	Own Neg.	Carbon County
12/11	Frank Mayash	57	Mistaken Id.	Park County

Montana Hunting Fatalities By Year

1930

9/28	Chls Montgomery	39	Own Neg.	Beaverhead Co.
11/24	Andy J. Marouthas	38	Water Death	Cascade Co.

1931

10/3	Steve Chrisman		Health	Yellowstone Co
10/26	Hollis B. Wiggin		Own Neg.	Missoula Co.
11/10	Wallace Stone	23	Own Neg.	Custer County
11/11	Adolph A. Coverdell	31	Mistaken Id.	Flathead Co.
11/13	Floyd Marble	31	Own Neg.	Gallatin Co.
11/22	John C. Holland		Own Neg.	Gallatin Co.
1931	William B. Burkhart	43	Own Neg.	Missoula Co.

1932

10/4	Clarence E. Fahlgren		Own Neg.	Sweet Grass Co
11/2	Lewis W. Maynard	15	Companion	Ravalli County
11/2	Oliver M. Johnson	45	Own Neg.	Deer Lodge Co.
11/8	Orville Briner	21	Mistaken Id.	Sweet Grass Co
11/14	Edgely Mills	21	Mistaken Id.	Granite County
11/14	Harvey H. Mills		Mistaken Id.	Granite County
11/27	Jack Carlisle	40	Lost/Missing	Glacier County
11/29	Everett Hoar	11	Other Causes	Silver Bow Co.
11/29	Robert M. Bell	45	Own Neg.	Silver Bow Co.
12/16	John Hinz	52	Lost/Missing	Deer Lodge Co.

1933

10/10	Vincent Walcott	17	Companion	Lake County
10/15	Ford R. Lake	30	Water Death	Teton County
10/19	Walter L. Kulbeck	47	Companion	Flathead Co.
10/31	James Vern Booth	40	Other Causes	Missoula Co.
11/4	Charles Midboe	22	Companion	Dawson Co.
11/6	Homer Schuchmann		Mistaken Id.	Ravalli County
11/7	Carl Burnston	30	Mistaken Id.	Madison Co.
11/7	Melvin Evenson	54	Mistaken Id.	Flathead Co.
11/8	George Armitage	57	Lost/Missing	Madison Co.

Montana Hunting Fatalities By Year

1933 (continued)

Date	Name	Age	Cause	County
11/10	Donald Campbell		Own Neg.	Lincoln County
11/14	Robert Harkness	63	Health	Missoula Co.

1934

Date	Name	Age	Cause	County
9/30	Harry Hines	60	Health	Lewis & Clark
10/29	Emmitt C. Watters	24	Other Causes	Granite County
10/29	Charles Jacobs	33	Own Neg.	Yellowstone Co

1935

Date	Name	Age	Cause	County
10/24	William Powell	80	Health	Judith Basin Co
11/4	Lawrence Dean	34	Own Neg.	Gallatin Co.
11/6	Lawrence Carmack	33	Own Neg.	Gallatin Co.
11/7	Hugo Benedetti	35	Water Death	Cascade Co.
11/8	Sam Kahl	17	Own Neg.	Lake County
11/10	George Westfall	69	Lost/Missing	Silver Bow Co.
11/20	Wilbur Coe		Mistaken Id.	Flathead Co.
11/27	Philip S. Terrio	19	Own Neg.	Beaverhead Co.

1936

Date	Name	Age	Cause	County
8/2	Harry E. Stradtzeck	12	Own Neg.	Flathead Co.
10/4	John Fink	18	Own Neg.	Deer Lodge Co.
10/11	Edgar Hicks	16	Own Neg.	Ravalli County
10/14	Clifford Smith	30	Companion	Lewis & Clark
10/17	Ruth Fraunhofer	18	Own Neg.	Cascade Co.
10/19	Aurel Tucker	14	Companion	Missoula Co.
10/22	Edward Neumann	33	Own Neg.	Fergus County
11/10	Albert Booth	27	Own Neg.	Gallatin Co.
11/10	Elmer E. Stockman	35	Own Neg.	Ravalli County
11/10	Thomas Weir	45	Mistaken Id.	Powell County
11/10	Bruce Schwenneker	27	Mistaken Id.	*Absb/Brtooh
11/12	Albert Westberg	28	Lost/Missing	Meagher Co.
11/15	Arthur T. Ridgeway	45	Own Neg.	Fergus County
11/16	Ray V. Doney	35	Own Neg.	Missoula Co.
11/30	George Reissing	14	Companion	Teton County

Montana Hunting Fatalities By Year

1937

7/13	Andrew Danielson	69	Own Neg.	Flathead Co.
10/18	Ralph Longpre	23	By Animal	Mineral Co.
10/22	Alfonse Chourand	21	Lost/Missing	Missoula Co.
10/22	Ed Cameron	42	Health	Fergus County
10/23	George T. Westover		Water Death	Madison Co.
11/23	Berton Thompson	50	Own Neg.	Broadwater Co
12/19	Herman Merene	35	Other Causes	Park County

1938

9/13	Vernon Ward		Other Causes	Missoula Co.
9/23	Earl Lyght	20	Own Neg.	Flathead Co.
10/17	James A. Parrish		Health	Lewis & Clark
10/19	Clarence Dorey	25	Lost/Missing	Missoula Co.
10/21	William Hauskamaa	20	Lost/Missing	Judith Basin Co
10/23	Mark Kaulbach	19	Own Neg.	Chouteau Co.
10/31	Carl Anderson	19	Companion	Chouteau Co.
11/1	Forrest Smurr	22	Own Neg.	Lake County
11/3	Grover Pace	44	By Animal	Sanders County
11/4	Frank Thompson		Health	Flathead Co.
11/14	George Mcleslie	34	Lost/Missing	Blaine County
11/15	Dick Powell	20	Lost/Missing	Gallatin Co.
11/15	Howard V. Little		Mistaken Id.	Ravalli County
11/18	Dan Mitchell		Other Causes	Toole County
11/18	John J. Marshall	35	Other Causes	Granite County
11/22	Robert Felieous	24	Companion	Silver Bow Co.
11/23	Frank Seiller	17	Companion	Lake County
12/3	Fred Grinde	23	Own Neg.	Cascade Co.

1939

10/5	William L. Wyrick	27	Other Causes	Yellowstone Co
10/9	Wesley Burger Coley	15	Other Causes	Yellowstone Co
10/16	Robert Phoenix	21	Own Neg.	Madison Co.
10/20	William Smith	21	Own Neg.	Ravalli County
11/3	Chauncey Bowdin		Own Neg.	Lake County
11/30	Clarence Baker		Mistaken Id.	Gallatin Co.

Montana Hunting Fatalities By Year

1940

8/29	Charles V. Lambert	67	Other Causes	Valley County
10/4	Dennis F. Kohner		Own Neg.	Ravalli County
10/5	George Eckelberry	42	Water Death	Flathead Co.
10/8	Edward Duby	28	Mistaken Id.	Missoula Co.
10/17	Grover C. Bryan	54	Companion	Sweet Grass Co
10/20	Robert Reesman	12	Own Neg.	Missoula Co.
10/21	Donald P. Knapp	37	Other Causes	Missoula Co.
11/9	Gus Stean	60	Lost/Missing	Mineral Co.
11/11	Claude S. Averill	54	Health	Lake County
11/18	Carl Shepka	13	Own Neg.	Deer Lodge Co.
11/19	Frank Howell	50	By Animal	Flathead Co.
11/22	James Brice	14	Own Neg.	Yellowstone Co
12/3	Benjamin Mahr	36	Other Causes	Yellowstone Co

1941

10/30	Hezekiah VanDorn	62	Companion	Lake County
11/8	Riley Ray	56	Own Neg.	Musselshell Co.
11/16	Charles McElroy	49	By Animal	Flathead Co.
11/17	George W. Flamm	58	Companion	Carbon County
11/17	Oliver Gaston	70	Health	Flathead Co.
11/29	James McBride	70	Lost/Missing	Lincoln County

1942

10/27	Elmer Buck	28	Companion	Flathead Co.
10/30	Frank Pogacher		Lost/Missing	Musselshell Co.
11/5	Arthur S. Borden		Health	Lincoln County
11/7	John Eichstadt	54	Own Neg.	Deer Lodge Co.
11/7	Alley C. McGilvrey	78	Health	Missoula Co.
11/10	Walter Grimes	46	Companion	Cascade Co.
11/10	Paul Praast		Lost/Missing	Powell County

1943

10/17	Albert Mora	18	Mistaken Id.	Lewis & Clark
11/1	Oscar Bye	51	Health	Silver Bow Co.
11/1	James Bowden	11	Own Neg.	Ravalli County

Montana Hunting Fatalities By Year

1943 (continued)

11/9	Henry W. Bassett	64	Health	Flathead Co.
11/15	Gilbert J. Pochervina	14	Own Neg.	Madison Co.

1944

10/14	Orit T. Forbes	40	Own Neg.	Pondera Co.
11/21	Bryon C. Wilson	54	Lost/Missing	Flathead Co.

1945

10/5	Wlm R. Reymerson	56	Health	Ravalli County
10/17	J.H. Meiers		Companion	Lincoln County
10/20	J. W. Redlingshafer	32	Companion	Flathead Co.
10/22	Creed R. Morgan		Companion	Ravalli County
10/23	Vern Simaro	35	Health	Lincoln County
11/10	James Callaway	47	Lost/Missing	Lewis & Clark
11/13	Clifford Courtney	44	Water Death	Yellowstone Co
11/13	Emmett Courtney	15	Water Death	Yellowstone Co
11/14	Henry Staffan	51	Health	Beaverhead Co.
11/15	Charles White	27	Other Causes	Park County
11/25	Monty Leavitt	9	Companion	Toole County

1946

10/16	William Kercher Jr.	17	Own Neg.	Cascade Co.
10/18	Frank Meyers	39	Other Causes	Gallatin Co.
10/20	Ed Bloodgood		Lost/Missing	Park County
10/24	George Johnson	30	Other Causes	Silver Bow Co.
10/28	Jack E. Parmillee		Water Death	Callatin Co.
10/28	G.A. Zink		Water Death	Gallatin Co.
10/29	John N. Thomas		Health	Park County
11/21	Richard Busler		Water Death	Lake County
11/25	Robert Rodine	23	Water Death	Missoula Co.

1947

10/8	Louis Camp	66	Health	Ravalli County
10/9	Ross Collins	47	Health	Ravalli County
10/12	Robert Longnecker	39	Health	Ravalli County

Montana Hunting Fatalities By Year

1947 (continued)

10/16	Clifford G. Hogan	42	Water Death	Missoula Co.
10/16	Albert L. Richardson	29	Water Death	Missoula Co.
10/27	Henry A. True	64	Health	Pondera Co.
10/28	Benedict D. Perga	44	Health	Madison Co.
10/29	Charles Masker	19	Companion	Judith Basin
11/6	George D. Mason		By Animal	Valley County
11/8	Ralph T. Grosswiler	40	Own Neg.	Flathead Co.
11/9	George Lofftus	38	Lost/Missing	Ravalli County
11/16	Robert A. Ryan	63	Health	Sweet Grass Co
11/16	Ralph Adkins	57	Health	Granite County
11/16	Charles M. Brewster	58	Health	Cascade Co.
11/29	Girrald E. Townsend	55	Health	Gallatin Co.

1948

10/12	Freddy Pitsch	14	Other Causes	Big Horn Co.
10/16	Walter Laughfranere	25	Mistaken Id.	Park County
10/31	Donald J. Bertoglio	15	Companion	Silver Bow Co.
11/1	Jerry Brown	24	Own Neg.	Powder River
11/1	Arne Haugse	76	Health	Teton County
11/19	Raymond Necklace		Companion	Roosevelt Co.

1949

10/12	Floyd E. Stiles	54	Health	Missoula Co.
10/12	Fred Jaqueth	51	Health	Flathead Co.
10/12	Jesse L. Odelle	64	Health	Pondera Co.
10/17	William Patterson	27	Own Neg.	Beaverhead Co
10/18	Charles Kirby	52	Water Death	Fergus County
10/20	George L. Russell	51	Health	Silver Bow Co.

1950

9/27	Charles F. Maris		Health	Musselshell Co.
10/9	Caroline J. Ullery	23	Companion	Custer County
10/23	Alvin Austin		Companion	Sanders County
10/24	Horace H. Snider		Water Death	Phillips County
10/24	William A. Olsen	64	Health	Phillips County

Montana Hunting Fatalities By Year

1950 (continued)

10/24	Oscar Butts	59	Health	Missoula Co.
10/24	Frederick Portman	43	Own Neg.	Lewis & Clark
11/3	Mrs. Mary Winkley	40	Lost/Missing	Beaverhead Co.
11/15	Robert Brown W.	17	Companion	Missoula Co.
11/17	Elmer A. Findall	65	Heath	Missoula Co.

1951

10/15	E.C. Humphrey	85	Lost/Missing	Fergus County
10/18	Edward Robinson	14	Companion	Roosevelt Co.
10/19	Lowell Webb		Mistaken Id.	Ravalli County
10/21	James Wishart	21	Lost/Missing	Flathead Co.
10/23	Curtis Westrum	31	Own Neg.	Flathead Co.
10/27	Ray A. Kuaffman	16	Own Neg.	Flathead Co.
10/27	Rudolph B. Krutar		Health	Deer Lodge Co.
10/27	Bernard V. Urich		Health	Sweet Grass Co
10/27	John Heiland		Health	Lake County
10/27	Ernest Dubie		Health	Beaverhead Co.
10/28	Guy Long	40	Mistaken Id.	Flathead Co.
11/1	Fred Anderson	39	Health	Flathead Co.
11/5	Gerald Hays		Companion	Lincoln County
11/6	Arthur Foster	53	Health	Gallatin Co.
11/7	Thomas E. McClure	65	Health	Stillwater Co.
11/14	Roy Rush		Health	Flathead Co.
11/14	Marvin H. Wagner	24	Companion	Sanders County
11/16	Charles Webber	17	Mistaken Id	Missoula Co.

1952

10/11	Orville Clancy	17	Own Neg.	Roosevelt Co.
10/18	Rev. Charles Bolin	35	Mistaken Id.	Flathead Co.
10/20	William F. Johnson	69	Health	Lewis & Clark
10/21	Frank Yale	50	Health	Flathead Co.
10/22	Richard W. Gilber	60	Own Neg.	Lincoln County
10/29	Alfred Sterner	70	Health	Lake County
11/4	Kenneth Newton	17	Own Neg.	Phillips County
12/1	George F. Delisle	52	Companion	Yellowstone Co

Montana Hunting Fatalities By Year

1953

10/8	Donald Ray Fain	13	Lost/Missing	Madison Co.
10/13	Clarence Sivertson	20	Own Neg.	Blaine County
10/17	Edwin Charles Ham	16	Companion	Powell County
10/17	William Lowney	62	Health	Silver Bow Co.
10/21	Al Kruzon	32	Companion	Mineral County
10/23	William Syblon	37	Own Neg.	Musselshell.Co.
10/25	Francis Norquay	55	Companion	Flathead Co.
11/3	Harry Howard	84	Mistaken Id.	Lincoln County
11/8	Art Sanders	16	Companion	Musselshell Co.
11/8	Bert Bailey	47	Health	Ravalli County
11/19	Ben Reimer	45	Lost/Missing	Flathead Co.

1954

10/15	Jackie Shandy	16	Water Death	Carbon County
10/19	Leonard R. Schmidt	39	Health	Musselshell Co.
10/19	Charles T. Case	50	Health	Beaverhead Co.
10/28	David W. Saltsman	24	Companion	Lincoln County
11/1	Dean Williams	18	Own Neg.	Richland Co.
11/1	John Earl Murphy	63	Health	Lewis & Clark
11/1	William Orr	21	Mistaken Id.	Beaverhead Co.
11/2	John Synnes	70	Health	Lewis & Clark
11/15	Ray Johns	49	Companion	Lake County
11/20	John H. Mueller	72	Health	Lewis & Clark

1955

10/16	Harry Luce	58	Health	Cascade Co.
10/16	Silas H. Jerome	66	Health	Missoula Co.
10/19	William N. Hughley	64	Health	Lewis & Clark
10/27	Joseph K. Harbison	55	Health	Park County
10/30	Clair C. Hood	65	Other Causes	Richland Co.
10/31	Rudolph Pries	82	Health	Wibaux County
11/9	William Jones	60	Heath	Madison Co.
11/9	Henry J. Jondrow	78	Health	Sweet Grass Co
11/12	Mrs. Robert Pulse	19	Other Causes	Lincoln County
11/15	Thomas Melton	47	Health	Ravalli County

Montana Hunting Fatalities By Year

1955 (continued)

11/15	Thomas Melton	47	Health	Ravalli County
11/15	Thomas Melton	47	Health	Ravalli County
11/20	Ross Nelson	19	Companion	Broadwater Co.
11/20	John Burvich	19	Mistaken Id.	Silver Bow Co.

1956

10/17	Miles Spaich	41	Own Neg.	Mineral County
10/17	Ralph Younglove	32	Mistaken Id.	Lewis & Clark
10/18	William R. Clark	56	Health	Beaverhead Co.
10/18	Clarence Skaggs	22	Mistaken Id.	Powder River
10/18	Raymond H. White	42	Own Neg.	Yellowstone Co
10/22	Clark Russell Lane	10	Other Causes	Jefferson Co.
10/22	William K. Scott	29	By Animal	*Bob Marshall
10/28	George Henry Mills	61	Health	Ravalli County
10/29	Herbert Goecks	47	Health	Broadwater Co.
10/30	Pearl Herndon	63	Health	Missoula Co.
11/6	Jim Hankinson	25	Companion	Mineral County
11/7	Gary Mosback	9	Companion	Park County
11/12	June C. Edmondson	69	Health	Custer County
11/13	Burton Davenport	50	Health	Sanders County
11/13	John F. Detz	50	Health	Gallatin Co.

1957

10/7	Arthur Shoberg	15	Own Neg.	Lewis & Clark
10/13	Gerald Barney	25	Lost/Missing	Granite County
10/22	Jack Kosola	48	Health	Deer Lodge Co.
10/28	Kenneth Schmidt	28	Other Causes	Beaverhead Co.
10/28	Frank West	48	Companion	Park County
11/4	Albert Hardie	21	Companion	Lewis & Clark
11/4	Robert Jennings	17	Mistaken Id.	Ravalli County
11/12	Walter B. Sokoloski	18	Companion	Ravalli County
11/12	John W. Dowling		Health	Ravalli County
11/13	Elias Hoch	40	Companion	Garfield Co.
11/16	Herb Martinich	48	Health	Cascade Co.

Montana Hunting Fatalities By Year

1958

10/1	John Gust Anderson	71	Companion	Dawson Co.
10/20	Howard Gleason	77	Own Neg.	Richland Co.
10/23	Clyde F. Williams	74	Lost/Missing	Powder River
10/23	Robert Pittman	28	Lost/Missing	Rosebud Co.
10/24	John Stone	75	Health	Flathead Co.
10/24	Clyde Escher	19	Lost/Missing	Powder River
10/24	Tony Stepanek	19	Lost/Missing	Powder River
10/26	Ralph W. Harbaugh	64	Health	Garfield Co.
10/28	Walter Lee Collins	66	Health	Sanders County
10/31	Samuel Adams	39	By Animal	Powell County
11/10	Ivan L. Gamett	27	Health	Lewis & Clark
11/15	Robert C. Brewer	35	Heath	Teton County
11/17	Walter Talbot	44	Health	Madison Co.
11/22	LeRoy Tucker	41	Own Neg.	Blaine County
11/23	Clyde Jenkins	45	Health	Sanders County
11/24	Harold T. Farron	57	Own Neg.	Granite County
11/30	Reuben Gomke	15	Companion	Hill County

1959

1/30	Dale Robinson	20	Companion	Musselshell Co.
10/12	Westley P. Stace	29	Companion	Blaine County
10/19	Robert W. Smith	22	Companion	Judith Basin Co
10/19	Donald Marko	26	Mistaken Id.	Cascade Co.
10/19	James Farstad	16	Other Causes	Phillips County
10/26	James Garey	64	Other Causes	Bob Marshall
10/27	Fred E. Kent	30	Lost/Missing	Judith Basin Co
11/1	John Edward Grady	44	Own Neg.	Lewis & Clark
11/1	Gary Sorenson	17	Companion	Phillips County
11/7	Clarence Trader	29	Lost/Missing	Big Horn Co.
11/8	John A. Robinson	47	Health	Lewis & Clark
11/8	Wesley H. Elbert	33	Mistaken Id.	Beaverhead Co.
11/11	John B. Bourassa	64	Health	Meagher Co.
11/14	Joseph P. Jansen Jr.	44	Health	Toole County
11/17	Adrian Dick Joki		Lost/Missing	Gallatin Co.
11/18	Aloysius Racine	14	Own Neg.	Glacier County

Montana Hunting Fatalities By Year

1959 (continued)

Date	Name	Age	Cause	County
11/22	George Wood	50	Health	Lincoln County
11/22	Neil Christenson	30	Mistaken Id.	Flathead Co.
11/22	Ernest Hammer		Mistaken Id.	Pondera Co.
11/28	Arthur D. Jordan	59	Lost/Missing	Missoula Co.

1960

Date	Name	Age	Cause	County
10/15	Harvey E. Hewitt		Lost/Missing	Roosevelt Co.
10/24	Judith Marie Walker	22	Companion	Valley County
11/1	John R. Dahl	41	Own Neg.	Deer Lodge Co.
11/16	Fritz Fry	65	Lost/Missing	Missoula Co.
11/20	Walter Franke	52	Mistaken Id.	Sanders County

1961

Date	Name	Age	Cause	County
10/2	James Gregory	17	Own Neg.	Carbon County
10/16	Kenneth Rawson		Health	Chouteau Co.
10/16	Jack R. Burger	34	Companion	Mineral County
10/17	Emil L. Rozuoi	51	Health	Rosebud Co.
10/18	Troy E. Thacker	58	Health	Flathead Co.
10/18	Robert Zeuler	52	Health	Yellowstone Co
10/21	James Miller	21	Mistaken Id.	Richland Co.
10/22	Norm G. Thrasher	21	Mistaken Id.	Cascade Co.
10/23	Egbert Zyp Jr.	49	Health	Fergus County
10/24	Michael Long-Tree	16	Companion	Roosevelt Co.
11/5	Thomas Kelsey	39	Mistaken Id.	Lincoln County
11/6	William J. Batten	26	Water Death	Madison Co.
11/7	Don Cattnach	46	Companion	Petroleum Co.

1962

Date	Name	Age	Cause	County
9/11	Duayne Murray	29	Other Causes	Fergus County
9/11	Ben Peterson Jr.	27	Other Causes	Fergus County
9/19	Burton O. Burrell	54	Other Causes	Lincoln County
10/2	John Higgins	47	Other Causes	Missoula Co.
10/29	Fred Hamilton	74	Lost/Missing	Lake County
10/30	Kenneth Lynnes		Other Causes	Blaine County
11/5	James Gibbons	29	Mistaken Id.	Big Horn Co.

Montana Hunting Fatalities By Year

1962 (continued)

11/12	Richard Austad	17	Other Causes	Lewis & Clark
11/12	Dennis Eaton	42	Other Causes	Park County
11/12	Leo B. Johnson		Other Causes	Park County
11/13	Edward Olson		Own Neg.	Gallatin Co.
11/13	David Klien	15	Lost/Missing	Lake County
11/24	Kenneth Eickoff	13	Own Neg.	Fergus County
11/25	Steve Annas	11	Other Causes	Lewis & Clark
12/2	Joe Bernard Cowdrey	20	Other Causes	Hill County
12/16	Kenneth H. Fraser	31	Water Death	Flathead Co.
12/16	Floyd F. Knopes	29	Water Death	Flathead Co.

1963

9/21	Clifford M. Ware	63	Health	Richland Co.
9/27	Charles W. West	53	Own Neg.	Silver Bow Co.
9/27	Billy Johnson	15	Own Neg.	Phillip County
10/15	Theodore Haynes	19	Own Neg.	Yellowstone Co
10/18	Dr. G. O. Sweum	62	Health	Custer County
11/2	Victor Vermillion	25	Lost/Missing	Gallatin Co.
11/13	Calvin L. Seeley	42	Health	Fergus County
11/14	Charles Nelson	63	Own Neg.	Lake County
11/22	Robert A. Gruber	68	Health	Sanders County

1964

10/19	Frank L. Anderson	42	Companion	Park County
10/20	Earl James Gaw	57	Health	Custer County
10/22	Albert Altman	52	Other Causes	Gallatin Co.
10/26	Lindy Walla	6	Companion	Wheatland Co
11/2	Floyd Greenup	52	Health	Sanders County
11/16	Frank McCauley	64	Health	Jefferson Co.
11/20	William Popish	48	Own Neg.	Missoula Co.

1965

1/15	Carl Martin	23	Companion	Toole County
10/4	William Townsend	50	Mistaken Id.	Gallatin Co.
10/5	Ward A. Staats Sr.		Health	Lewis & Clark

1965 (continued)

10/9	Jeff Thomas	50	Mistaken Id.	Ravalli County
10/11	Egon Wagerer	38	Own Neg.	Lewis & Clark
10/26	Wallace Mack	70	Health	Custer County
11/2	Regan Hoyt	14	Companion	Carbon County
11/7	Daniel A. Jewett	17	Companion	Madison Co.
11/8	Reino Nikula Jr.	23	Mistaken Id.	Carbon County
11/24	Eugene E. Eggert	40	Health	Lincoln County
11/24	Larry Kruger	18	Lost/Missing	Mineral Co.

1966

10/10	Richard Ertz	24	Water Death	Flathead Co.
10/24	William A. Young	32	Own Neg.	Meagher Co.
10/25	Vern McKay	50	Health	Madison Co.
10/26	Donald L. Kelly	51	Health	Judith Basin Co
11/1	Lester R. Comstock	58	Health	Lewis & Clark
11/15	Stewart White	55	Health	Jefferson Co.
11/21	George V. Doherty	48	Health	Hill County
11/22	Leonard Gilbertson	38	Other Causes	Teton County

1967

10/1	Michael P. Milelich	22	Own Neg.	Silver Bow Co.
10/8	George Kapp	15	Water Death	Fergus County
10/16	Roy F. Warwood	18	Own Neg.	Gallatin Co.
10/24	Carl Willis	66	Health	Flathead Co.
11/8	Peter R. Lesofski	44	Health	Lewis & Clark
11/11	Robert Mike Barnes	17	Other Causes	Missoula Co.
11/18	Clarence Stokes	57	Own Neg.	Flathead Co.

1968

10/30	Raymond Rebich	17	Own Neg.	Beaverhead Co.
10/20	Albert Haglund	52	Water Death	Lewis & Clark
11/17	Tassie H. Farmer	41	Lost/Missing	Lake County
11/19	Amber Spence	18	Companion	Lincoln County
11/19	John E. Anderson	41	Other Causes	Powell County
11/24	Wayne E. Obert	44	Health	Powell County

Montana Hunting Fatalities By Year

1969

Date	Name	Age	Cause	Location
3/31	Gary Raunig	14	Other Causes	Lewis & Clark
9/19	John A. McFarland	73	Health	Missoula Co.
9/21	Hans I. Ericksen	52	Mistaken Id.	*Bob Marshall
10/5	George R. Frank	22	Companion	Missoula Co.
10/7	Raymond E. Rathie	41	Mistaken Id.	Ravalli County
10/20	Sgt. G. F. Thompson	35	Health	Silver Bow Co.
10/21	William Lovell	63	Health	Lewis & Clark
10/23	Roswell L. Breakus	50	By Animal	Gallatin Co.
10/26	Dave L. Schonenbach	16	Own Neg.	Rosebud Co.
10/26	Daniel Herron	42	Own Neg.	Lewis & Clark
10/29	Robert L. Kleist	50	Other Causes	Powder River
11/5	Clay Morris	73	Lost/Missing	Beaverhead Co.
11/7	Earl E. Talbert	43	Mistaken Id.	Sanders County
11/13	Norris Thompson	19	Companion	Valley County

1970

Date	Name	Age	Cause	Location
10/1	Carl Knutson		Health	Lewis & Clark
10/20	Morris C. Holton	52	Health	Garfield Co.
10/24	Michael Fadness	16	Companion	Park County
10/29	William Dillabaugh	55	Health	Sheridan Co.
11/2	Charles W. Fuller Jr.	40's	Other Causes	Wibaux County
11/2	Howard H. Hanifl	56	Other Causes	Wibaux County
11/4	Eugene Chapman	49	Other Causes	Missoula Co.
11/22	Annie M. Hammond	19	Lost/Missing	Sanders County
11/22	Ross DuPuis	63	Lost/Missing	Sanders County

1971

Date	Name	Age	Cause	Location
10/18	Erland B. Whaley	48	Water Death	Sanders County
10/19	Leonard H. Strand	68	Health	Fergus County
10/19	Robert L. Marshall	80	Health	Fergus County
10/31	Gerald W. Giesick	33	Water Death	Yellowstone Co
11/5	Dennis A. Steffes	29	Other Causes	Sweet Grass Co
11/21	Lt. Charles Guin	24	Other Causes	Cascade Co.
11/21	Sgt Dickie Grisham	41	Other Causes	Cascade Co.
11/21	Sgt Erle Webster	48	Other Causes	Cascade Co.

Montana Hunting Fatalities By Year

1971 (continued)
11/21	Larry Webster	14	Other Causes	Cascade Co.
11/23	James B. Palmer	54	Health	Ravalli County
11/28	Douglas A. Madigan	32	Mistaken Id.	Ravalli County

1972
10/16	Mark Allen Lueder	15	Companion	Cascade Co.
10/26	Merle Berggren	50	Health	Custer County
10/26	Fred Hellman	64	Lost/Missing	Flathead Co.
11/3	Revie W. Luce	42	Other Causes	Stillwater Co.
11/3	Richard S. Rusidak	38	Other Causes	Stillwater Co.
11/19	Louis Burrell	62	Water Death	Lincoln County
11/21	Nadine J. Riedl	20	Companion	Powder River

1973
10/23	Kenneth Harvey	44	Other Causes	Fergus County
10/29	Gary L. Palmer	23	Water Death	Madison Co.
10/29	Steve Bullock	21	Water Death	Madison Co.
11/1	Herman Skagen	59	Lost/Missing	Fergus County
11/1	Dr. Charles McJilton	77	Water Death	Lewis & Clark
11/8	T. N. Chamberlain	48	Lost/Missing	Powell County
11/8	Kenneth L. Fultz	54	Lost/Missing	Ravalli County
11/8	David Nelson	41	Other Causes	Ravalli County
11/14	Wesley Drollinger	42	Own Neg.	Flathead Co.
11/23	Wade Drollinger	18	Companion	Flathead Co.
11/24	Gordon Dressel	40	Water Death	Park County
11/25	Paul D. Buck	57	Health	Fergus County

1974
10/18	R. L. Middleton	17	Own Neg.	Park County
10/23	Sam McDonald	22	Own Neg.	Broadwater Co.
11/8	Donald R. Kimberlin	37	Lost/Missing	Mineral County
11/24	Don Harkin	13	Other Causes	Gallatin Co.
11/25	Louis Callender	62	Lost/Missing	Ravalli County

Montana Hunting Fatalities By Year

1975

10/20	Robert Wright	23	Own Neg.	Madison Co.
10/22	Linda Palbykin	25	Other Causes	Madison Co.
10/28	Donald Harper	50	Lost/Missing	Park County
11/26	Timothy Schock	22	Lost/Missing	Cascade Co.

1976

3/30	Kenneth R. Barnes	17	Other Causes	Teton County
10/9	Barry Drake	16	Other Causes	Treasure Co.
10/12	Ralph Steinberg	66	Health	Custer County
10/12	Roger Lee Jorgenson	27	Companion	Stillwater Co.
10/25	Max Clayton Hoff	33	Other Causes	Yellowstone Co
10/26	Mark S. Koefod	27	Companion	Hill County
11/22	Ed W. Langford	67	Other Causes	Fergus County
11/27	Richard Jacobson	27	Lost/Missing	Flathead Co.

1977

10/2	Louis Paul Sprattler	22	Companion	Teton County
10/18	Jerry Scott Kroh		Companion	Yellowstone Co
10/24	William J. Pierson	13	Own Neg.	Powell County
11/16	Paul S. Wininger	54	Health	Madison Co.

1978

10/23	Richard McGillis	24	Other Causes	Cascade Co.
10/26	James Boor	30	Other Causes	Lincoln Co.
11/3	Stanley Wood	38	Other Causes	Powell County
11/3	Earnest A. Hahnert	42	Other Causes	Powell County

1979

10/22	Mitchell Kelley	22	Other Causes	Carbon County
10/22	Darcy Satterfield	21	Other Causes	Carbon County
10/23	James W. Jackson	13	Other Causes	Valley County
10/29	Jordan S. Sorenson	15	Companion	Flathead Co.
11/5	D. W. Christianson	17	Own Neg.	Blaine County
11/30	Rodney McKenzie	17	Other Causes	Sanders County

Dying to Hunt in Montana
Montana Hunting Fatalities By Year

1980

10/29	Walter Campbell	58	Own Neg.	Teton County
11/12	J.K. Bowling	66	Health	Ravalli County
12/1	Lee Faw	15	Companion	Sweet Grass

1981

10/26	James Hugh O'Neill	64	Health	Lewis & Clark
10/26	Harold Quarles Sr.	59	Health	Silver Bow Co.
11/30	Wilbur H. Stedman	20	Lost/Missing	Rosebud Co.
11/30	Vicki K. Stedman	19	Lost/Missing	Rosebud Co.

1982

6/28	Shannon Weatherly	28	Mistaken Id.	Park County
11/2	Clyde C. Richardson	79	Health	Hill County

1983

2/16	Tracy Cray	25	Lost/Missing	Park County
2/16	William G. Nemeth	62	Health	Park County
10/26	Holis M. Broderick	45	Companion	Fergus County

1984

11/1	Glenn Carr	46	Lost/Missing	*Bob Marshall
11/21	Daniel Michael Davy	35	Mistaken Id.	Missoula Co.

1985

11/11	Leslie O'Neill	27	Other Causes	Silver Bow Co.

1986

9/30	Jeff Thompson	24	Own Neg.	Flathead Co.
10/2	Mark Lowell Burgett	12	Own Neg.	Madison Co.
11/6	Raymond C. Eagle	29	Own Neg.	Roosevelt Co.

1987

Jan 2	Wade Otto Stuber	28	Companion	Choteau Co.
10/26	Kenneth Reinhart	48	Companion	Missoula Co.
10/30	Kary Schanz	32	Companion	Custer County

Montana Hunting Fatalities By Year

1987 (continued)

11/2	James Drury	41	Health	Lincoln County
11/10	Alan K. Kitchel	22	By Animal	Gallatin Co.
11/17	John Doyle	24	Lost/Missing	Ravalli County
11/17	James A. Steging	24	Lost/Missing	Ravalli County
12/27	Taylor Buck	25	Own Neg.	Carter County

1988

4/23	Gerald B. Jensen	48	Own Neg.	McCone Co.
10/10	Randy L. Anderson	17	Water Death	Cascade Co.
10/26	Jack Love	53	Health	Lake County
10/28	Arthur L. Schmidt	57	Health	Ravalli County

1990

5/28	Ryan Voerman	17	Other Causes	Flathead Co.
8/23	Eric Watson	14	Companion	Lake County
10/4	Susan Adams	42	Lost/Missing	Ravalli County
10/22	Kay Fairservice	35	Companion	Cascade Co.
10/24	Scott L. Jorgenson	36	Own Neg.	Valley County
10/25	Anita L. Greenlee	34	Own Neg.	Carbon County
10/31	Anthony Kar Tuss	44	Own Neg.	Gallatin Co.
11/9	Merle D. Wood	65	Other Causes	Lewis & Clark
11/26	Troy S. Goldston	18	Own Neg.	Lake County

1991

10/18	Donald B. Hambrick	43	Own Neg.	Ravalli County
11/1	Lucas Johnson	13	Own Neg.	Broadwater Co.
11/4	Charles E. Miller	41	Lost/Missing	Park County
11/4	Tom E. McDaniel	44	Lost/Missing	Park County
11/5	James M. Jackson	29	Own Neg.	Mineral County
11/11	Dana M. Fallsdown	15	Other Causes	Big Horn Co.
11/19	Mahlon Gunn Jr.	12	Companion	Hill County
12/12	James Telegan	59	Lost/Missing	Madison Co.
12/20	Harry D. Hilyard	52	Own Neg.	Sheridan Co.

Dying to Hunt in Montana
Montana Hunting Fatalities By Year

1992

11/4	James Burrell		Water Death	Jefferson Co.
11/4	Herman C. Saari	41	Health	Missoula Co.
11/8	Mike Dahl	34	Other Causes	Big Horn Co.
11/8	Stanley Andrzejek	49	Other Causes	Cascade Co.
11/10	Roger A. English	61	Health	Ravalli County

1993

11/19	Lamar Rasmussen	42	Water Death	Flathead Co.

1994

10/5	Mitchell K. Bonko	16	Other Causes	Big Horn Co.
11/7	Nathan M. Cox	20	Companion	Carbon County
11/7	Ernest L. Houghton	78	Lost/Missing	Teton County
11/30	Wendi L. Weisgerber	21	Companion	Yellowstone Co

1995

7/19	Chad R. Haugen	11	Other Causes	Blaine County
9/15	Ronald S. Molback	41	Mistaken Id.	Meagher Co.

1996

5/20	Michael G. Privett	11	Companion	Ravalli County
11/18	Randall P. Moses	39	Mistaken Id.	Flathead Co.
11/26	Kieran Pat Grant	41	Health	Lake County

1997

11/23	Todd Slauson	29	Own Neg.	Missoula Co.
12/23	Chris D. Weaver	14	Companion	Flathead Co.

1998

11/17	Scott Bettle	36	Other Causes	Beaverhead Co.
11/23	Steve W. Hoscheid	36	Other Causes	Granite County
11/29	Robert Torgrimson	38	Other Causes	Fergus County

1999

11/21	Roger A. Wagner	36	Mistaken Id.	Powell County

Montana Hunting Fatalities By Year

2000

5/7	William E. Cantrell	76	Own Neg.	Flathead Co.
10/23	Daniel Ova	50	Health	Beaverhead Co.
10/25	Dale Gummer	50	Other Cause	Silver Bow Co.
10/26	Gus Barber	9	Other Causes	Madison Co.
11/13	Raymond LaRoche	20	Other Causes	Richland Co.

2001

10/31	Dennis R. Nelson	45	Own Neg.	Gallatin Co.
11/1	Timothy A. Hilston	50	By Animal	Powell County
12/11	Kodi Chapman	12	Lost/Missing	Flathead Co.

2002

10/30	Thomas Asbridge	39	Companion	Missoula Co.
11/19	Chaskay Ricker	12	Companion	Richland Co.

2003

5/14	Joshua N. Lee	22	Companion	Flathead Co.
2/21	Jeff Puente	33	Other Causes	Big Horn Co.
11/6	Bob P. Rasmusson	48	Other Causes	Beaverhead Co.
11/7	Gary Lee Truax	55	Own Neg.	Missoula Co.
12/3	Robert Simonich	45	Other Causes	Lewis & Clark

2004

6/4	Zachary W. Mienk	21	Own Neg.	Lake County
10/20	Michael LaMere	62	Lost/Missing	Hill County
11/29	Joseph Holzapfel	14	Own Neg.	Flathead Co.
12/7	Francis C. Plante Jr.	16	Mistaken Id.	Lake County

2005

2/3	Bruce J. King	53	Own Neg.	Sheridan Co.

Location of Incident

This section indicates the location, county, region or general area where the hunting accident occurred. Since many of the county lines have changed over the years and most of the locations were not reported precisely, some of the counties listed here in may not be accurate.

Beaverhead County

Date	Victim	Cause of Death
January 30, 1832	Flthd Indian trapper[6]	Other Causes
August 26, 1906	Miss Ruth Bean	By Companion
September 5, 1913	Leslie Dodds	Own Negligence
December 2, 1914	Wallace Brown	Lost or Missing
September 27, 1917	Gladys Bradley	By Companion
November 23, 1920	Carl Osmand	Lost or Missing
September 18, 1926	James Keefe	Water Death
September 28, 1930	Chrles Montgomery	Own Negligence
November 27, 1935	Philip S. Terrio	Own Negligence
November 14, 1945	Henry Staffan	Health Reasons
October 17, 1949	William Patterson	Own Negligence
November 3, 1950	Mrs. Mary Winkley	Lost or Missing
October 27, 1951	Ernest Dubie	Health Reasons
October 19, 1954	Charles T. Case	Health Reasons
November 1, 1954	William Orr	Mistaken Identity
October 18, 1956	William R. Clark	Health Reasons
October 28, 1957	Kenneth Schmidt	Other Causes
November 8, 1959	Wesley H. Elbert	Mistaken Identity
October 30, 1968	Raymond Rebich	Own Negligence
November 5, 1969	Clay Morris	Lost or Missing
November 17, 1998	Scott Bettle	Other Causes
October 23, 2000	Daniel Ova	Health Reasons
November 6, 2003	Robert P. Rasmusson	Other Causes

Big Horn County
October 12, 1948	Freddy Pitsch	Other Causes
November 7, 1959	Clarence Trader	Lost or Missing
November 5, 1962	James Gibbons	Mistaken Identity
November 11, 1991	Dana M. Fallsdown	Other Causes
November 8, 1992	Mike Dahl	Other Causes
October 5, 1994	Mitchell K. Bonko	Other Causes
February 21, 2003	Jeff Puente	Other Causes

Blaine County
November 2, 1901	James Gamble	Own Negligence
November 14, 1938	George McLeslie	Lost or Missing
October 13,1953	Clarence Sivertson	Own Negligence
November 22, 1958	LeRoy Tucker	Own Negligence
October 12, 1959	Westley P. Stace	By Companion
October 30, 1962	Kenneth Lynnes	Other Causes
November 5, 1979	D. W. Christianson	Own Negligence
July 19, 1995	Chad R. Haugen	Other Causes

Broadwater County
September 23, 1893	Tom Tregoning	By Companion
September 30, 1923	John Szasv	Own Negligence
September 30, 1927	Burr W. Clark	Own Negligence
November 23, 1937	Berton Thompson	Own Negligence
November 20, 1955	Ross Nelson	By Companion
October 29, 1956	Herbert Goecks	Health Reasons
October 23, 1974	Sam McDonald	Own Negligence
November 1, 1991	Lucas Johnson	Own Negligence

Carbon County
January 23, 1912	Leon Stevenson	Other Causes
August 7, 1922	Andrew Lubardo	Own Negligence
October 1, 1924	Larcey M. Lakar	Own Negligence

Locations of Montana Hunting Fatalities

Carbon County (continued)
November 25, 1929	Richard Allen	Own Negligence
November 17, 1941	George W. Flamm	By Companion
October 15, 1954	Jackie Shandy	Water Death
October 2, 1961	**James Gregory**	**Own Negligence**
November 2, 1965	Regan Hoyt	By Companion
November 8, 1965	Reino Nikula Jr.	Mistaken Identity
October 22, 1979	Mitchell Kelley	Other Causes
October 22, 1979	Darcy Satterfield	Other Causes
October 25, 1990	Anita L. Greenlee	Own Negligence
November 7, 1994	Nathan Michael Cox	By Companion

Carter County
December 29, 1912	George Goss	Mistaken Identity
December 27, 1987	Taylor Buck	Own Negligence

Cascade County
May 4, 1823	Unknown Trapper	Other Causes
May 4, 1823	Unknown Trapper	Other Causes
May 4, 1823	Unknown Trapper	Other Causes
May 4, 1823	Unknown Trapper	Other Causes
Feb 1874	28 U.S. Army troops	Other Causes
April 2, 1874	Rock	Other Causes
December 8, 1890	Harry Emery	Mistaken identity
September 7, 1893	Stan Crewlslenski	Water Death
December 28, 1895	Paul Zias	By Companion
October 11, 1896	LeGrand Contalou	Water Death
October 27, 1896	William W. White	Other Causes
August 11, 1897	William Keogh	By Companion
September 2, 1901	Henry C. Love	By Companion
December 8, 1901	Frank Swingley	By Companion
October 5, 1902	Arthur Sharpe	Own Negligence
September 9, 1904	Iverson Vaughn	By Companion
September 12, 1904	Charles Wiitala	Mistaken Identity
September 14, 1904	Lucien A. Enders	Water Death

Cascade County (continued)

September 2, 1905	Frank Gonsior	Own Negligence
March 16, 1908	Ray Lefebvre	Other Causes
October 26, 1908	Andrew J. Martin	Own Negligence
November 15, 1909	George C. Beckman	Own Negligence
October 2, 1912	Martin McGraw	Own Negligence
October 10, 1912	Thomas Stark	Lost or Missing
July 29, 1914	Ervin M. Hilton	Other Causes
September 22, 1914	Carl Pearson	Other Causes
October 7, 1916	Joseph F. House	By Companion
October 12, 1916	Ralph Belgrade	Own Negligence
November 23, 1917	Frank Carlson	Lost or Missing
October 2, 1921	Floyd Lewis	Other Causes
September 21, 1924	Everett Kaoski	By Companion
November 11, 1927	Kenneth Gardner	Mistaken Identity
September 25, 1928	Carlton Whitsell	By Companion
October 17, 1928	Henry L. Houston	Other Causes
November 12, 1928	Herschel A. Dockery	Own Negligence
October 21, 1929	Otto Garrison	Water Death
October 21, 1929	Clifford Harrison	Water Death
October 23, 1929	Evert Applegate	Water Death
November 24, 1930	Andrew J. Marouthas	Water Death
November 7, 1935	Hugo Benedetti	Water Death
October 17, 1936	Ruth Fraunhofer	Own Negligence
December 3, 1938	Fred Grinde	Own Negligence
November 10, 1942	Walter Grimes	By Companion
October 16, 1946	William Kercher Jr.	Own Negligence
November 16, 1947	Charles M. Brewster	Health Reasons
October 16, 1955	Harry Luce	Health Reasons
November 16, 1957	Herb Martinich	Health Reasons
October 19, 1959	Donald Marko	Mistaken Identity
October 22, 1961	Norman G. Thrasher	Mistaken Identity
November 21, 1971	Lt. Charles Guin	Other Causes
November 21, 1971	Sgnt. Dick Grisham	Other Causes
November 21, 1971	Sgnt. Erle Webster	Other Causes
November 21, 1971	Larry Webster	Other Causes

Cascade County (continued)

October 16, 1972	Mark Allen Lueder	By Companion
November 26, 1975	Timothy Schock	Lost or Missing
October 23, 1978	Richard McGillis	Other Causes
October 10, 1988	Randy L. Anderson	Water Death
October 22, 1990	Kay Fairservice	By Companion
November 8, 1992	Stanley Andrzejek	Other Causes

Chouteau County

Fall of 1866	Charles Carofel	Other Causes
September 27, 1907	William Powell	Own Negligence
November 14, 1910	Walter Schultz	Lost or Missing
November 14, 1910	Amos Schultz	Lost or Missing
October 24, 1918	M.F. Stoughton	Own Negligence
November 4, 1928	Walter Griesbach	Own negligence
October 23, 1938	Mark Kaulbach	Own Negligence
October 31, 1938	Carl Anderson	By Companion
October 16, 1961	Kenneth Rawson	Health Reasons
January 2, 1987	Wade Otto Stubber	By Companion

Custer County

February 5, 1881	Calvin Bryon	Lost or Missing
February 11, 1881	Jonathan Erickson	Other Causes
November 10, 1931	Wallace Stone	Own Negligence
October 9, 1950	Caroline J. Ullery	By Companion
November 12, 1956	June Edmondson	Health Reasons
October 18, 1963	Dr. G. O. Sweum	Health Reasons
October 20, 1964	Earl James Gaw	Health Reasons
October 26, 1965	Wallace Mack	Health Reason
October 26, 1972	Merle Berggren	Health Reasons
October 12, 1976	Ralph Steinberg	Health Reasons
October 30, 1987	Kary Schanz	By Companion

Dying to Hunt in Montana
Locations of Montana Hunting Fatalities

Dawson County
December 31, 1928	Leroy Jensen	Other Causes
November 4, 1933	Charles Midboe	By Companion
October 1, 1958	John Gust Anderson	By Companion

Deer Lodge County
September 10, 1881	Peter Helstrom	By Animal
October 17, 1927	Joseph J. Kosena	Own Negligence
November 19, 1929	Andrew Kola	Water Death
November 2, 1932	Oliver M. Johnson	Own Negligence
December 16, 1932	John Hinz	Lost or Missing
October 4, 1936	John Fink	Own Negligence
November 18, 1940	Carl Shepka	Own Negligence
November 7, 1942	John Eichstadt	Own Negligence
October 27, 1951	Rudolph B. Krutar	Health Reasons
October 22, 1957	Jack Kosola	Health Reasons
November 1, 1960	John R. Dahl	Own Negligence

Fergus County
May 6, 1899	John Wills	Other Causes
September 19, 1902	Louis Gardape	Mistaken Identity
September 20, 1903	Jesse Hodges	Mistaken Identity
November 22, 1904	Percy Glenn	Own Negligence
November 10, 1906	S.E. Wilson	Mistaken Identity
May 7, 1912	Floyd Ritch	Own Negligence
October 13, 1916	Oswald K. Sellar	By Companion
November 24, 1916	Geza Ottopal	Health Reasons
September 16, 1917	Sullivan Berger	Mistaken Identity
December 14, 1925	Clifford W. Ofstie	By Companion
October 13, 1928	Olive Shaw	By Companion
October 22, 1936	Edward Neumann	Own Negligence
November 15, 1936	Arthur T. Ridgeway	Own Negligence
October 22, 1937	Ed Cameron	Health Reasons
October 18, 1949	Charles Kirby	Water Death

Fergus County (continued)

October 15, 1951	E.C. Humphrey	Lost or Missing
October 23, 1961	Egbert Zyp Jr.	Health Reasons
September 11, 1962	Duayne Murray	Other Causes
September 11, 1962	Ben Peterson Jr.	Other Causes
November 24, 1962	Kenneth Eickoff	Own Negligence
November 13, 1963	Calvin L. Seeley	Health Reasons
October 8, 1967	George Kapp	Water Death
October 19, 1971	Leonard H. Strand	Health Reasons
October 19, 1971	Robert L. Marshall	Health Reasons
October 23, 1973	Kenneth Harvey	Other Causes
November 1, 1973	Herman Skagen	Lost or Missing
November 25, 1973	Paul D. Buck	Health Reasons
November 22, 1976	Ed W. Langford	Other Causes
October 26, 1983	Holis M. Broderick	By Companion
November 29, 1998	Robert Torgrimson	Other Causes

Flathead County

May 20, 1893	Olof Olson	Water Death
January 6, 1896	Walter Joy	Water Death
February 17, 1900	Robert Waddell	Other Causes
August 23, 1900	August Lerch	Other Causes
November 5, 1902	John Malloy	Own Negligence
November 7, 1902	Benjamin F. Egan	Lost or Missing
August 5, 1903	Eddie Collins	By Companion
September 15, 1906	Aaron McGuire	Mistaken Identity
December 20, 1907	Charles R. Peterson	Mistaken Identity
December 3, 1910	Ray Forcum	Health Reasons
November 30, 1911	Walter B. Munroe	Own Negligence
November 23, 1912	Joe Waigel	Lost or Missing
September 3, 1913	Mrs. H.E. Houston	Own Negligence
October 21, 1915	David A. Long	Lost or Missing
October 26, 1918	Jack Smith	Own Negligence
October 2, 1919	Leroy S. Tupper	By Companion
October 29, 1919	P.L. Woods	Health Reasons

Flathead County (continued)

December 1, 1920	Ernest Balke	Mistaken Identity
November 4, 1921	James Pullman	By Companion
November 23, 1923	Cecil Trusty	By Companion
October 27, 1925	H.F. Betts	Other Causes
November 20, 1925	James Geer	Other Causes
November 16, 1927	George Kennedy	Own Negligence
November 11, 1931	Adolph A. Coverdell	Mistaken Identity
October 19, 1933	Walter L. Kulbeck	By Companion
November 7, 1933	Melvin Evenson	Mistaken Identity
November 20, 1935	Wilbur Coe	Mistaken Identity
August 2, 1936	Harry E. Stradtzeck	Own Negligence
July 13, 1937	Andrew Danielson	Own Negligence
September 23, 1938	Earl Lyght	Own Negligence
November 4, 1938	Frank Thompson	Health Reasons
October 5, 1940	George Eckelberry	Water Death
November 19, 1940	Frank Howell	By Animal
November 16, 1941	Charles McElroy	By Animal
November 17, 1941	Oliver Gaston	Health Reasons
October 27, 1942	Elmer Buck	By Companion
November 9, 1943	Henry W. Bassett	Health Reasons
November 21, 1944	Bryon C. Wilson	Lost or Missing
October 20, 1945	J. W. Redlingshafer	By Companion
November 8, 1947	Ralph T. Grosswiler	Own Negligence
October 12, 1949	Fred Jaqueth	Health Reasons
October 21, 1951	James Wishart	Lost or Missing
October 23, 1951	Curtis Westrum	Own Negligence
October 27, 1951	Ray A. Kuaffman	Own Negligence
October 28, 1951	Guy Long	Mistaken Identity
November 1, 1951	Fred Anderson	Health Reasons
November 14, 1951	Roy Rush	Health Reasons
October 18, 1952	Rev. Charles Bolin	Mistaken Identity
October 21, 1952	Frank Yale	Health Reasons
October 25, 1953	Francis Norquay	By Companion
November 19, 1953	Ben Reimer	Lost or Missing
October 24, 1958	John Stone	Health Reasons

Locations of Montana Hunting Fatalities

Flathead County (continued)

November 22, 1959	Neil Christenson	Mistaken Identity
October 18, 1961	Troy E. Thacker	Health Reasons
December 16, 1962	Kenneth H. Fraser	Water Death
December 16, 1962	Floyd F. Knopes	Water Death
October 10, 1966	Richard Ertz	Water Death
October 24, 1967	Carl Willis	Health Reasons
November 18, 1967	Clarence Stokes	Own Negligence
November 3, 1972	Fred Hellman	Lost or Missing
November 14, 1973	Wesley Drollinger	Own Negligence
November 23, 1973	Wade Drollinger	By Companion
November 27, 1976	Richard Jacobson	Lost or Missing
October 29, 1979	Jordan S. Sorenson	By Companion
September 30, 1986	Jeff Thompson	Own Negligence
May 28, 1990	Ryan Voerman	Other Causes
November 19, 1993	Lamar Rasmussen	Water Death
November 18, 1996	Randall P. Moses	Mistaken Identity
December 23, 1997	Chris D. Weaver	By Companion
May 7, 2000	William E. Cantrell	Own Negligence
December 11, 2001	Kodi Chapman	Lost or Missing
May 14, 2003	Joshua N. Lee	By Companion
November 29, 2004	Joseph Holzapfel	Own Negligence

Gallatin County

April 10, 1810	George Drouillard	Other Causes
April 10, 1810	Del. Indian Trapper[7]	Other Causes
April 10, 1810	Del. Indian Trapper[8]	Other Causes
April 12, 1810	James Cheeks	Other Causes
April 12, 1810	Ayers	Other Causes
April 12, 1810	Freehearty	Other Causes
April 12, 1810	Hull	Other Causes
April 12, 1810	Rucker	Other Causes
April 12, 1810	Blackfeet Warrior	Other Causes
June 15, 1901	George Reiter	Lost or Missing
December 30, 1903	G.W. Bowen	Other Causes

Gallatin County (continued)

November 19, 1904	Harry Nagard	By Companion
January 1, 1909	Otto Roll	By Companion
May 17, 1916	Sam G. Massey	Mistaken Identity
December 16, 1916	Wilbert Shipman	By Companion
October 26, 1918	John J. Robertson	Water Death
October 25, 1919	Norman Winchell	Mistaken Identity
November 2, 1919	Thomas C. Page	Health Reasons
November 5, 1920	Thomas A. Towery	Own Negligence
November 14, 1923	James H. Boling	By Companion
October 23, 1925	J.H. Waddell	By Companion
November 13, 1931	Floyd Marble	Own Negligence
November 22, 1931	John C. Holland	Own Negligence
November 4, 1935	Lawrence Dean	Own Negligence
November 6, 1935	Lawrence Carmack	Own Negligence
November 10, 1936	Albert Booth	Own Negligence
November 15, 1938	Clarence Baker	Mistaken Identity
November 15, 1938	Dick Powell	Lost or Missing
October 18, 1946	Frank Meyers	Other Causes
October 28, 1946	Jack E. Parmillee	Water Death
October 28, 1946	G.A. Zink	Water Death
November 29, 1947	G. E. Townsend	Health Reasons
November 6, 1951	Arthur Foster	Health Reasons
November 13, 1956	John F. Detz	Health Reasons
November 17, 1959	Adrian Dick Joki	Lost or Missing
November 13, 1962	Edward Olson	Own Negligence
November 2, 1963	Victor Vermillion	Lost or Missing
October 22, 1964	Albert Altman	Other Causes
October 4, 1965	William Townsend	Mistaken Identity
October 16, 1967	Roy F. Warwood	Own Negligence
October 23, 1969	Roswell L. Breakus	By Animal
November 24, 1974	Don Harkin	Other Causes
November 10, 1987	Alan K. Kitchel	By Animal
October 31, 1990	Anthony Kar Tuss	Own Negligence
October 31, 2001	Dennis R. Nelson	Own Negligence

Dying to Hunt in Montana
Locations of Montana Hunting Fatalities

Garfield County
November 13, 1957   Elias Hoch   By Companion
October 26, 1958   Ralph W. Harbaugh   Health Reasons
October 20, 1970   Morris C. Holton   Health Reasons

Glacier County
December 4, 1908   Alexander MacAulay   Other Causes
September 22, 1921   Harry G. Hawkins   Water Death
September 27, 1923   Fred Mock   Other Causes
November 27, 1932   Jack Carlisle   Lost or Missing
November 18, 1959   Aloysius Racine   Own Negligence

Granite County
December 29,1895   John Whiting   Own Negligence
November 8, 1903   Bridge Williams   Water Death
November 8, 1903   Max Wright   Water Death
November 7, 1917   Fred H. Batts   Water Death
November 19, 1923   Andrew Hakke   Water Death
November 14, 1932   Edgely Mills   Mistaken Identity
November 14, 1932   Harvey H. Mills   Mistaken Identity
October 29, 1934   Emmitt C. Watters   Other Causes
November 18, 1938   John J. Marshall   Other Causes
November 16, 1947   Ralph Adkins   Health Reasons
October 13, 1957   Gerald Barney   Lost or Missing
November 24, 1958   Harold T. Farron   Own Negligence
November 23, 1998   S. W. Hoscheid   Other Causes

Hill County
January 12, 1881   Private Severance   Lost or Missing
May 30, 1902   White-Boy   Other Causes
October 2, 1913   Mrs. James Morris   Other Causes

Hill County (continued)

October 23, 1918	Louie Hoop	Water Death
November 23, 1921	Archie Blair	Own Negligence
November 30, 1958	Reuben Gomke	By Companion
December 2, 1962	Joe B. Cowdrey	Other Causes
November 21, 1966	George V. Doherty	Health Reasons
October 26, 1976	Mark S. Koefod	By Companion
November 2, 1982	C. C. Richardson	Health Reasons
November 19, 1991	Mahlon Gunn Jr.	By Companion
October 21, 2004	Michael LaMere	Lost or Missing

Jefferson County

September 17, 1912	Edward Michaels	By Companion
September 17, 1926	Richard Driscoll	Other Causes
October 22, 1956	Clark Russell Lane	Other Causes
November 16, 1964	Frank McCauley	Health Reasons
November 15, 1966	Stewart White	Health Reasons
November 4, 1992	James Burrell	Water Death

Judith Basin County

May 10, 1899	Hugh Hutchinson	Other Causes
December 11, 1927	Anton Schafer	Own Negligence
October 24, 1935	William Powell	Health Reasons
October 21, 1938	William Hauskamaa	Lost or Missing
October 29, 1947	Charles Masker	By Companion
October 19, 1959	Robert W. Smith	By Companion
October 27, 1959	Fred E. Kent	Lost or Missing
October 26, 1966	Donald L. Kelly	Health Reasons

Lake County

November 9, 1922	Lee Combs	Water Death
November 9, 1922	Lyle Combs	Water Death

Lake County (continued)

November 9, 1922	William Combs	Water Death
September 29, 1924	Peter Irvine	Health Reasons
October 10, 1933	Vincent Walcott	By Comparison
November 8, 1935	Sam Kahl	Other Causes
November 1, 1938	Forrest Smurr	Own Negligence
November 23, 1938	Frank Seiller	By Companion
November 3, 1939	Chauncey Bowdin	Own Negligence
November 11, 1940	Claude S. Averill	Health Reasons
October 30, 1941	Hezekiah VanDorn	By Companion
November 21, 1946	Richard Busler	Water Death
October 27, 1951	John Heiland	Health Reasons
October 29, 1952	Alfred Sterner	Health Reasons
November 15, 1954	Ray Johns	By Companion
October 29, 1962	Fred Hamilton	Lost or Missing
November 13, 1962	David Klien	Lost or Missing
November 14, 1963	Charles Nelson	Own Negligence
November 17, 1968	Tassie H. Farmer	Lost or Missing
October 26, 1988	Jack Love	Health Reasons
August 23, 1990	Eric Watson	By Companion
November 26, 1990	Troy S. Goldston	Own Negligence
November 26, 1996	Kieran Pat Grant	Health Reasons
June 4, 2004	Zachary W. Mienk	Own Negligence
December 7, 2004	Francis C. Plante Jr.	Mistaken Identity

Lewis and Clark County

October 21, 1899	William Longstaff	Lost or Missing
October 21, 1907	T. Stewart	Water Death
October 21, 1907	Arthur Donegan	Water Death
October 21, 1907	James Brown	Water Death
October 8, 1908	Louis Deckerville	Own Negligence
October 25, 1908	Harry Heath	Lost or Missing
September 29, 1912	Richard Jones	Own Negligence
December 10, 1916	Joseph A. Stuesse	Own Negligence
October 31, 1927	Frank Balkovich	Water Death

Locations of Montana Hunting Fatalities

Lewis and Clark County (continued)

November 6, 1928	Bozo Masanovich	Own Negligence
September 30, 1934	Harry Hines	Health Reasons
October 14, 1936	Clifford Smith	By Companion
October 17, 1938	James A. Parrish	Health Reasons
October 17, 1943	Albert Mora	Mistaken Identity
November 10, 1945	James Callaway	Lost or Missing
October 24, 1950	Fred Portman Jr.	Own Negligence
October 20, 1952	William F. Johnson	Health Reasons
November 1, 1954	John Earl Murphy	Health Reasons
November 2, 1954	John Synnes	Health Reasons
November 20, 1954	John H. Mueller	Health Reasons
October 19, 1955	Wm N. Hughley	Health Reasons
October 17, 1956	Ralph Younglove	Mistaken Identity
October 7, 1957	Arthur Shoberg	Own Negligence
November 4, 1957	Albert Hardie	By Companion
November 10, 1958	Ivan L. Gamett	Health Reasons
November 1, 1959	John Ed Grady	Own Negligence
November 8, 1959	John A. Robinson	Health Reasons
November 12, 1962	Richard Austad	Other Causes
November 25, 1962	Steve Annas	Other Causes
October 5, 1965	Ward A. Staats Sr.	Health Reasons
October 11, 1965	Egon Wagerer	Own Negligence
November 1, 1966	Lester R. Comstock	Health Reasons
November 8, 1967	Peter R. Lesofski	Health Reasons
October 20, 1968	Albert Haglund	Water Death
March 31, 1969	Gary Raunig	Other Causes
October 21, 1969	William Lovell	Health Reasons
October 26, 1969	Daniel Herron	Own Negligence
October 1, 1970	Carl Knutson	Health Reasons
November 1, 1973	Dr. C. McJilton	Water Death
October 26, 1981	James H. O'Neill	Health Reasons
November 9, 1990	Merle D. Wood	Other Causes
December 3, 2003	Robert Simonich	Other Causes

Locations of Montana Hunting Fatalities

Liberty County

May 16, 1902	5-yr-old Kyolle boy	Other Causes
October 10, 1919	Alexander Stronach	Own Negligence

Lincoln County

May 20, 1893	Charles F. Foley	Water Death
August 3, 1905	Mr. Barnaby	Lost or Missing
December 19, 1908	Robert A. Taylor	Mistaken Identity
November 10, 1912	John Easlack	Mistaken Identity
October 5, 1913	J. Dulen	Other Causes
November 2, 1914	George Standiford	Mistaken Identity
November 21, 1915	Henry Divis	Other Causes
December 14, 1916	Dan Murr	Mistaken Identity
September 19, 1917	Edward L. Volcour	Health Reasons
December 9, 1922	Paul Russell	By Companion
October 20, 1923	Harold Wallinder	Mistaken Identity
November 10, 1933	Donald Campbell	Own Negligence
November 29, 1941	James McBride	Lost or Missing
November 5, 1942	Arthur S. Borden	Health Reasons
October 17, 1945	J.H. Meiers	By Companion
October 23, 1945	Vern Simaro	Health Reasons
November 5, 1951	Gerald Hays	By Companion
October 22, 1952	Richard W. Gilber	Own Negligence
November 3, 1953	Harry Howard	Mistaken Identity
October 28, 1954	David W. Saltsman	By Companion
November 12, 1955	Mrs. Bob Pulse	Other Causes
November 22, 1959	George Wood	Health Reasons
November 5, 1961	Thomas Kelsey	Mistaken Identity
September 19, 1962	Burton O. Burrell	Other Causes
November 24, 1965	Eugene E. Eggert	Health Reasons
November 19, 1968	Amber Spence	By Companion
November 19, 1972	Louis Burrell	Water Death
October 26, 1978	James Boor	Other Causes
November 2, 1987	James Drury	Health Reasons

Madison County

Fall of 1808	John Potts	Other Causes
Fall of 1808	Blackfeet Warrior[9]	Other Causes
October 14, 1832	Henry Vanderburgh	Other Causes
October 14, 1832	Monsieur Pilou	Other Causes
October 14, 1832	Blackfeet Warrior	Other Causes
February 10, 1900	George Humphrey	Other Causes
September 19, 1903	Nick Simons Jr.	Own Negligence
July 13, 1908	A.J. Moody	By Companion
November 7, 1933	Carl Burnston	Mistaken Identity
November 8, 1933	George Armitage	Lost or Missing
October 23, 1937	George T. Westover	Water Death
October 16, 1939	Robert Phoenix	Own Negligence
November 15, 1943	G. J. Pochervina	Own Negligence
October 28, 1947	Benedict D. Perga	Health Reasons
October 8, 1953	Donald Ray Fain	Lost or Missing
November 9, 1955	William Jones	Health Reasons
November 17, 1958	Walter Talbot	Health Reasons
November 6, 1961	William J. Batten	Water Death
November 7, 1965	Daniel A. Jewett	By Companion
October 25, 1966	Vern McKay	Health Reasons
October 29, 1973	Gary L. Palmer	Water Death
October 29, 1973	Steve Bullock	Water Death
October 20, 1975	Robert Wright	Own Negligence
October 22, 1975	Linda Palbkin	Other Causes
November 16, 1977	Paul S. Wininger	Health Reasons
October 2, 1986	Mark L. Burgett	Own Negligence
December 12, 1991	James Telegan	Lost or Missing
October, 26, 2000	Gus Barber	Other Causes

McCone County

October 28, 1924	Cavyell 6-yr-old boy	Other Causes
April 23, 1988	Gerald B. Jensen	Own Negligence

Locations of Montana Hunting Fatalities

Meagher County

August 4, 1901	George E. Hailey	Own Negligence
September 10, 1902	Rev. L. E. Armitage	Own Negligence
November 16, 1926	William Lawrence	Own Negligence
November 12, 1936	Albert Westberg	Lost or Missing
November 11, 1959	John B. Bourassa	Health Reasons
October 24, 1966	William A. Young	Own Negligence
September 15, 1995	Ronald S. Molback	Mistaken Identity

Mineral County

February 9, 1898	M.C. Beach	Mistaken Identity
November 21, 1903	M.M. Johnson	Lost or Missing
November 15, 1925	Charles Donally	Health Reasons
November 17, 1928	Sgt. Paul B. Portis	By Companion
October 18, 1937	Ralph Longpre	By Animal
November 9, 1940	Gus Stean	Lost or Missing
October 21, 1953	Al Kruzon	By Companion
October 17, 1956	Miles Spaich	Own Negligence
November 6, 1956	Jim Hankinson	By Companion
October 16, 1961	Jack R. Burger	By Companion
November 24, 1965	Larry Kruger	Lost or Missing
November 8, 1974	Don R. Kimberlin	Lost or Missing
November 5, 1991	James M. Jackson	Own Negligence

Missoula County

October 15, 1884	David Austin	Own Negligence
September 9, 1893	Eli Paulin	Own Negligence
December 19, 1904	Carroll E. Brooks	By Companion
October 20, 1908	Charles B. Peyton	Other Causes
October 20, 1908	Camille Paul	Other Causes
October 20, 1908	Antoine Stousee	Other Causes
October 20, 1908	Frank Stousee	Other Causes
October 20, 1908	M. Yellow-Mountain	Other Causes
October 29, 1917	Adelore Lafrinire	Other Causes

Missoula County (continued)

November 13, 1921	Andrew Brae	By Companion
October 31, 1925	Frank A. Matt	Lost or Missing
September 25, 1926	Samuel B. Clark	Own Negligence
November 19, 1926	John Ben Hougland	Lost or Missing
October 26, 1931	Hollis B. Wiggin	Own Negligence
January 2,1932	William B. Burkhart	Own Negligence
October 31, 1933	James Vern Booth	Other Causes
November 14, 1933	Robert Harkness	Health Reasons
October 19, 1936	Aurel Tucker	By Companion
November 16, 1936	Ray V. Doney	Own Negligence
October 22, 1937	Alfonse Chourand	Lost or Missing
September 13, 1938	Vernon Ward	Other Causes
October 19, 1938	Clarence Dorey	Lost or Missing
October 8, 1940	Edward Duby	Mistaken Identity
October 20, 1940	Robert Reesman	Own Negligence
October 21, 1940	Donald P. Knapp	Other Causes
November 7, 1942	Alley C. McGilvrey	Health Reasons
November 25, 1946	Robert Rodine	Water Death
October 16, 1947	Clifford G. Hogan	Water Death
October 16, 1947	Albert L. Richardson	Water Death
October 12, 1949	Floyd E. Stiles	Health Reasons
October 24, 1950	Oscar Butts	Health Reasons
November 15, 1950	Robert W. Brown	By Companion
November 17, 1950	Elmer A. Findall	Health Reasons
November 16, 1951	Charles Webber	Mistaken Identity
October 16, 1955	Silas H. Jerome	Health Reasons
October 30, 1956	Pearl Herndon	Health Reasons
November 28, 1959	Arthur D. Jordan	Lost or Missing
November 16, 1960	Fritz Fry	Lost or Missing
October 2, 1962	John Higgins	Other Causes
November 20, 1964	William Popish	Own Negligence
November 11, 1967	Robert Mike Barnes	Other Causes
September 19, 1969	John A. McFarland	Health Reasons
October 5, 1969	George R. Frank	By Companion

Missoula County (continued)

November 4, 1970	Eugene Chapman	Other Causes
November 21, 1984	Daniel M. Davy	Mistaken Identity
October 26, 1987	Kenneth Reinhart	By Companion
November 4, 1992	Herman C. Saari	Health Reasons
November 23, 1997	Todd Slauson	Own Negligence
October 30, 2002	Thomas Asbridge	By Companion
November 7, 2003	Gary Lee Truax	Own Negligence

Musselshell County

April 12, 1919	Elijah Linn	By Companion
November 8, 1941	Riley Ray	Own Negligence
October 30, 1942	Frank Pogacher	Lost or Missing
September 27, 1950	Charles F. Maris	Health Reasons
October 23, 1953	William Syblon	Own Negligence
November 8, 1953	Art Sanders	By Companion
October 19, 1954	Leonard R. Schmidt	Health Reasons
January 30, 1959	Dale Robinson	By Companion

Park County

September 1, 1894	B.T. "Curly" Rogers	Other Causes
1894	Unknown Hunter	By Animal
September 5, 1905	Mrs. Coventry	Mistaken Identity
October 26, 1909	E. Lund	Lost or Missing
May 5, 1912	John Austin	By Animal
November 26, 1912	Harrison Allan	Own Negligence
December 16, 1916	Ernest Carlisle	Other Causes
December 20, 1916	Nick Carr	Other Causes
September 21, 1919	Clyde Fryer	Other Causes
December 11, 1929	Frank Mayash	Mistaken Identity
December 19, 1937	Herman Merene	Other Causes
November 15, 1945	Charles White	Other Causes
October 20, 1946	Ed Bloodgood	Lost or Missing

Park County (continued)

October 29, 1947	John N. Thomas	Health Reasons
October 16, 1948	Walt Laughfranere	Mistaken Identity
October 27, 1955	Joseph K. Harbison	Health Reasons
November 7, 1956	Gary Mosback	By Companion
October 28, 1957	Frank West	By Companion
November 12, 1962	Dennis Eaton	Other Causes
November 12, 1962	Leo B. Johnson	Other causes
October 19, 1964	Frank L. Anderson	By Companion
October 24, 1970	Michael Fadness	By Companion
November 24, 1973	Gordon Dressel	Water Death
October 18, 1974	R. L. Middleton	Own Negligence
October 28, 1975	Donald Harper	Lost or Missing
June 28, 1982	Shannon Weatherly	Mistaken Identity
February 16, 1983	Tracy Cray	Lost or Missing
February 16, 1983	William G. Nemeth	Health Reasons
November 4, 1991	Charles E. Miller	Lost or Missing
November 4, 1991	Tom E. McDaniel	Lost or Missing

Petroleum County

November 7, 1961	Don Cattnach	By Companion

Phillips County

August 15, 1904	William Malard	Own Negligence
October 24, 1950	William A. Olsen	Health Reasons
October 24, 1950	Rev H. H. Snider	Water Death
November 4, 1952	Kenneth Newton	Own Negligence
October 19, 1959	James Farstad	Other Causes
November 1, 1959	Gary Sorenson	By Companion
September 27, 1963	Billy Johnson	Own Negligence

Locations of Montana Hunting Fatalities

Pondera County

September 21, 1914	R. W. Rheinackle	Water Death
November 30, 1924	John Vanden Wall	By Companion
October 14, 1944	Orit T. Forbes	Own Negligence
October 27, 1947	Henry A. True	Health Reasons
October 12, 1949	Jesse L. Odelle	Health Reasons
November 22, 1959	Ernest Hammer	Mistaken Identity

Powder River County

November 1, 1948	Jerry Brown	Own Negligence
October 18, 1956	Clarence Skaggs	Mistaken Identity
October 23, 1958	Clyde F. Williams	Lost or Missing
October 24, 1958	Clyde Escher	Lost or Missing
October 24, 1958	Tony Stepanek	Lost or Missing
October 29, 1969	Robert L. Kleist	Other Causes
November 21, 1972	Nadine J. Riedl	By Companion

Powell County

September 7, 1886	Robert Whipple	Water Death
January 11, 1896	Charlie Housman	Other Causes
February 22, 1896	James Bingley	Lost or Missing
October 29, 1914	Roy Blow	Health Reason
October 23, 1919	Cpt. Wm Strong	Mistaken Identity
November 3, 1919	James McWhethey	Mistaken Identity
November 10, 1935	Thomas Weir	Mistaken Identity
November 10, 1942	Paul Praast	Lost or Missing
October 17, 1953	Edwin C. Ham	By Companion
October 31, 1958	Samuel Adams	By Animal
November 19, 1968	John E. Anderson	Other Causes
November 24, 1968	Wayne E. Obert	Health Reasons
November 8, 1973	T. N. Chamberlain	Lost or Missing
October 24, 1977	William J. Pierson	Own Negligence
November 3, 1978	Stanley Wood	Other Causes
November 3, 1978	E. A. Hahnert	Other Causes

Powell County (continued)

| November 21, 1999 | Roger A. Wagner | Mistaken Identity |
| November 1, 2001 | Timothy A. Hilston | By Animal |

Ravalli County

January 5, 1902	William Stuart	Own Negligence
November 15, 1927	Rex Roberts	Own Negligence
November 2, 1932	Lewis W. Maynard	By Companion
November 6, 1933	H. Schuchmann	Mistaken Identity
October 11, 1936	Edgar Hicks	Own Negligence
November 10, 1936	E. E. Stockman Jr.	Own Negligence
November 15, 1938	Howard V. Little	Mistaken Identity
October 20, 1939	William Smith	Own Negligence
October 4, 1940	Dennis F. Kohner	Own Negligence
November 1, 1943	James Bowden	Own Negligence
October 5, 1945	Wm R. Reymerson	Health Reasons
October 22, 1945	Creed R. Morgan	By Companion
October 8, 1947	Louis Camp	Health Reasons
October 9, 1947	Ross Collins	Health Reasons
October 12, 1947	Robert Longnecker	Health Reasons
November 9, 1947	George Lofftus	Lost or Missing
October 19, 1951	Lowell Web	Mistaken Identity
November 8, 1953	Bert Bailey	Health Reasons
November 15, 1955	Thomas Melton	Health Reasons
October 28, 1956	George Henry Mills	Health Reasons
November 4, 1957	Robert Jennings	Mistaken Identity
November 12, 1957	W. B. Sokoloski Jr.	By Companion
November 12, 1957	John W. Dowling	Health Reasons
October 9, 1965	Jeff Thomas	Mistaken Identity
October 7, 1969	Ray Edward Rathie	Mistaken Identity
November 23, 1971	James B. Palmer	Health Reasons
November 28, 1971	Doug A. Madigan	Mistaken Identity
November 8, 1973	Kenneth L. Fultz	Lost or Missing
November 8, 1973	David Nelson	Other Causes
November 25, 1974	Louis Callender	Lost or Missing

Ravalli County (continued)

November 12, 1980	J.K. Bowling	Health Reasons
November 17, 1987	John Doyle	Lost or Missing
November 17, 1987	James A. Steging	Lost or Missing
October 28, 1988	Arthur L. Schmidt	Health Reasons
October 4, 1990	Susan Adams	Lost or Missing
October 18, 1991	Don B. Hambrick	Own Negligence
November 10, 1992	Roger A. English	Health Reasons
May 20, 1996	Michael G. Privett	By Companion

Richland County

November 1, 1926	Buffalo Hunter	Other Causes
November 1, 1954	Dean Williams	Own Negligence
October 30, 1955	Clair C. Hood	Other Causes
October 20, 1958	Howard Gleason	Own Negligence
October 21, 1961	James Miller	Mistaken Identity
September 21, 1963	Clifford M. Ware	Health Reasons
November 13, 2000	Ray A. LaRoche	Other Causes
November 19, 2002	Chaskay Ricker	By Companion

Roosevelt County

July 11, 1884	Seth Whipple	Lost or Missing
November 14, 1926	James Royan	Other Causes
November 19, 1948	Ray Necklace	By Companion
October 18, 1951	Ed Robinson	By Companion
October 11, 1952	Orville Clancy	Own Negligence
October 15, 1960	Harvey E. Hewitt	Lost or Missing
October 24, 1961	Michael Long-Tree	By Companion
November 6, 1986	Raymond C. Eagle	Own Negligence

Rosebud County

October 23, 1958	Robert Pittman	Lost or Missing
October 17, 1961	Emil L. Rozuoi	Health Reasons
October 26, 1969	D. L. Schonenbach	Own Negligence

Rosebud County (continued)

November 30, 1981	Wilbur H. Stedman	Lost or Missing
November 30, 1981	Vicki K. Stedman	Lost or Missing

Sanders County

November 17, 1904	Warren Hulbert	By Companion
December 2, 1914	F. E. Woodworth	By Companion
September 4, 1915	Ernest B. Clark	Mistaken Identity
November 3, 1938	Grover Pace	By Animal
October 23, 1950	Alvin Austin	By Companion
November 14, 1951	Marvin H. Wagner	By Comparison
November 13, 1956	Burton Davenport	Health Reasons
October 28, 1958	Walter L. Collins	Health Reasons
November 23, 1958	Clyde Jenkins	Health Reasons
November 20, 1960	Walter Franke	Mistaken Identity
November 22, 1963	Robert A. Gruber	Health Reasons
November 2, 1964	Floyd Greenup	Health Reasons
November 5, 1969	Earl E. Talbert	Mistaken Identity
November 22, 1970	Annie M. Hammond	Lost or Missing
November 22, 1970	Ross DuPuis	Lost or Missing
October 18, 1971	Erland B. Whaley	Water Death
November 30, 1979	Rodney McKenzie	Other Causes

Sheridan County

October 29, 1970	Wm Dillabaugh	Health Reasons
December 20, 1991	Harry D. Hilyard	Own Negligence
February 3, 2005	Bruce J. King	Own Negligence

Silver Bow County

October 5, 1909	Mike Friel	By Companion
September 9, 1912	John Sagar	Own Negligence
November 9, 1921	Knute Knuteson	Own Negligence
September 2, 1923	Ralph Ryan	Own Negligence

Locations of Montana Hunting Fatalities

Silver Bow County (continued)

November 29, 1932	Everett Hoar	Other Causes
November 29, 1932	Robert M. Bell	Own Negligence
November 10, 1935	George Westfall	Lost or Missing
November 22, 1938	Robert Felieous	By Companion
November 1, 1943	Oscar Bye	Health Reasons
October 24, 1946	George Johnson	Other Causes
October 31, 1948	Donald J. Bertoglio	By Companion
October 20, 1949	George L. Russell	Health Reasons
October 17, 1953	William Lowney	Health Reason
November 20, 1955	John Burvich	Mistaken Identity
September 27, 1963	Charles W. West	Own Negligence
October 1, 1967	Michael P. Milelich	Own Negligence
October 20, 1969	Sgt. G. F. Thompson	Health Reasons
October 26, 1981	Harold Quarles Sr.	Health Reasons
November 11, 1985	Leslie O'Neill	Other Causes
October 25, 2000	Dale Gummer	Other Causes

Stillwater County

September 17, 1926	Farney L. Coles	By Companion
November 7, 1951	Thomas E. McClure	Health Reasons
November 3, 1972	Revie W. Luce	Other Causes
November 3, 1972	Richard S. Rusidak	Other Causes
October 12, 1976	Roger L. Jorgenson	By Companion

Sweet Grass County

November 2, 1929	Alva Williams	Other Causes
October 4, 1932	C. E. Fahlgren	Own Negligence
November 8, 1932	Orville Briner	Mistaken Identity
October 17, 1940	Grover C. Bryan	By Companion
November 16, 1947	Robert A. Ryan	Health Reasons
October 27, 1951	Bernard V. Urich	Health Reasons
November 9, 1955	Henry J. Jondrow	Health Reasons
November 5, 1971	Dennis A. Steffes	Other Causes
December 1, 1980	Lee Faw	By Companion

Teton County

April 30, 1881	John Brown	Own Negligence
November 26, 1920	Charles L. Torrence	Own Negligence
November 26, 1923	Ted Ellis	Water Death
September 17, 1927	Huston C. Peters	By Companion
October 15, 1933	Ford R. Lake	Water Death
November 30, 1936	George Reissing	By Companion
November 1, 1948	Arne Haugse	Health Reasons
November 15, 1958	Robert C. Brewer	Health Reasons
November 22, 1966	Leonard Gilbertson	Other Causes
March 30, 1976	Kenneth Ray Barner	Other Causes
October 2, 1977	Louis Paul Sprattler	By Companion
October 29, 1980	Walter Campbell	Own Negligence
November 7, 1994	Ernest L. Houghton	Lost or Missing

Toole County

December 6, 1917	James Donald Ashe	Other Causes
November 17, 1928	Von Hartso	Water Death
November 18, 1938	Dan Mitchell	Other Causes
November 25, 1945	Monty Leavitt	By Companion
November 14, 1959	Joseph P. Jansen Jr.	Health Reasons
January 15, 1965	Carl Martin	By Companion

Treasure County

October 9, 1976	Barry Drake	Other Causes

Valley County

December 12, 1923	Peter Henningson	By Companion
August 29, 1940	Charles V. Lambert	Other Causes
November 6, 1947	George D. Mason	By Animal
October 24, 1960	Judith M. Walker	By Companion
November 13, 1969	Norris Thompson	By Companion
October 23, 1979	James W. Jackson	Other Causes
October 24, 1990	Scott L. Jorgenson	Own Negligence

Wheatland County

| October 26, 1964 | Lindy Walla | By Companion |

Wibaux County

October 31, 1955	Rudolph Pries	Health Reasons
November 2, 1970	C. W. Fuller Jr.	Other Causes
November 2, 1970	Howard Hanifl	Other Causes

Yellowstone County

May 31, 1823	Michael Immel	Other Causes
May 31, 1823	Robert Jones	Other Causes
May 31, 1823	Unknown Trapper	Other Causes
May 31, 1823	Unknown Trapper	Other Causes
May 31, 1823	Unknown Trapper	Other Causes
May 31, 1823	Unknown Trapper	Other Causes
May 31, 1823	Unknown Trapper	Other Causes
Early 1833	Hugh Glass	Other Causes
Early 1833	Edward Rose	Other Causes
Early 1833	Menard	Other Causes
November 15, 1917	Andrew Craig	Water Death
October 8, 1924	Walter Wersall	Own Negligence
December 2, 1924	Hunt Coy	Other Causes
November 25, 1929	Wm Baumgartner	By Companion
October 3, 1931	Steve Chrisman	Health Reasons
November 29, 1934	Charles Jacobs	Own Negligence
October 5, 1939	William L. Wyrick	Other Causes
October 9, 1939	Wesley B. Coley	Other Causes
November 22, 1940	James Brice	Own Negligence
December 3, 1940	Benjamin Mahr	Other Causes
November 13, 1945	Clifford Courtney	Water Death
December 1, 1952	George F. Delisle	By Companion
October 18, 1956	Raymond H. White	Own Negligence
October 18, 1961	Robert Zeuler	Health Reasons
October 15, 1963	Theodore Haynes	Own Negligence

Yellowstone County (continued)

October 31, 1971	Gerald W. Giesick	Water Death
October 25, 1976	Max Clayton Hoff	Other Causes
October 18, 1977	Jerry Scott Kroh	By Companion
November 30, 1994	Wendi Weisgerber	By Companion

Absaroke Beartooth

November 10, 1936	Bruce Schwenneker	Mistaken Identity

Bob Marshall Wilderness

October 22, 1956	William K. Scott	By Animal
October 26, 1959	James Garey	Other Causes
September 21, 1969	Hans I. Erickson	Mistaken Identity
November 1, 1984	Glenn Carr	Lost or Missing

Northern Montana (Near the Canadian Border)

June of 1876	Jim Fowler	Other Causes

VICTIM INDEX

Victim	Date	Cause	Location
AAAAAAAAAAAAAAAAAAAAAAAAAAAAAAAAAAAAAAAAAAAAAAA			
Adams, Samuel	10/31/1958	By Animal	Powell County
Adams, Susan	10/4/1990	Lost/Missing	Ravalli County
Adkins, Ralph	11/16/1947	Health	Granite County
Allen, Harrison	11/26/1912	Own Neg.	Park County
Allen, Richard	11/25/1929	Own Neg.	Carbon County
Altman, Albert	10/22/1964	Other Causes	Gallatin Co.
Anderson, Carl	10/31/1938	Companion	Chouteau Co.
Anderson, Frank L.	10/19/1964	Companion	Park County
Anderson, Fred	11/1/1951	Health	Flathead Co.
Anderson, John E.	11/19/1968	Other Causes	Powell County
Anderson, John Gust	10/1/1958	Companion	Dawson Co.
Anderson, Randy Lee	10/10/1988	Water Death	Cascade Co.
Andrzejek, Stanley	11/8/1992	Other Causes	Cascade Co.
Annas, Steve	11/25/1962	Other Causes	Lewis & Clark
Applegate, Evert	10/23/1929	Water Death	Cascade Co.
Armitage, George	11/8/1933	Lost/Missing	Madison Co.
Armitage, Leslie E.	9/10/1902	Own Neg.	Meagher Co.
Asbridge, Thomas	10/30/2002	Companion	Missoula Co.
Ashe, James Donald	12/6/1917	Other Causes	Toole County
Austad, Richard	11/12/1962	Other Causes	Lewis & Clark
Austin, Alvin	10/23/1950	Companion	Sanders County
Austin, David	10/15/1884	Own Neg.	Missoula Co.
Austin, John	5/5/1912	By Animal	Park County
Averill, Claude S.	11/11/1940	Health	Lake County
Ayers	4/12/1810	Other Causes	Gallatin Co.
BBBBBBBBBBBBBBBBBBBBBBBBBBBBBBBBBBBBBBBBBBBBB			
Bailey, Bert	11/8/1953	Health	Ravalli County
Baker, Clarence	11/30/1939	Mistaken Id	Gallatin Co.
Balke, Ernest	12/1/1920	Mistaken Id	Flathead Co.
Balkovich, Frank	10/31/1927	Water Death	Lewis & Clark
Barber, Gus	10/26/2000	Other Cause	Madison Co.
Barnaby	8/3/1905	Lost/Missing	Lincoln County

433

Barner, Kenneth Ray	3/30/1976	Other Causes	Teton County
Barnes, Robert Mike	11/11/1967	Other Cause	Missoula Co.
Barney, Gerald	10/13/1957	Lost/Missing	Granite County
Bassett, Henry W.	11/9/1943	Health	Flathead Co.
Batten, William John	11/6/1961	Water Death	Madison Co.
Batts, Fred H.	11/7/1917	Water Death	Granite County
Baumgartner, W.	11/25/1929	Companion	Yellowstone Co
Beach, M.C.	2/9/1898	Mistaken Id	Mineral Co.
Bean, Ruth	8/26/1906	Companion	Beaverhead Co.
Beckman, Goerge C.	11/15/1909	Own Neg.	Cascade Co.
Belgrade, Ralph	10/12/1916	Own Neg.	Cascade Co.
Bell, Robert M.	11/29/1932	Own Neg.	Silver Bow Co.
Benedetti, Hugo	11/7/1935	Water Death	Cascade Co.
Berger, Sullivan	9/16/1917	Mistaken Id	Fergus County
Berggren, Merle	10/26/1972	Health	Custer County
Bertoglio, Donald J.	10/31/1948	Companion	Silver Bow Co.
Bettle, Scott	11/17/1998	Other Causes	Beaverhead Co.
Betts, H.F.	10/27/1925	Other Causes	Flathead Co.
Bingley, James	2/22/1896	Lost/Missing	Powell County
Blackfeet Warrior	Fallof 1808	Other Causes	Madison Co.
Blackfeet Warrior	4/12/1810	Other Causes	Gallatin Co.
Blackfeet Warrior	10/14/1832	Other Causes	Madison Co.
Blair, Archie	11/23/1921	Own Neg.	Hill County
Bloodgood, Ed	10/20/1946	Lost/Missing	Park County
Blow, Roy	10/29/1914	Health	Powell County
Bolin, Charles Rev.	10/18/1952	Mistaken Id	Flathead Co.
Boling, James H.	11/14/1923	Companion	Gallatin Co.
Bonko, Mitchell K.	10/5/1994	Other Causes	Big Horn Co.
Boor, James	10/26/1978	Other Causes	Lincoln County
Booth, Albert	11/10/1936	Own Neg.	Gallatin Co.
Booth, James Vernon	10/31/1933	Other Causes	Missoula Co.
Borden, Arthur S.	11/5/1942	Health	Lincoln County
Bourassa, John B.	11/11/1959	Health	Meagher Co.
Bowden, James	11/1/1943	Own Neg.	Ravalli County
Bowdin, Chauncey	11/3/1939	Own Neg.	Lake County
Bowen, G.W.	12/30/1903	Other Causes	Gallatin Co.
Bowling, J.K.	11/12/1980	Health	Ravalli County

Bradley, Gladys	9/27/1917	Companion	Beaverhead Co.
Brae, Andrew	11/13/1921	Companion	Missoula Co.
Breakus, Roswell L.	10/23/1969	By Animal	Gallatin Co.
Brewer, Robert C.	11/15/1958	Health	Teton County
Brewster, Charles	11/16/1947	Health	Cascade Co.
Brice, James	11/22/1940	Own Neg.	Yellowstone Co
Briner, Orville	11/8/1932	Mistaken Id	Sweet Grass Co
Broderick, Holis M.	10/26/1983	Companion	Fergus County
Brooks, Carroll E.	12/19/1904	Companion	Missoula Co.
Brown, James	10/21/1907	Water Death	Lewis & Clark
Brown, Jerry	11/1/1948	Own Neg.	Powder River
Brown, John	4/30/1881	Own Neg.	Teton County
Brown, Robert W.	11/15/1950	Companion	Missoula Co.
Brown, Wallace	12/2/1914	Lost/Missing	Beaverhead Co.
Bryan, Grover C.	10/17/1940	Companion	Sweet Grass Co
Bryon, Calvin	2/5/1881	Lost/Missing	Custer County
Buck, Elmer	10/27/1942	Companion	Flathead Co.
Buck, Paul D.	11/25/1973	Health	Fergus County
Buck, Taylor	12/27/1987	Own Neg.	Carter County
Buffalo Hunter	11/1/1926	Other Causes	Richland Co.
Bullock, Steve	10/29/1973	Water Death	Madison Co.
Burger, Jack R.	10/16/1961	Companion	Mineral Co.
Burgett, Mark L.	10/2/1986	Own Neg.	Madison Co.
Burkhart, William B.	(1931) p 29	Own Neg.	Missoula Co.
Burnston, Carl	11/7/1933	Mistaken Id.	Madison Co.
Burrell, Burton O.	9/19/1962	Other Causes	Lincoln County
Burrell, James	11/4/1992	Water Death	Jefferson Co.
Burrell, Louis	11/19/1972	Water Death	Lincoln County
Burvich, John	11/20/1955	Mistaken Id	Silver Bow Co.
Busler, Richard	11/21/1946	Water Death	Lake County
Butts, Oscar	10/24/1950	Health	Missoula Co.
Bye, Oscar	11/1/1943	Health	Silver Bow Co.

CCCCCCCCCCCCCCCCCCCCCCCCCCCCCCCCCCCCCCCCCC

Callaway, James	11/10/1945	Lost/Missing	Lewis & Clark
Callender, Louis	11/25/1974	Lost/Missing	Ravalli County
Cameron, Ed	10/22/1937	Health	Fergus County

Camp, Louis	10/8/1947	Health	Ravalli County
Campbell, Donald	11/10/1933	Own Neg.	Lincoln County
Campbell, Walter	10/29/1980	Own Neg.	Teton County
Cantrell, William E.	5/7/2000	Own Neg.	Flathead Co.
Carlisle Jack	11/27/1932	Lost/Missing	Glacier County
Carlisle, Ernest	12/16/1916	Other Causes	Park County
Carlson, Frank	11/23/1917	Lost/Missing	Cascade Co.
Carmack, Lawrence	11/6/1935	Own Neg.	Gallatin Co.
Carofel, Charles	Fall of 1866	Other Causes	Chouteau Co.
Carr, Glenn	11/1/1984	Lost/Missing	*Bob Marshall
Carr, Nick	12/20/1916	Other Causes	Park County
Case, Charles T.	10/19/1954	Health	Beaverhead Co.
Cattnach, Don	11/7/1961	Companion	Petroleum Co.
Cavyell 6-yr-old boy	10/28/1924	Other Causes	McCone Co.
Chamberlain, T. N.	11/8/1973	Lost/Missing	Powell County
Chapman, Kodi	12/11/2001	Lost/Missing	Flathead Co.
Chapman, Eugene	11/4/1970	Other Causes	Missoula Co.
Cheeks, James	4/12/1810	Other Causes	Gallatin Co.
Chourand, Alfonse	10/22/1937	Lost/Missing	Missoula Co.
Chrisman, Steve	10/3/1931	Health	Yellowstone Co
Christenson, Neil	11/22/1959	Mistaken Id	Flathead Co.
Christianson, David	11/5/1979	Own Neg.	Blaine County
Clancy, Orville	10/11/1952	Own Neg.	Roosevelt Co.
Clark, Burr W.	9/30/1927	Own Neg.	Broadwater Co.
Clark, Ernest B.	9/4/1915	Mistaken Id	Sanders County
Clark, Samuel B.	9/25/1926	Own Neg.	Missoula Co.
Clark, William R.	10/18/1956	Health	Beaverhead Co.
Coe, Wilbur	11/20/1935	Mistaken Id	Flathead Co.
Coles, Farney L.	9/17/1926	Companion	Stillwater Co.
Coley, Wesley B.	10/9/1939	Other Causes	Yellowstone Co
Collins, Eddie	8/5/1903	Companion	Flathead Co.
Collins, Ross	10/9/1947	Health	Ravalli County
Collins, Walter Lee	10/28/1958	Health	Sanders County
Combs, Lee	11/9/1922	Water Death	Lake County
Combs, Lyle	11/9/1922	Water Death	Lake County
Combs, William	11/9/1922	Water Death	Lake County
Comstock, Lester R.	11/1/1966	Health	Lewis & Clark

Contalou, LeGrand	10/11/1896	Water Death	Cascade Co.
Courtney, Clifford	11/13/1945	Water Death	Yellowstone Co
Courtney, Emmett	11/13/1945	Water Death	Yellowstone Co
Coventry, Mrs.	9/5/1905	Mistaken Id	Park County
Coverdale, Adolph	11/11/1931	Mistaken Id	Flathead Co.
Cowdrey, Joe B.	12/2/1962	Other Causes	Hill County
Cox, Nathen M.	11/7/1994	Companion	Carbon Co.
Coy, Hunt	12/2/1924	Other Causes	Yellowstone Co
Craig, Andrew	11/15/1917	Water Death	Yellowstone Co
Cray, Tracy	2/16/1983	Lost/Missing	Park County
Crelslenski Stanisloff	9/7/1893	Water Death	Cascade Co.

DDDDDDDDDDDDDDDDDDDDDDDDDDDDDDDDDDDDDD

Dahl, John R.	11/1/1960	Own Neg.	Deer Lodge Co
Dahl, Mike	11/8/1992	Other Causes	Big Horn Co.
Danielson, Andrew	7/13/1937	Own Neg.	Flathead Co.
Davenport, Burton	11/13/1956	Health	Sanders County
Davy, Daniel M.	11/21/1984	Mistaken Id	Missoula Co.
Dean, Lawrence	11/4/1935	Own Neg.	Gallatin Co.
Deckerville, Louis	10/8/1908	Own Neg.	Lewis & Clark
Delisle, George F.	12/1/1952	Companion	Yellowstone Co
Detz, John F.	11/13/1956	Health	Gallatin Co.
Dillabaugh, William	10/29/1970	Health	Sheridan Co.
Divis, Henry	11/21/1915	Other Causes	Lincoln County
Dockery, Herschel A.	11/12/1928	Own Neg.	Cascade Co.
Dodds, Leslie	9/5/1913	Own Neg.	Beaverhead Co.
Doherty, George V.	11/21/1966	Health	Hill County
Donally, Charles	11/15/1925	Health	Mineral County
Donegan, Arthur	10/21/1907	Water Death	Lewis & Clark
Doney, Ray V.	11/16/1936	Own Neg.	Missoula Co.
Dorey, Clarence	10/19/1938	Lost/Missing	Missoula Co.
Dowling, John W.	11/12/1957	Health	Ravalli County
Doyle, John	11/17/1987	Lost/Missing	Ravalli County
Drake, Barry	10/9/1976	Other Causes	Treasure Co.
Dressel, Gordon	11/24/1973	Water Death	Park County
Driscoll, Richard	9/17/1926	Other Causes	Jefferson Co.
Drollinger, Wade	11/23/1973	Companion	Flathead Co.

<u>Drollinger, Wesley</u>	11/14/1973	Own Neg.	Flathead Co.
<u>Drouillard, George</u>	4/10/1810	Other Causes	Gallatin Co.
<u>Drury, James</u>	11/2/1987	Health	Lincoln County
<u>Dubie, Ernest</u>	10/27/1951	Health	Beaverhead Co.
<u>Duby, Edward</u>	10/8/1940	Mistaken Id	Missoula Co.
<u>Dulen, J.</u>	10/5/1913	Other Causes	Lincoln County
<u>DuPuis, Ross</u>	11/22/1970	Lost/Missing	Sanders County

EEEEEEEEEEEEEEEEEEEEEEEEEEEEEEEEEEEEEEEEEEEEEEEE

<u>Eagle, Raymond C.</u>	11/6/1986	Own Neg.	Roosevelt Co.
<u>Easlack, John</u>	11/10/1912	Mistaken Id	Lincoln County
<u>Eaton, Dennis</u>	11/12/1962	Other Causes	Park County
<u>Eckelberry, George</u>	10/5/1940	Water Death	Flathead Co.
<u>Edmondson, June C.</u>	11/12/1956	Health	Custer County
<u>Egan, Benjamin F.</u>	11/7/1902	Lost/Missing	Flathead Co.
<u>Eggert, Eugene E.</u>	11/24/1965	Health	Lincoln County
<u>Eichstadt, John</u>	11/7/1942	Own Neg.	Deer Lodge Co.
<u>Eickoff, Kenneth</u>	11/24/1962	Own Neg.	Fergus County
<u>Elbert, Wesley H.</u>	11/8/1959	Mistaken Id	Beaverhead Co.
<u>Ellis, Ted</u>	11/26/1923	Water Death	Teton County
<u>Emery, Harry</u>	12/8/1890	Mistaken Id.	Cascade Co.
<u>Enders, Lucien A.</u>	9/14/1904	Water Death	Cascade Co.
<u>English, Roger Allen</u>	11/10/1992	Health	Ravalli County
<u>Erickson, Jonathan</u>	2/11/1881	Other Causes	Custer County
<u>Eriksen, Hans I.</u>	9/21/1969	Mistaken Id	*Bob Marshall
<u>Ertz, Richard</u>	10/10/1966	Water Death	Flathead Co.
<u>Escher, Clyde</u>	10/24/1958	Lost/Missing	Powder River
<u>Evenson, Melvin</u>	11/7/1933	Mistaken Id	Flathead Co.

FFFFFFFFFFFFFFFFFFFFFFFFFFFFFFFFFFFFFFFFFFFFFFFFFFF

<u>Fadness, Michael</u>	10/24/1970	Companion	Park County
<u>Fahlgren, Clarence</u>	10/4/1932	Own Neg.	Sweet Grass Co
<u>Fain, Donald R.</u>	10/8/1953	Lost/Missing	Madison Co.
<u>Fairservice, Kay</u>	10/22/1990	Companion	Cascade Co.
<u>Fallsdown, Dana M.</u>	11/11/1991	Other Causes	Big Horn Co.
<u>Farmer, Tassie H.</u>	11/17/1968	Lost/Missing	Lake County
<u>Farron, Harold T.</u>	11/24/1958	Own Neg.	Granite County

Farstad, James	10/19/1959	Other Causes	Phillips County
Faw, Lee	12/1/1980	Companion	Sweet Grass Co
Felieous, Robert	11/22/1938	Companion	Silver Bow Co
Findall, Elmer A.	11/17/1950	Health	Missoula Co.
Fink, John	10/4/1936	Own Neg.	Deer Lodge Co.
Flamm, George W.	11/17/1941	Companion	Carbon County
Flthd Indn. Trapper	1/30/1832	Other Causes	Beaverhead Co.
Foley, Charles F.	5/20/1893	Water Death	Lincoln County
Forbes, Orit T.	10/14/1944	Own Neg.	Pondera Co.
Forcum, Ray	12/3/1910	Health	Flathead Co.
Foster, Arthur	11/6/1951	Health	Gallatin Co.
Fowler, Jim	June 1876	Other Causes	*Northern MT.
Frank, George R.	10/5/1969	Companion	Missoula Co.
Franke, Walter	11/20/1960	Mistaken Id	Sanders County
Fraser, Kenneth H.	12/16/1962	Water Death	Flathead Co.
Fraunhofer, Ruth	10/17/1936	Own Neg.	Cascade Co.
Freehearty	4/12/1810	Other Causes	Gallatin Co.
Friel, Mike	10/5/1909	Companion	Silver Bow Co.
Fry, Fritz	11/16/1960	Lost/Missing	Missoula Co.
Fryer, Clyde	9/21/1919	Other Causes	Park County
Fuller, Charles W.	11/2/1970	Other Causes	Wibaux County
Fultz, Kenneth L.	11/8/1973	Lost/Missing	Ravalli County

GGGGGGGGGGGGGGGGGGGGGGGGGGGGGGGGGGGGGGG

Gamble, James	11/2/1901	Own Neg.	Blaine County
Gamett, Ivan L.	11/10/1958	Health	Lewis & Clark
Gardape, Louis	9/19/1902	Mistaken Id	Fergus County
Gardner, Kenneth	11/11/1927	Mistaken Id	Cascade Co.
Garey, James	10/26/1959	Other Causes	*Bob Marshall
Garrison, Otto	10/21/1929	Water Death	Cascade Co.
Gaston, Oliver	11/17/1941	Health	Flathead Co.
Gaw, Earl James	10/20/1964	Health	Custer County
Geer, James	11/20/1925	Other Causes	Flathead Co.
Gibbons, James	11/5/1962	Mistaken Id	Big Horn Co.
Giesick, Gerald W.	10/31/1971	Water Death	Yellowstone Co
Gilber, Richard W.	10/22/1952	Own Neg.	Lincoln County
Gilbertson, Leonard	11/22/1966	Other Causes	Teton County

Glass, Hugh	Early 1833	Other Causes	Yellowstone Co
Gleason, Howard	10/20/1958	Own Neg.	Richland Co.
Glenn, Percy	11/22/1904	Own Neg.	Fergus County
Goecks, Herbert	10/29/1956	Health	Broadwater Co.
Goldston, Troy S.	11/26/1990	Own Neg.	Lake County
Gomke, Reuben	11/30/1958	Companion	Hill County
Gonsior, Frank	9/2/1905	Own Neg.	Cascade Co.
Goss, George	11/14/1912	Mistaken Id	Carter County
Grady, John Edward	11/1/1959	Own Neg.	Lewis & Clark
Grant, Kieran P.	11/26/1996	Health	Lake County
Greenlee, Anita L.	10/25/1990	Own Neg.	Carbon County
Greenup, Floyd	11/2/1964	Health	Sanders County
Gregory, James	10/2/1961	Own Neg.	Carbon County
Griesbach, Walter	11/4/1928	Own Neg.	Chouteau Co.
Grimes, Walter	11/10/1942	Companion	Cascade Co.
Grinde, Fred	12/3/1938	Own Neg.	Cascade Co.
Grisham, Dickie Sgt	11/21/1971	Other Causes	Cascade Co.
Grosswiler, Ralph T.	11/8/1947	Own Neg.	Flathead Co.
Gruber, Robert A.	11/22/1963	Health	Sanders Co.
Guin, Lieutenant C.	11/21/1971	Other Causes	Cascade Co.
Gummer, Dale	10/25/2000	Other Causes	Silver Bow Co.
Gunn, Mahlon Jr.	11/19/1991	Companion	Hill County

HHHHHHHHHHHHHHHHHHHHHHHHHHHHHHHHHHHHHH

Haglund, Albert	10/20/1968	Water Death	Lewis & Clark
Hahnert, Earnest A.	11/3/1978	Other Causes	Powell County
Hailey, George E.	8/4/1901	Own Neg.	Meagher Co.
Hakke, Andrew	11/19/1923	Water Death	Granite Co.
Ham, Edwin C.	10/17/1953	Companion	Powell County
Hambrick, Donald	10/18/1991	Own Neg.	Ravalli County
Hamilton, Fred	10/29/1962	Lost/Missing	Lake County
Hammer, Ernest	11/22/1959	Mistaken Id	Pondera Co.
Hammond, Annie	11/22/1970	Lost/Missing	Sanders Co.
Hanifl, Howard H.	11/2/1970	Other Causes	Wibaux County
Hankinson, Jim	11/6/1956	Companion	Mineral County
Harbison, Joseph K.	10/27/1955	Health	Park County
Harbaugh, Ralph W.	10/26/1958	Health	Garfield Co.

Hardie, Albert	11/4/1957	Companion	Lewis & Clark
Harkin, Don	11/24/1974	Other Causes	Gallatin Co.
Harkness, Robert	11/14/1933	Health	Missoula Co.
Harper, Donald	10/28/1975	Lost/Missing	Park County
Harrison, Clifford	10/21/1929	Water Death	Cascade Co.
Hartso, Von	11/17/1928	Water Death	Toole County
Harvey, Kenneth	10/23/1973	Other Causes	Fergus County
Haugen Chad R.	7/19/1995	Other Causes	Blaine County
Haugse, Arne	11/1/1948	Health	Teton County
Hauskamaa, Wlm	10/21/1938	Lost/Missing	Judith Basin Co
Hawkins, Harry G.	9/22/1921	Water Death	Glacier County
Haynes, Theodore	10/15/1963	Own Neg.	Yellowstone Co
Hays, Gerald	11/5/1951	Companion	Lincoln County
Heath, Harry	10/25/1908	Lost/Missing	Lewis & Clark
Heiland, John	10/27/1951	Health	Lake County
Hellman, Fred	10/26/1972	Lost/Missing	Flathead Co.
Helstrom Peter	9/10/1881	By Animal	Deer Lodge Co.
Henningson, Peter	12/12/1923	Companion	Valley County
Herndon, Pearl	10/30/1956	Health	Missoula Co.
Herron, Daniel	10/26/1969	*Own Neg.*	*Lewis & Clark*
Hewitt, Harvey E.	10/15/1960	Lost/Missing	Roosevelt Co.
Hicks, Edgar	10/11/1936	Own Neg.	Ravalli County
Higgens, John	10/2/1962	Other Causes	Missoula Co.
Hilston, Timothy A.	11/1/2001	By Animal	Powell County
Hilton, Ervin M.	7/29/1914	Other Causes	Cascade Co.
Hilyard, Harry D.	12/20/1991	Own Neg.	Sheridan Co.
Hines, Harry	9/30/1934	Health	Lewis & Clark
Hinz, John	12/16/1932	Lost/Missing	Deer Lodge Co.
Hoar, Everett	11/29/1932	Other Causes	Silver Bow Co.
Hoch, Elias	11/13/1957	Companion	Garfield Co.
Hodges, Jesse	9/20/1903	Mistaken Id	Fergus County
Hoff, Max Clayton	10/25/1976	Other Causes	Yellowstone Co
Hogan, Clifford G.	10/16/1947	Water Death	Missoula Co.
Holland, John C.	11/22/1931	Own Neg.	Gallatin Co.
Holton, Morris C.	10/20/1970	Health	Garfield Co.
Holzapfel, Joseph	11/29/2004	Own Neg.	Flathead Co.

Hood, Clair C.	10/30/1955	Other Causes	Richland Co.
Hoop, Louie	10/23/1918	Water Death	Hill County
Hoscheid, Stephen	11/23/1998	Other Causes	Granite County
Houghton, Ernest L.	11/7/1994	Lost/Missing	Teton County
Hougland, John Ben	11/19/1926	Lost/Missing	Missoula Co.
House, Joseph F.	10/7/1916	Companion	Cascade Co.
Housman, Charlie	1/11/1896	Other Causes	Powell County
Houston, H. Mrs.	9/3/1913	Own Neg.	Flathead Co.
Houston, Henry L.	10/17/1928	Other Causes	Cascade Co.
Howard, Harry	11/3/1953	Mistaken Id	Lincoln County
Howell, Frank	11/19/1940	By Animal	Flathead Co.
Hoyt, Regan	11/2/1965	Companion	Carbon County
Hughley, William N.	10/19/1955	Health	Lewis & Clark
Hulbert, Warren	11/17/1904	Companion	Sanders County
Hull	4/12/1810	Other Causes	Gallatin Co.
Humphrey, E.C.	10/15/1951	Lost/Missing	Fergus County
Humphrey, George	2/10/1900	Other Causes	Madison Co.
Hutchinson, Hugh	5/10/1899	Other Causes	Judith Basin Co

IIIIIIIIIIIIIIIIIIIIIIIIIIIIIIIIIIIIIIIIIIIIIIIIIIIIIIIIIIIIIIIIIIIIIIIIIIIIIIIIIIIIIIIIIII

Immel, Michael	5/31/1823	Other Causes	Yellowstone Co
Irvine, Peter	9/29/1924	Health	Lake County

JJJJJJJJJJJJJJJJJJJJJJJJJJJJJJJJJJJJJJJJJJJJJJJJJJJJJJJJJJJJJJJJJJJJJJJJJJJJ

Jackson, James M.	11/5/1991	Own Neg.	Mineral Co.
Jackson, James W.	10/23/1979	Other Causes	Valley County
Jacobs, Charles	10/29/1934	Own Neg.	Yellowstone Co
Jacobson, Richard	11/27/1976	Lost/Missing	Flathead Co.
Jansen, Joseph P. Jr.	11/14/1959	Health	Toole County
Jaqueth, Fred	10/12/1949	Health	Flathead Co.
Jenkins, Clyde	11/23/1958	Health	Sanders County
Jennings, Robert	11/4/1957	Mistaken Id	Ravalli County
Jensen, Gerald B.	4/23/1988	Own Neg.	McCone Co.
Jensen, Leroy	12/31/1928	Other Causes	Dawson Co.
Jerome, Silas H.	10/16/1955	Health	Missoula Co.
Jewett, Daniel Allen	11/7/1965	Companion	Madison Co.
Johns Ray	11/15/1954	Companion	Lake County

Johnson, Billy	9/27/1963	Own Neg.	Phillips County
Johnson, George	10/24/1946	Other Causes	Silver Bow Co.
Johnson, Leo B.	11/12/1962	Other Causes	Park County
Johnson, Lucas	11/1/1991	Own Neg.	Broadwater Co.
Johnson, M.M.	11/21/1903	Lost/Missing	Mineral Co.
Johnson, Oliver M.	11/2/1932	Own Neg.	Deer Lodge Co.
Johnson, William F.	10/20/1952	Health	Lewis & Clark
Joki, Adrian Dick	11/11/1959	Lost/Missing	Gallatin Co.
Jondrow, Henry J.	11/9/1955	Health	Sweet Grass Co
Jones, Richard	9/29/1912	Own Neg.	Lewis & Clark
Jones, Robert	5/31/1823	Other Causes	Yellowstone Co
Jones, William	11/9/1955	Health	Madison Co.
Jordan, Arthur D.	11/28/1959	Lost/Missing	Missoula Co.
Jorgenson, Roger L.	10/12/1976	Companion	Stillwater Co.
Jorgenson, Scott L.	10/24/1990	Own Neg.	Valley County
Joy, Walter	1/6/1896	Water Death	Flathead Co.

KKKKKKKKKKKKKKKKKKKKKKKKKKKKKKKKKKKKKK

Kahl, Sam	11/8/1935	Own Neg.	Lake County
Kaoski, Everett	9/21/1924	Companion	Cascade Co.
Kapp, George	10/8/1967	Water Death	Fergus County
Kauffman (see Kuaffman)			
Kaulbach, Mark	10/23/1938	Own Neg.	Chouteau Co.
Keefe, James	9/18/1926	Water Death	Beaverhead Co.
Kelly, Donald L.	10/26/1966	Health	Judith Basin Co
Kelley, Mitchell	10/22/1979	Other Causes	Carbon County
Kelsey, Thomas	11/5/1961	Mistaken Id	Lincoln County
Kennedy, George	11/16/1927	Own Neg.	Flathead Co.
Kent, Fred E.	10/27/1959	Lost/Missing	Judith Basin Co
Keogh, William	8/11/1897	Companion	Cascade Co.
Kercher, William	10/16/1946	Own Neg.	Cascade Co.
Kimberlin, Don R.	11/8/1974	Lost/Missing	Mineral County
King, Bruce J.	2/3/2005	Own Neg.	Sheridan Co.
Kirby, Charles	10/18/1949	Water Death	Fergus County
Kitchel, Alan K.	11/10/1987	By Animal	Gallatin Co.
Kleist, Robert L.	10/29/1969	Other Causes	Powder River
Klien, David	11/13/1962	Lost/Missing	Lake County

Knapp, Donald P.	10/21/1940	*Other Causes*	Missoula Co.
Knopes, Floyd F.	12/16/1962	Water Death	Flathead Co.
Knuteson, Knute	11/9/1921	Own Neg.	Silver Bow Co.
Knutson, Carl	10/1/1970	Health	Lewis & Clark
Koefod, Mark S.	10/26/1976	Companion	Hill County
Kola, Andrew	11/19/1929	Water Death	Deer Lodge Co.
Kohner, Dennis F.	10/4/1940	Own Neg.	Ravalli County
Kosena, Joseph J.	10/17/1927	Own Neg.	Deer Lodge Co.
Kosola, Jack	10/22/1957	Health	Deer Lodge Co.
Kroh, Jerry Scott	10/18/1977	Companion	Yellowstone Co
Kruger, Larry	11/24/1965	Lost/Missing	Mineral County
Krutar, Rudolph B.	10/27/1951	Health	Deer Lodge Co.
Kruzon, Al	10/21/1953	Companion	Mineral County
Kuaffman, Raymond	10/27/1951	Own Neg.	Flathead Co.
Kulbeck, Walter L.	10/19/1933	Companion	Flathead Co.
Kyolle, 5-yr-old boy	5/16/1902	Other Causes	Liberty County

LLLLLLLLLLLLLLLLLLLLLLLLLLLLLLLLLLLLLLLLLLLLLLLL

Lafrinire, Adelore	10/29/1917	Other Causes	Missoula Co.
Lakar, Larcey M.	10/1/1924	Own Neg.	Carbon County
Lake, R. Ford	10/15/1933	Water Death	Teton County
Lambert, Charles V.	8/29/1940	Other Causes	Valley County
LaMere, Michael	10/20/2004	Lost/Missing	Hill County
Lane, Clark Russell	10/22/1956	Other Causes	Jefferson Co.
Langford, Edward	11/22/1976	Other Causes	Fergus County
LaRoche, Raymond	11/13/2000	Other Causes	Richland Co.
Laughfranere, Walt	10/16/1948	Mistaken Id	Park County
Lawrence, William	11/16/1926	Own Neg.	Meagher Co.
Leavitt, Monty	11/25/1945	Companion	Toole County
Lee, Joshua N.	5/14/2003	Companion	Flathead Co.
Lefebvre, Ray	3/16/1908	Other Causes	Cascade Co.
Lerch, August	8/23/1900	Other Causes	Flathead Co.
Lesofski, Peter R.	11/8/1967	Health	Lewis & Clark
Lewis, Floyd	10/2/1921	Other Causes	Cascade Co.
Linn, Elijah	4/12/1919	Companion	Musselshell Co.
Little, Howard V.	11/15/1938	Mistaken Id	Ravalli County
Lofftus, George	11/9/1947	Lost/Missing	Ravalli County

Long, David A.	10/21/1915	Lost/Missing	Flathead Co.
Long, Guy	10/28/1951	Mistaken Id	Flathead Co.
Longenecker, Robert	10/12/1947	Health	Ravalli County
Longpre, Ralph	10/18/1937	By Animal	Mineral County
Longstaff, William	10/21/1899	Lost/Missing	Lewis & Clark
Long-Tree, Michael	10/24/1961	Companion	Roosevelt Co.
Love, Henry C.	9/2/1901	Companion	Cascade Co.
Love, Jack	10/26/1988	Health	Lake County
Lovell, William	10/21/1969	Health	Lewis & Clark
Lowney, William	10/17/1953	Health	Silver Bow Co.
Lubardo, Andrew	8/7/1922	Own Neg.	Carbon County
Luce, Harry	10/16/1955	Health	Cascade Co.
Luce, Revie W.	11/3/1972	Other Causes	Stillwater Co.
Lueder, Mark Allen	10/16/1972	Companion	Cascade Co.
Lund, E.	10/26/1909	Lost/Missing	Park County
Lyght, Earl	9/23/1938	Own Neg.	Flathead Co.
Lynnes, Kenneth	10/30/1962	Other Causes	Blaine County

MMMMMMMMMMMMMMMMMMMMMMMMMMMMMMMM

MacAulay, Alex	12/4/1908	Other Causes	Glacier County
Mack, Wallace	10/26/1965	Health	Custer County
Madigan, Douglas A.	11/28/1971	Mistaken Id	Ravalli County
Mahr, Benjamin	12/3/1940	Other Causes	Yellowstone Co
Malard, William	8/15/1904	Own Neg.	Phillips County
Malloy, John	11/5/1902	Own Neg.	Flathead Co.
Marble, Floyd	11/13/1931	Own Neg.	Gallatin Co.
Maris, Charles F.	9/27/1950	Health	Musselshell Co.
Marko, Donald	10/19/1959	Mistaken Id	Cascade Co.
Marouthas, Andrew	11/24/1930	Water Death	Cascade Co.
Marshall, John J	11/18/1938	Other Causes	Granite County
Marshall, Robert L.	10/19/1971	Health	Fergus County
Martin, Andrew J.	10/26/1908	Own Neg.	Cascade Co.
Martin, Carl	1/15/1965	Companion	Toole County
Martinich, Herb	11/16/1957	Health	Cascade Co.
Masanovich, Bozo	11/6/1928	Own Neg.	Lewis & Clark
Masker, Charles	10/29/1947	Companion	Judith Basin Co
Mason George Dan	11/6/1947	By Animal	Valley County

Massey, Samuel G. a.k.a.

(Sam S. Conboy S.)	5/17/1916	Mistaken Id	Gallatin Co.
Matt, Frank A.	10/31/1925	Lost/Missing	Missoula Co.
Mayash, Frank	12/11/1929	Mistaken Id	Park County
Maynard, Lewis W.	11/2/1932	Companion	Ravalli County
McBride, James	11/29/1941	Lost/Missing	Lincoln County
McCauley, Frank	11/16/1964	Health	Jefferson Co.
McClure, Thomas E.	11/7/1951	Health	Stillwater Co.
McDaniel, Tom E.	11/4/1991	Lost/Missing	Park County
McDonald, Sam	10/23/1974	Own Neg.	Broadwater Co.
McElroy, Charles	11/16/1941	By Animal	Flathead Co.
McFarland, John A.	9/19/1969	Health	Missoula Co.
McGillis, Richard	10/23/1978	Other Causes	Cascade Co.
McGilvery, Alley C.	11/7/1942	Health	Missoula Co.
McGraw, Martin	10/2/1912	Own Neg.	Cascade Co.
McGuire, Aaron	9/15/1906	Mistaken Id	Flathead Co.
McJilton, Charles	11/1/1973	Water Death	Lewis & Clark
McKay, Vern	10/25/1966	Health	Madison Co.
McKenzie, Rodney	11/30/1979	Other Causes	Sanders County
Mcleslie, George	11/14/1938	Lost/Missing	Blaine County
McWhethey, James	11/3/1919	Mistaken Id	Powell County
Meirs J.H.	10/17/1945	Companion	Lincoln County
Melton, Thomas	11/15/1955	Health	Ravalli County
Menard	Early 1833	Other Causes	YellowstoneCo
Merene, Herman	12/19/1937	Other Causes	Park County
Meyers, Frank	10/18/1946	Other Causes	Gallatin Co.
Michaels, Edward	12/29/1912	Companion	Jefferson Co.
Midboe, Charles	11/4/1933	Companion	Dawson Co.
Middleton, Richard	10/18/1974	Own Neg.	Park County
Mienk, Zachary W.	6/4/2004	Own Neg.	Lake County
Milelich, Micheal P.	10/1/1967	Own Neg.	Silver Bow Co
Miller, Charles E.	11/4/1991	Lost/Missing	Park County
Miller, James	10/21/1961	Mistaken Id	Richland Co.
Mills, Edgely	11/14/1932	Mistaken Id	Granite County
Mills, George Henry	10/28/1956	Health	Ravalli County
Mills, Harvey H.	11/14/1932	Mistaken Id	Granite County
Mitchell, Daniel	11/18/1938	Other Causes	Toole County

Victim Index

Mock, Fred	9/27/1923	Other Causes	Glacier County
Molback, Ronald S.	9/15/1995	Mistaken Id	Meagher Co.
Montgomery, Chrls	9/28/1930	Own Neg.	Beaverhead Co.
Moody, A.F.	7/13/1908	Companion	Madison Co.
Mora, Albert	10/17/1943	Mistaken Id	Lewis & Clark
Morgan, Creed R.	10/22/1945	Companion	Ravalli County
Morris, Clay	11/5/1969	Lost/Missing	Beaverhead Co.
Morris, Mrs. James	10/2/1913	Other Causes	Hill County
Mosback, Gary	11/7/1956	Companion	Park County
Moses, Randall P.	11/18/1996	Mistaken Id	Flathead Co.
Mueller, John H.	11/20/1954	Health	Lewis & Clark
Munroe, Walter B.	11/30/1911	Own Neg.	Flathead Co.
Murphy, John Earl	11/1/1954	Health	Lewis & Clark
Murr, Dan	12/14/1916	Mistaken Id	Lincoln County
Murray, Duayne	9/11/1962	Other Causes	Fergus County

NNNNNNNNNNNNNNNNNNNNNNNNNNNNNNNNNNNNNNNN

Nagard, Harry	11/19/1904	Companion	Gallatin Co.
Necklace, Raymond	11/19/1948	Companion	Roosevelt Co.
Nelson, Charles	11/13/1963	Own Neg.	Lake County
Nelson, David	11/8/1973	Other Causes	Ravalli County
Nelson, Dennis R.	10/31/2001	Own Neg.	Gallatin Co.
Nelson, Ross	11/20/1955	Companion	Broadwater Co.
Nemeth, William G.	2/16/1983	Health	Park County
Neumann, Edward	10/22/1936	Own Neg.	Fergus County
Newton, Kenneth	11/4/1952	Own Neg.	Phillips County
Nikula, Reino Jr.	11/8/1965	Mistaken Id	Carbon County
Norquay, Francis	10/25/1953	Companion	Flathead Co.

OOOOOOOOOOOOOOOOOOOOOOOOOOOOOOOOOOOOOOO

Obert, Wayne E.	11/24/1968	Health	Powell County
Odelle, Jesse L.	10/12/1949	Health	Pondera Co.
Ofstie, Clifford W.	12/14/1925	Companion	Fergus County
Olson, Edward	11/13/1962	Own Neg.	Gallatin Co.
Olson, Olof	5/20/1893	Water Death	Flathead Co.
Olson, William A.	10/24/1950	Health	Phillips County
O'Neill, James H.	10/26/1981	Health	Lewis & Clark

O'Neill, Leslie | 11/11/1985 | Other Causes | Silver Bow Co.
Orr, William | 11/1/1954 | Mistaken Id | Beaverhead Co.
Osmand, Carl | 11/23/1920 | Lost/Missing | Beaverhead Co.
Ottopal, Geza | 11/24/1916 | Health | Fergus County
Ova, Daniel | 10/23/2000 | Health | Beaverhead Co.

PPPPPPPPPPPPPPPPPPPPPPPPPPPPPPPPPPPPPPPPPP

Pace, Grover	11/3/1938	By Animal	Sanders County
Page, Thomas C.	11/2/1919	Health	Gallatin Co.
Palbykin, Linda	10/22/1975	Other Causes	Madison Co.
Palmer, Gary L.	10/29/1973	Water Death	Madison Co.
Palmer, James B.	11/23/1971	Health	Ravalli County
Parmillee, Jack E.	10/28/1946	Water Death	Gallatin Co.
Parrish, James A.	10/17/1938	Health	Lewis & Clark
Patterson, William	10/17/1949	Own Neg.	Beaverhead Co.
Paul, Camille	10/20/1908	Other Causes	Missoula Co.
Paulin, Eli	9/9/1893	Own Neg.	Missoula Co.
Pearson, Carl	9/22/1914	Other Causes	Cascade Co.
Perga, Benedict D.	10/28/1947	Health	Madison Co.
Peters, Huston C.	9/17/1927	Companion	Teton County
Peterson, Ben Jr.	9/11/1962	Other Causes	Fergus County
Peterson, Charles R.	12/20/1907	Mistaken Id	Flathead Co.
Peyton, Charles B.	10/20/1908	Other Causes	Missoula Co.
Phoenix, Robert	10/16/1939	Own Neg.	Madison Co.
Pierson, William J.	10/24/1977	Own Neg.	Powell County
Pilou, Monsieur	10/14/1832	Other Causes	Madison Co.
Pitsch, Freddy	10/12/1948	Other Causes	Big Horn Co.
Pittman, Robert	10/23/1958	Lost/Missing	Rosebud Co.
Plante, Francis Carl	12/7/2004	Mistaken Id	Lake County
Pochervina, Gilbert	11/15/1943	Own Neg.	Madison Co.
Pogacher, Frank	10/30/1942	Lost/Missing	Musselshell Co.
Popish, William	11/20/1964	Own Neg.	Missoula Co.
Portis, Paul B. Sgt	11/17/1928	Companion	Mineral County
Portman, Frederick	10/24/1950	Own Neg.	Lewis & Clark
Potts, John	Fall of 1808	Other Causes	Madison Co.
Powell, Dick	11/15/1938	Lost/Missing	Gallatin Co.
Powell, William	9/27/1907	Own Neg.	Chouteau Co.

Powell, William   10/24/1935   Health   Judith Basin Co
Praast, Paul   11/10/1942   Lost/Missing   Powell County
Pries, Rudolph   10/31/1955   Health   Wibaux County
Privett, Michael G.   5/20/1996   Companion   Ravalli County
Puente, Jeff   2/21/2003   Other Causes   Big Horn Co.
Pullman, James   11/4/1921   Companion   Flathead Co.
Pulse, Robert Mrs.   11/12/1955   Other Causes   Lincoln County

QQQQQQQQQQQQQQQQQQQQQQQQQQQQQQQQQQQQQQQQQQ
Quarles, Harold Sr.   10/26/1981   Health   Silver Bow Co.

RRRRRRRRRRRRRRRRRRRRRRRRRRRRRRRRRRRRRRRRRR
Racine, Aloysius   11/18/1959   Own Neg.   Glacier County
Rasmussen, Lamar   11/19/1993   Water Death   Flathead Co.
Rassmusson, Robert   11/6/2003   Other Causes   Beaverhead Co.
Rathie, Raymond   10/7/1969   Mistaken Id   Ravalli County
Raunig, Gary   3/31/1969   Other Causes   Lewis & Clark
Rawson, Kenneth   10/16/1961   Health   Chouteau Co.
Ray, Riley   11/8/1941   Own Neg.   Musselshell Co.
Rebich, Raymond   10/30/1968   Own Neg.   Beaverhead Co.
Redlingshafer, John   10/20/1945   Companion   Flathead Co.
Reesman, Robert   10/20/1940   Own Neg.   Missoula Co.
Reimer, Ben   11/19/1953   Lost/Missing   Flathead Co.
Reinhart, Kenneth   10/26/1987   Companion   Missoula Co.
Reissing, George   11/30/1936   Companion   Teton County
Reiter, George   6/15/1901   Lost/Missing   Gallatin Co.
Reymerson, William   10/5/1945   Health   Ravalli County
Rheinackle, Robert   9/21/1914   Water Death   Pondera Co.
Richardson, Albert L.   10/16/1947   Water Death   Missoula Co.
Richardson, Clyde   11/2/1982   Health   Hill County
Ricker, Chaskay   11/19/2002   Companion   Richland Co.
Ridgeway, Arthur T.   11/15/1936   Own Neg.   Fergus County
Riedl, Nadine J.   11/21/1972   Companion   Powder River
Ritch, Floyd   5/7/1912   Own Neg.   Fergus County
Roberts, Rex   11/15/1927   Own Neg.   Ravalli County
Robertson, John J.   10/26/1918   Water Death   Gallatin Co.
Robinson, Dale   1/30/1959   Companion   Musselshell Co.

Robinson, Edward	10/18/1951	Companion	Roosevelt Co.
Robinson, John A.	11/8/1959	Health	Lewis & Clark
Rock	4/2/1874	Other Causes	Cascade Co.
Rodine, Robert	11/25/1946	Water Death	Missoula Co.
Rogers, B.T. "Curly"	9/1/1894	Other Causes	Park County
Roll, Otto	1/1/1909	Companion	Gallatin Co.
Rose, Edward	Early 1833	Other Causes	Yellowstone Co
Royan, James	11/14/1926	Other Causes	Roosevelt Co.
Rozuoi, Emil L.	10/17/1961	Health	Rosebud Co.
Rucker	4/12/1810	Other Causes	Gallatin Co.
Rush, Roy	11/14/1951	Health	Flathead Co.
Rusidak, Richard S.	11/3/1972	Other Causes	Stillwater Co.
Russell, George L.	10/20/1949	Health	Silver Bow Co.
Russell, Paul	12/9/1922	Companion	Lincoln Co.
Ryan, Ralph	9/2/1923	Own Neg.	Silver Bow Co.
Ryan, Robert A.	11/16/1947	Health	Sweet Grass Co

SSSSSSSSSSSSSSSSSSSSSSSSSSSSSSSSSSSSSSSSSSSSSSSSSSSSSSSSSSSS

Saari, Herman C.	11/4/1992	Health	Missoula Co.
Sagar, John	9/9/1912	Own Neg.	Silver Bow Co.
Saltsman, David W.	10/28/1954	Companion	Lincoln County
Sanders, Art	11/8/1953	Companion	Musselshell Co.
Satterfield, Darcy	10/22/1979	Other Causes	Carbon County
Schafer, Anton	12/11/1927	Own Neg.	Judith Basin Co
Schanz, Kary	10/30/1987	Companion	Custer County
Schmidt, Arthur L.	10/28/1988	Health	Ravalli County
Schmidt, Kenneth	10/28/191957	Other Causes	Beaverhead Co.
Schmidt, Leonard R.	10/19/1954	Health	Musselshell Co.
Schock, Timothy	11/26/1975	Lost/Missing	Cascade Co.
Schonenbach, David	10/26/1969	Own Neg.	Rosebud Co.
Schuchmann, Homer	11/6/1933	Mistaken Id	Ravalli County
Schultz, Amos	11/14/1910	Lost/Missing	Chouteau Co.
Schultz, Walter	11/14/1910	Lost/Missing	Chouteau Co.
Schwenneker, Bruce	11/10/1936	Mistaken Id	*Absk/Br-tooh
Scott, William K.	10/22/1956	By Animal	*Bob Marshall
Seeley, Calvin L.	11/13/1963	Health	Fergus County
Seiller, Frank	11/23/1938	Companion	Lake County

Sellar, Oswald K.	10/13/1916	Companion	Fergus County
Severance, Private	1/12/1881	Lost/Missing	Hill County
Shandy, Jackie	10/15/1954	Water Death	Carbon County
Sharp, Arthur	10/5/1902	Own Neg.	Cascade Co.
Shaw, Olive	10/13/1928	Companion	Fergus County
Shepka, Carl	11/18/1940	Own Neg.	Deer Lodge Co.
Shipman, Wilbert	12/16/1916	Companion	Gallatin Co.
Shoberg, Arthur	10/7/1957	Own Neg.	Lewis & Clark
Simaro, Vern	10/23/1945	Health	Lincoln County
Simonich, Robert	12/3/2003	Other Causes	Lewis & Clark
Simons, Nick Jr.	9/19/1903	Own Neg.	Madison Co.
Sivertson, Clarence	10/13/1953	Own Neg.	Blaine County
Skagen, Herman	11/1/1973	Lost/Missing	Fergus County
Skaggs, Clarence	10/18/1956	Mistaken Id	Powder River
Slauson, Todd	11/23/1997	Own Neg.	Missoula Co.
Smith, Clifford	10/14/1936	Companion	Lewis & Clark
Smith, Jack	10/26/1918	Own Neg.	Flathead Co.
Smith, Robert W.	10/19/1959	Companion	Judith Basin Co
Smith, William	10/20/1939	Own Neg.	Ravalli County
Smurr, Forrest	11/1/1938	Own Neg.	Lake County
Snider, Horace H.	10/24/1950	Water Death	Phillips County
Sokoloski, Walter B.	11/12/1957	Companion	Ravalli County
Sorenson, Gary	11/1/1959	Companion	Phillips County
Sorenson, Jordan S.	10/29/1979	Companion	Flathead Co.
Spaich, Miles	10/17/1956	Own Neg.	Mineral County
Spence, Amber	11/19/1968	Companion	Lincoln County
Sprattler, Louis Paul	10/2/1977	Companion	Teton County
Staats, Ward A.	10/5/1965	Health	Lewis & Clark
Stace, Westley P.	10/12/1959	Companion	Blaine County
Staffan, Henry	11/14/1945	Health	Beaverhead Co.
Standiford, George	11/2/1914	Mistaken Id	Lincoln County
Stark, Thomas	10/10/1912	Lost/Missing	Cascade Co.
Stedman, Vicki K.	11/30/1981	Lost/Missing	Rosebud Co.
Stedman, Wilbur H.	11/30/1981	Lost/Missing	Rosebud Co.
Stean, Gus	11/9/1940	Lost/Missing	Mineral County
Steffes, Dennis A.	11/5/1971	Other Causes	Sweet Grass Co
Steging, James A.	11/17/1987	Lost/Missing	Ravalli County

Steinberg, Ralph	10/12/1976	Health	Custer County
Stepanek, Tony	10/24/1958	Lost/Missing	Powder River
Sterner, Alfred	10/29/1952	Health	Lake County
Stevenson, Leon	1/23/1912	Other Causes	Carbon County
Stewart, T.	10/21/1907	Water Death	Lewis & Clark
Stiles, Floyd E.	10/12/1949	Health	Missoula Co.
Stockman Elmer E.	11/10/1936	Own Neg.	Ravalli County
Stokes, Clarence	11/18/1967	Own Neg.	Flathead Co.
Stone, John	10/24/1958	Health	Flathead Co.
Stone, Wallace	11/10/1931	Own Neg.	Custer County
Stoughton, M.F.	10/24/1918	Own Neg.	Chouteau Co.
Stousee, Antoine	10/20/1908	Other Causes	Missoula Co.
Stousee, Frank	10/20/1908	Other Causes	Missoula Co.
Stradtzeck, Harry E.	8/2/1936	Own Neg.	Flathead Co.
Strand, Leonard H.	10/19/1971	Health	Fergus County
Stronach, Alexander	10/10/1919	Own Neg.	Liberty County
Strong, Captain W.	10/23/1919	Mistaken Id	Powell County
Stuart, William	1/5/1902	Own Neg.	Ravalli County
Stubber, Wade Otto	1/2/1987	Companion	Choteau Co.
Stuesse, Joseph A.	12/10/1916	Own Neg.	Lewis & Clark
Sweum, Dr. Gunder	10/18/1963	Health	Custer County
Swingley, Frank	12/8/1901	Companion	Cascade Co.
Syblon, William	10/23/1953	Own Neg.	Musselshell Co.
Synnes, John	11/2/1954	Health	Lewis & Clark
Szasv, John	9/30/1923	Own Neg.	Broadwater Co.

TTTTTTTTTTTTTTTTTTTTTTTTTTTTTTTTTTTTTTTTTTT

Talbert, Earl E.	11/7/1969	Mistaken Id	Sanders County
Talbot, Walter	11/17/1958	Health	Madison Co.
Taylor, Robert A.	12/19/1908	Mistaken Id	Lincoln County
Telegan, James	12/12/1991	Lost/Missing	Madison Co.
Terrio, Philip S.	11/27/1935	Own Neg.	Beaverhead Co.
Thacker, Troy E.	10/18/1961	Health	Flathead Co.
Thomas, Jeff	10/9/1965	Mistaken Id	Ravalli County
Thomas, John N.	10/29/1946	Health	Park County
Thompson, Berton	11/23/1937	Own Neg.	Broadwater Co.
Thompson, Frank	11/4/1938	Health	Flathead Co.

Thompson, Gerald F	10/20/1969	Health	Silver Bow Co.
Thompson, Jeff	9/30/1986	Own Neg.	Flathead Co.
Thompson, Norris	11/13/1969	Companion	Valley County
Thrasher, Norman	10/22/1961	Mistaken Id	Cascade Co.
Torgrimson, Robert	11/29/1998	Other Causes	Fergus County
Torrence, Charles L.	11/26/1920	Own Neg.	Teton County
Towery, Thomas A.	11/5/1920	Own Neg.	Gallatin Co.
Townsend, Eddy G.	11/29/1947	Health	Gallatin Co.
Townsend, William	10/4/1965	Mistaken Id	Gallatin Co.
Trader, Clarence	11/7/1959	Lost/Missing	Big Horn Co.
Trapper, Del. Indian	4/10/1810	Other Causes	Gallatin Co.
Trapper, Del. Indian	4/10/1810	Other Causes	Gallatin Co.
Trapper, Unknown	5/4/1823	Other Causes	Cascade Co.
Trapper, Unknown	5/4/1823	Other Causes	Cascade Co.
Trapper, Unknown	5/4/1823	Other Causes	Cascade Co.
Trapper, Unknown	5/4/1823	Other Causes	Cascade Co.
Trapper, Unknown	5/31/1823	Other Causes	Yellowstone Co
Trapper, Unknown	5/31/1823	Other Causes	Yellowstone Co
Trapper, Unknown	5/31/1823	Other Causes	Yellowstone Co
Trapper, Unknown	5/31/1823	Other Causes	Yellowstone Co
Trapper, Unknown	5/31/1823	Other Causes	Yellowstone Co
Tregoning, Tom	9/23/1893	Companion	Broadwater Co.
Truax, Gary Lee	11/7/2003	Own Neg.	Missoula Co.
True, Henry A.	10/27/1947	Health	Pondera Co.
Trusty, Cecil	11/23/1923	Companion	Flathead Co.
Tucker, Aurel	10/19/1936	Companion	Missoula Co.
Tucker, LeRoy	11/22/1958	Own Neg.	Blaine County
Tupper, Leroy S.	10/2/1919	Companion	Flathead Co.
Tuss, Anthony	10/31/1990	Own Neg.	Gallatin Co.

UUUUUUUUUUUUUUUUUUUUUUUUUUUUUU

Ullery, Caroline J.	10/9/1950	Companion	Custer County
Unknown Hunter	1894[10]	By Animal	Park County
Urich, Bernard V.	10/27/1951	Health	Sweet Grass Co
U.S. Soldiers (28)	Feb 1874	Other Causes	Cascade Co.

VVVVVVVVVVVVVVVVVVVVVVVVVVVVVVV

<u>Vanden-Wall, John</u>	11/30/1924	Companion	Pondera Co.
<u>Vanderburgh, Henry</u>	10/14/1832	Other Causes	Madison Co.
<u>VanDorn, Hezekiah</u>	10/30/1941	Companion	Lake County
<u>Vaughn, Iverson</u>	9/9/1904	Companion	Cascade Co.
<u>Vermillion, Victor</u>	11/2/1963	Lost/Missing	Gallatin Co.
<u>Voerman, Ryan</u>	5/28/1990	Other Causes	Flathead Co.
<u>Volcour, Edward L.</u>	9/19/1917	Health	Lincoln County

WWWWWWWWWWWWWWWWWWWWWWWWWWWWWW

<u>Waddell, J.H.</u>	10/23/1925	Companion	Gallatin Co.
<u>Waddell, Robert</u>	2/17/1900	Other Causes	Flathead Co.
<u>Wagerer, Egon</u>	10/11/1965	Own Neg.	Lewis & Clark
<u>Wagner, Marvin H.</u>	11/14/1951	Companion	Sanders County
<u>Wagner, Roger A.</u>	11/21/1999	Mistaken Id	Powell County
<u>Waigel, Joe</u>	11/23/1912	Lost/Missing	Flathead Co.
<u>Walcott, Vincent</u>	10/10/1933	Companion	Lake County
<u>Walker, Judith M.</u>	10/24/1960	Companion	Valley County
<u>Walla, Lindy</u>	10/26/1964	Companion	Wheatland Co
<u>Wallinder, Harold</u>	10/20/1923	Mistaken Id	Lincoln County
<u>Ward, Vernon</u>	9/13/1938	Other Causes	Missoula Co.
<u>Ware, Clifford M.</u>	9/21/1963	Health	Richland Co.
<u>Warwood, Roy F.</u>	10/16/1967	Own Neg.	Gallatin Co.
<u>Watson, Eric</u>	8/23/1990	Companion	Lake County
<u>Watters, Emmitt C.</u>	10/29/1934	Other Causes	Granite Co.
<u>Weatherly, Shannon</u>	6/28/1982	Mistaken Id	Park County
<u>Weaver, Christopher</u>	12/23/1997	Companion	Flathead Co.
<u>Web, Lowell</u>	10/19/1951	Mistaken Id	Ravalli County
<u>Webber, Charles</u>	11/16/1951	Mistaken Id	Missoula Co.
<u>Webster, Erle Sgt</u>	11/21/1971	Other Causes	Cascade Co.
<u>Webster, Larry</u>	11/21/1971	Other Causes	Cascade Co.
<u>Weir, Thomas</u>	11/10/1936	Mistaken Id	Powell County
<u>Weisgerber, Wendi</u>	11/30/1994	Companion	Yellowstone Co
<u>Wersall, Walter</u>	10/8/1924	Own Neg.	Yellowstone Co
<u>West, Charles W.</u>	9/27/1963	Own Neg.	Silver Bow Co.
<u>West, Frank</u>	10/28/1957	Companion	Park County
<u>Westberg, Albert</u>	11/12/1936	Lost/Missing	Meagher Co.

<u>Westfall, George</u>	11/10/1935	Lost/Missing	Silver Bow Co
<u>Westover, George T.</u>	10/23/1937	Water Death	Madison Co.
<u>Westrum, Curtis</u>	10/23/1951	Own Neg.	Flathead Co.
<u>Whaley, Erland B.</u>	10/18/1971	Water Death	Sanders County
<u>Whipple, Robert</u>	9/7/1886	Water Death	Powell County
<u>Whipple, Seth</u>	7/11/1884	Lost/Missing	Roosevelt Co.
<u>White-Boy</u>	5/30/1902	Other Causes	Hill County
<u>White, Charles</u>	11/15/1945	Other Causes	Park County
<u>White, Raymond H.</u>	10/18/1956	Own Neg.	Yellowstone Co
<u>White, Stewart</u>	11/15/1966	Health	Jefferson Co.
<u>White, William W.</u>	10/27/1896	Other Causes	Cascade Co.
<u>Whiting, John</u>	12/29/1895	Own Neg.	Granite County
<u>Whitsell, Carlton</u>	9/25/1928	Companion	Cascade Co.
<u>Wiggin, Hollis B.</u>	10/26/1931	Own Neg.	Missoula Co.
<u>Williams, Alva</u>	11/2/1929	Other Causes	Sweet Grass Co
<u>Williams, Bridge</u>	11/8/1903	Water Death	Granite County
<u>Williams, Clyde F.</u>	10/23/1958	Lost/Missing	Powder River
<u>Williams, Dean</u>	11/1/1954	Own Neg.	Richland Co.
<u>Willis, Carl</u>	10/24/1967	Health	Flathead Co.
<u>Wills, John</u>	5/6/1899	Other Causes	Fergus County
<u>Willson, Bryon C.</u>	11/21/1944	Lost/Missing	Flathead Co.
<u>Wilson, S.E.</u>	11/10/1906	Mistaken Id	Fergus County
<u>Winchell, Norman</u>	10/25/1919	Mistaken Id	Gallatin Co.
<u>Wininger, Paul S.</u>	11/16/1977	Health	Madison Co.
<u>Winkley, Mary</u>	11/3/1950	Lost/Missing	Beaverhead Co.
<u>Wishart, James</u>	10/21/1951	Lost/Missing	Flathead Co.
<u>Wiitala, Charles</u>	9/12/1904	Mistaken Id	Cascade Co.
<u>Wood, George</u>	11/22/1959	Health	Lincoln County
<u>Wood, Merle D.</u>	11/9/1990	Other Causes	Lewis & Clark
<u>Wood, Stanley</u>	11/3/1978	Other Causes	Powell County
<u>Woods, P.L.</u>	10/29/1919	Health	Flathead Co.
<u>Woodworth, Fred</u>	12/2/1914	Companion	Sanders County
<u>Wright, Max</u>	11/8/1903	Water Death	Granite County
<u>Wright, Robert</u>	10/20/1975	Own Neg.	Madison Co.
<u>Wyrick, William L.</u>	10/5/1939	Other Causes	Yellowstone Co

YY

Yale, Frank	10/21/1952	Health	Flathead Co.
Yellow-Mountain, M	10/20/1908	Other Causes	Missoula Co.
Young, William A.	10/24/1966	Own Neg.	Meagher Co.
Younglove, Ralph	10/17/1956	Mistaken Id	Lewis & Clark

ZZZZZZZZZZZZZZZZZZZZZZZZZZZZZZZZZZZZZZZZZZZZZ

Zeuler, Robert	10/18/1961	Health	Yellowstone Co
Zias, Paul	12/28/1895	Companion	Cascade Co.
Zink, G.A.	10/28/1946	Water Death	Gallatin Co.
Zyp, Egbert Jr.	10/23/1961	Health	Fergus County

(Endnotes)
[1] Unknown Blackfeet Warrior killed by John Potts in 1808.
[2] One of the two unknown Delaware Indian trappers who were killed with George Drouillard in 1810.
[3] One of the two unknown Delaware Indian trappers who were killed with George Drouillard in 1810.
[4] Unknown Blackfeet Warrior killed by James Cheeks in 1810
[5] Unknown Blackfeet Warrior killed by Henry Vanderburgh in 1832
[6] Flathead Indian Trapper
[7] One of the two unknown Delaware Indian trappers who were killed with George Drouillard in 1810.
[8] One of the two unknown Delaware Indian trappers who were killed with George Drouillard in 1810.
[9] Unknown Blackfeet warrior killed by John Potts in 1808
[10] Reported in Billings Gazette 12/7/1897